*Oracle Press*™

Oracle8: A Beginner's Guide

Michael Abbey
Michael J. Corey

Osborne **McGraw-Hill**

Berkeley New York St. Louis
San Francisco Auckland Bogotá Hamburg London Madrid
Mexico City Milan Montreal New Delhy Panama City
Paris São Paulo Singapore Sydney Tokyo Toronto

Osborne/**McGraw-Hill**
2600 Tenth Street
Berkeley, California 94710
U.S.A.

For information on translations or book distributors outside the U.S.A.,
or to arrange bulk purchase discounts for sales promotions, premiums, or
fundraisers, please contact Osborne/**McGraw-Hill** at the above address.

Oracle8: A Beginner's Guide

4567890 AGM 99

ISBN 0-07-882393-5

Publisher
Brandon A. Nordin

Editor In Chief
Scott Rogers

Project Editor
Mark S. Karmendy

Editorial Assistant
Ann Sellers

Technical Editor
Ian Abramson

Technical Reviewer
David Teplow

Copy Editors
Michelle Khazai, Dennis Weaver

Proofreaders
Pat Mannion, Karen Mead,
Rhonda Holmes

Indexer
Richard Shrout

Computer Designer
Peter Hancik

Illustrator
Peter Hancik

Series Design
Jani Beckwith

This book is dedicated to my four wonderful children: Jordan Noah, Nathan Mordecai, Ben James, and Naomi Liba. I fantasize about how wonderful it is going to be to meet my childrens' children.

Michael Abbey

About the Authors...

Michael Abbey has lived and breathed Oracle Software for the past 11 years. His forte is Oracle\UNIX installation, performance tuning, and instance management. Michael's services have been in demand from Italy to California and Florida to Eastern Canada. With Mike Corey, he directed IOUG—Alive in Dallas, Texas, USA, in April 1997. Michael Abbey can be reached via email at masint@istar.ca.

Mike Corey, co-owner of Database Technologies, Inc. in Newton, MA, has collected quite a following in the Oracle community. He has dedicated numerous hours, months, and years to helping ensure the user community has the active ear of Oracle Corporation. Mike possesses a well-rounded knowledge of Oracle the company and Oracle the software. He offers over 11 years of experience to the Corey\Abbey team. Mike can be reached via email at mcorey@dbtinc.com.

Contents

Foreword

racle has always been a source of computing technology innovation and leadership. It started with portable relational database technology brought to market in the late 1970s. In 1984, Oracle accomplished what was claimed to be impossible and successfully ported its relational database to the desktop computer. Oracle's next release, Version 5, awakened the marketplace to the possibilities of distributed data, client/server architecture, and the viability of downsizing mainframe applications. Oracle's Version 6 relational database, released with its revolutionary row level locking model, innovative PL/SQL language, and support of clustered and symmetrical multiprocessor computers, took relational database applications into an entirely new marketplace. Oracle7 provided the necessary technology to build industrial strength, high availability, network enabled workgroup, and enterprise class applications.

Using Oracle8, Oracle's newest technology, today's system designers and developers can build 21st century enabled applications ranging from mission critical online transaction processing systems supporting thousands of users to multi-terabyte data warehouses for decision support. Oracle8, an integral component of Oracle's Network Computing Architecture, provides a common foundation for both client/server and World Wide Web-based applications. Oracle's Network Computing Architecture provides developers with the construction tools, database servers, and computing architectures needed to build functionally rich applications that will run on any combination of stand-alone, client/server, or web-enabled computing environment. This technology empowers end users through intuitive methods and visually oriented tools to easily access and manipulate massive amounts of data. Enterprise class applications can break away from the restraints of centralized data models and move quickly towards distributed, interactive information-on-demand environments. The legacy data of yesterday's applications can now be migrated to today's more cost-effective and end-user accessible computing architecture. Oracle has developed a scaleable, extensible, and distributed architecture that can transparently cross the technical and expertise chasms that naturally exist between on-line transaction processing and decision support applications.

As this book will explain in considerable detail, the robust features of Oracle8 open a new chapter in the development of client/server and web-enabled enterprise class applications. End users will find this book to be a road map to understanding and harnessing Oracle's power to efficiently manipulate massive amounts of heterogeneous data containing complex interrelationships. Application designers and developers will find insight into leveraging technology where object-relational applications can be developed and deployed onto the computing platform of choice with virtually no change to code or functionality. The authors, both experienced application developers, database administrators, and system managers, show a simple but effective approach to understanding Oracle8 and its vast capabilities.

Oracle8 leverages the synergy that exists between the advancing technologies of object databases and web-enabled computing. This book will be an excellent introduction to this technology for developers, managers, and end users seeking more effective use and control of data management information technology. Oracle would like to thank the authors for providing a great starting point to understanding Oracle8 and the exciting, new information systems of the 21st century.

Gary E. Damiano
Senior Director
Oracle Corporation

Acknowledgments

Michael Abbey

would like to thank the countless number of people who have helped get this work out the door. Sue Phipps (Phipps Consulting Enterprises-Ottawa) has been there for me when I need that extra burst of energy to tackle yet another chapter update to the original work. Thanks to my fellow author Mike Corey. Thanks to Darryl Smith for writing the chapter on Oracle Forms. Mike Teske helped with some VMS commands in a few areas where my VAX skills were deficient. I enjoyed working with Scott Rogers, Mark Karmendy, Wendy Rinaldi, and Ann Sellers at Osborne McGraw-Hill. Other names that come to mind: Sydney and Rhoda Abbey, David Teplow and Ian Abramson (your friendly neighborhood technical editors), Kevin Canady, Dave Kreines, Per Brondum, Jamie Best, Sue Cunningham, Gary Damiano, Nancy Taslitz, Carl Dudley, Ira Greenblatt, Glen McLeod - thanks! Ken Jacobs and Yvonne Park were so kind to help Mike and me get a hold of Oracle8 for Windows NT software and documentation while the bits and bytes were still wet on the CD.

I would also like to mention the late Herman Wong who worked for Oracle Corporation in Toronto—a wonderful man who "held my hand" through many sessions wrestling with the Oracle software. The kind of guy you meet once and feel you've known all your life—only the good die young.

Michael J. Corey

ow having co-authored two books, it is very clear to me why most acknowledgments start off with "Thanks to my wife and family...." It is true, the family suffers the most. Writing a book has the ability to drain all your time, your personal time, your friends' time, your associates' time and anyone else around you. Well, to bring this book to press required a lot of time and effort from a lot of people. This list does not begin to do it justice.

A special thanks to my wife Juliann (a woman with a lot of understanding), and my children John, Annmarie, and Michael. Special thanks to Michael Abbey, my co-author. This book would not have been possible without his many phone calls/emails night after night. This book is a great example of the technology highway at work. You have one author in Hingham, MA, USA, the other in Ottawa, Canada, and the publisher in Berkeley, CA, USA—each able to communicate electronically.

I would also like to thank my friend and partner (at Database Technologies Inc., Newton, MA, USA) David Teplow. I consider myself very fortunate to be associated with David both professionally and personally. David has been using Oracle since version 2.0. He is probably the best application developer in all of New England.

Another associate of mine at Database Technologies Inc. deserves special mention: Darryl Smith. He was the key source of talent for our Oracle Forms 4.5 chapter. One of the things you realize after working with Oracle as long as I have—you can't know all the answers. When I first started working with the product, there were three manuals. Now I could easily fill a book case and have. So when we decided to do this book, we looked to the best Forms developer I know to help us. Well, judge for yourself.

I would also like to extend a special thanks to all my colleagues at Database Technologies. Don Briffett has nicknamed me "Hurricane man," as I have been known to send my office into a whirlwind when I arrive. Thanks to all for their patience.

Thanks to my many friends at Oracle whose talents and capabilities never fail to amaze me. Here is a short but in no way complete list: Ray Lane (Mr. Blues), Andy Laursen (Mr. Parallel Server/Media Server), Mark Porter (Video Lad), Scott Martin (Mr. SQL*TRAX), Rama Velpuri

(Mr. Backup/Recovery), Stephanie Herle (Ms. Events), Gail Peterson
(Ms. Road Block Breaker), David Anderson (a True Californian), Judy Boyle,
(Ms. Usergroup 93), Joe Didonato (Mr. Education).

A special thanks to a friend/associate at Oracle Corporation, Gary
Damiano.

Thanks to my many friends at the Oracle Users Groups. Here is a small
but incomplete list: Dave Kreines, Marty Greenfield, Geoff Girvin, Merrilee
Nohr, Buff Emslie, Bert Spencer, Warren Capps, Julie Silverstein, Emily
Bersin, Chris Wooldridge (WIZOP on CompuServe), Mark Farnham
(great comments on *Tuning Oracle*) and so many more.

Thanks to the people at Osborne/McGraw-Hill; without them you
would never have received the finished product. A special thanks to
everyone who purchased *Tuning Oracle*. Your comments and
encouragement have been tremendous.

Introduction

nformation technology products are the hot commodities in the marketplace. Many vendors deliver one-stop-shopping solutions that permit users to view and techies to manage very large volumes of data. Online transaction processing systems demand high throughput and users demand speed, accuracy, and reasonable time-to-market. Data warehousing solutions now deal with muli-terabytes of information and users need to get at that information quickly.

Oracle is a major player in the database market and, as of late, has launched initiatives to address Internet-based products and solutions. The heart of Oracle's offering is their Cooperative Server Technology. It is the backbone of just about everything they distribute. *Oracle8: A Beginner's Guide* offers an overview of the Server technology for the beginner as well as other Oracle-savvy personnel wanting to take their understanding of Oracle a step further.

We discuss the relational approach to database management, look at new bells and whistles in the Oracle8 offering, as well as introduce the reader to the Structured Query Language (SQL) and a handful of Oracle tools designed to retrieve information from an Oracle 7/8 repository. We pay special attention to the work of the Oracle Database Administrator—a person so key to the smooth operation and optimal performance of any system running with the Oracle Server.

Oracle8: A Beginner's Guide introduces and explains the phenomenon called "network computing" and discusses Oracle's offering and their Network Computer Architecture. Oracle is a major player in this environment, and we provide the reader with a foundation to understand the choices looming on the horizon as vendors push us towards the thin client.

Oracle8: A Beginner's Guide leads the reader through many step-by-step exercises to manage the Oracle7/8 database, write reports using SQL*Plus and Oracle Reports, and build interactive screens using Oracle Forms.

As you go...

Throughout this book, important points are emphasized:

NOTE

These sections provide extra information about the material in the text.

TIP and VIP

These sections give you an extra insider know-how.

CAUTION

These tell you when to watch out for potential pitfalls.

CHAPTER

1

What Is Oracle?

hy bother to learn Oracle or even read this book? Perhaps you have picked up this book because you keep seeing the big O word, **Oracle**. This is the same word you keep seeing in the help wanted section of your local newspaper. This is also the same word you keep seeing in your favorite trade journal. Seeing this word makes you think about the big C word, **Career**. Of course all this thinking links up with the big M word, **Money**.

You have your reasons—career and money, for instance, or you just want to be part of the current technology movement. You have an area of interest—be it Web-enabled computing, data warehousing, the Network Computer, rightsizing, network computing architecture, client/server, or even video on demand. One thing is very clear: Oracle Corporation (and its technology) is a major player in today's technology movement and promises to be an even bigger player tomorrow.

This chapter introduces Oracle Corporation, its tools and its major initiatives including many of the interesting areas we mentioned above. We will first discuss the basics of the relational database model Oracle has implemented and its core development tools SQL*Plus, Oracle Developer 2000 (including Oracle Forms, Oracle Reports, and Oracle Graphics), Designer/2000, Oracle Book, and Oracle Loader. If you understand these items, you are well on your way to understanding the technology movement of which Oracle is a major part. We will then discuss how Oracle the company has grown. We will introduce you to SQL*Connect, the tool that allows Oracle to talk to other data sources. We'll also explain how Oracle started to use its own tools to build applications that cater to customers' standard business requirements. We will then move on to Oracle, the company today, highlighting the advancement and various flavors of the core database. We will pay special attention to data warehousing, Oracle's Web initiatives, Oracle's move toward an Object-Oriented Database (Oracle8), and Oracle's move into the Network Computer. We will then end with an overview of Oracle user groups.

VIP

Joining an Oracle user group is your best insurance policy for making the most out of your investment in Oracle and its growing lists of technologies.

So here we go—you will learn what Oracle is, how it really works, and how you can use it.

NOTE
Most of you have either heard of or worked with the Oracle7 Server for some time. In this chapter and throughout the rest of the book, most of the material we discuss is applicable to both Oracle7 and Oracle8.

Terminology

The following definitions will arm you with the technical jargon you need to make it through this chapter.

■ An *object-oriented database* allows object extensions to be built into classic relational database technology.

■ *Client/server computing* has three components. Users work with a PC (client), and communicate with a larger central computer (server). An assortment of network software is the third component, allowing communication between the client and the server.

■ *Cyberspace* is another name for the World Wide Web.

■ A *data warehouse* is a collection of corporate information, derived directly or indirectly from operational systems and some external data sources. Its specific purpose is to support business decisions, not business operations. To learn more about data warehouses, we suggest you obtain a copy of *Oracle Data Warehousing* (Oracle Press 1997, ISBN 0-07-882242-4, Corey & Abbey), where we strive to give you a practical guide to building a data warehouse.

■ *Fault tolerance* refers to the ability of some computers to initiate automatic corrective activities when a component or program malfunctions. The classic example is the machine that falls back to a backup disk when an online disk fails. The fall back happens with no human intervention, and a message is sent to a central location to inform of the corrective action.

■ Programs are *event-driven* when portions of code initiate special activities when a certain event happens. For example, when exiting your favorite word processor, there is an event mapped to the Exit command. When the event occurs, the software checks to see if your document should be saved, and brings up the Save dialog box, if necessary.

■ A *fat client* is your traditional PC system. If purchased today, it would have at least 16 megabytes of memory, 1.2 gigabytes of disk storage, a Pentium-based chip and an internal CD-ROM drive—in other words, your typical PC purchase. In the client/server world, a fat client would contain all the code/programs locally.

■ Programs are *function key/keypad-driven* when pressing certain function keys or keys on the number keypad initiate special activities.

■ *GUI (graphical user interface)* is a drag-and-drop-type interface. This means it was written to take advantage of a mouse.

■ A *telnet session* is the ability to run a connection on a server that emulates the functionality of a dumb terminal.

■ A *firewall* is another term for a router. It primary purpose is to inspect network traffic and prevent unauthorized traffic from passing through. The router inspects requests coming from external sources and determines if they are appropriate to pass into internal systems. For example, an e-mail message sent to George Noll would only be allowed to enter into the system if the company actually has an employee with that name. In addition, a firewall can also determine what types of services will be allowed through. For example, it might not allow access to a remote client via telnet, but would still allow e-mail to pass through its filter.

■ An *intranet site* is where one or more applications reside that were built using Internet technologies. To access the application, you use one of the universal browsers like Netscape Navigator or Internet Explorer. Since it is an intranet site, the applications reside within the firewall and are accessed using Internet technologies, like TCP/IP, HTML, or Java. The primary purpose of intranet sites is to service internal customers.

■ An *Internet site* is where one or more applications reside that were built using Internet technologies. In addition, the sites would typically be accessed by a universal browser, just as you do with the intranet site. Since it is an Internet site, the applications reside outside the firewall and are accessed using the same Internet technologies. The primary purpose of Internet sites is to service external customers. A typical Internet URL, or address, is *http://www.dbtinc.com*. An average Internet site typically contains marketing information.

■ A *master file* is used by computer systems to store information that is used across multiple applications. In a billing system, the name, address, and other contact information may be stored in a master file and used by accounts receivable, inventory, and accounts payable.

■ *MOLAP* refers to data that is stored in a multidimensional database format. In order for the data to become multidimensional, the various dimensions/attributes of the data are identified. Then a transformation of the data happens, where it is physically stored based on the intersections of those dimensions. Each intersection represents a unique point within the data.

■ A *network computer,* or *"NC,"* is a thin client by nature with as little as 4 megabytes of memory, no hard drive, containing one of any range of microprocessors, from a Pentium to a 32-bit RISC chip and will retail for under $1000. Since the average PC owner only uses his or her PC for functions like e-mail and word processing, why put an expensive "FAT Client/PC" on the desktop when only 10 percent of its functionality is ever really being used? Instead, you can put a machine on the desktop that only has to deal with the presentation of information, which means it only needs a very small operating system, a small amount of memory, a very fast processor and little or no disk storage. Unlike the dumb terminals of the past, this machine does have its own processor. The best analogy to this device is the telephone: it might have some limited functionality on its own, but it is useless unless it is hooked up to the phone network.

■ The *Network Computing Architecture* is Oracle's answer to surviving the information-enabled age. With the introduction and establishment of the Internet as a viable commercial platform for computing, Oracle took a hard look at what architecture would be needed to harness and manage software development and deployment in the age of network computing. They established a three-tiered architecture comprised of a thin client for the presentation layer, an application server for business rules, and a database server for data storage and manipulation. The goal is to create a common set of technologies that will allow all PCs, network computers, and any other client devices to work with all database servers, application servers and Web servers over any network.

■ *Oracle Applications* is a suite of off-the-shelf programs written by Oracle that provide electronic solutions to clients' business requirements. Applications satisfy Oracle customers' needs in areas such as financial management, human resources, manufacturing, and inventory.

■ *OLAP* stands for online analytical processing of data. It is a category of technology that enables users to gain insight into the data in a fast, interactive, easy-to-use manner.

■ *ROLAP* is where the data is stored in the relational database format, but is accessible via technology geared to online analytical processing or OLAP.

■ *Rightsizing* is an exercise companies go through when they assess their existing computer hardware and software, and decide on future direction. Given the direction the industry is taking toward smaller, more powerful computers, a great deal of rightsizing exercises conclude with choosing a flavor of client/server computing.

■ Applications are called *turnkey* when they can do everything the users ever wanted and then some. They are easy to learn and can be used with little or no training. The metaphor refers to turning the key in an automobile's ignition and the car (or application in this case) springs to life. Turnkey also means the complete solution; when a project or application is turnkey, the developer has done all the work and the client only needs to start it up and use it.

■ A *thin client* is a device with minimal internal memory and little or no hard disk storage, but that typically contains a microprocessor of some sorts. In the future, thin clients will range from Personal Data Assistants (PDAs) to Network Computers.

■ A *URL* is an Internet address. An example of an URL is *http://home.istar.ca/~masint/.* Think of this as your roadmap to any given Internet site. URL actually stands for *Universal Resource Locator.*

■ The *World Wide Web* is the graphical portion of the Internet (see Figure 1-1). Since the creation of universal browser(s) like Netscape Navigator and the Internet Explorer, the Internet can now easily deal with all types of data from sound to video to text. With this newfound graphical capability, anyone can easily navigate the Internet. The Web has taken the Internet from the once-sacred realm of only the highly technical person to John and Jane Q. Public. Now that the Internet has gained massive, broad-based use, we have a very viable commercial platform with which to do business.

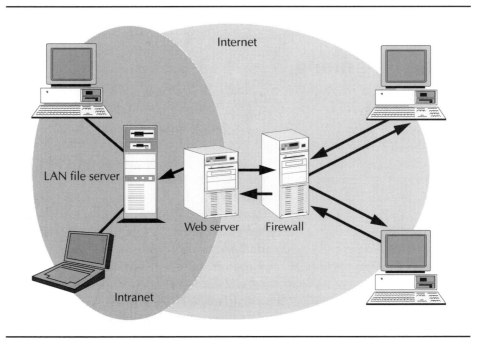

FIGURE 1-1.   *The intranet and the Internet*

What Is Oracle?

What a great question! We wish this question had been asked when we first started working with the product in version 3, when the entire documentation set for Oracle consisted of three or four books. Back then, Oracle was primarily a database company that offered few or no services. In addition, Oracle had no canned applications. Today, the picture is quite different. This multibillion-dollar company has lots of products, lots of services, and even more applications.

What makes Oracle so special is its demonstrated ability to overcome all obstacles, whether they be technological challenges or the challenges associated with rapid growth. Oracle has also demonstrated a continuous ability to build products that help us exceed the demands of the information-enabling age we live in. It's this uncanny ability to see the future of technology year after year that will help it continue to lead the charge from defining the Web computing of tomorrow to what will be the future of network computing. Chapter 20 is dedicated to a detailed explanation of the network computer. To help you understand Oracle the company, we will go back to its roots and its foundation—the database. From there, we will return to Oracle the company and how it is structured today.

In the Beginning

In the beginning, Oracle was just a database company—a relational database company, to be specific. At that time, relational databases were a new way of thinking about how data should be structured and stored. The key to this type of database is an understanding of the relationships between data, and then structuring the information base to reflect those relationships. In this way, an information base would be built that could stand the test of time. The goal in a relational database is to build a database in which only the data changes, not the underlying structures themselves. The old way of doing things is called the *traditional approach*. To illustrate the difference between these two approaches, we will start by taking a look at the traditional customer master file compared to its relational database counterpart. We will then look at characteristics of both approaches, and how changes are made using each. Finally, we will examine the differences between the two models, and show why the relational approach is the preferred way to store information. In this and the next few sections, we use the terminology "approach" and "model" when discussing "traditional" and "relational." These terms can be used synonymously; they have the same meaning.

The Traditional Approach

Figure 1-2 illustrates a traditional customer master file. It contains all the normal fields you would expect to see: customer name, address, city, state, home phone, and work phone. There is a separate slot for each item of information; thus, the number of slots depends on the number of different types of data being recorded.

This traditional design was adequate until the use of fax machines became widespread. Incorporating a fax number into the old model required an additional phone field, which in turn required a complete restructuring of the database. Also necessary was a complete redesign of the application code (i.e., a rewrite of large portions if not all of the application) associated with the customer master file (not to mention the prohibitive cost of implementing the change). Using a traditional design, managers had to make the following decisions:

■ If the application code was changed, there were high costs associated with adding new functionality to applications. Installations hoped their staff could facilitate the change rapidly; a mistake could cause an interruption in their ability to deal with customers and carry on business.

■ If the application code was left as is, all the money associated with making the change was not spent. Money was saved, but there was a price to pay: you did business without access to fax machine phone numbers. Of course, if this continued to happen, your business was taking a great technological risk. In the long run, the competition (who made the change) might pass you by.

■ Or, you could try to replace an existing data element with the needed fax number field. The saying that best describes this is "*Robbing Peter to pay Paul.*" In the business, this is called spaghetti code of a hack. This approach may work for a short while, but always costs a lot more in the long run.

Customer master file
customer_name
address
city
state
home_phone
work_phone

FIGURE 1-2. *A traditional customer master file*

At this point, you might be sitting back and saying, "What's the big deal? Who cares if the application has to be changed every once in a while?" The reality is that we live in a changing world, and businesses that don't keep up risk dying. Fact: for over 100 years, the Swiss dominated the world's watch industry. When a new type of watch was invented using quartz movement, the Swiss didn't react. Today, the Swiss make a very small portion of the world's watches. In today's world, businesses have to change constantly. Twenty years ago, the life expectancy of a computer line was three to five years. Today, a new line of hardware comes out every year. The business model and its computer systems must be able to keep pace. Using the traditional approach, had we altered the customer master file to include fax numbers, we would have had to reload the file (to populate the fax number field). On top of this, all the programs that used data in the customer master file would need modifying. At this point, we should also mention how data in traditional systems is stored. A traditional database might contain the customer master file, the payroll master file, the health insurance master file, and so on. Each one of these master files is separate. This is a problem when an event affects more than one of the files.

To illustrate how cumbersome the traditional approach can get (not to mention how expensive), look at the following scenario. Traditional systems keep redundant information in multiple locations. The employee benefits application stores employee names in a benefits master file. The payroll people maintain employee names in a payroll master file. On top of this, the long distance system stores employee names in the telecommunications master file. Suppose an employee changes his or her last name and needs a paycheck written with the new last name. The name might be changed in the payroll master file but it may not be changed elsewhere.

VIP
Synchronizing changes to the same data in multiple locations is the single most difficult function to ensure in the traditional approach.

In the traditional database, it might take months to ensure the name is properly changed in every place it is stored, not to mention the time and effort it takes just to make the changes. Wouldn't Sally be upset if she got married and lost her health insurance benefits!

Traditional systems are *design-driven*: they require design changes when one needs to capture new kinds of data. Whenever a new business need is identified (i.e., the need to store fax, cell phone, or car phone numbers), a high-end systems analyst or database administrator (highly technical, not to mention highly priced) is required to review the existing application design and make the necessary design modifications. The bottom line: the design changes are expensive, and worse still, many installations don't make the changes for that very reason!

Now, let's examine how the relational approach handles this problem.

The Relational Approach

Using this approach, system designers isolate types of information that need capturing. They then identify the relationships between those information types, and implement a database structure similar to that shown in Figure 1-3. Using the relational model, what was previously referred to as master files are called tables. Notice how Figure 1-3 shows a customer table, a phone_number table, and a phone_number_types table. Each is a separate table within the database.

In Figure 1-3, the relationship between customer and phone_number is represented by the crow's feet, which shows that a customer may have one or more phone numbers. We also show a relationship between phone_number_types and phone_number. This single line represents the fact that a phone_number must be associated with one type of phone. Thus,

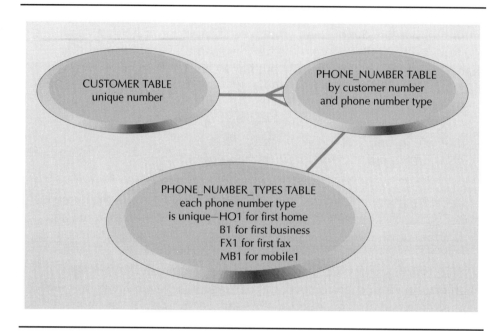

FIGURE 1-3. *Three tables (master files) using the relational model*

we have some rules governing the relationships between our customer and phone number data:

- Each customer may have one or more phone number(s).

- Each phone number belongs to one and only one customer.

- Each phone number must be one and only one type (e.g., a home voice number, a business number, a fax number, or a mobile phone).

Now that we have designed the database to understand these relationships and to enforce our rules, all we have to do to add fax numbers is to add a row of data to the phone_number_types entity. There is no need to restructure the database; there is no need to do a complete redesign of the application programs; and there is no need to program any new functionality. Using this approach, the work required to implement the storing of fax numbers is trivial.

Think back to poor Sally and her health insurance benefits. In the relational model (as illustrated in Figure 1-3), Sally's name is stored in one location. When the benefits application reads Sally's name, it gets it from the customer table. Likewise, when the payroll and telecommunications systems need Sally's name, they get it from the customer table as well.

Systems built using the relational model store information once. Changes and additions to that central repository are reflected immediately.

VIP

In a relational database, synchronizing changes to data is a non-issue since all data resides in one and only one location.

Relational systems are *data-driven*; you pay a highly technical person to come in and build a system so that the key relationships are identified and built into the system (e.g., a person may have one or more phone numbers). Then, when it becomes necessary to capture additional phone number types, it is not necessary to redesign the system. You don't need a high-priced analyst to effect changes—you add a new phone number type to the phone_number_types table.

In the relational database model, the relationship between customer and phone number stays the same. You merely need to register a new phone number type in the phone_number_types table.

Differences Between the Two Approaches

Table 1-1 summarizes how traditional and relational systems are built, and shows how they differ, using the fax number example.

In the Beginning: Summary of Points

To summarize the features of a relational database:

■ A relational database is data-driven, not design-driven. It is designed once, and the data changes over time without affecting the applications.

- The data is self-describing. For example, the phone number type is identified as phone_number_type.

- Data is stored in one place, read from one place, and modified in one place. Data is stored once, so maintaining consistency among all applications is easier.

VIP

In a distributed computing environment, it is conceivable that data may be stored in more than one place; in this case, it is the responsibility of the relational database management system and applications to ensure data is always in synch.

Task	Traditional	Relational
Design applications	Figure what applications need what types of information, then set up a series of master files.	Define the types of data that will be collected and define their relationships.
Implement applications	Load data into master files, placing one item of information into each slot in each master file.	Load types of data into their respective tables, ensuring each item ends up stored in one and only one location.
Modify applications (i.e., allow for capturing of more types of data)	Redesign the database and modify all programs to reflect the change. Reload any master files affected by the change.	Isolate the table where the type of data affected is defined (i.e., the phone_number_types table). The data that exists in the tables remains unaffected.
Modify a subset of data	Read each master file from start to finish. If a row is part of the subset to be modified, process it, otherwise go on to the next record.	Isolate the set of rows that are part of the subset, and implement the change in one SQL statement.

TABLE 1-1. *Differences Between Traditional and Relational Models*

■ Rules that control how the data will be stored are defined and enforced.

Oracle Today

Today, Oracle Systems Corporation, based in Redwood Shores, California, manufactures software products and delivers services for the electronic management of information. Oracle is a worldwide provider of computer software, with 1997 revenues in excess of $5 billion. Oracle does business in over 90 countries around the world, and their software runs on upwards of 100 different computers. They are a major player on the information superhighway.

With the innovation of the Media Server and a number of cooperative agreements with worldwide communications giants, Oracle is actively participating in the race to bring video on demand to your living room.

With its recent agreement with Netscape Corporation, Oracle is actively participating in the race to dominate the World Wide Web. Let's take a closer look at this relationship and what it means.

In October 1996 Oracle and Netscape corporation signed a "strategic agreement to integrate and distribute flagship products." Specifically, Oracle will bundle Netscape Navigator with its Intel-based Network Computer software operating environment.

NOTE
This agreement also includes Oracle's fully owned subsidiary, Network Computer, Inc.

Oracle also agreed not to offer other third-party browser products bundled with its Intel-based Network computers. This agreement also established Netscape Navigator as Oracle's preferred third-party Internet client for selected future Oracle products. Netscape Corporation agreed that Oracle's enterprise and workgroup database servers will be the only databases bundled with Netscape commercial applications, including Netscape Merchant System, Netscape Publishing System, and Netscape Community System. A press release on the agreement went on to state: "These agreements combine the companies' complementary market-leading products. Netscape Navigator is credited with 80 percent market share according to recent industry reports and Netscape Commercial

Applications are used by many leading sites on the Internet. Oracle's Universal Server is the industry's leading database with 42 percent market share according to International Data Corp. (1996)." Oracle's recent agreement with Netscape positions it uniquely to dominate the World Wide Web. The real power of the Web is yet to be harnessed. Today most people are not very impressed with a majority of Web sites they visit. They are nothing more than static applications—in other words, they are glorified billboards. When your Web site is able to harness the power of a database, watch out. Imagine a Web site that knew who you were and could tailor itself to your needs and wants. That would be a very powerful tool, indeed. Once again, Oracle Corporation sees the future and is positioning itself to get there first.

What these two examples show us is that Oracle corporation is part of the never-ending race to bring the very best technology to its customers. The ability to see the future trends in technology and the ability to embrace key technology early on not only help Oracle survive, but are key reasons it continues to make giant strides ahead of the competition. The foundation of this house is the Oracle Server. Let's take a closer look at the Oracle Server and how it has been able to manufacture a suite of products that revolve around it.

Oracle8 Server

The Oracle8 Server is a state-of-the-art information management environment. It is a repository for very large amounts of data, and gives users rapid access to that data. The Oracle8 Server allows for the sharing of data between applications; the information is stored in one place and used by many systems. At first, the Oracle8 Server was available on Sun Solaris and Windows NT. The Oracle7 Server runs on dozens of different computers, supporting the following configurations:

- **Host-based** Users are connected directly to the same computer on which the database resides.

- **Client/server** Users access the database from their personal computer (client) via a network, and the database sits on a separate computer (server).

- **Distributed processing**   Users access a database that resides on more than one computer. The database is spread across more than one machine, and the users are unaware of the physical location of the data they work with.

- **Web-enabled computing**   The ability to access data from an Internet-based application.

We believe the Oracle7 Server has helped position Oracle the company at the top of the list of successful information vendors, and Oracle8 will continue the tradition.

Why Oracle Is Where It Is Today

There are many significant features that have catapulted Oracle to the top of the growing information management vendor community.

Security Mechanisms

Oracle's sophisticated security mechanisms control access to sensitive data by an assortment of privileges. Users are given rights to view, modify, and create data based on the name they use to connect to the database. Customers use these mechanisms to ensure specified users get to see sensitive data, while others are forbidden.

Backup and Recovery

Oracle provides sophisticated backup and recovery routines. Backup creates a secondary copy of Oracle data; recovery restores a copy of data from that backup. Oracle's backup and recovery strategy minimizes data loss and downtime when and if problems arise. Oracle Server also provides backup and recovery schemes that can allow uninterrupted access to the data 7 days a week, 24 hours a day, and 365 days a year.

Space Management

Oracle offers flexible space management. You can allocate disk space for storage of data and control subsequent allocations by instructing Oracle how much space to set aside for future requirements. It also has a series of special abilities that were designed with very large databases in mind. In fact, many of the latest features in Oracle8 and 7.3 were designed with data warehouses in mind. By design, these are typically very large databases.

Open Connectivity

Oracle provides open connectivity to and from other vendors' software. Using add-ons to the Oracle database, you can work with information that resides in other data repositories, such as IBM's DB2, Sybase, or Microsoft Access. Also, you are permitted to store your data in Oracle's database and access it from other software, such as Microsoft Visual Basic, Powersoft's PowerBuilder, and Gupta's SQL*Windows.

Development Tools

The Oracle Server, commonly referred to as the database engine, supports a wide range of development tools, end-user query tools, off-the-shelf applications, and office-wide information management tools.

Components of the Oracle7/8 Server

Oracle sells its server technology with a number of add-on options that enhance the server capabilities. The base product provides all the functionality to support the requirements of most of Oracle's customers. When customers require additional functionality Oracle has a series of options they can purchase which include:

- Video
- WebServer
- Enterprise Manager
- Spatial Data
- ConText
- OLAP
- Messaging
- Advance Networking
- Parallel Server

Let's take a closer look at the Oracle8 Server itself, and then we will review some of the Oracle8 Server components and options and look at the functionality they provide for you.

The Oracle Server is the foundation of the entire Oracle product and application suite. The Server is where the data gets stored. Data in its simplest sense is numbers and letters. As we are all learning very quickly, access to information is critical if corporations want to survive the information-enabling age we all live in. The Oracle Server is where all this data is stored. Data or information, as we all know, takes on many more forms than just letters and numbers. With the Oracle Server and its additional options, you will be able to store, manipulate, and present data in whatever form it resides. You will learn how data ranges from numbers and letters, to video and sound, to structured and unstructured forms. The Oracle Server is a repository for holding and manipulating data very quickly.

Data Accessibility

When you purchase the Oracle Server, you get a whole host of core functionality to help you store and keep your data accessible. It provides utilities for backing up the data. These include the ability to back up the information while the user community is still using it. The term we like to use to explain this concept is "hot backup." The official Oracle term for this ability to back up live data is "archive mode backups." No longer does an organization have to shut down access to the applications while a backup is being made of the database. The bottom line is that you can keep your Oracle database up 7 days a week, 24 hours a day.

The Oracle Server also provides for data integrity. If, while a user is changing data within an Oracle database, a failure of any sort happens, the database has the ability to undo or rollback any suspected transaction. With Oracle Server, you are never in doubt as to the status of any transaction. It also includes a full, row level, locking of all data that resides within it.

For example, if you were working on a stock purchase application built on an Oracle repository and two users wanted to buy lot #5, which is 100 shares of a Database Technologies stock, the database would not allow that to happen. Since there is only one lot left to purchase, the database would allow one user to have access to purchasing and the other user would have to wait. When the second user received the go-ahead to proceed, he or she would see the new status of the lot as sold. The Oracle Server transparently handles these situations, maintaining the integrity of the data.

Procedural Component

With release 7.1 of the Oracle7 server, this option became part of the core Oracle7 Server at no additional cost. All of the procedural features are in the Oracle Server product and then some. The foundation of this option is Oracle's programming language, PL/SQL, which is discussed in Chapter 7. With this option, you can implement the following features.

■ **Stored Procedures** Programs (or code segments) are stored in the Oracle database and perform central functions for your installation. For example, in a cable television billing application, you may use a stored procedure to create a reminder letter to customers with delinquent accounts. The execution of that procedure is triggered by the creation of a customer's monthly statement when unpaid charges are due for over 60 days.

■ **Database Triggers** These are code stored in the database triggered by events that occur in your applications. In a human resources application, for example, when a new employee is hired, the creation of a new set of personnel information could use a database trigger to create messages to be sent to other parts of the company. These messages, triggered by the new employee being added to the database, could alert the operators of the message center to the existence of the new individual.

■ **Packages** Procedures are grouped together and store the code as a single program unit in the database. For example, a central warehouse for a chain of bookstores could design a package that takes care of the routing of special orders to the appropriate retail location. There would be procedures within this package to initiate the transfer of goods, process notifications of short orders, process reorders, and so on.

VIP

This component coupled with distributed processing, replication, and parallel query used to be separate options purchased separately from the Oracle7/8 Server. They are now all components of the base product.

Distributed Processing Component

In many installations, portions of corporate data reside on different computers in different cities. Accounts receivable may be based in Dallas, procurement in Toronto, research and development in Jakarta, and the head office might be in Lisbon. Each location has a segment of the corporate data, yet users need to access that information as if it all resided on the same central computer. The Oracle Server's distributed capability permits this scenario to become a reality. There is *location transparency*, such that a user in Yokohama working with the information stored in Toronto is unaware of the physical location of the data. The physical location of the procurement data is unknown to all users. Oracle's distributed option permits this to work.

Parallel Query Component

The parallel query feature allows customers to take advantage of processing queries on computers with more than one central processing unit (commonly referred to as a CPU). On single CPU machines (or multi-CPU machines without the parallel query option), a single process accesses the database and displays the data that qualifies based on the selection criteria. The processing is handled as shown in Figure 1-4.

When using the parallel query option on multi-CPU machines, Oracle dispatches a number of query processes that work alongside one another. They partition the query processing and work simultaneously; the results are merged and presented to the user when ready. Figure 1-5 shows the basics of this option.

With this ability to run parallel queries, a query that used to take an hour can run in minutes by taking advantage of all the available CPU power.

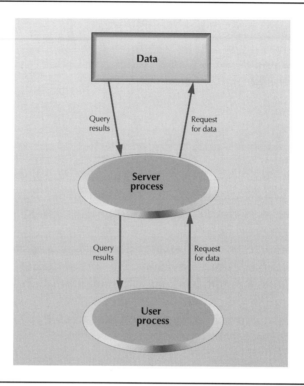

FIGURE 1-4. *Query processing without the parallel query feature*

Summary of Points

- The procedural component of the Oracle8 Server delivers PL/SQL, as well as stored procedures, database triggers, packages, and functions. These code segments reside in the database, and can be shared by applications.

- The distributed component allows users to work with data in a remote database as if it resided locally.

- The parallel query component caters to computers with multiple CPUs, and allows query processing to be split between multiple server processes.

■ Provided with the Oracle8 Server are a multitude of functions that insure data integrity. This includes the locking capability needed to prevent two users from trying to update the same database object at the same time. The above example of purchasing shares of stock best illustrates this point.

■ The Oracle8 server provides functionality that can maintain data accessibility 7 days a week, 24 hours a day.

Parallel Server Option

Some manufacturers make clustered computers: each machine in the cluster has its own memory, yet they have common disk storage devices. The parallel server option allows Oracle to operate with this configuration.

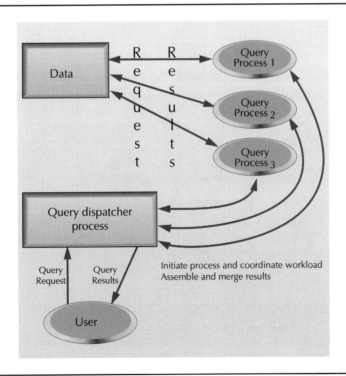

FIGURE I-5. *Query processing with the parallel query feature*

Each machine is referred to as a node in the cluster, and the term loosely coupled is used to refer to the nodes. Figure 1-6 shows how this works.

The bottom line of this option is that you can have two or more computers talking to the same database at the same time. This provides you with near fault tolerance performance at a fraction of the cost. If one machine fails for any reason, just reroute your users onto the other machine. It is near fault tolerance in that it approaches 99.9 percent availability. The only time the Oracle8 Server won't be available is when both machines are experiencing hardware failure. Also, you have the power of two or more computers at your disposal. If you run out of horsepower on one machine, add another.

VIP

The Parallel Server option is NOT part of the base product and is purchased separately.

Video Option

Recognizing the fact that a whole new set of applications are emerging with requirements that go way beyond traditional data and text, Oracle has developed the video option. The video option extends the ability of the

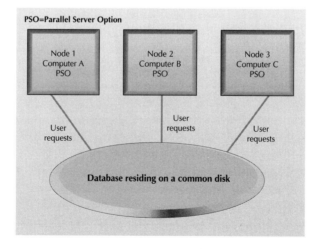

FIGURE 1-6. *Loosely coupled nodes in a cluster*

core database (Oracle8 Server) so that it is now able to store, manage, and deliver real-time, full-screen video and high-quality sound to clients over the network. Today, this ability is not needed by most businesses, so it does not make sense to make this part of the core database implementation. What is clear, however, is that the applications of the future need to be more media and medium-rich.

A good example of an application that would benefit from the Oracle video option is a sales kiosk system. Today, a kiosk-based application is a very static application designed to only deal with a pre-determined path. What if a sales kiosk were built that could look into the corporate database, determine who the customers are, their likes and dislikes, and then provide a specially-developed kiosk display which includes full-motion video and sound and delivered this all over a network. To price the products displayed on the kiosk, it would go across the network and retrieve from the corporate database the current up-to-date pricing and description data. To determine a discount schedule, it would look at all the information known about the prospective customer within the corporate databases and then build a kiosk application on the fly, offering customers unique discounts tailored to their needs.

Imagine another application, a computer-based training system, that had full access to video on demand with a full Oracle8 Server behind it. It could determine how well you were doing on the training materials and only display the expert portion of the materials if you are doing very well, or decide you need extended help and display more detailed class material. Since it would have access across the network to all the corporate data currently stored about a student, the class can be tailored to the student. This would be true interactive training. Since the interactive class had the rich medium of full-motion video and sound, it would be able to convey much more information to the student than traditional computer-based training, commonly referred to as *CBT*.

Imagine true video on demand on your TV set. Today, people think cable is the latest and greatest, yet with over one hundred channels at our disposal, you still cannot find anything worth watching. People in general like the quality of the picture and the variety of the channels available on cable. Actually, we like the fact that we can rent recent movies right from home through the pay-per-view channels. Until we got cable, we were the number one reason the local video store made money: the late fees we were charged every time we returned a rental late.

Well, if you think cable is great, imagine true video on demand, accessible from your home. There you are, sitting at home bored. You decide you want to watch a movie or simply cannot find anything worth watching. It's 2:12 p.m.—without video on demand, you would be stuck watching the movies the local cable company had decided to make available to their customers. As if that weren't enough, you either have to start watching a movie late or hope a movie you want to watch is starting at 2:30 p.m. Another issue is quality—it's not a digital signal, so you are stuck with the picture you get. Finally, what if you want to watch a particular movie that is out of season? For example, you feel like watching a Christmas movie, but it's the middle of May. Most likely, the movie you want to see won't be available. In the world of video on demand, this would be a very different situation.

You decide you want to watch a movie. In fact, you want to watch a John Wayne movie. Stored in digital form on an Oracle8 Server with the video option is every John Wayne movie ever produced. The Server allows you to search for movie information by title, genre, stars, co-stars, or whatever criteria you choose. You can see your all-time favorite movie, *Mary Poppins*! You order up the movie, and a video stream is displayed on your TV set. Whenever you like, you can stop, replay, or fast-forward the movie.

NOTE
Before you get too excited, remember that the vendors of this product will ensure you cannot watch the movie over and over again without paying more than once!

You have complete control of the picture—in other words, true video on demand. Think it's a dream? It is currently under trial in several areas in the world. The Oracle video software powers some of the world's largest interactive television deployments.

Any database that is going to survive our information-enabling age must be able to manipulate data types that extend way beyond client/server applications of today, and having the ability to manipulate full-motion video and sound makes a whole new class of applications possible. The two examples used are just the tip of the iceberg.

As with anything Oracle corporation does, it is fully scaleable and deployable across its product line. Today, you can embed video technology into Oracle Media Objects, Oracle Power Objects, and Microsoft's Visual Basic. This means you can deploy video on demand technology in the applications you build today.

When you purchase Oracle7 release 7.3 Video option you get the following components:

- **Oracle Video Option** The extensions needed to allow your Oracle7 server to handle and service video on demand requests.

- **Oracle Video Client** The software needed by your application developers to embed and utilize networked video applications in their applications.

- **Oracle Media Net** The software components which allow clients and servers to communicate over a distributed computing environment.

Enterprise Manager

One of the things we always found ironic about the move toward open systems was the lack of everyday tools that existed. For example, we would be working on one of the fastest UNIX machines/open systems that ever existed, and yet we would have no tape management system. The reason we did not have it is that it did not yet exist. There was no vendor we could purchase the tape solutions from.

Over the past few years, this has all changed. Many a company has rebuilt itself by taking the tools it sold in the mainframe arena and making them available in UNIX. The reason these tools were built in the first place still applies in the open system arena: you still need good tape management software, since backing up your computer system to an inexpensive medium like tape is very important. Being able to find those tapes and manage those tapes is a very critical need. Platinum Corporation is a great example of a company that has rebuilt itself in the open system arena. Platinum has taken many of the tools they built for the IBM mainframe and rebuilt the equivalent for open systems/UNIX. For example, we now see transaction log analyzers being sold for the Oracle marketplace. These are crucial tools when you deploy mission-critical applications. When a need (or vacuum) arises in the marketplace, there are always companies to fill that need. This is the basic law of supply and demand at work. Overall, we think these are the good signs of a maturing marketplace, which is the type of environment you want when the application is mission-critical.

It's important to recognize the fact that one of the most difficult skill sets to find in the Oracle marketplace is the knowledge that good, solid database administrators bring to their jobs. It's also important to note that without solid management tools in place, Oracle customers will not be able to deploy larger, more complex databases. Oracle has built its own answer to this problem, Oracle Enterprise Manager (or *OEM*). With this type of tool in place, your database administrator can be more productive, and a weak database administrator will have a very strong tool to help supplement his or her ability.

VIP

Solid system management tools are critical to keeping your Oracle database running smoothly. We recommend you take the time to evaluate all system management options available. The correct choice for you should be based on your budget and needs.

Oracle Enterprise Manager is a set of management tools designed to help you manage the complete Oracle environment, which includes systems, applications, networks, and databases. In addition to being able to manage different Oracle environments from one tool, you also have intelligent agents and an open interface to help you leverage third-party products.

From the Manager console, the database administrator through a GUI interface has the ability to manage the complete Oracle environment. There are four major components to the Oracle Enterprise Manager Console:

- Navigator allows you to view and manipulate all network nodes and services in a family tree-like manner.

- Map Window allows the database administrator to view and map subsets of objects in a graphical manner. For example, if you worked in a major hospital, with quite a few Oracle databases, you might look at your Oracle environments in three distinct ways—admitting, emergency room, and lab results. This tool allows you to take a very complex environment and map it into more cohesive subsets.

■ Job Scheduling System allows database administrators to automate repetitive tasks. This can be done in one location, to automate a task at a remote site. For example, the database administrator might automate the backups, which frees them up for other tasks.

■ Event Management System allows the database administrator to remotely monitor system and database events, and then, based on some preset thresholds, kick off corrective jobs working with the job scheduling system. For example, you might set up an event to monitor database free space to ensure that you never allow a database to run out of space.

Every Oracle database that is being managed has an intelligent agent process running. This process monitors the database(s) known to OEM, gathers statistics about database performance, and stores information in the Oracle8 repository to feed to OEM for perusal and corrective action by the database administrator. Through this agent, OEM can make things happen. It is also open, so that third-party products can take advantage of it. When the Oracle8 Server is installed, you end up with the Enterprise Manager base product.

Spatial Data Option

With the spatial data option you are able to store and manipulate both spatial and attribute data in a single database. It allows you to have both Oracle8 Spatial Data option tables in your database with any mix of standard Oracle8 tables. You can then access both table types using the standard Oracle tool sets.

To understand what spatial data is and means to your Oracle8 Server, let's take a look at how the Oracle8 server normally accesses data stored within it. A traditional Oracle database is made up of data stored within a database object called a *table*. A table is made up of many columns of data. These columns of data are the attributes of the table.

For example, by looking at Table 1-2, we have a table called the state. It is made up of six attributes, which are columns of data.

Many of the applications that need access to state names and codes are not interested in any of the attributes associated with governor information.

State_code	State_name	Gov_Lname	Gov_fname	Gov_Mi	Party_Code
MA	Massachusetts	Weld	Bill	I	R
CA	California	Smith	Darryl	E	R
ID	Idaho	Head	Potato	A	D
WI	Wisconsin	Head	Cheese	A	D
NH	New Hampshire	Farnham	Mark	O	R
VT	Vermont	Jerry	Ben	A	D
RI	Rhode Island	Chapman	Cindy	W	D

TABLE I-2. *Traditional "Attribute" Relational Database Table*

So in the traditional Oracle8 server, you are able to create a database object called an *index*.

An index is a database object that contains just the subset of data a typical application is interested in. When creating the index, you specify those columns you wish to be able to search upon. Those columns are called *keys*.

By looking at Table 1-3, you see an example of an index named State_Index. It is much quicker to retrieve data from the index for two reasons.

1. It is much quicker, since the data set is much smaller. Remember, you have fewer columns/attributes of data to deal with. The entries in the index are stored in such a way that it is quicker to find locations within the data set when specifying the key.

2. This method of data retrieval has worked quite well, for most applications. Your database performance was a factor of database size and index efficiency. As very large databases become more prevalent and the trend toward large data warehouses grows, the existing Oracle indexing mechanisms have not been able to keep up with a new class of users' performance needs.

To meet this new class of users' needs, Oracle engineered the spatial data option. Performance is now a factor of how much data you actually retrieve, not the size of the data set. In a spatial database, the data is the

State_code	State_name
MA	Massachusetts
CA	California
ID	Idaho
WI	Wisconsin
NH	New Hampshire
VT	Vermont
RI	Rhode Island

TABLE 1-3.   *Index on a Traditional Relational Database Table*

index. In a spatial database table, you identify all the dimensions you are interested in. The spatial database option is able to take these various dimensions and merge them into a single value that represents the intersections of all desired dimensions. Every combination of these dimensions leads to a single unique point. Once the dimensions are identified, the data is encoded and grouped together in an appropriate manner. The greater the relationship between data, the closer it is stored in the database. When a request is made to access the data, any data that is not relevant is outside the bounds of the query. Since the data is the index, data outside of your interest is ignored. A query that looks at a megabyte of data takes the same time to retrieve the data on a 10 megabyte table as it does a 1 terabyte table. The factor that has the greatest impact on performance is the data set in which you are interested.

Spatial Data Option Summary

In summary, the spatial data option is a new way to store and retrieve data. Since the data is the index and is stored based on the relationship of the dimensions and each dimension represents a unique location of the associated dimensions, a query is only forced to look at the data that is of interest. The major determinant of database performance is the size of the data set you are interested in. This is very useful in a very large database of a typical data warehouse.

ConText Option

The Oracle8 Server Context option is a text management solution that enables you to manage unstructured text information resources as quickly as you manage structured data. Structured data is data stored in columns, like the state_cd column. An example of your unstructured text data is a contract, or a magazine article. Figure 1-7 and Figure 1-8 illustrate the difference between structured and unstructured data. With the context option, you are able to build and deploy text-based applications with a SQL-like interface.

What's ironic is that organizations for the past ten years have invested very heavily in building applications that enable us to rapidly retrieve structured data. Yet most of the data in the world is unstructured: many studies state that 90 percent of the world's data is unstructured. Good examples of unstructured data are magazine articles, Web pages, faxes, e-mails, contracts, and documentation. Think of all the valuable information that is stored within these documents. What if your data warehouse application could easily have access to every contract you ever signed. What if you could store and retrieve data from every e-mail message you ever sent based on a theme search. Would this be useful? In today's information-enabled world, access to data is key. It would be foolish to ignore 90 percent of the world's textual information. The ConText allows your Oracle8 server to deal with unstructured data, giving your organization access to an estimated 90 percent of the world's data, today.

WebServer

The true power of the World Wide Web is not static data pages, which are the majority of Web sites today. The true power of the Web can only be realized when you can marry it to your database. When we go out and navigate the World Wide Web, what we typically see are a lot of very sophisticated billboards. Yes, they have sound and enhanced graphics, but they are still glorified billboards. The only difference? Instead of being behind the wheels of our cars, we are sitting at our desks in front of a PC.

Imagine a Web site that had access to the corporate database. It could retrieve facts about you, your likes and dislikes. It could then dynamically build a Web site on the fly to meet your needs. Imagine a Web site that could be maintained by a low-end clerk instead of a very highly

	A	B	C	D	E
1	Timecard Number	Start Date	End Date	Employee Name	Employee Number
2					
3					
4					
5					
6					
7					
8					
9					
10					

Spreadsheets

FIGURE 1-7.   *Unstructured data*

compensated Web specialist. Every time you wanted to make a price change, you could make that change to your corporate database and the Web site would automatically be updated. That's what the Oracle WebServer technology is all about. It allows your Oracle8 Server to talk to

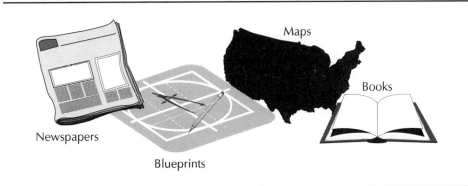

FIGURE 1-8.   *Structured data*

the current state of Web software from JAVA to HTML. WebServer can let you do all of the things we mentioned in this paragraph and more.

This is just the tip of the iceberg. There are many works out there that explain the direction of Web-based electronic technology.

OLAP Option

With this option, OLAP users can express their data in the same way they think about it. Rather than thinking of the data in terms of flat files or spreadsheets, the OLAP option allows you to look at the data in terms of its many dimensions. This ability to organize data in the way that users think about it is known as multidimensionality. Then, based on these dimensions, the data is transformed into a multidimensional database. Oracle Corporation recognizes the fact that the relational model is not always the optimal choice for storing all types of data. The OLAP options extend the Oracle8 server with the capabilities to store data in the relational model (ROLAP) or in the multidimensional model (MOLAP). Oracle8 Server gives you the best of all worlds—full OLAP support with the physical data inside the relational model or inside the multidimensional model or both.

WHAT ARE DIMENSIONS?   *Dimensions* are the key components or attributes of the way that data is categorized. For example, you could classify a sale by "the time when the product was purchased"; "the particular product that was purchased"; "where the purchase occurred"; and "the price of the product." Each one of these items could be thought of as a dimension within the database. In this example, time, products, geography, and measures are the dimensions. The intersection of these dimensions produces a *cell*. A cell is defined as a single data point that occurs at the intersection defined by selecting one value from each of the dimensions in a multidimensional array. When one visualizes a multidimensional database, one might see a Rubik's cube. Rubik's cube was a game that originated in the Soviet Union, in which you had a series of blocks, and you moved the various cells of the cube to line up the colors.

Locating the value of sales in a car dealership application for Boston is quite easy. You think in terms of its position within the database as opposed to thinking about which columns you might have to join. With the OLAP option, you are given the capability of physically storing the data in the multidimensional model or storing it in the relational model.

Advance Networking Option

The advance networking option provides a single source of integration with enterprise directory services, such as single sign-on services, network encryption, token and user authentication. Previous releases called this option the Oracle Secure Network Services.

Think of the networking option as the peanut butter in a peanut butter sandwich. One slice of bread is Oracle and all its related software, and the other slice of bread is a third party vendor's network software. By separating Oracle from the network layer, you never have to rewrite your applications to take advantage of a new network layer. For example, if the U.S. government mandates that all installations worldwide must start using a 1 terabit encryption package, this Networking Option Layer would help ensure that you would not have to change a line of application code.

Oracle recognizes the fact that these enterprise network services are constantly changing, and Oracle implementation allows it to be "technology neutral." Simply put, the Oracle Network option allows you to support any protocol, any application, and any data by integrating the connected session with the network layer transparently. With the advance networking option, you will be positioned to take advantage of new communication technologies as they become available.

SQL*Plus—The User-friendly Interface

So far we have talked about the Oracle Universal Server. Let's move on to SQL*Plus—the way you define and manipulate data in Oracle's relational database. SQL (Structured Query Language) is the industry standard adopted by all database vendors. (Some people pronounce SQL as "sequel"; others pronounce each letter separately.) Oracle's SQL*Plus is a superset of standard SQL: it conforms to the standards of a SQL-compliant language, and it has some Oracle-specific add-ons, leading to its name (SQL and Plus). In the old days, SQL*Plus was called UFI, the user-friendly interface. Compared to writing in a typical programming language like FORTRAN, friendly it is.

The Oracle Server only understands statements worded using SQL—when tools such as Oracle Forms interact with the database, they pass nothing other than SQL statements for processing. Oracle's implementation of SQL through SQL*Plus is compliant with ANSI (American National Standards Institute) and ISO (International Standards Organization) standards. Almost all Oracle tools support identical SQL syntax.

SQL is tailored to harness the power of the relational model. Since all your data is stored via the relationship, it is possible to work with your data in sets, versus independent rows of data. With SQL*Plus, much of the work associated with retrieving data out of a traditional database goes away. For example, you no longer read a record. Instead, you write a program that deals with all the records associated with an entity. No one record is different than another. In SQL*Plus, whatever action you decide to take is done as a complete set. We demonstrate how this is done in Chapter 6 and Chapter 11.

VIP
All the vendors have gone the relational database route. The relational model is here to stay.

SQL*Plus: Summary of Points

Let's summarize what we have learned about Oracle's base programming language:

- SQL*Plus is Oracle's flavor of SQL. "Plus" refers to Oracle's addition to the SQL language.

- All work with a relational database is done with a SQL-based programming language.

- SQL*Plus is user-friendly.

- When programming with SQL*Plus, you work on sets of data (i.e., information is not processed one record at a time).

- Using the "Plus" component of SQL*Plus, it is easy to write useful reports (Chapters 6 and 11 highlight report writing using SQL*Plus).

Oracle Forms—The Front End

With the foundation of a strong database and complemented by a strong
language for reporting (SQL*Plus), it was only natural that Oracle would
expand into a screen generator, since this is the primary way most users
deal with the database. Oracle Forms is part of the Developer/2000 suite of
tools and typically the front end tool of choice for mission-critical
applications. It runs in a graphical user interface (GUI) environment, with
the look and feel of Microsoft Windows (3.x, NT, or Windows 95).

Application developers design data entry and query screens with Oracle
Forms; end users can then use these screens to manipulate data in the
Oracle database. The interface with the user is event-driven or function
key/keypad-driven. As summarized in Table 1-4, there are three types of
modules one writes with Oracle Forms. Rolled together, they provide the
developer and end user with a complete forms-based corporate data entry
solution. Combining an assortment of these three types of programs into a
full-blown application is part of the art of working with Oracle Forms. In
Chapter 8 we discuss this tool in greater detail.

Oracle Reports—The Report Writer

With the foundation of a strong relational database and complemented by a
robust suite of core development tools, Oracle continued to expand. While
SQL*Plus is a great reporting tool, it was not designed with just reporting in
mind. So Oracle developed various tools just for generating reports,

Program type	Contents
forms	Allows update, creation, and deletion of data within Oracle objects.
menu	Defines an assortment of main menus and an optional subset of any number of submenus.
library	A repository for centralized PL/SQL code accessed by other types of Oracle Forms modules.

TABLE I-4.   *Oracle Forms Module Types*

including SQL*QMX, RPT, and Easy*SQL. Oracle Reports (and its predecessor SQL*Reportwriter) is the flagship report writer tool for the Developer/2000 suite. We discuss Oracle Reports in Chapter 9 and show you how to build a few simple reports.

Oracle Reports is a successor to SQL*Reportwriter that appeared with Oracle version 6. SQL*Reportwriter provides a reporting environment with which the developer designs reports and the end user executes them; it evolved into Oracle Reports as users insisted they wanted a Windows-based mouse-driven interface. With Oracle Reports, you can create graphical report representations of the data in your Oracle database.

Oracle Reports (starting with version 2.0) is a true multimedia reporting environment. You can include images, sound, and charts, and you can present reports in a variety of colors using an assortment of fonts. You can easily create popular report output styles with Oracle Reports. Using its powerful default features, developers can create master/detail reports, matrix reports, and form letters with little programming.

Master/Detail Reports

When designing master/detail reports, the programmer defines a hierarchy of the data assembled for the report; you display all data for the first level, then the second level data it is related to. The following simple master/detail report uses automobile manufacturers as an example. The manufacturer is called the master; when a master is displayed, all of its associated detail information appears.

```
Manufacturer:  Nissan
Model          Style        Price Class
Quest          Minivan      D
Maxima         Sedan        G
Ultima         Sport        F


Manufacturer:  GM
Model          Style        Price Class
Safari         Minivan      D
Impala         Sedan        G
TransAm        Sport        F
```

Matrix Reports

In matrix reports, you use the values of rows and columns as labels. For example, let's consider the following set of data:

```
Salesperson              Quarter              Commission
10                       1                    500
10                       2                    400
20                       1                    600
20                       2                    900
20                       3                    350
30                       2                    900
30                       3                    235
```

That data would be presented in the following way in a matrix report:

```
          1           2           3
10        500         400
20        600         900         350
30                    900         235
```

Notice how the quarter column values appear as column headers and the salesperson numbers appear as row headers.

Form Letters

With form letters, you take information from the database and include it in the body of a letter. Sometimes, one simply gets name and address information from the database. Other times, the text in the body of the letter is extracted from the database. In the next example, the text in italics has been printed based on address information stored in the database; the text in bold and italics forms part of the letter's body and comes from the database too.

```
...
Dear Ms. Stroud:
This is to inform you that ...... no later than the end of May,
1998.
...
Dear Mr. Flaherty:
This is to inform you that ...... no later than the middle of
July, 1999.
...
```

VIP
Oracle Reports is a report writer. Unlike SQL*Plus, it is very graphically based. Using the power of a computer and its mouse, you are able to point and click to build very powerful reports.

Oracle Book

Oracle Book is an online document viewing facility for the sharing of text across Oracle products. Since version 7.1 of the Oracle Server, Oracle has supplied a set of online documentation you can read using Oracle Book. Oracle Book has three components:

- *Designer* provides for the creation and maintenance of online documents.

- *Converter* takes older formats of Book documents and converts them to the latest release.

- *Runtime* provides viewing capabilities and is used to propagate Book documents to the user community.

The Runtime environment permits customization of user preferences, though the documents' contents cannot be changed. Oracle now distributes the majority of its products with electronic online documentation read using Oracle Book. Developers use Oracle Book Designer to create and modify documents, and users run Oracle Book to access them.

NOTE
Over time we expect to see Oracle migrate toward universal browsers. We expect the use of Oracle Book to dissipate. Since the product is still for sale we felt it made sense to mention it. In some ways it was one of the first generic browsers.

VIP

With the industry trend towards universal browser technology, it makes more sense to look at deploying an application built on Netscape Navigator than to buy and deploy one using Oracle Book .

Oracle Loader and SQL*Connect

In the old days, Oracle had a special tool called ODL (Oracle Data Loader). Over time, this has evolved into Oracle Loader, a tool that very quickly allows you to load data into an Oracle database. (It should be noted you get this tool as part of the standard toolset.) Tools like this are very important to an Oracle database. In the real world, a great deal of customers' systems still use the traditional approach. Most agree that a relational database is a great tool, but migrating traditional systems to relational systems requires conversion of your existing systems' data. Well, that's what Oracle Loader is all about. It is a tool you use to move data into an Oracle database.

VIP

Oracle Loader is a great tool to use when you need to move data into your data warehouse.

Like any good capitalistic company, Oracle grew its supply to meet the demands of the marketplace. A big demand exists in the industry for tools that enable you to move data from a traditional database to a relational database, just as we are seeing an even bigger demand for tools to migrate data into the data warehouse. There is also a great demand for tools that enable a relational database to talk to a traditional database. That is the thrust behind tools like SQL*Connect, which enables an Oracle database to connect and talk to a traditional database, be it an IBM mainframe or a DEC Alpha system. The trick is that it treats these external data sources as extensions of the database. You can even run SQL commands against these sources.

In fact, the SQL*Connect product became so popular that it now has the ability to talk to over 30 external data sources. It also has a new name, the Oracle Open Gateways, and three product families: the Oracle Transparent

Gateways, the Oracle Procedural Gateways and finally, the Oracle Access Managers. The functionality ranges from being able to access SQL commands to an external data source, to being able to run procedures on an external data source. The name of the game is connectivity and the Oracle suite of products do it better than anyone else.

It's also clear that once the data is placed in an Oracle database with the Developer/2000 suite, it is very easy to generate reports and screens to manipulate the contents. It is also the reality that this migration might take years to accomplish. Oracle has developed tools to move your data into Oracle, like Oracle Loader, or tools to talk to a traditional database, like SQL*Connect.

Oracle Using Its Own Tools—the Applications

As time went on, Oracle Corporation realized that there was a strong business opportunity available for off-the-shelf generic applications. So Oracle started to build financial applications. This had two major impacts on the rest of the Oracle environments (i.e., Oracle customers using the same products Oracle the company itself was using).

For the first time, Oracle Corporation was actually using its own tools to build applications. The more they used the tools, the more the tools improved. The company started to live, eat, and breathe their own tools. The more Oracle used their own tools, the more they found ways to improve them. So, very quickly, we started to see major improvements in the quality and functionality of the tools.

Second, as soon as Oracle Corporation started to build applications based on the relational database model, companies started to use the Oracle software for mission-critical business functions (e.g., payroll). This accelerated the proliferation of Oracle's database software, and more and more companies started to reap the benefits of the new technology Oracle had developed.

Today, Oracle has a division that puts out applications in every major product area—from accounting to manufacturing to industry-specific solutions. Administrative support of today's application customer can be done using Oracle InterOffice, which we discuss next. In addition, Oracle application has a whole list of industry solutions from education to pharmaceuticals.

Oracle InterOffice

On June 20, 1996 Oracle Corporation announced Oracle InterOffice, the world's first fully-scaleable, Web-based collaboration software built on the Oracle7/8 Server. The roots of this software go back to previous Oracle products from its document management software to Oracle Office, the traditional Office automation tool. What's different about Oracle InterOffice is that it was built with the World Wide Web in mind. As our society becomes more electronic in nature, you will be able to use Oracle InterOffice to incorporate your business partners and suppliers into your business processes.

Just like its predecessor, this product will help automate the paper flow process, only this time within the total electronic community. For example, an employee might put in a request for office supplies. That request would automatically be routed to the manager for approval, then sent off to the supplier to be filled. This would all be done electronically. Workflow management processing like this now has the capability to extend into the electronic community.

This product includes full messaging support (e-mail, rules-based filtering), scheduling support (to-do lists, daily/weekly/monthly schedules), directory services (distribution lists, alias support), document management and many more features.

Developer/2000 and Designer/2000

Developer/2000 and Designer/2000 offer a complete solution when Oracle clients need to design, program, implement, and maintain systems. They provide for rapid application development in a client/server Windows environment. Their advanced functionality supports BPR (Business Process Reengineering) and mechanisms to take advantage of the server processing that can be done using Oracle's database engine; both are tightly integrated with the Oracle Server and share a common repository. Designer/2000 has three major components.

■   Business process reengineering

- Modellers
- Generators

Developer/2000 has four major components.

- Oracle Reports
- Oracle Forms
- Oracle Graphics
- Procedure Builder

Since Developer/2000 and Designer/2000 share the same repository of information, communication is nearly seamless. As you are gathering your requirements and recording the information, the repository is being populated. Then, based on that information, the models can be developed and the code generated. When the form is created, it utilizes the common repository.

SQL*Net Common GUI functionality, as embedded in Oracle's latest generation of reporting and forms development tools, provides the interface between the analyst and Developer/2000 or Designer/2000. The development can be done in small workgroups and applications easily deployed to hundreds of users. Developer/2000 offers automatic code generation as well as automated software distribution. PL/SQL, the language that Oracle has embedded in all its development products, offers Designer/2000 and Developer/2000 the same program development environment on client as well as server. Designer/2000 supports a wide range of business model functionality that enables companies to build systems ranging from the simplest to the most complex. Designer/2000 is the next generation of Oracle's suite of CASE products whose version number climbed as high as 5.1. Many readers are familiar with the obsolete line of Oracle CASE called CASE*Dictionary and CASE*Designer.

Oracle Reports Generator takes the information in the Designer/2000 repository and creates Oracle Reports. As the system evolves and changes, you go back and regenerate your reports. Changes made in the dictionary ripple through the reports as they are regenerated.

Personal Oracle

Since early 1995, Oracle has produced Oracle for personal computers in both DOS and Microsoft Windows environments. The following configuration is required for running Personal Oracle.

- A 386 or stronger central processing unit (CPU), though a 486 or Pentium is preferred

- At least 60 megabytes (or 62,914,560 bytes) of available disk space

- A 40MHz or faster processor—speeds of 66 or better are preferable

- At least 16 megabytes of extended memory

- MS-DOS or PC-DOS versions 5 or 6, or Digital Research's DR-DOS version 6 or higher

- Microsoft Windows 3.1, 3.11, Windows 95, or NT

Personal Oracle on NT is a full-blown Oracle8 Server implementation; most of the topics we discuss in this book apply to the PC as well. Throughout this book, we include a section in most chapters that deals with Personal Oracle specifics. Most operations with Personal Oracle use the Windows point-and-click interface you may be familiar with already. Most of the tools vended with Personal Oracle are Windows-based. You will not be able to run these from your DOS command line—you will get the error you have probably seen all too many times: "This program requires Microsoft Windows." Export and Import, to name a few, are DOS-based utilities with Personal Oracle 32-bit, and when you run them you will bring up a DOS Window.

The Services

The services wing of Oracle Corporation is a major component of what Oracle has to offer the marketplace. These services offer the following:

- **Education** Skilled instructors teach about the wide range of the Oracle product set as well as some of the relational database modeling, design, and analysis theory.

■ **Consulting** Trained professionals are at your disposal to help facilitate corporate system solutions using Oracle's products and Oracle's partners' technology. There is a network of companies that develop and market their own products that work alongside Oracle's products; Oracle partners with these companies.

■ **Industries** Solutions to industry-specific business requirements, with special attention to addressing key issues with Oracle-based technology.

The services Oracle provides to the marketplace can be grouped into four components: Oracle worldwide customer support, Oracle Education, Oracle Industries, and Oracle Consulting.

■ Oracle worldwide customer support provides technical assistance to clients in the care and feeding of Oracle products. Support services are specifically geared to match customer needs, with a suite of support levels from around-the-clock personalized service (Oracle Gold) to online electronic support through the private support forum on CompuServe (Oracle SupportLink).

■ Oracle Education offers a wide range of courses on the full suite of products and applications. It can provide pre-classroom learning via the computer-based training (CBT) electronic medium. There are centers in over 50 countries that provide classroom and in-house training to end users, developers, analysts, and IT (information technology) managers.

■ Oracle Alliance works with specific pockets of industry to identify key issues, using Oracle technology to create system solutions. It works alongside industry professionals to refine business system goals and to build systems that help companies stay one step ahead of the competition.

■ Oracle Consulting helps customers realize critical solutions by providing expert guidance and technology transfer. It assists with business process re-engineering exercises, the transformation to open systems, and application development, to name a few. Oracle Expert Services offers management (e.g., strategic planning), technical (e.g., performance tuning), development (e.g., custom systems), and Oracle applications implementation services.

An increasing portion of Oracle business is generated in the services area each year. Oracle services enable customers to implement dependable, state-of-the-art technology systems that deploy the Oracle Universal Server technology. Services are geared toward knowledge transfer and lasting success of system solutions realized in partnership with Oracle professionals.

Oracle User Groups—Events and Publications

There is a significant number of Oracle user groups and events around the world. Oracle Corporation, as well as the user group community, has aligned itself on a tricontinental basis: the Americas, Europe/Africa/Middle East, and Asia-Pacific. Contact information for all of these central user communities can be obtained through the headquarters of the International Oracle Users Group (IOUG)-Americas in Chicago on the Web at *http://www.ioug.org* at +1(312) 245-1579.

User groups around the world meet regularly to discuss technical issues related to using Oracle. There are presentations over a wide range of Oracle-related subjects from the user community, third-party vendors, and Oracle Corporation.

The three continental user groups' central contacts are in the U.S., Austria, and Australia. Each geographical area has one or more Oracle conferences in a year, the largest of which are the following:

- The Americas holds IOUG-A Live, in the spring of each year in the USA.

- The Asia-Pacific user forum is held in Australia or New Zealand, usually in November of each year.

- Europe/Middle East/Africa holds the European Oracle User Forum (EOUF), usually in March or April of each year.

A number of Oracle user groups around the world publish newsletters and magazines with articles on Oracle products and services. As examples: *Select* magazine is published quarterly by the IOUG-Americas, *Relate* magazine is published quarterly by the UK Oracle Users Group, and the

Digital Special Interest Group in the U.S. publishes the *Lighthouse* newsletter periodically.

Data Warehousing with Oracle

It is a fact that we live in the information-enabled age, and that information is power. We are seeing a major trend toward corporations building data warehouses and data marts. In this book we will cover what data warehouses and data marts are, and we will also explain the two current views on the best way to implement a data warehouse strategy for your business. Then, we will talk techie and go over the new data warehousing features in Oracle. The goal of Chapter 19 is to teach you all you need to know to understand the concepts and the key features in Oracle that help you support data warehousing.

Network Computing

In this book we will discuss the network computer, or *NC,* and the network computing architecture *NCA.* This is HOT stuff. Ever since Larry Ellison, Oracle's CEO, started talking about the NC computer, the world is trembling. Every single PC vendor has announced price cuts, a new product offering, new strategic alliances, and even Microsoft is changing its tune. Chapter 20 of this book is where you learn about the shot heard around the world. So read on to find out what is making Microsoft change course and every PC vendor redefine its strategy. By now, you've probably already guessed that the World Wide Web is caught up in all this, too.

What's Next

Enough said! From reading this chapter, we trust you have a basic knowledge of what Oracle is and what they produce. You should have a clear understanding that Oracle Corporation's roots are based on the database. From this base, Oracle has branched out to become a full-service vendor that can supply a database that will run on a PC all the way up to an IBM 3090. Oracle also offers a core set of tools that will fully migrate up or down. In addition, Oracle is a full-service provider of turnkey applications, consulting, education, and new technologies, such as building Web-enabled applications to leading the industry on the Network Computer. Now it's time to get your feet wet. Read on!

CHAPTER
2

Oracle8 Overview and
Object Oriented
Databases

n this chapter, we will review the concepts of object-oriented databases (the foundation of Oracle8), discuss the object-relational database model, and then transition into an overview of Oracle8 and its new features. We relate back to examples whenever possible.

Terminology

The following definitions will arm you with the technical jargon to make it through this chapter:

- An *array* in Oracle8 is an ordered set of built-in types or objects, called elements. Each array element is of the same type. Each element has an index, which is a number corresponding to the element's position in the array.

- *Encapsulation* means that each object within the database has a well-defined interface with distinct borders. This has the direct benefit of preventing illegal access to the data.

- *Inheritance* is the ability to create new classes of objects as specializations of existing classes.

- *Nested tables* are another new collection type provided with Oracle8. A nested table is a table that appears as a column in another table, yet you can perform the same operations on it as on other tables.

- *Objects* are software representations of real-world entities.

- *Object views* are an extension of the traditional relational view mechanism that allows you to treat relational data as if it were object entities.

- *Object-relational database* is the term used to describe a database that is the evolution of a relational database, that now has object-oriented capabilities embedded within it. In other words, it is a database that is a hybrid between the relational model and the object-oriented model. Most analysts believe this is the future of computing.

- *Polymorphism* is the ability of objects to react differently to an identical message.

■ Every row in an Oracle table has a unique *rowid*. This rowid uniquely identifies that row of data within the database. Before Oracle8, a rowid could be remembered using the acronym *BARF*. BARF means block, adddress, record, and file id. (We learned this trick from Scott Martin, who in a previous life was an Oracle Kernel Developer.) When you put these all together, you have BARF—the unique physical location of a row within the database. In the following listing you will see the output of a SQL statement that selected rowid from an Oracle8 database:

```
select rowid, substr(rowid,1,8) "BLOCK",
       substr(rowid,15,4) "FILE", substr(rowid,10,4) "ROW"
  from tablex;
  ROWID                   BLOCK      FILE    ROW
  ------------------      --------   ----    ----
  00000DD5.0000.0001   00000DD5   0001    0000
  00000DD5.0001.0001   00000DD5   0001    0001
```

■ *VARRAY* is a new type recognized by Oracle8. Remember, an array is an ordered set of built-in types or objects, called elements. Oracle8 implementation of arrays is of variable size, which is why arrays are called VARRAYs. In Oracle8, when you create the array, you must always specify the maximum size. The statement **create type price as varray(100) of number;** is an example of a VARRAY declaration. Remember when you create a new type, the database does not actually go out and allocate any database space, it merely defines a new type and stores it in the system catalog. For example, you might use the **type** clause in a **create table** statement. You would use it as the data type of a column. **create table car (car_name varchar2(25), car_value price);** is how this user-defined type is used.

VIP
Oracle8 incorporates a new extended rowid format, which supports new features in Oracle8 such as table partitions, index partitions, and clusters. If you have an application that references rowid, be very careful. We like to call this new rowid OBARF—Object, Block, Address, Row, and File.

■ The Oracle8 Server incorporates a new *extended ROWID format,* which supports new features in Oracle8 such as table partitions, index partitions, and clusters. Remember, rowid uniquely identifies a row of data within an Oracle database. The extended rowid in Oracle8 includes the information in the Oracle7 rowid, plus the data object number. The data object number is an identification number that the server assigns to schema objects in the database, such as nonpartitioned tables or partitions. The following listing shows the look of this extended rowid:

```
SQL*Plus: Release 4.0.3.0.0 - Production on Sun May 11 12:20:12 1999
Copyright (c) Oracle Corporation 1979, 1994, 1996. All rights
     reserved.
Connected to:
Oracle8 Server Release 8.0.3.0.1 - Production
With the distributed, heterogeneous, replication, objects
and parallel query options
PL/SQL Release 3.0.3.0.1 - Production
SQL> create table sales
  2   (invoice_no number,
  3     sale_year     int not null,
  4     sale_month int not null,
  5     sale_day      int not null)
  6   partition by range (sale_year,sale_month,sale_day)
  7   (partition p1 values less than (1994,04,01) tablespace p1,
  8    partition p2 values less than (1994,07,01) tablespace p2);
Table created.
SQL> insert into sales values (100,1994,2,1);
1 row created.
SQL> insert into sales values (200,1994,6,1);
1 row created.
SQL>
SQL> select rowid from sales;
ROWID
------------------
AAAAfOAAFAAAAADAAA
AAAAfPAAGAAAAADAAA
```

Every row in a nonclustered table of an Oracle database is assigned a unique rowid that corresponds to the physical address of a row's row piece (the initial row piece if the row is chained among multiple row pieces). In the case of clustered tables, rows in different tables that are in the same data block can have the same rowid.

What Is an Object-Oriented Database

As we have all heard many times before, Oracle8 is Oracle's first version of the database to incorporate object-oriented technology. Oracle8 is the corporation's first object-relational database. Notice we used the term *object-relational database* since this implementation is not a pure object-oriented database, nor is it just a relational database. It now represents a hybrid of the two, so let's call it an object-relational database.

VIP

An object-relational database is a term used to describe a database that has evolved from the relational model into a hybrid database that contains both relational technology and object technology.

For many years there have been debates as to whether the next generation of mainstream database technology would be an object-oriented database or whether it would be a SQL-based database with object-oriented extensions. We feel that there are several reasons that the object-relational approach will dominate:

- Object-relational databases such as Oracle8 are upward-compatible with users' current relational databases, so users can migrate their current relational databases and applications to Oracle8 without rewriting them, and then migrate their databases and applications to the object-oriented features of Oracle8 when they choose.

- Previous pure object-oriented databases did not support the standard ad hoc query capabilities of SQL databases; this can be a major problem when needs arise that had not been anticipated in the original design. It was also a problem in interfacing standard SQL tools to pure object-oriented databases. In fact, one of the major reasons the corporate world was so quick to embrace relational databases was this ability to create ad hoc queries.

■ The integration of object-oriented and relational representations in Oracle8 is semantically clean, and considerably more powerful then either relational or object-oriented representations alone. This makes the design of compact, efficient databases much easier.

As you can see, there are many compelling factors that will cause the industry to adopt the evolution of the relational database into the object-relational database. One of our favorite reasons is based on the simple rule: *water will always follow the path of least resistance and so will people*. In other words, people will go with what they feel most comfortable with. Remember the Apple computer law that Apple corporation tried to pass in the United States? They tried to get a law passed in the United States that would give them special tax treatment, to help them donate computers into the schools. They learned as a corporation that by getting children familiar with Apple computers early on, as they moved into the corporate world, they would want to use Apple computers. This would result in future business.

Today, Oracle has won over the enterprise. People already see Oracle as a mission-critical database able to get them the results they need. People are very comfortable with the technology they bring to the corporate world. Their preference will be to go with the Oracle implementation of the relational database as long as they can bring the key features of object-oriented technologies. Well, Oracle8 represents just that. At this point, we feel they have won the battle and the war. It's also interesting to note that many of the industry leaders would now concur with this.

To help you appreciate and understand what Oracle8 means to the industry and why object-relational database will become the standard, we will first discuss object-oriented technologies and then provide an overview of Oracle8 and its key changes.

VIP

An object-oriented database is one that can store data, the relationship of the data, and the behavior of the data (i.e., the way it interacts with other data).

Unlike the relational database approach—which deals with data at the lowest possible level, a series of columns and rows—the object-oriented approach deals with data at a much higher level; it deals with the objects surrounding the data. In an object-oriented database, when dealing with the customer, you deal with an object called "customer". When dealing with an order, you reference an object called "order". Since an object database understands the object customer and all its relationships, it can easily deal with the object customer and all that is needed to work with it.

In the relational model, order is really a combination of many different tables, with intersection tables holding all the attributes needed to support and maintain an order. Unlike the object model, where the database has intelligence about the interrelationships, this is not the case in the relational model. When a change is made to the relational model, it usually translates into a whole new series of tables that must be developed if the model is to continue to work. These relationships must be recrafted by a database designer.

Lets take a closer look at when a customer places an order in a relational database. There are a number of tables needed to support that activity. There might be a customer table, an inventory table, a price table, an inventory_price table, a line_item_table, a customer_history table, and so on. In order to manipulate these tables, the programmer must craft the needed code with the required links between tables.

As you can see, the simple act of placing an order requires a number of tables. Rows and columns in tables contain information required for the assembly of the order. A single change to the order process can have a major impact on the underlying tables that support it, requiring a database designer to come in and craft the new relationships and their associated tables to represent those relationships. In the object-oriented model, this is not the case. In fact, it assumes the model will change, and that change is just a natural occurrence and progression.

What Is an Object?

Objects are software representations of real-world entities. To capture the features and capabilities of the real world, objects consist of both attributes and operational information. Remember, in an object-oriented database, the data dictionary not only stores (and allows you to understand) the relationship of one object to other, but it also understands the behaviors of the object.

VIP

Objects are software representations of real-world entities.

What Is a Class?

When objects are similar to one another in behaviors and other attributes, they can be put together into a class. This concept of classes, parent classes, subclasses, and superclasses allows for a level of abstraction for grouping objects. Think of a *class* as a template for objects. This helps you in managing very complex objects. This ability to group by class also allows objects to take advantage of similarities of behaviors and other characteristics they share.

VIP

Classes are templates for objects.

Encapsulation

One of the basics to the object-oriented model is the support of encapsulation. *Encapsulation* is where the data is bound to the object so that access to the data can only happen through the behaviors approved or accepted by that object. This has the direct benefit of protecting the data from illegal access.

VIP

Encapsulation means that each object within the database has a well-defined interface with distinct borders.

From a developer's perspective, objects are an encapsulation of data and behaviors. They can be thought of as programming black boxes. Think of objects as collections of code and data that have the ability to function independently. This is a very powerful capability.

A question that springs up immediately is "does encapsulation violate the relational rule of data independence?" We think not. One of the pillars of object-oriented programming is encapsulation. Encapsulation includes the ability to only access objects and its data through the behaviors approved or accepted by that object. This is contradictory to the fundamental principle of relational databases, known as *data independence*. According the relational model as defined by Dr. Codd and Chris Date, any data can be accessed in an ad hoc, independent manner.

At first glance, you might think it was impossible to have data that was independent from the application while allowing encapsulation. One easily jumps to the conclusion that these two differences would make the relational model noncompatible with the object-oriented model, but this is not the case.

In the object-oriented model, the data behaviors are stored within the database, and they are not external from the database. Since the data behaviors are within the database, it does not jeopardize the independence of applications from the data. This is the basis of the law of data independence—the applications, be it SQL or other ad hoc tools, are independent of the data itself.

Database Triggers

We suppose a case could be made to say that relational databases have always had a form of encapsulation through the use of database triggers. But then, to support encapsulation, that would mean creating a trigger for every possible method of accessing the data. Our experience has taught us this would not be practical. In fact, if you were to try and implement encapsulation through database triggers, overall database performance would degrade.

 VIP
Our experience has shown that the use of too many database triggers will degrade overall database performance.

Every time you accessed a table, a corresponding trigger would need to fire. This fact alone causes the database to do twice the work it normally would to access the data. The other problem we commonly see is that many times these triggers are not well written, which will very quickly destroy database performance in itself. So, in practice, we see very limited use of database triggers.

We do want to make the point that triggers are a very powerful tool within a relational database when used correctly. But they were never intended as a tool to give you the power of encapsulation.

Extensibility

Extensibility is the ability of an object-oriented database to add new objects and their associated behaviors without affecting the other objects and applications. Since data can be encapsulated with objects, this ability of extensibility gives the object model the ability to handle nonstandard data situations. This is a very powerful feature.

Inheritance

Think of *inheritance* as a form of code sharing. As a new class of objects is defined, it can be defined in terms of an existing class or what is known as the base class. So, as lower-level objects are created, they inherit or access the data and behaviors associated with all classes above it.

The class of objects derived from the base class typically augments or redefines the existing structure and behavior of the base class. Another way of thinking of inheritance is that you typically create new classes as a specialization of existing classes. You usually derive classes for the following reasons:

■ You want to implement the same code but have different behaviors associated with it. For example, a nurse class might be treated differently than a doctor class, even though they all belong to the class of hospital employees.

■ You might want to incrementally extend the behavior of the base class. Now that you have created a specialized class called doctor, you can now tailor code segments to give the doctor class special abilities. This is a way to add functionality to the system.

■ You might want to provide for different implementations of the system.

VIP

Inheritance is the ability to create new classes of objects as specializations of existing classes.

There are two different types of inheritance:

- **Data inheritance:** This is where a data element can inherit additional attributes from other data elements in the class.

- **Function/object inheritance:** This is where an object can inherit data and attributes from another object in its class.

Think of inheritance as building blocks of code; you can take advantage of behaviors that have already been developed. Suppose you have created an object called "states". When you create another object called "east_of _Mississippi", it is able to inherit all the things the base class understands about states and build from there. Fact—all states have capitals; therefore, the east_of_Mississippi object, having inherited characteristics of the state class, has a capital.

Polymorphism

Polymorphism is the ability of two different objects to behave differently when receiving the same message. The concept of polymorphism really parallels the real world, where identical messages are received every day, yet are reacted to differently.

Let's take the simple act of sitting on the beach in the sun for an hour. I am a very fair-skinned person. If I sit on the beach in the sun for an hour, I will come out looking as red as a boiled lobsta (remember, I am from New England, where lobster is pronounced "lobsta"). My neighbor is of Caribbean heritage; she looks as tanned as can be. Yet we both received the same dose of sun.

VIP

Polymorphism is the ability of objects to react differently to an identical message. An object reacts differently based on the information supplied, and understands the context of the information that has been input.

Object Oriented Technologies Summary

The cornerstone of object oriented technology consists of the following:

- Objects
- Classes
- Encapsulation
- Extensibility
- Inheritance
- Polymorphism

As you can see, these types of capabilities allow for a very powerful database capability. This database can learn from itself and reuse elements where it makes sense. As well, it can deal with very complex objects at a very simplistic level. This overview of object-oriented technologies will help you better understand Oracle8 and where the future of database technologies is headed. Oracle8 is an implementation of an object-relational database whose beginnings are in relational technology. This database's future is an evolution into object-oriented technologies. This is just the tip of the iceberg of the object-oriented features in Oracle8. To appreciate and understand Oracle8 abilities to support mission-critical, enterprise-wide applications go beyond the ability to create objects. Using your foundation of object-oriented technology, let's take a closer look at Oracle8.

Oracle8—An Overview

The goal when building Oracle8 was to manage your corporate data, no matter what type of data type it is. This includes structured data and nonstructured data. Oracle8 can store that data in the most appropriate model for your applications and situation. If that means the pure relational model, then leave it that way. If that means taking advantage of objects, then Oracle8 has object support. If it means storing it in a multidimensional format, that is fine too. Whatever makes it easy for you to be successful in your enterprise, Oracle8 can handle.

Oracle Corporation recognizes that there are many ways corporations use technologies. For some, it is online transaction processing; for others, it is decision support. Whatever the needs of your business, Oracle8 has been developed to deal with your corporate applications. Table 2-1 illustrates features that Oracle Corporation built into the Oracle8 database that allow it to be your source of one-stop shopping for the enterprise.

Any	Supports
Data Type	Scalar, text, video, spatial, image, user-defined
Data Model	Relational, multidimensional, object-oriented
Application	Operations, decision support, collaboration, commerce

TABLE 2-1.   *Oracle8 Is Designed to Support*

Key Focus Areas of Oracle8

The key areas of focus when building Oracle8 are expected to be the following:

- High-end online transaction processing (*OLTP*) and data warehouse requirements

- Object-relational extensions

- Performance, manageability, and functional enhancements throughout

It should be no surprise to anyone that Oracle wants to own the corporate enterprise database. Oracle wants to manage all your data. Oracle recognizes that to do this, to attain this goal, it must be able to manage very large databases; this is the key to managing the demanding needs of the data warehouse as well as large high-end OLTP systems. Today no one runs an airline reservation system on a relational database, yet with Oracle8, this would be possible.

Oracle8: How Many Users and How Big Can It Get

Today, of the 20 largest databases in the world, 15 run on DB2. Oracle8 will be changing the landscape. Today, Oracle8 can scale to support over 10,000 users. Today, Oracle8 can support a database over 100 terabytes (where a terabyte is 1,048,576,000,000 bytes) in size. These abilities are critical to supporting high-end OLTP environments and very large data warehouse projects. Oracle8 has greatly improved availability features and utilities to improve manageability; these features are crucial to keeping very large databases running.

VIP
*With Oracle8, you can now support 10,000+
users on a single node with a database over
100 terabytes in size.*

Partitioning and Parallelism

One of the easiest ways we have found to work on a complicated problem
is to break it into smaller, simpler problems. That is what partitioning is all
about—the ability to break the database into smaller, more manageable
pieces, then to work with those pieces independently. With Oracle8, you
now have this ability.

We find that when we want a job done quickly, we inevitably ask for
help. A team effort will always accomplish the task much quicker than an
individual working alone. This is what parallel execution is all about—the
ability to break a job into many smaller jobs that can be worked on in
parallel. Jobs that used to take hours can now be accomplished in minutes.
Let's take a closer look at Oracle8 and partitioning.

ORACLE8: TABLE AND INDEX PARTITIONING   With Oracle8,
you have now the ability to partition tables and indexes. With this ability to
partition, Oracle8 now has provided you with the tools you need to work
with very large tables and indexes.

VIP
*Partitioning is the ability to break tables and
indexes into smaller, more manageable pieces.*

When a table or index is partitioned, the column definitions, the
constraint definitions, and the index column definitions must stay the same.
For example, if you **create index life_cereal** consisting of column
corey_col, abbey_col, ault_col, this definition of the index will be the same
for each partitioned piece.

What can change, and most likely will, is the storage definition and
other physical attributes. For example, you can fine-tune the storage
characteristics for each separate partition.

VIP
Under Oracle8, partitions can have different physical attributes. In other words, partitions can be placed in physically different locations.

For example, you would typically break a very large table into separate partitions, each stored on a separate tablespace. You do this many times to achieve the following:

■ Allow for better I/O load balancing. This is why you would typically have each partition mapped to a physically separate disk drive.

■ Improve and enhance backup and recovery capability. Oracle supports the concept of partition independence; we will go over this in more detail later in this chapter.

■ Minimize the possibility of data corruption. A corruption is local to one partition.

■ Assist the archiving process by allowing the oldest information to be stored in its own partition and more easily moved elsewhere.

The following listing illustrates the syntax on how to partition a table into one or more pieces:

```
create table ...
( col1    number,
  col2    number,
  ...           )
partition by range ( col1, col2 )
  ( partition p1 values less than ( ...,... ) tablespace p1,
    partition p2 values less than ( ...,... ) tablespace p2);
```

Based on data stored within a table, you are able to determine how and where the information will be loaded. For example, you might have all customers' last names beginning with the letters "A-C" go into partition one, and all customers that have a last name beginning with the letters "D-Z" go into partition two.

The following listing shows you an example of a index being partitioned into two pieces. All customers with last names less than "N" end up in tablespace ts1. All other customers end up in tablespace ts2. Notice the use of **maxvalue**.

```
create index customer_idx
    on customer (customer_last_name, customer_first_name)
  partition by range (customer_last_name)
            partition values less than ('N') tablespace ts1,
            partition values less than (maxvalue) tablespace ts2;
```

With Oracle8, you also gain the ability to create both global indexes and local indexes. A *local index* is one that is only local to a particular partition. A *global index* is one that spans many partitions. It is outside the scope of this book to get into the many grueling details of local indexes versus global indexes and all the derivatives. Suffice it to say that when an index is localized to a particular partition, you can use this fact to your advantage. You can fine-tune performance on a particular partition. You can also minimize the impact of certain activities down to a particular partition.

Let's now take a closer look at the concept of partition independence. We hinted at some of this functionality when we talked about why you would partition.

PARTITION INDEPENDENCE   Oracle8 supports the concept of *partition independence*. As we discussed earlier in this chapter, partitioning can make backup and recovery easier. With Oracle8, it is possible to recover just a partition since it supports partition independence. This makes it possible to perform concurrent maintenance operations on different partitions of the same table or index. With Oracle8, it is also possible to support **select** and DML operations that are unaffected by maintenance operations.

This means it is possible to be loading data using the direct path load. This method of loading data writes directly to the partition and eliminates database logging. This is the fastest possible way to load data into an Oracle database. This is a critical capability to support very large databases. While the load is running, other partitions have applications issuing **select** and DML operations against them.

VIP

Oracle8 supports partition independence. This means operations such a database recovery or direct path loading can be happening on one partition while applications are running DML and SQL operations on other partitions.

Partition independence is particularly important for operations that involve data movement. Such operations may take a long time (minutes, hours, or even days). Partitioning can reduce the window of unavailability on other partitions to a short time (few seconds) during operations that involve data movement, provided there are no interpartition stored constructs (global indexes and referential integrity constraints).

This ability to take a database and break its tables and indexes into partitions is a very powerful capability. It makes it possible to deploy mission-critical applications on multiterabyte databases. It makes it possible to support thousands of users. To put it bluntly, partitioning is a very big deal.

The fact is Murphy's law always strikes when you least expect it. Remember Murphy's law—"what can go wrong will, at the worst possible moment." The bigger the database, the more likely a problem. Another way of saying it—the good news is that your disk drives only have a 1 in 100 failure rate over a one-year period. The bad news is that you have 500 disk drives. The point is that you will have database disasters strike in very large databases. There will be times you will have to rebuild portions of the database. With Oracle8, it is now possible to break the database into smaller, more manageable pieces and load those partitions without affecting the rest of the database. The ability to back up and recover independently is critical. Again, partitioning is a very big deal.

REFERENCING A PARTITION   With Oracle8, partition names can optionally be referenced in DDL and DML statements. They can also be referenced when using import and export utility. This ability to specify partition names in DDL and DML commands coupled with the concept of partition independence is why you can backup and recover partitions independently.

VIP

Oracle8 supports incomplete tablespace recovery. This should only be done with the help of trained experts. This is a very difficult operation to perform.

The following listing illustrates some SQL statements against partitioned information:

```
alter table sales drop partition prt4;
alter table sales add partition prt4 values
      less than ('970523') tablespace ts4;
alter table sales drop partition prt4;
alter table sales modify partition prt4 unusable local indexes;
alter table sales modify partition prt4 rebuild unusable local indexes;
alter table sales rename partition prt4 to sale_prt4;
alter table sales truncate partition prt4 drop storage;
alter index cust_idx rebuild partition prt4 nologging;
alter index cust_idx modify partition prt4 unusable;
export scott/tiger file=exp.dmp
      tables=(scott.sales:prt4, scott.sales:prt2)
```

As you can see from this listing, Oracle8 partition names can optionally be referenced in DDL and DML statements. Yes, it is now possible to manage 100-terabyte databases.

Parallelism

As we stated earlier, parallelism is the ability to break a task into many smaller jobs that can be worked on in parallel. Jobs that used to take hours can now be accomplished in minutes.

Oracle8 Parallel Server

Oracle8 supports many different forms of parallelism. Figure 2-1 illustrates the ability to have loosely coupled machines all talking to the same database and disk farm. When we use the term *loosely coupled*, we mean the machines do not share memory. This ability to configure Oracle8 in Parallel Server mode provides the customer a combination of high availability combined with high performance.

Oracle8 Parallel Server provides you with enhanced very high availability, since you now have 2+ machines doing the work normally

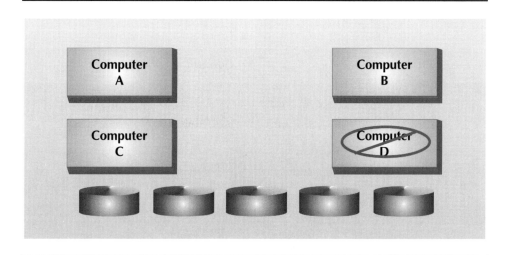

FIGURE 2-1.   *Oracle8 Parallel Server*

done by one. In Figure 2-1, we illustrate the fact that one machine is unavailable, yet you still have three other machines able to access the database. This configuration gives you near fault tolerance using a nonproprietary platform.

You also get the expanded capability or additional processing power. If your organization outgrows one machine's capability, add a second machine. Oracle8 Parallel Server scales in performance as you add additional nodes.

Oracle8—More Parallelism

Oracle8 supports parallel **select**, **insert**, **update**, **delete**, and recovery. This means that you can instruct the database to make certain operations work in parallel. An operation that is working in parallel works something like this:

1. The given task (**insert**, **update**, **delete**, **select**) is broken into smaller, separate tasks based upon the degree of parallelism chosen.

2. If the degree chosen was 3 for the given task (let's say **select** is broken into 3 separate **select** statements), each parallel **select** statement would work on a separate portion of the whole.

3. The tasks are executed.

4. The tasks are finished and the results are merged together.

5. The results are presented back to the user.

Figure 2-2 illustrates this process. If a typical **select** takes an hour, by having three separate tasks working on it, Oracle8 can bring its execution and processing time down substantially. Tasks that never could be run in a day can now be run in parallel in a fraction of the time.

Oracle8—How to Use Parallelism

Oracle8 now supports parallelism to a degree never possible before. The following listing shows a few of the many ways to invoke parallelism. Oracle8 supports this capability in every major functionality of the database. When a table is created, you can choose to assign it a level of parallelism so that whenever a statement is executed against it, the parallelism happens transparently.

```
create table sales nologging parallel (degree 4) as select * from sales_ne;
create index sales_idx on sales (sale_dt)  nologging parallel (degree 3);
update /*+ parallel(sales,4) */ sales set c1=c1+1;
insert /*+ parallel(sales,2) */ into sales ...
select /*+ parallel(sales,4) */ * from sales;
```

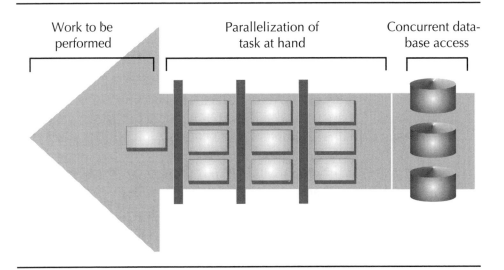

FIGURE 2-2. *Parallel execution*

Parallelism is completely configurable in Oracle8. You can now use it to help you get information out of the database in minutes; you can also use it to recover a database in parallel in a fraction of the time it used to take.

Oracle8 Backup and Recovery

The backup and recovery process has been reengineered in Oracle8. It has more automation and more audit trails than ever before. In addition, Oracle is working more closely with third-party vendors to provide you with more options than ever before. Oracle realizes that in order to be successful in this arena, they need the best possible tools.

Oracle8: Objects and New Database Objects

As we have discussed earlier, the relational model is used to represent data as a series of tables with columns and attributes. Oracle8 is an object-relational database. This means it has object-oriented technologies embedded within it. With this in mind, we would expect to be able to build complex object types in Oracle8 (complex in the sense we would expect you to be able to have objects within objects, and some ability to bind or encapsulate methods with those objects). Well, you won't be disappointed. Oracle8 does support complex object types.

VIP
A method is a procedure or function that is part of the object type definition and that can operate on the object type data attributes.

In Oracle8, you have the ability to declare an object type by specifying a name with one or more attributes, coupled with some PL/SQL code. These attributes can be as simple as a varchar2 field to reference another object. These object types are complex in nature, since you can have objects referencing objects. The object you reference can also have embedded objects. Once these objects are created, they can be referenced elsewhere. As you can see, this ability to support complex objects is the basis of the object-relational database. Lets take a closer look at some object types supported in Oracle8.

Nested Objects

Oracle8 supports the concept of *nested objects*. With the **create type** command, you are able to create additional data types, and then reference those data types within other objects. The following listing demonstrates creating a new data type called room_capacity_type.

```
create type room_capacity_type (
     auditorium_setting           integer,
     table_setting                integer,
     standing_room_setting        integer);
```

The following listing references the newly created type in the conference_facility table. The type room_capacity_type exists with or without the table conference_facility. This type can be used in many different ways and in many different locations. This ability to extend the database with additional types is a very powerful capability. It is also a very powerful capability to help simplify the complexity of dealing with complex data types.

```
SQL*Plus: Release 4.0.3.0.0 - Production on Sun May 11 12:20:12 1999
Copyright (c) Oracle Corporation 1979, 1994, 1996.  All rights reserved.
Connected to:
Oracle8 Server Release 8.0.3.0.1 - Production
With the distributed, heterogeneous, replication, objects
and parallel query options
PL/SQL Release 3.0.3.0.1 - Production
SQL>
SQL> create table conference_facility (
  2      room_name                    varchar2(20),
  3      room_settings                room_capacity_type);
Table created.
SQL> -- ** now let's insert into the table **
SQL> insert into conference_facilty values (
  2      'GREAT HALL',  room_capacity_type(500, 200, 1000));
1 row created.
```

VIP
Data types created with the **create type** *command exist independently of any table.*

VARRAY

A new type recognized in Oracle8 is VARRAY. An array is an ordered list of elements. In Oracle8, they are called VARRAY since the array is of variable size. When we think of an array, we think of the mail boxes you see at old hotels when you check in. Each room in the hotel would have a slot in this big box holding the room keys. In Oracle8, an *array* is an ordered set of built-in types or objects called elements. Since the array is variable size, when you create it in Oracle8, you must always specify the maximum size. This listing uses VARRAY:

```
create type price as varray(100) of number;
```

It is interesting to note that when you create this array in Oracle8, the database does not actually go out and allocate any database space, it merely defines a new type and stores it in the system catalog. It is possible to reference this array in another table, as the data type of a column. For example,

```
create table car (car_name varchar2(25), car_val price);
```

This ability to support arrays of variable size is a very nice enhancement in Oracle8. Many times as a developer, this functionality would have made my job much easier. We look forward to using this newfound ability to manipulate order sets of objects.

TYPES Within TYPES

With Oracle8, it is possible to use types within types. Another way of saying this is that a type can be an attribute of another type. The following listing shows the address type being referenced by the employee_type:

```
SQL*Plus: Release 4.0.3.0.0 - Production on Sun May 11 12:20:12 1999
Copyright (c) Oracle Corporation 1979, 1994, 1996.  All rights reserved.
Connected to:
Oracle8 Server Release 8.0.3.0.1 - Production
With the distributed, heterogeneous, replication, objects
and parallel query options
PL/SQL Release 3.0.3.0.1 - Production
```

```
SQL> create type address_type (
    2       street                    varchar2(40),
    3       city                      varchar2(30),
    4       state                     varchar2(2),
    5       zip_cd                    number(5));
Table created.
SQL> create type employee_type (
    2       name                      varchar2(30),
    3       hire_date                 date,
    4       address                             address_type,
    5       member procedure          give_raise
    6       member function                     get_salary return number;
Table created.
SQL>
```

This ability to create new types is a very powerful feature in Oracle8. This is a great tool to help you standardize the type of like objects. By creating common types for frequently used items such as an address, you can avoid a lot of issues up the road. We all know that standards are a wonderful tool for keeping production environments up and running. Types can be referenced across the database. The following listing shows types being used in a variety of different ways:

```
declare
    p1           person_type;
    addr         address;
    begin
      create procedure get_emp_id
          (employee               emp_type) as ...
      create function get_emp (name varchar2)
          return emp_type as ...
```

Methods and Types

Another strength of Oracle8 is the ability to bind code to data. We call these *code segment methods*. Remember our definition of method. A *method* is a procedure or function that is part of the object type definition and can operate on the data attributes of the object type. This is approaching the capability of encapsulation, one of the foundations of object-oriented databases. The following listing shows a type definition linked to some methods:

```
SQL*Plus: Release 4.0.3.0.0 - Production on Sun May 11 12:20:12 1999
Copyright (c) Oracle Corporation 1979, 1994, 1996.  All rights reserved.
Connected to:
Oracle8 Server Release 8.0.3.0.1 - Production
With the distributed, heterogeneous, replication, objects
and parallel query options
PL/SQL Release 3.0.3.0.1 - Production
SQL> create type good_bad_type
  2        (good_guy                   integer,
  3         bad_guy                    integer,
  4         map member function good_or_bad return real,
  5         member procedure           normalize,
  6         member function            neutral (x good_bad_type)
  7         return good_bad_type);
Type created.
SQL>
```

As you can see by looking at this listing, Oracle8 gives you the very powerful ability to bind code and data together. In this example, we create a new data type that is specific to this business. Since it is a data type, we can reference it throughout our database, to ensure consistency. We also show the data type good_bad_type being bound together with some code. In this case it is being bound together with a function called Neutral. We have code and data being tightly joined together. This is much more powerful than traditional database triggers. This ability to have objects within objects, code joined together with data, makes Oracle8 a very power tool.

Experience has shown us that standardization is a very desirable trait in a mission-critical environment. The ability to bind methods to types should help avoid many of the data consistency problems of the past. Perhaps it makes sense to develop a valid state lookup method and bind it to the state_type.

Object Views

Oracle8 object views are an extension of the traditional relational view mechanism that allows you to treat relational data as if it were object entities. Simply put, object views allow use of relational data in object-oriented applications. This means you can **select**, **update**, **insert**, and **delete** relational data as if the data were stored as object entities.

This means your current applications can coexist with new applications that use object-oriented features. With this mechanism in Oracle8, you have the best of both worlds. You can continue to run your applications, at the same time building new applications that take advantage of object-relational features of Oracle8. This allows for a gradual migration path. This is a very desirable feature as the databases continue to get bigger and bigger.

Summary

By covering the foundation of an object-oriented database, we hope to give you an understanding of where Oracle8 is headed. It is the first pass at object-relational database—a very big step in the right direction. Coming out of the gate, all the features of an object-oriented database are not there. But you have to learn how to crawl before you can walk.

We believe that Oracle has already crossed the biggest hurdle it had to face by implementing object views. It has provided a mechanism to support objects without breaking the existing applications. From this foundation, Oracle corporation can add additional object technology capabilities. Look to the features we have discussed and you can see where Oracle is headed.

We feel objects are just a tiny part of the story to tell. Oracle now has a database that can support 100+ terabytes and over 10,000+ users on a node. It has **select**, **insert**, **update**, **delete**, and recovery parallelism and full partition support. If and when your 100+ terabyte database fails, you can restore just the failed partition. You can tune down to the partition itself. These are very powerful capabilities.

What's Next

Enough said! Let's now move on to a discussion of Oracle, the software, and highlight the means by which Oracle has crafted support for very large relational and object-relational databases. In the next chapter, we cover the gamut of objects stored in the Oracle8 database, from tables to synonyms.

CHAPTER
3

Architecture

fter memorizing Chapters 1 and 2, you now know about the Oracle Corporation and some of the products it sells to its worldwide user community. We spent a great deal of time on the Oracle Server—it is the foundation of everything Oracle has out there. We feel the major reason Oracle is such a force in modern information technology is its staying power. Oracle corporation has been down a number of times in its history and always bounces back up to bigger and better heights. This chapter delves further into Oracle8 database architecture. After reading this chapter, you will understand the following:

- Components of an Oracle8 database

- Tablespaces

- Rollback segments

- Online redo logs

- Control files

- Processes associated with an Oracle8 database

- System global area (SGA)

- An Oracle instance

Terminology

The following definitions will arm you with the technical jargon to make it through this chapter:

- An *application* is a set of Oracle programs that solve a company's or person's business needs. In more day-to-day terms, the computer system that generates bills for a hydroelectric utility could be referred to as a billing application.

- An *instance* is a portion of computer memory and auxiliary processes required to access an Oracle database.

- *Objects* are software representations of real-world entities.

- A *datafile* is a file on your disk that stores information. For example, when working with a word processor, you could call your document a datafile.

- A *DBA* or database administrator is a technical wizard who manages the complete operation of the Oracle database. The DBA's job is highlighted in Chapters 14 and 18.

- A *dirty data block* is a portion of computer memory that contains Oracle data whose value has changed from what was originally read from the database. If a personnel application read the name "Julie Cohen" into a data block in memory and the name was changed to "Julie Anderson", the block in memory containing the new name is called a dirty data block. Think of dirty data blocks as data sitting in memory that has been changed but not yet written back to the database.

- A *hot data block* is a block whose data is changed frequently. In an inventory application, a popular part's quantity_on_hand would be in a hot data block since its value undergoes constant change.

- *LRU* (least recently used) is an algorithm Oracle uses when it needs to make room for more information in memory than will fit in the memory space allocated. Let's say Oracle has five slots in memory holding information, and it needs to put some additional information into memory. Since the five slots are full, Oracle flushes the information that has sat idle for the longest period of time.

- A *table* holds Oracle data. It contains space allocated to hold application-specific data in your database.

- A *tablespace* is a collection of one or more datafiles. All database objects are stored in tablespaces. It is called a tablespace because it typically holds a database object called a table.

- *Rollback* is the activity Oracle performs to restore data to its prior state before a user started to change it. For example, you change the value for someone's location from "AL" to "MN" and then decide that you made a mistake—a rollback activity could change the location back to "AL."

■ *Undo information* is the information the database needs to undo or rollback a user transaction due to a number of reasons. For example, when you change a customer's credit limit from $2,000 to $3,000, undo information is kept in case you decide not to save the change.

Why Bother to Learn the Architecture?

We have found in our travels that many users do not see the need for understanding the internal architecture of the Oracle database. They just go out and code the application (the official term for this is rapid prototyping). The Oracle relational database and its tools make application building look easy—much the way a pro athlete makes a sport look easy. However, we all know from experience that what looks easy in theory might not be easy in practice.

Here's an analogy to illustrate why you should take the time to understand the Oracle database architecture. It all started a year ago, when I helped the plumber put a new heating system in our home. By helping the plumber, I was able to bring the installation cost way down; being a Yankee at heart, I found that money was a very strong motivator to do manual labor! The heating system installed was forced hot water: after the water is heated, electric pumps move it through the pipes. During the installation process, I expended a great deal of effort bleeding the air pockets out of the heating system, as air prevents the heated water from circulating through the pipes. A few weeks later, the bedrooms were not getting enough heat. With some knowledge of the heating system, I was able to determine that an air pocket must be in the pipes. I took the time to bleed the air out, and shortly after, heat was restored.

A month later, a "Nor'easta" (in Boston, lobster is pronounced "lobsta" and chowder is pronounced "chowda") snowstorm hit Boston and we lost our power. Within a few hours, without electricity to work the electric pumps, the house started to get very cold. With three small children at home, this was not a good situation. I kept thinking there must be a way to get the remaining hot water in the heating system to circulate through the pipes without electricity. Again, applying my limited knowledge of the architecture of a hot-water heating system, I came up with the solution:

by opening up the return pipes, the cold water was replaced with the remaining hot water. Heat was then restored. Yes Super Dad was able to Save the Day !

There is a point to the analogy: we are not plumbers. But a good understanding of how things were designed helped in ways we had never anticipated. With this in mind, you may want to take the time to read the rest of this chapter.

TIP

When starting to work with complex software such as Oracle, take the time to learn the architecture. Down the road, taking this time at the beginning will pay off.

What Is a Database?

We posed the question "What is a database?" to Scott Martin, one of the Oracle core developers who helped write the Oracle Parallel Server and who most recently engineered his own product called SQL*Trax. Scott replied: "It's a bunch of programs that manipulate datafiles." Scott's statement is absolutely correct. A database is a collection of datafiles and the software that manipulates it. So let's take a closer look at the Oracle database using Scott's definition as our starting point. We start at the datafile level.

Datafiles

Datafiles contain all the database data. The Oracle database is made up of one or more datafiles; datafiles are grouped together to form a tablespace. Especially important to note here is that the datafiles contain all of the data information stored in the database. Think of disk drives on a PC. The files contained on those disk drives represent all the information currently available to that PC.

User Data and System Data

Two types of data or information are stored within the datafiles associated with a database: user data and system data.

■ *User data* is your application data, with all of the applications' relevant information. This is the information your organization stores in the database. Table 3-1 shows typical types of user data.

■ *System data* is the information the database needs to manage the user data and to manage itself. For example, with system data, Oracle tells itself that the Social Security field in a table consists of all numbers and no letters and that it is a mandatory field. System data also tells Oracle the valid users of the database, their passwords, how many datafiles are part of the database, and where these datafiles are located. Table 3-2 shows typical system data.

What Is a Database? Summary of Points

To summarize what we have learned about databases:

■ A database is a collection of programs that manipulate datafiles.

■ Two types of information are stored in an Oracle database:

1. User data is your particular application data (e.g., a customer invoice).

2. System data is the data that the database needs to manage itself (e.g., the name and location of all the datafiles associated with a particular database).

Type of Data	Contains Information About
Customer Information	Last name, first name, phone number
Product Information	Product name, availability, price
Medical Information	Lab results, doctor's name, nurse's name
Inventory Information	Quantity in stock, quantity backordered
Financial Information	Stock price, interest rate

TABLE 3-1. *Common Types of User Data*

Type of Data	Contains Information About
Tables	The fields of the table and the type of information they hold
Space	Amount of physical space the database objects take
Users	Names, passwords, privileges
Datafiles	Number, location, time last used

TABLE 3-2. *Common Types of System Data*

Tablespaces—Oracle's Manila Folder

Since a database is a collection of datafiles, it's very important that you understand how an Oracle database groups these files together. It does this under the umbrella of a database object called a tablespace. Before you can insert data into an Oracle database, you must first create a tablespace, then an object within that tablespace to hold the data. When you create the object, you must include all the information about the type of data you want to hold. This is similar to the COBOL programmer defining a record layout. Look at the following code used to create the customer table; it illustrates how Oracle stores information about the type of data it will record. In the next listing, we give the table a name (i.e., customer), give a descriptive name to each element of information we wish to store (i.e., first_name or last_name), and tell Oracle the type of data we wish to capture (i.e., number and varchar2).

```
create table customer
   (first_name        varchar2(15),
    last_name         varchar2(15),
    phone_area_code   number,
    phone_number      number)
tablespace users;
```

Now that you understand why it is called a tablespace, let's try to understand why we need tablespaces to group datafiles together. The best analogy to explain a database, tablespace, datafile, table, and data is an image of a filing cabinet. Think of the database as the filing cabinet; the drawers within the cabinet are tablespaces; the folders in those drawers are datafiles; the pieces of paper in each folder are the tables and other database objects; the information written on the paper in each folder is the data. Tablespaces are a way to group datafiles.

Keep this in mind: as with your own filing cabinet, you would not intentionally put your homeowner's insurance policy in a drawer called "school records." On the other hand, you might put your homeowner's policy in a drawer called "insurance." The same commonsense rules should apply to naming the tablespaces within your database.

VIP

Do not mix application data in the same tablespace. When you create tablespaces for your applications, give them a descriptive name (e.g., your federal tax data may be held in the intern_rev_bound tablespace).

If you follow the previous recommendation, you will find out in no time how easy it is to manage your database—separate applications mean separate tablespace.

VIP

Keep in mind the limits placed on the length of filenames when working with Oracle on multiple platforms of which one may be DOS. The eight-character filename and three-character extension in DOS may impact on the names of the datafiles you select.

Tablespace Names and Contents

Let's take a look at a typical database and the tablespace names you might see. Since you have a lot of freedom in Oracle when naming tablespaces, notice how we use a descriptive name for each tablespace that describes the type of data it contains. The names we give you are merely an accepted convention; your site's DBA is not required to use them. Remember—the whole point of tablespaces is to help you organize your database.

System Tablespace

The system tablespace is a required part of every Oracle database. This is where Oracle stores all the information it needs to manage itself, such as names of tablespaces and what datafiles each tablespace contains.

Temp Tablespace

The temp tablespace is where Oracle stores all its temporary tables. This is the database's whiteboard or scratch paper. Just as you sometimes need a place to jot down some numbers so you can add them up, Oracle also has a need for some periodic disk space. In the case of a very active database, you might have more than one temp tablespace; for example, TEMP01, TEMP02, and TEMP03.

Tools Tablespace

The tools tablespace is where you store the database objects needed to support tools that you use with your database, such as Oracle Reports, with its own set of tables (Oracle Reports is discussed in Chapter 9). Like any Oracle application, Oracle Reports needs to store tables in the database. Most DBAs place the tables needed to support tools in this tablespace.

Users Tablespace

The users tablespace holds users' personal information. For example, when you are learning how to use Oracle, you might want to create some database objects. This is where the DBA will typically let you place your database object.

Data and Index Tablespaces

From here, anything goes. In some installations, you see tablespace names such as DATA01, DATA02, DATA03, which represent different places to hold data. In other sites, you might see DATA01, INDEX01, etc. Think of a database index as the index in a book: to find a particular reference in the book, you look in the index for its location, rather than reading the whole book from page one. Indexes are a special database object that enable Oracle to quickly find data stored within a table.

   In Oracle, looking at every row in a database is called a full table scan. (We expect that the term full table scan will go away over time, now that Oracle8 supports objects) Using an index search is called an index scan.

Many other shops name their tablespaces after the application data they hold. For example, in a hospital, the tablespace names might be lab_system or research.

Rollback Tablespace

All Oracle databases need a location to store undo information. This tablespace, which holds your rollback segments, is typically called rollback or rbs. One of the primary reasons you use a database management system such as Oracle is for its ability to recover from incomplete or aborted transactions as part of the core functionality. Recovery is discussed in more detail in the "Redo Logs—The Transaction Log" section of this chapter.

Back to Scott's original definition of a database: you start to realize that a database is certainly made up of lots of datafiles. Creating tablespaces and adding space to existing tablespaces are covered in Chapter 14 and Chapter 18.

Tablespaces: Summary of Points

To summarize what we have learned about tablespaces:

- A tablespace is a collection of one or more datafiles.

- The following tablespaces are either required or common to many databases:

  - The system tablespace contains the information Oracle needs to manage itself and your data. This tablespace name is mandatory.

  - The temp tablespace is Oracle's scratch area. On certain occasions, Oracle needs disk space to manage its own transaction or a transaction on your behalf.

  - The tools tablespace stores the objects needed by tools that run against an Oracle database.

  - The users tablespace keeps users' personal database objects.

  - The rollback tablespace is where the database object rollback segments are typically stored.

- The data and index tablespaces store your application data.

- An index is a special type of database object. Oracle uses indexes to speed up data retrieval. We discuss indexes and how they enhance Oracle's performance in Chapter 13.

- A full table scan means that Oracle reads every row of data associated with a given object.

- Undo information is stored in a special database object called a rollback segment. A rollback segment is used to roll back the old value of a database object in case of a failure or aborted transaction.

Redo Logs—The Transaction Log

In addition to the datafiles associated with a tablespace, Oracle has other operating system files associated with it called online redo logs. Another common term for redo logs is transaction logs. These are special operating system files in which Oracle records all changes or transactions that happen to the database. As changes are made to the database, these changes occur in memory. Oracle handles these changes in memory for performance reasons. A disk I/O (input/output) is 1,000 times slower than an action in memory. Since a copy of all transactions is always recorded to the online redo logs, Oracle can take its time recording back to the original datafile the changes to data that occurred in memory. Eventually, the final copy of the change to the data is recorded back to the physical datafile. Since all the transactions are recorded in the online redo logs, the database is always able to recover itself from these transaction logs. It is a requirement that every Oracle database have at least two online redo logs.

How Redo Logs Work

Redo logs work in a circular fashion. Let's say you have a database with two online redo logs, logA and logB. As transactions create, delete, and modify the data in the database, they are recorded first in logA. When logA is filled up, a log switch occurs. All new transactions are then recorded in logB. When logB fills up, another log switch occurs. Now all transactions are recorded in logA again. This is shown in Figure 3-1.

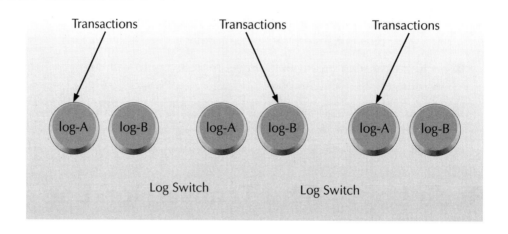

FIGURE 3-1.   *How redo logs work*

VIP
Since redo logs are used in a cyclical fashion,
when Oracle reuses logA, the transaction
information sitting in logA is overwritten.

This point leads us into the discussion of how the Oracle database runs
in either ARCHIVELOG or NOARCHIVELOG mode; these have a direct
correlation to the online redo logs.

ARCHIVELOG Mode: Full Recoverability

When a database is running in ARCHIVELOG mode, all transaction redo
logs are kept. This means that you have a copy of every transaction that
runs against the database, so even though the redo logs work in a circular
fashion, a copy of the redo log is made before it is overwritten. In the event
that the database needs to switch before the copy has been made, Oracle
will freeze up until this action has completed. Oracle will not allow the old
transaction log to be overwritten until it has a copy of it. By having a copy
of all transactions, the database is now able to protect you against all types

of failures, including user error or a disk crash. This is the safest mode to run your database in.

VIP
A database running in ARCHIVELOG mode will save a copy of the redo logs before they are overwritten. This allows for extended recovery capability, including point-in-time recovery.

NOARCHIVELOG Mode

When a database is running in NOARCHIVELOG mode (the default), old redo logs are not kept. Because not all the transaction logs are kept, you are only protected from events such as a power failure (remember that a fill-up of the log causes it to switch—when it circles around to the original, the previous information is lost).

VIP
A database running in NOARCHIVELOG mode will not save a copy of the redo logs before they are overwritten. NOARCHIVELOG mode allows for the bare minimum level of recovery. It is primarily designed to protect you from instance failure.

Redo Logs: Summary of Points

To summarize what we have learned so far about redo logs:

- An Oracle database is made up of two types of files:
  - Datafiles grouped together into tablespaces
  - Datafiles grouped under the family of redo logs
- A database must have at least two redo logs.
- A redo log contains all the transactions that have occurred against the database.
- Another common name for the redo log is the transaction log.

- The transaction logs are necessary to protect your data against loss. Their sole purpose is for recovery against unexpected failures.

- An Oracle database runs in two modes:

  - ARCHIVELOG mode saves all transaction logs.

  - In NOARCHIVELOG mode, old redo logs are not kept.

Control Files

Every database must have at least one control file, though it is highly recommended that you have two or more.

VIP

It is good to have two or more control files in case one is damaged while the database operates. If you have a single control file, you will be in trouble without an additional control file to keep the database accessible to your users.

A control file is a very small file that contains key information about all the files associated with an Oracle database. Control files maintain the integrity of the database and help to identify which redo logs are needed in the recovery process.

The best analogy we can think of to illustrate this point is getting your yearly car inspection. Every year in the state of Massachusetts, residents must get their cars inspected to make sure they meet all safety and pollution guidelines.

Before the database is allowed to begin running, it goes to the control file to determine if the database is in acceptable shape. For example, if a datafile is missing or a particular file has been altered while the database was not using it, then the control file informs the database that it has failed inspection. If this happens, as in a car inspection, you will not be allowed to continue until the problem is corrected.

VIP
If Oracle reads the control file and, based on the information it contains, determines the database is not in acceptable shape, it will not permit the database to run.

Whenever a database checkpoint occurs or there is a change to the structure of the database, the control file is updated. If you do not have a valid control file, your database will not start.

VIP
Have at least two control files for your database and store them on different disks.

VIP
*In the event you lose all your control files, Oracle7/8 supports a **create controlfile** command that can, under most circumstances, be used to recreate a control file.*

Control File: Summary of Points

To summarize what we have learned so far about control files:

- Every database must have at least one control file. You are strongly advised to have at least two control files, and they should be on separate disks.

- All major changes to the structure of the database are recorded in the control file.

Programs

We have defined a database as being "a bunch of programs that manipulate datafiles." It's now time to discuss the programs; we prefer to call them processes since every time a program starts against the database, it communicates with Oracle via a process. Later in this chapter we talk about support processes required to run the Oracle database (see the section "Database Support Processes"). There are two types of Oracle processes you should know about: user and server.

User (Client) Processes

User processes work on your behalf, requesting information from the server processes. Examples of user processes are Oracle Forms (Chapter 8), Oracle Reports (Chapter 9), and SQL*Plus (Chapter 6 and Chapter 12). These are common tools any user of the data within the database uses to communicate with the database.

Server Processes

Server processes take requests from user processes and communicate with the database. Through this communication, user processes work with the data in the database.

The best analogy we have ever heard comes to us compliments of a company called J3 that makes training videos. A good way to think of the client/server process is to imagine yourself in a restaurant. You, the customer, communicate to the waiter who takes your order. That person then communicates the request to the kitchen. The kitchen staff's job is to prepare the food, let the waiter know when it is ready, and stock inventory. The waiter then delivers the meal back to you. In this analogy, the waiter represents the client process, and the kitchen staff represents the server processes.

Programs: Summary of Points

There are two types of programs or processes:

- One type is the user (client) process. Examples include SQL*Plus, Oracle Forms, and Oracle Reports—in other words, any tools you might use to access the database.

- Server processes take requests from client processes and interact with the database to fill those requests.

Database Support Processes

As we stated before, server processes take requests from user (client) processes; they communicate with the database on behalf of user processes. Let's take a look at a special set of server processes that help the database operate.

Database Writer (DBWR)

The database writer is a mandatory process that writes changed data blocks back to the database files. It is one of the only two processes that are allowed to write to the datafiles that make up your Oracle database. On certain operating systems, Oracle allows you to have multiple database writers. This is done for performance reasons.

Checkpoint (CKPT)

Checkpoint is an optional process. When users are working with an Oracle database, they make requests to look at data. That data is read from the database files and put into an area of memory where users can look at it. Some of these users eventually make changes to the data that must be recorded back onto the original datafiles. Earlier in the chapter, we talked about redo logs and how they record all transactions. When the redo logs switch, a checkpoint occurs. When this switch happens, Oracle goes into memory and writes any dirty data blocks' information back to disk. In addition, it notifies the control file of the redo log switch.

These tasks are normally performed by the log writer (lgwr) discussed in the next section. For performance reasons, the DBA can make changes to the database to enable the checkpoint process. This process's sole job is to take the checkpoint responsibility away from the log writer.

Log Writer (LGWR)

The log writer is a mandatory process that writes redo entries to the redo logs. Remember, the redo logs are a copy of every transaction that occurs in the database. This is done so that Oracle is able to recover from various types of failure. In addition, since a copy of every transaction is written in the redo log, Oracle does not have to spend its resources constantly writing data changes back to the datafiles immediately. This results in improved performance. The log writer is the only process that writes to the redo logs. It is also the only process in an Oracle database that reads the redo logs.

System Monitor (SMON)

System monitor is a mandatory process that performs any recovery that is needed at startup. In the parallel server mode (Oracle databases on different computers sharing the same disk farm—see Figure 3-2), it can also perform recovery for a failed database on another computer. Remember, the two databases share the same datafiles.

Process Monitor (PMON)

Process monitor is a mandatory process that performs recovery for a failed user of the database. It assumes the identity of the failed user, releasing all the database resources that user was holding, and it rolls back the aborted transaction.

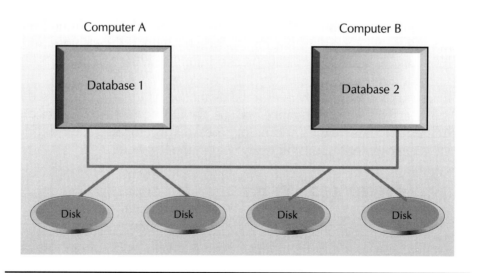

FIGURE 3-2. *Oracle in parallel server mode*

Archiver (ARCH)

Archiver is an optional process. As we discussed earlier in the "Redo Logs" section, the redo (transaction) logs are written to in a sequential manner. When a log fills up, there is a log switch to the next available redo log. When you are running the database in ARCHIVELOG mode, the database goes out and makes a copy of the redo log. This is done so that when the database switches back to this redo log, there is a copy of the contents of this file for recovery purposes. This is the job of the archiver process. Similar to a copy machine, it makes a copy of the file.

Lock (LCKn)

Lock is an optional process. When you are running the Oracle database in the parallel server mode, you will see multiple lck processes. In parallel server mode (see Figure 3-2), these locks help the databases communicate.

Recoverer (RECO)

You only see this optional process when the database is running the Oracle distributed option. The distributed transaction is one where two or more locations of the data must be kept in synch. For example, you might have one copy of data in Boston and another copy of the data in Mexico City. Let's say that while updating the data, the phone line to Mexico goes down due to a severe rainstorm, and a mud slide washes the phone line away. It is the job of the reco process to resolve transactions that may have completed in Boston but not in Mexico City. These transactions are referred to as in-doubt until they are resolved by this reco process.

Dispatcher (Dnnn)

Dispatchers are optional background processes, present only when a multithreaded server configuration is used. At least one dispatcher process is created for every communication protocol (i.e., TCP/IP, SNA) in use (D000, . . ., Dnnn). Each dispatcher process is responsible for routing requests from connected user processes to available shared server processes and returning the responses back to the appropriate user processes. Towards the end of this chapter, we spend more time discussing this important facility.

Database Support Processes: Summary of Points

There are a number of support processes that help communication between the user processes and the database server. These support processes are responsible for the following:

- Writing data back to the datafiles when a checkpoint occurs (dbwr)

- Ensuring dirty data blocks are written back to disk when a checkpoint occurs (ckpt)

- Reading from and writing to the redo logs (lgwr)

- Running any database recovery that may be required at startup (smon)

- Releasing resources that a user acquired if that user's session ends abnormally (pmon)

- Archiving a copy of a redo log when a log switch occurs when running ARCHIVELOG mode (arch)

- Managing locking in a parallel server configuration (lck)

- Recovering in-doubt transactions when using the Oracle distributed option (reco)

This list of processes we gave you is not the complete list. What we gave you are the processes you were most likely to see in 90% of the installations. If you understand the purpose behind these processes, you have the fundamentals you need to understand how the Oracle8 database works. If your shop is running the database in parallel server mode, then you will see some additional processes to help the database share locks. Let's now discuss memory structures, the way many processes communicate with each other.

Memory Structure—The Phone Line

Up to this point, we have talked about the datafiles and the programs. We have also talked about server processes and client processes. Now we will talk about how the client and server processes communicate to each other and themselves through memory structures. Just as the name implies, this is an area of memory set aside where processes can talk to themselves or to other processes.

Oracle uses two types of memory structures: the system global area, or SGA (think of it as an old-fashioned telephone party line or the conference calling option on your phone), and program global area, or PGA (think of this as an intercom system).

System Global Area (SGA)

SGA is a place in memory where the Oracle database stores pertinent information about itself. It does this in memory, since memory is the quickest and most efficient way to allow processes to communicate. This memory structure is then accessible to all the user processes and server processes. Figure 3-3 shows how the SGA is in the center of all communication.

Since the SGA is the mechanism by which the various client and server processes communicate, it is important that you understand its various components. The Oracle Server SGA is broken into the following key components.

Data Buffer Cache

The data buffer cache is where Oracle stores the most recently used blocks of database data. In other words, this is your data cache. When you put information into the database, it is stored in data blocks. The data buffer cache is an area of memory in which Oracle places these data blocks so that a user process can look at them. Before any user process can look at a

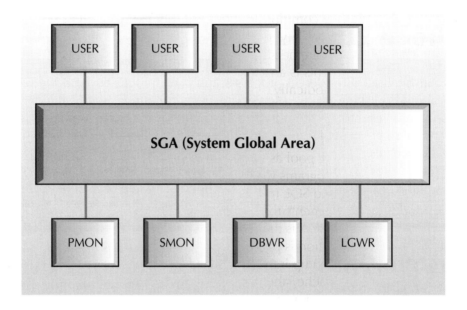

FIGURE 3-3. *SGA: the great phone line*

piece of data, the data must first reside in the data buffer cache. There is a physical limit on the size of the data buffer cache. Thus, as Oracle fills it up, it leaves the hottest blocks in the cache and moves out the cold blocks. It does this via the least recently used (LRU) algorithm.

An important point to clarify: if a client process needs information that is not in the cache, the database goes out to the physical disk drive, reads the needed data blocks, then places them in the data buffer cache. It does this so that all other client and server processes get the benefit of the physical disk read.

Dictionary Cache (Row Cache)

A dictionary cache contains rows out of the data dictionary. The data dictionary contains all the information Oracle needs to manage itself, such as what users have access to the Oracle database, what database objects they own, and where those objects are located.

Redo Log Buffer

Remember that another common name for the online redo logs is the transaction log. So, before any transaction can be recorded into the redo log (the online redo logs are needed for recovery purposes), it must first reside in the redo log buffer. This is an area of memory set aside for this event. Then, the database periodically flushes this buffer to the online redo logs.

Shared SQL Pool

Think of the shared SQL pool as your program cache. This is where all your programs are stored. Programs within an Oracle database are based on a standard language called SQL (pronounced "sequel"). This cache contains all the parsed SQL statements that are ready to run.

To summarize, the SGA is the great communicator. It is the place in memory where information is placed so that client and server processes can access it. It is broken up into major areas: the data cache, the redo log cache, the dictionary cache, and the shared SQL cache. Figure 3-4 shows the caches Oracle maintains in the SGA—we call the SQL cache the sqlarea; these two terms can be used synonymously.

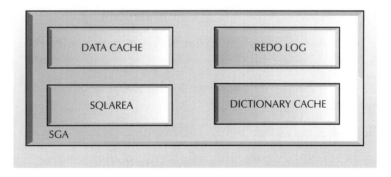

FIGURE 3-4. *SGA—a closer look*

Program Global Area (PGA)

PGA is an area of memory that is used by a single Oracle process. The program global area is not shared; it contains data and control information for a single process. It contains information such as process session variables and internal arrays. Like an intercom system in your home, the various parts of the process can communicate to each other but not to the outside world.

Memory Structure: Summary of Points

To summarize what we have learned so far about memory structure:

- There are two types of memory areas:
  - System global area (SGA)
  - Program global area (PGA)
- The SGA is shared by all server and client processes.
- The SGA has four major components:
  - The data buffer cache is your data cache.
  - The dictionary cache (rows cache) is the information Oracle needs to manage itself.
  - The redo log buffer is the transaction cache.
  - The shared SQL pool is your program cache.
- Before a user process can look at information out of the database, it must first reside in the SGA.
- The SGA is the great communicator by which all processes can share information.
- The PGA is not shared between processes.
- The PGA contains data and process control information.

What Is an Oracle Instance?

Simply put, an Oracle instance is a set of Oracle server processes that have
their own system global area and a set of database files associated with
them. For example, let's say you have a computer with two databases on
it, called prd and tst. If these databases each have their own SGA and a
separate set of Oracle server processes, then you have two instances of
the database. This is shown in Figure 3-5.

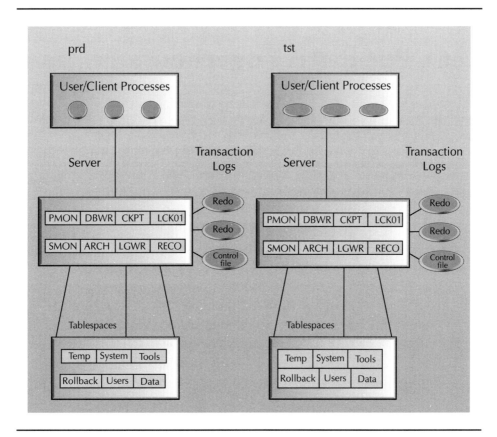

FIGURE 3-5.   *Two Oracle instances*

So that the database does not get confused, each instance is identified by what's known as the SID (system identifier). On most UNIX computers, it is set by the variable "ORACLE_SID." Then, each of the server processes is named to match the SID. For example, on the tst database, the processes would be named

```
ora_tst_dbwr
ora_tst_pmon
ora_tst_smon
ora_tst_lgwr
```

Let's Put It All Together

Now that we understand the Oracle architecture, we'll follow a transaction. Let's say we are strolling through Freeport and we approach a bank machine to see if we have enough money for a bottle of wine. Let's go through the transaction:

1. We ask for an account balance. The machine is running a program called SQL*Plus as the client process. It takes our question and formulates it into the following SQL statement:

```
select account_balance
  from bank_table
 where account_number = '1112222333'
   and account_type = 'SAVINGS';
```

SQL statements are passed to the server processes through the SGA. The server processes check the shared pool for the executable version of the program. If it's not there, it places a parsed "Ready to Run" version there and then executes the program. The account balance "Data Block" is then read from the datafiles and placed into the data cache portion of the SGA. Once in the data cache, the client process is able to read the balance and pass it back to the customer. We're told the balance is $325.00.

2. We see the balance and request a $25 withdrawal. The client process takes our request and formulates it into the following SQL statement:

```
update bank_table
   set account_balance = 300
where account_number = '1112222333'
   and account_type = 'SAVINGS';
```

In closing, here is a summary of the processing that Oracle does with this update statement:

1. The client process passes the statement to the server process through the SGA.

2. The server processes look in the shared pool for an executable version of the program. If one is found, proceed to step #4; if not, proceed to step #3.

3. Process this SQL statement and move its executable version into the pool.

4. Execute the SQL statement.

5. Is the data this statement manipulates in the data cache? If it is, proceed to step #7; if it is not, proceed to step #6.

6. Read the data from the database file into the data cache.

7. Record the old value of the data in a rollback segment (the rollback segment holds the old balance of $325).

8. Create a copy of the transaction in the redo logs.

9. Change the data in the data cache to reflect the new balance of $300.

10. The bank machine signals through the SGA that all is complete.

11. Record the completion of the transaction in the redo log.

12. Free up the undo information in the rollback segment.

13. Deliver money to customer.

14. Buy a great bottle of wine for half the price we would pay in Boston!

VIP
*In step #7 of this process, if the user cancels
the transaction OR the system comes down
during the transaction, the information held in
the rollback segment is used to restore the
original balance.*

VIP
*As with every transaction, eventually the
database writer writes the data cache copy of
the data block back to the original datafile.*

As you can see, a lot goes on for your client process to be able to
access the database. After you work with Oracle for a while, its value
becomes clear.

A Closer Look at the Multithreaded Server (MTS)

As we stated earlier, the multithreaded server allows numerous connections
to the database to all share memory and resources. This minimizes the
memory overhead associated with supporting many users.

Before we had the MTS configuration, each process that connected
to the Oracle8 database required a separate process with its own allocation
of memory. Due to the overhead of creating these connections, and
maintaining these connections, this way of managing connections
became a major performance bottleneck.

The multithreaded server configuration allows processes to share
memory and connections. This eliminates much of the overhead associated
with supporting large amounts of users trying to access the database. This is
a major feature that allows Oracle to support a large number of users.

NOTE
MTS is one of many features in Oracle8 that make it possible to support the 10,000+ concurrent user community. Not all clients will use MTS, but it is a component in the startegy to support such a large number of users.

VIP
The multithreaded server feature is not necessarily the best way to go with all applications. Familiarize yourself with its features and speak with colleagues and fellow techies before running out and implementing it on all your Oracle8 instances.

The multithreaded server has pools of connections, called *shared server processes*, that are constantly established and that allow users to share those open connections. This method of connection is much faster than its predecessor, a dedicated connection. To help illustrate this concept, let's look at an example. Consider an order entry system with dedicated server processes. A customer places an order as a clerk enters the order into the database. For most of the transaction, the clerk is on the telephone talking to the customer and the server process dedicated to the clerk's user process remains idle. The server process is not needed during most of the transaction, yet the system is forced to support the connection, draining needed resources for other users. The multithreaded server configuration eliminates the need for a dedicated server process for each connection. A pool of connections is maintained. As the clerk needs to talk to the database, that clerk is allocated a connection. The time and resources needed to create connections are eliminated. The time and resources needed to maintain the connection are shared by all users. This frees up very valuable, scarce resources.

To set up your system to use the multithreaded server, you must make some changes in the instance initialization parameter file, then shut down and restart the database. The appropriate number of dispatcher processes for each instance depends upon the performance you want from your database, the host operating system's limit on the number of connections per process, and the number of connections required per network protocol.

The instance must be able to provide as many connections as there are concurrent users on the database system; the more dispatchers you have, the better potential database performance users will see, since they will not have to wait as long for dispatcher service. Think of dispatchers as the dispatcher at your local taxi cab company. When you call up, the dispatcher answers the phone and assigns the work to a cab. The more dispatchers you have, the more calls that can be answered.

We have discussed the multithreaded server on its own based on the importance of the feature and its mission—supporting lots of user connections very effectively. Just like the rest of the Oracle8 database, it is highly tunable. With Oracle8's ability to support 10,000+ concurrent users, perhaps more of us will end up experimenting and becoming fluent with MTS.

What's Next

We leave this chapter with two suggestions:

- Ingest the information we have discussed here and look at your database configuration and try to recognize all the components we have highlighted. Walk through the chapter again, and as you cross into a new section, ensure you can identify the components as they appear in your database. For example, where we discuss database support processes, stop and run a program status command on your machine and identify every process by name.

NOTE

*In UNIX, this would be done using the command **ps -ef | grep oracleprd** for a database with an ORACLE_SID of prd. In VMS, the command is **sho system/out=temp.lis** followed by **search temp.lis ora_**.*

■ Keep running back to parts of this chapter as you read the rest of the book. It is remarkable how much you will understand about Oracle having this chapter as a foundation.

In the next chapter, we discuss the assortment of objects stored in the Oracle database and the jobs some special objects perform as your database operates.

CHAPTER
4

Database Objects

his chapter deals with all the major database objects you will encounter while working with Oracle8. Each of these objects has a specific purpose or job to do. In this chapter, we will explain what each object is used for and give you an example of how to use it. We will provide details on tables, views, indexes, synonyms, and snapshots to name a few. In Chapter 1, we discussed how Oracle stores information in one place. If a payroll application needs personnel information for a firm's employees, rather than capture the required information itself, the payroll system reads data from the personnel system. Since data is stored in one place and read by all, we will also introduce object privileges in this chapter, and show you how privileges are used to control who can do what with data.

Terminology

The following definitions will arm you with the technical jargon to make it through this chapter:

- A *table* is a database object that holds your data. Information about every table is stored in the data dictionary; with this information, Oracle allows you to maintain data residing in your table.

- A *view* allows you to see a customized selection of one or more tables, and it uses a SQL query that is stored in the database. When using views, the SQL statement that defines the view is executed as if you had coded the defining statement yourself.

- An *index* is a minicopy of a table. Index entries for a table allow Oracle rapid access to the data in your tables.

- A *synonym* is an alternate name for an object in the database. Think of a synonym as a nickname for an object—somewhat like calling a woman named Margaret by the name Maggie instead.

- *Grants* are privileges given out by owners of objects, allowing other users to work with their data.

- The *data dictionary* is maintained by Oracle and contains information relevant to the tables that reside in the database. For example, in a telecommunications system, the data dictionary records the fact that a North American area code is three digits long.

- A *role* is a group of privileges that are collected together and granted to users. Once privileges are granted to a role, a user inherits the role's privileges by becoming a member of that role. This way, instead of updating every user's account on an individual basis, you can just manage the role.

- A *remote database* is an Oracle8 instance that runs on a computer different than the one you may currently be logged onto. Picture a network where a database server resides in Newton, and communicates with another server in Toronto. Users logged on to the machine in Toronto may access a remote database in Newton using a network transport mechanism to enable the communication.

- A *snapshot* is a read-only copy of data stored in one or more tables. Using Oracle8's scheduling features, the DBA instructs Oracle to regularly refresh a snapshot on a remote database from the contents of the data in the tables that serve as the inputs to the snapshot.

- *Contention* occurs when two or more database users are waiting for data or a resource (e.g., memory required to perform a sort or CPU time to perform some calculation). Closely hooked to contention are situations that cause users to wait for one another to complete their activity before they can take their turn using the resource in question.

Tables—Where Oracle Stores Your Data

A table is the database object that holds your data. The data dictionary holds information about every table; Oracle uses its data dictionary to ensure the correct type of data (e.g., number or character) is placed in Oracle tables. The best analogy is to think of a table as a spreadsheet. The cells of the spreadsheet equate to the columns of the table. Just like the cells of a spreadsheet, the columns of a table have a data type associated with them. If the number data type is associated with a spreadsheet cell, then you would not be allowed to store letters in the spreadsheet cell. The same applies to a table's columns. Table columns that are of a number data type cannot accept letters. Data types are covered in detail in Chapter 6.

The way you create tables in Oracle is through the **create table** command. Let's take a closer look at an example of this command in its simplest form:

```
SQL*Plus: Release 4.0.3.0.0 - Production on Sun May 11 12:20:12 1999
Copyright (c) Oracle Corporation 1979, 1994, 1996.  All rights reserved.
Connected to:
Oracle8 Server Release 8.0.3.0.1 - Production
With the distributed, heterogeneous, replication, objects
and parallel query options
PL/SQL Release 3.0.3.0.1 - Production
SQL> create table customer
  2    (last_name  varchar2(30),
  3     state_cd   char(2),
  4     sales      number);
Table created.
SQL>
```

In this example, we create a table called customer. The columns associated with the table are last_name, state_cd, and sales. Each of these columns has a data type associated with it.

The column last_name has a data type of varchar2. Its maximum length is 30, which means the column cannot hold a name larger than 30 characters. The data type varchar2 tells the database that this column can accept letters, numbers, and special characters. In addition, varchar2 tells the database to store the information internally in a variable-length format. For example, the last name Lane takes less room to store than the last name Ellison. In other words, Oracle only uses the amount of space it needs to hold the name.

The column state_cd has a data type of char. The 2 tells us it has a length of two characters. The data type of char tells the database that this column can accept letters, numbers, and special characters. In addition, char tells the database to store the information internally in a fixed-length format. No matter how big the state_cd is, it can take up no more and no less space than it takes to hold two characters.

The column sales has a data type of number. This data type tells the database it can only accept numbers. In addition, since they are numbers, you can add, subtract, multiply, and divide the contents. In fact, Oracle has an extensive set of mathematical functions you can apply to columns of data type number.

VIP
A table is a database object that holds your data. It is made up of many columns. Each of those columns has a data type associated with it. This data type is the roadmap that Oracle follows so it knows how to correctly manipulate the contents.

Views—A Special Look at Your Data

A view is a database object that allows you to create a customized slice of a table or a collection of tables. Unlike a table, a view contains no data, just a SQL query. The data that is retrieved from this query is presented like a table. In fact, if you did not create the view, you would think you were dealing with a table. Like a table, you may **insert**, **update**, **delete**, and **select** data from a view.

VIP
You can always select data from a view, but, in some situations there are restrictions on other ways data in a view can be manipulated.

Why Use Views?

It is important to know how to use views, since you will probably require views for one or all of the following reasons:

- Views can provide an additional level of security. For example, you might have an employee table within your company, and you might want to create a view that allows managers to see information on only their employees.

- Views allow you to hide data complexity. An Oracle database is made up of many tables. You can retrieve information from two or more tables by performing a join, and these joins can get very confusing for a typical end user and even a seasoned veteran. Many times, you will create a view that is the combination of many tables. For example, you might have a view that is a combination of the customer table and order table. Thus, the user of the database would only have to make a simple select off of the view called cust_ord. They would never know that this might actually be based on two tables.

■ Views help you maintain naming sanity. Often, when we create column names for an Oracle table, we forget that people actually have to type them when wording SQL statements. For example, we might have a column named middle_initial_of_person. In the view, we could rename the column "mi."

■ Views allow the flexibility of changing the makeup of one or more tables that make up the view without the need to change application code. Suppose a view joins two tables, displaying three columns from one table and four from the next. If the first table is altered to contain an extra column, the view definition is not affected and any applications that reference the view require no attention.

Creating Views

You create a view using the command **create view** while connected to Oracle. This is usually done via SQL*Plus. Let's try creating a simple view:

```
SQL*Plus: Release 4.0.3.0.0 - Production on Sun May 11 12:20:12 1999
Copyright (c) Oracle Corporation 1979, 1994, 1996.  All rights reserved.
Connected to:
Oracle8 Server Release 8.0.3.0.1 - Production
With the distributed, heterogeneous, replication, objects
and parallel query options
PL/SQL Release 3.0.3.0.1 - Production
SQL> create or replace view cust as
  2   select last_name, state_cd
  3     from customer;
View created.
SQL>
```

If users want to access the last_name and state_cd information stored in the customer table using the cust view, they could issue the command **select * from cust;** rather than **select last_name,state_cd from customer;**.

When the command is issued, Oracle runs the SQL statement associated
with the view. This query brings back the data from the customer table,
missing any columns not mentioned in the **create view** statement. The
order by command is covered in Chapter 6.

Since this view did not include the column sales, you can allow people
access to the customer data without giving them access to the sensitive data
stored within the sales column. Like a table, you have complete control
over who has access to the view.

VIP

*A view is just a SQL query that is stored in the
database. The results of that query are returned
in the form of a table.*

Indexes—A Quick Way to Speed Access to Your Data

Just like an index in a book, which helps you find information faster, an
index placed on a table helps you retrieve your data faster. If your
application is running slow, a well-placed index will make it run quicker.

VIP

*A well-placed index on a table will help the
database retrieve your data faster.*

It has been our experience that if you think of indexes as minitables,
you will be able to understand how they work. Let's imagine we have the
following table (the four dots in the listing represent the definition of
column d through column z, giving the table 26 columns):

```
SQL*Plus: Release 4.0.3.0.0 - Production on Sun May 11 12:20:12 1999
Copyright (c) Oracle Corporation 1979, 1994, 1996.  All rights reserved.
Connected to:
Oracle8 Server Release 8.0.3.0.1 - Production
With the distributed, heterogeneous, replication, objects
and parallel query options
PL/SQL Release 3.0.3.0.1 - Production
SQL> create table sample_3
```

```
 2      (a      char2(30),
 3       b      char2(30),
 4       c      char2(30),
....
Table created.
SQL>
```

Every time you want to read the information stored in column c, Oracle must also bring back the information stored in columns a, b, and d through z. Like every resource in a computer, there is a limit to how much it can physically do at any point in time.

To understand the point we are making, let's say that when Oracle issues a request for data from the sample_3 table, it can only retrieve the equivalent of four records' worth of information. Since each of the 26 columns in the table is defined as data type char, Oracle reserves 30 spaces for each column in the table. Thus, when reading the equivalent of four records at a time, the buffer holds 3,120 characters (26 columns * 30 characters * 4 records) of information. So, even though you may only wish to see the information stored in column c, the database is forced to wade through all the information stored in the table. Well, you have a solution to this problem, and it is called an index.

Let's say you create an index on column c with the SQL statement **create index colc_ind on sample_3(colc);**. Oracle creates the index object. Think of this as a minitable that holds only the column c information from the table named sample_3. In addition, it will retrieve the information needed to point back to the actual row within the table called sample_3 where the particular column c information came from. Like Siamese twins, these two objects are now linked together. Whatever happens to one happens to the other. If you delete a column c item from the main table, you will also delete the corresponding index entry.

Now, say you want to retrieve just the information stored in column c of the table called sample_3. Oracle knows it can resolve that request from the index, so rather than wading through the table, it just looks at the index. Oracle performs that same physical read, which was limited to four records' worth of information (or 3,120 characters at a time). By using the index just created, Oracle now only has to hold column c information. So instead of four records' worth of information, you can now get 104 records each read, since column c is 30 characters and the buffer can hold 3,120 characters.

VIP
*Index entries contain information only about
the columns that are part of the index, not all
the columns in a table.*

That same read can bring back much more focused information. It's
limited to looking at what you need and not required to wade through all
the other columns in the table. Before moving on, let's look at some
features of and uses for indexes, since indexes are so important.

Indexes Have a Sorted Order

By design, the data stored in a relational database has no particular order.
The record you insert into a table goes into the next available slot. So,
when you issue a SQL query looking for a particular date or range of dates
(e.g., **select * from state where state_cd = 'MA';**), Oracle is required to
look at every row of data in the table.

An index, on the other hand, is in a sorted order. If you have a date data
type column in a table, you could create an index on that column. The
index created by Oracle would contain all the dates in sorted order. It is
typically much quicker for Oracle to go to the index, find all the records for
a desired date, then bring back the information to you.

Indexes Can Guarantee Uniqueness

There are two types of indexes you can create. You can create a unique
index and a nonunique index. A unique index does not allow duplicates; a
nonunique index allows duplicates. As we stated earlier, an index is like a
Siamese twin to the table. If you create a unique index on column c in a
table, then every time you try to insert a row into the actual table, the index
will check to make sure that column c is still unique. The SQL statement
create index colc_ind on sample_3 (colc); is used to create a nonunique
index, and the statement **create unique index colc_ind on sample_3 table
(colc);** creates a unique index.

Two Columns Are Better Than One

Oracle allows you to create concatenated indexes. These indexes are made
up of more than one column. Many times, you realize when looking at

your tables that you would never look at column a without looking at column b. So it makes sense to index both together using a concatenated index. Let's build a concatenated index using the SQL statement **create index colabc_ind on sample_3 table (cola, colb, colc);**. Once this concatenated index is built, Oracle manages the index just as it does with those built on single columns.

The where Clause and Your Indexes

Oracle determines which index it will use to satisfy a query based on how the **where** clause is worded (i.e., the columns referenced in the **where** and **and** part of a SQL statement). Oracle examines the available indexes, and selects the index that will provide the quickest results.

VIP
*Oracle determines which indexes it will use by looking at the **where** clause of the SQL query.*

As your experience with formulating queries increases, you will find yourself becoming quite adept at wording SQL to allow Oracle to process queries using the available indexes.

Synonyms—A New Identity

Just as many actors change their names to make themselves easier to remember, and more recognizable, you can do the same for an Oracle table. When we created the table sample_3, the complete identity it received was the name of the owner of the table (e.g., ops$coreymj) and the table name. Then, if you are connected to Oracle as ops$coreymj, when you issue a SQL query, Oracle is smart enough to realize you are connected as the user who owns the table. So, behind the scenes, Oracle places the owner's name in front of the table name. Let's say you want to retrieve a column from the table and you issue the SQL query **select cola from sample_3;** which Oracle translates into the following:

```
select colA from ops$coreymj.sample_3;
```

A synonym is a database object that allows you to create alternate names for Oracle tables and views. Using our sample_3 table as an example, suppose a user who did not own the table issued the command **select cola from sample_3;**. Oracle would not know what to do. However, if the user had a synonym for the table, Oracle could successfully execute the SQL statement using the synonym. This simple SQL statement illustrates how synonyms are used. When users who do not own a table wish to reference a table in a SQL statement, they must always use a synonym to refer to the table.

You may decide to set up synonyms for any Oracle table for a variety of reasons:

- You want to hide the true owner or name of a table.

- You want or need to hide the true location of a table. Some installations have one table in Boston and another table in Ottawa.

- You want to provide users with a table name less complicated than the real table name (e.g., s3 instead of sample_3).

With this in mind, let's create a synonym using the SQL statement **create synonym toast for ops$coreymj. sample_3;**. Now, the following statements will bring back the same rows from the same table:

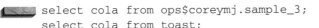

```
select cola from ops$coreymj.sample_3;
select cola from toast;
```

Private Synonyms and Public Synonyms

As you can see, you can use synonyms to give a table an alternate identity. This can greatly simplify SQL statement syntax. The synonym we created in the previous section is called a private synonym: normally ops$coreymj is the only one that can use the synonym toast to point to the table ops$coreymj.sample_3. Another type of synonym is a public synonym, which all Oracle users are able to use. You can create a public synonym with the SQL statement **create public synonym tonic for ops$coreymj.sample_3;**. Any Oracle user can now refer to the table using the public synonym tonic. Now users can issue the statement **select cola from tonic;** and Oracle would know they really mean **select cola from ops$coreymj.sample_3;**.

Grants—May I Please Have Access?

Up to now in this chapter, we may have given the impression that every database user has access to every other database users' objects and their contents. This is not true in the real world. Oracle gives you extensive control over what a user can see, modify, delete, or change. It is one of the real strengths of the Oracle Server. Combine this with views, and you can even control what data a user can look at.

VIP

Grants are used to give one user privileges to work with another user's data. Once privileges have been granted, recipients of the grant have the ability to work with someone else's objects.

We will now discuss some types of privileges and show how they are granted to other users.

Granting Privileges to Users

Granting of object privileges allows users to work with database objects and their contents.

VIP

When users are granted privileges on other users' tables, before they can reference those tables in SQL statements, there must be a public or private synonym through which Oracle can identify tne table.

Say user jrstocks owns a table called sample_b, and gives all database users access to the table. Along comes user coreyam and runs a statement against the sample_b table, and receives the following error message:

```
select * from sample_b;
             *
```

```
ERROR at line 1:
ORA-00942: table or view does not exist
```

Regardless of which privilege is being granted, there are three parts to each **grant** statement:

1. The keyword/privilege part is made up of the word **grant** followed by one or more privileges. When multiple privileges are placed in the same **grant** statement, they are separated by a comma.

2. The table name part starts with the keyword on and lists the table on which privileges are being given.

3. The recipient part lists one or more users who receive the privileges being given out.

Let's look at how four object privileges are given to users.

select

The select privilege allows other users to look at the contents of tables they do not own. The statement **grant select on sample_3 to public;** would allow all users to view the sample_3 table. The statement **grant select on sample_3 to ops$phippss,ops$abbeyms;** would allow the two users mentioned to look at sample_3. Notice when more than one user receives a grant, the usernames are separated in the list by a comma.

VIP
When public is the target of any grant, all users of the database receive the privileges specified. If your database had 15,000 users, granting a privilege to public would be the same as issuing 15,000 grants separately (one to each user!).

insert

The insert privilege allows one to create rows in other users' tables. The statement **grant insert on sample_a to public;** allows all users to create new rows in sample_a. Oracle allows stacking of privileges in a single grant statement—the SQL statement **grant insert, select on sample_a to public;** is the same as the two statements **grant select on sample_a to public;** followed by **grant insert on sample_a to public;**.

update
The update privilege allows other users to modify or change data in tables they do not own. The statement **grant update on sample_a to teplownd;** would permit user teplownd to modify information in sample_a.

delete
The delete privilege permits users to delete rows of information from specified tables. We recommend using caution giving out this privilege since it is very powerful. Picture the following that actually happened to one of our acquaintances. A programmer was connected to the production database while she thought she was logged into a test database. She issued the command **delete from people_master;** and Oracle responded with

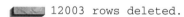 `12003 rows deleted.`

After exiting SQL*Plus, the next program that accessed people_master looking for a personnel record for Rick Bower was told the record did not exist!

The command **grant delete,update,select on sample_a to public;** gives the specified privilege to all database users. The command **grant select,update,insert,delete on sample_a to teplownd,greerw;** allows users teplownd and greerw to do the listed activities on the sample_a table.

Recipients of Grants
Throughout this section, we have shown a number of **grant** statements where the recipients were either public or an assortment of database users (e.g., teplownd). Imagine an installation where there are two distinct classes of users for a financial management system. One class of user is allowed to approve travel claims, cancel requisitions, and adjust quantities and unit prices on purchase orders. The other class is your everyday run-of-the-mill user who can only create requisitions. Say there was a list of 18 users in the first category, and over 900 in the second. Oracle uses roles to help manage grants to multiple users; we discuss roles in the next section.

Roles—A Way to Group Users Together

You can create a database object called a role, then grant privileges to that role, then grant that role to individual users. Sounds complicated, but it's very simple. For example, let's create a role called nurse by issuing the SQL statement **create role nurse;** and give the role some privileges by running the six commands:

```
grant insert on tableA to nurse;
grant insert on tableB to nurse;
grant insert, delete on tableC to nurse;
grant update on tableD to nurse;
grant delete on tableE to nurse;
grant select on tableF to nurse;
```

Now, let's give some users the nurse role by running the following three commands:

```
grant nurse to ops$abbey;
grant nurse to ops$teplow;
grant nurse to ops$lane;
```

When we want to effect a change to these three users, we just have to change the role nurse, and the users will automatically receive the change. If we want all three users to be able to delete from tablef, for example, we would issue the SQL statement **grant delete on tableF to nurse;**. All database users who have the role nurse would be affected by the new change.

Other Objects You May Encounter in Oracle8

Up until now, we have discussed objects in the Oracle8 database that all (or at least most) readers will become familiar with. This section features a number of objects that are closely related to the two main objects (tables and views), but some may never have the need or opportunity to create.

Snapshots

A snapshot is a recent copy of a table from another database or, in some cases, a subset of that table. The SQL statement that creates and subsequently maintains a snapshot normally reads data from a database residing on a remote server. In a distributed computing environment, DBAs define snapshots for one or both of the following reasons:

- Response time improves when a local read-only copy of a table exists—this can be many times faster than reading data directly from a remote database.

- Once a snapshot is built on a remote database, if the node containing the data from which the snapshot is built is not available, the snapshot can be used without the need to access the down database. Suppose the DBA has created a snapshot called zip_codes on a server in Boston. The data from which the snapshot is built is in Redwood Shores. If the Redwood Shores server is unavailable, the users of the Boston server can still access the zip_codes snapshot that resides in Boston.

The query that creates a snapshot closely resembles the code used to create a view as we discussed in the "Views—A Special Look at Your Data" section of this chapter. The secret to keeping a snapshot up-to-date is the specification of a refresh interval. When defining the snapshot, the DBA specifies this interval, and Oracle8 manages the propagation of data from the table(s) upon which the snapshot is built.

VIP
To define and incorporate snapshots into your applications, you must install Oracle8's distributed database feature.

Stored Objects

We first mentioned stored procedures, packages, and functions in the "Procedural Component" section of Chapter 1. The code for these special objects is written using Oracle's procedural SQL offering called PL/SQL, featured in Chapter 7. Just like tables and views, users of the Oracle8 database need privileges to run these code segments sitting in the database. Owners of stored objects must issue a SQL statement similar to the following to allow users to run their code:

```
grant execute on my_package to public; -- all users can execute the code
grant execute on my_func to nurse_role; -- all members of the role can run
    the code
grant execute on my_procedure to tom_scholz; -- user tom_scholz may run
    procedure
```

VIP
Just like tables and views, users need a synonym created to point at other users' stored objects before they can be executed.

Database Links

Database links are closely coupled to the distributed database feature. Database links allow users to work with data in remote databases without the need to know where that data resides. When a database link is created, logon information to the remote database is supplied, and each time the database link is used, a session is initiated on the distributed network to resolve the reference to a remote table or view. Interestingly enough, the ability to reference information without knowing (or caring) where it is stored is an extension of the relational theory of storing data once and reading it many times.

Sequences

Often in a relational or object-relational database, systems generate numeric column values that serve as primary keys. Sequences help relieve the need for disk I/O by caching numbers in memory, thereby making them available to systems requiring a sequential numbered primary key. In the past, before sequences appeared, application developers had to get a number from a single column table containing the ever-growing numeric value. This led to contention for the table, and required resources to lock the table while one session obtained the next available number. Unlike tables or views, applications do not select a value directly from a sequence.

Clusters

Clusters allow for a different method of storing table data. When applications continually work with a set of two or more tables, the DBA may consider using a cluster to store the data from the tables so commonly joined together. Tables in a cluster share the same data blocks; this cohabitation of the same physical area in the database files can enhance performance as the clustered data is retrieved, viewed, and perhaps updated.

Viewing Object Information in the Data Dictionary

Information about all the objects we have discussed in this chapter is stored in the Oracle8 data dictionary. The next listing points you at data dictionary information about objects:

```
ALL_CATALOG          All tables, views, synonyms, sequences accessible
                     to the user
ALL_INDEXES          Descriptions of indexes on tables accessible to
                     the user
ALL_IND_COLUMNS      COLUMNs comprising INDEXes on accessible TABLES
ALL_OBJECTS          Objects accessible to the user
ALL_SEQUENCES        Description of SEQUENCEs accessible to the user
ALL_SYNONYMS         All synonyms accessible to the user
ALL_TABLES           Description of tables accessible to the user
USER_CATALOG         Tables, Views, Synonyms and Sequences owned by the
                     user
USER_CLUSTERS        Descriptions of user's own clusters
USER_CLU_COLUMNS     Mapping of table columns to cluster columns
USER_INDEXES         Description of the user's own indexes
USER_IND_COLUMNS     COLUMNs comprising user's INDEXes or on user's TABLES
USER_OBJECTS         Objects owned by the user
USER_SEQUENCES       Description of the user's own SEQUENCEs
USER_SYNONYMS        The user's private synonyms
USER_TABLES          Description of the user's own tables
USER_VIEWS           Description of the user's own views
```

We have found one of the most useful items of information you can glean from the Oracle8 data dictionary is the interobject dependencies. The data dictionary view shown in the next listing is queried to display dependency information:

```
SQL> desc user_dependencies
 Name                            Null?    Type
 ------------------------------- -------- ----
 NAME                            NOT NULL VARCHAR2(30)
 TYPE                                     VARCHAR2(12)
 REFERENCED_OWNER                         VARCHAR2(30)
 REFERENCED_NAME                          VARCHAR2(64)
 REFERENCED_TYPE                          VARCHAR2(12)
 REFERENCED_LINK_NAME                     VARCHAR2(128)
 SCHEMAID                                 NUMBER
```

Inspect the output from the following query for a flavor of how useful we find this information:

```
SQL*Plus: Release 4.0.3.0.0 - Production on Sun May 11 12:20:12 1999
Copyright (c) Oracle Corporation 1979, 1994, 1996.  All rights reserved.
Connected to:
Oracle8 Server Release 8.0.3.0.1 - Production
With the distributed, heterogeneous, replication, objects
and parallel query options
PL/SQL Release 3.0.3.0.1 - Production
SQL> select name, referenced_owner, referenced_type
  2    from user_dependencies
  3   where referenced_name = 'ASSIGNMENT';
```

```
NAME                    REFERENCED_OWNER REFERENCED_TYPE
-------------------     ---------------- --------------------
DEPARTMENT              DEPT             TABLE
GET_END_DATE            COMMON           PROCEDURE
DURATION                COMMON           TABLE
SQL>
```

This query tells us that the DEPARTMENT and DURATION tables as well as the GET_END_DATE procedure are dependent on the assignment table. When maintenance activities begin that may affect the structure of the ASSIGNMENT table, it would be wise to visit these objects to see what affect the changes may have on them.

What's Next

We have given you an introduction to the most common database objects and their use. This list is not complete, but we have highlighted what is by far the most common. Every day that we work with the Oracle Server, we learn something new. As our experience has taught us, you will continually learn about Oracle's vast capabilities while you travel down its path. Just when you think you have learned it all, you will either discover a new product or something new you want to learn to do with an existing one.

The next chapter discusses how to install Oracle7 and Oracle8. Many of you may have Oracle and some of its products already installed on your personal computers. Nevertheless, Chapter 5 will teach you how to do it yourself next time. Part of the chapter discusses installing Oracle on large multiuser machines, referred to as minicomputers. Installation is where it all starts . . . carry on.

CHAPTER

5

Installation

o far, we have discussed Oracle the company, introduced you to Oracle architecture, and talked about the assortment of database objects. In this chapter, we will cover some installation issues and concepts, and we will provide you with some guidance about decisions you will have to make before, during, and after installation. This chapter is in two parts. First, we will show you how to install the Oracle Universal Server using the three most popular platforms—NT, UNIX, and Desktop—as examples. The first will feature the Oracle8 installer, and the other two release 7.3.2 of Oracle. Then we will look at installing Oracle products in the same environments using the same versions. By the end of this chapter, you will know how to:

- Install the Oracle8 Server in a Windows NT environment

- Install Oracle8 Client in a Windows 95 environment

- Install Oracle7 Server in a Windows 95 environment

- Install Personal Oracle7 for the first time in a UNIX environment

- Install Oracle products in a desktop and non-desktop environment

When reading this chapter and looking at the UNIX example, keep in mind that UNIX is case-sensitive; thus, the commands START.SH and start.sh are not the same. In addition, some of the commands are preceded with a period followed by a slash (./), which is a required part of the command.

Terminology

The following definitions will arm you with the technical jargon you need to make it through this chapter.

- *ORACLE_HOME* is the directory name under which all the Oracle software is installed. Think of it as the home of the Oracle database or as the location where the Oracle software resides on the machine on which it is installed.

- The *staging area* is made up of a number of locations on a disk (also called a directory structure) from where Oracle installs software. The files are sometimes stored in compressed format, to save disk space. Installation is often a two-stage process: from the distribution medium to the staging area, and then from the staging area to the ORACLE_HOME.

■ A *database administrator* or DBA is a technical wizard who manages the complete operation of the Oracle database.

■ A *DLL* is a dynamic link library used by all Windows software. These libraries contain routines that are enlivened at run time to manage the resources consumed by the programs.

■ The *ORACLE_SID* is an identifier unique to each Oracle database. When Oracle is installed, one specifies an ORACLE_SID to tell the database apart from others that may end up on the same machine. It's wise to choose a meaningful name for a database so that its purpose can be figured out from the ORACLE_SID (e.g., the SID "prd" may be used for production, and "tst" for a test database).

■ A *system administrator* is the person who manages computer resources and, with the DBA, manages hardware and computer peripherals.

■ A *local database* is one that resides on the same computer as the user. Accessing Personal Oracle from Windows 95 on the same machine is an example of a local database configuration.

■ A *remote database* is one that resides on a different computer than the one the user or developer is using. The remote database is accessed using a vendor's (e.g., Novell) network software and Oracle's network product called SQL*Net.

■ *Desktop* is the environment found on personal computers that accesses local or remote databases. The Apple Macintosh and Microsoft Windows are examples of desktop computing.

■ A *patch* is a fix applied to a program. Patches do not change the overall functionality of a program; they simply fix or enhance an existing product.

■ *Product bundling* is a method a vendor uses to package software components. Suppose two kinds of breakfast cereals were packaged together for a marketing promotion, and sold separately at other times; one could say the product bundling during the sale is different than under normal circumstances.

Universal Server—Oracle8

The installation we feature in this section begins with locating the setup program on the Oracle8 Server CD-ROM. There are two parts to an Oracle8 installation—the server portion and the client component. Let's get started.

NOTE

The series of steps you go through and questions asked by the Oracle8 installer depend on many factors. If Oracle8 is already on your machine, for example, the re-installation of the client portion may proceed through a set of different screens than those shown here.

Server Installation

While at the Windows NT Server console, place the Oracle8 CD in the CD-ROM. The installation then proceeds as follows:

1. When presented with the information box shown in Figure 5-1, click OK.

2. Most, though not all, installations are done in the English language. When Oracle displays the dialog box shown in Figure 5-2, click OK to accept English or select another language from the drop-down list beside the prompt.

3. Oracle then asks for the company name and the location of the Oracle Home folder. Most of the time the text "\ORANT" is suggested as the location of the folder, though it can be changed to anything you want. Fill in a name for Company, then click OK to continue.

4. The next dialog box, shown in Figure 5-3, wants you to specify the type of installation you wish to perform. The Programmer/2000 selection simply installs software that enables developers to access the Oracle8 Server data repository from some Oracle and non-Oracle tools. For the purpose of this exercise, we selected Oracle8 Server Products, which is most likely already highlighted. Click OK to carry on.

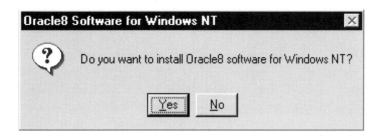

FIGURE 5-1.   *Oracle8 software for Windows NT confirmation*

5. Since this is an Oracle8 Server installation, the installer wants you to specify the nature of the starter database you want it to set up. Let's select the "Standard (30M minimum disk space)" option, shown in Figure 5-4. The Replication option and the discussion of what it entails are material best covered in another work.

6. The next choice is whether to copy the Oracle8 documentation to the server's hard drive, or read when necessary from the CD. Select the "Hard Drive (requires 66M bytes)" option, then click OK to continue.

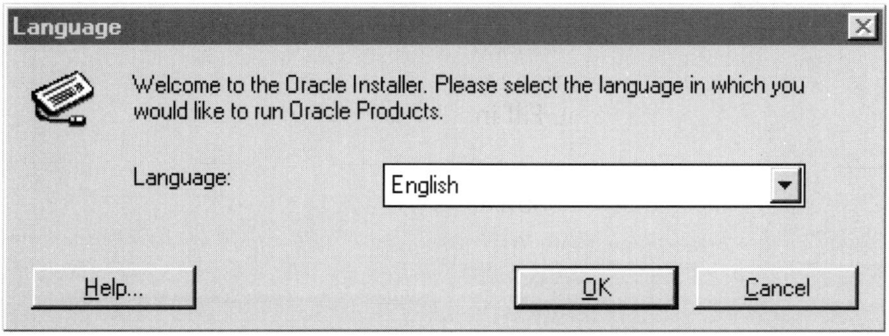

FIGURE 5-2.   *Language choice*

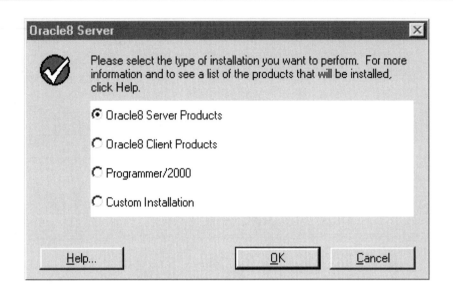

FIGURE 5-3. *Installation type selection*

FIGURE 5-4. *Starter database selection*

VIP
*To leave the server computer's CD-ROM
drive available for other uses, we recommend
allowing the installer to copy the
documentation files to disk. The
documentation is read using an Internet
browser like Netscape or Internet Explorer.
To use the JAVA version of the documentation,
the browser version numbers must be 3.0
or higher.*

7. The installer then starts the actual installation, continually updating
   a progress indicator, shown in Figure 5-5.

8. You are then presented with the Installation Completed information
   box encouraging you to consult release notes and displaying some
   information about Enterprise Manager and the Oracle Intelligent
   Agent, shown in Figure 5-6. Click OK to complete the Oracle8
   Server installation.

When you exit the installer, you will find two program groups have
been set up, as shown in Figure 5-7. The shortcuts in these groups point to
a number of text files containing useful information about the installation

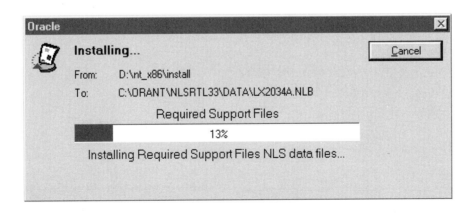

FIGURE 5-5.   *Progress indicator*

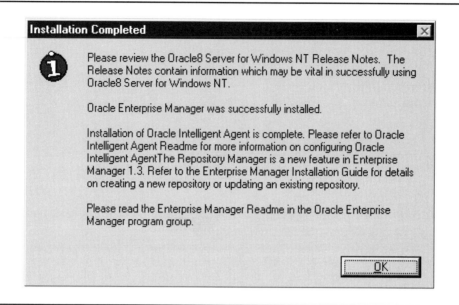

Installation Completed

Please review the Oracle8 Server for Windows NT Release Notes. The Release Notes contain information which may be vital in successfully using Oracle8 Server for Windows NT.

Oracle Enterprise Manager was successfully installed.

Installation of Oracle Intelligent Agent is complete. Please refer to Oracle Intelligent Agent Readme for more information on configuring Oracle Intelligent AgentThe Repository Manager is a new feature in Enterprise Manager 1.3. Refer to the Enterprise Manager Installation Guide for details on creating a new repository or updating an existing repository.

Please read the Enterprise Manager Readme in the Oracle Enterprise Manager program group.

OK

FIGURE 5-6. *Installation completed information*

just completed. You may find some of this material useful, but we have found most of it of little interest.

Client Installation

You may use a Windows NT or Windows 95 client for this installation.

VIP
Oracle will allow a client installation on Windows 95 but will NOT permit a Windows 95 installation of the Oracle8 Server.

The Oracle8 Client installation is performed as follows:

1. Place the Oracle8 Client CD in the drive, and the reader brings up the information box shown in Figure 5-8.

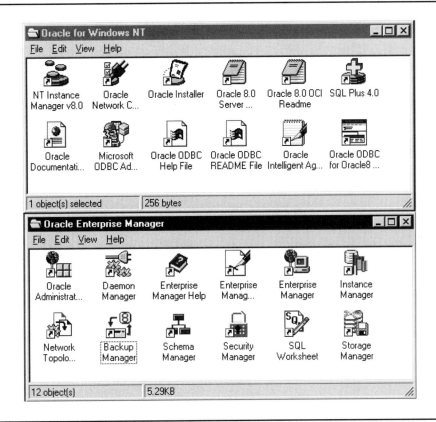

FIGURE 5-7. *Oracle8 Server program groups*

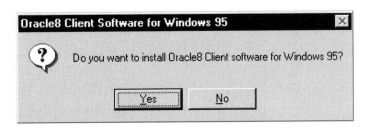

FIGURE 5-8. *Oracle8 Client software install confirmation*

2. The installer proceeds to do some checking on the client hard drive, then presents a series of questions, starting with the language confirmation screen shown in Figure 5-9. "English" is displayed, so simply click OK to proceed.

3. Oracle then asks for the company name and location of Oracle Home to proceed with the installation. Click on OK to make the dialog box shown in Figure 5-10 dissolve.

4. The installer then displays the option selection dialog box. The "Oracle8 Client Products" is more than likely selected. Click OK to continue as shown in Figure 5-11.

5. When asked about Oracle Documentation, ask the installer to place the documents on your hard disk. Click OK to continue.

6. Oracle then proceeds along its merry way and ends up completing its work as we have specified throughout the series of dialog boxes presented. Don't forget to study the screen as the installer does its work—some of the information may prove helpful! When the installation is completed, click OK to finish. When the installer finishes its work, you will find a program group like the one shown in Figure 5-12.

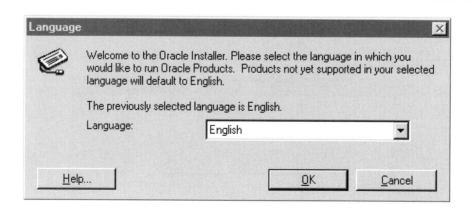

FIGURE 5-9. *Language choice dialog box*

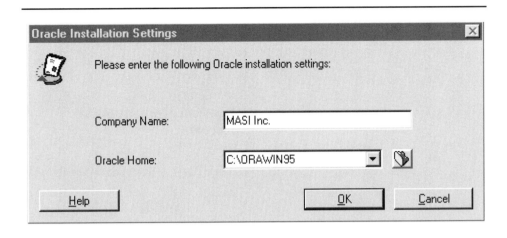

FIGURE 5-10. *Specification of company and Oracle home*

Installing Oracle—UNIX

We have chosen the Hewlett-Packard (or HP) UNIX operating system for our first example of an Oracle7 installation, since such a large portion of Oracle installations are running one form or another of UNIX. If you are

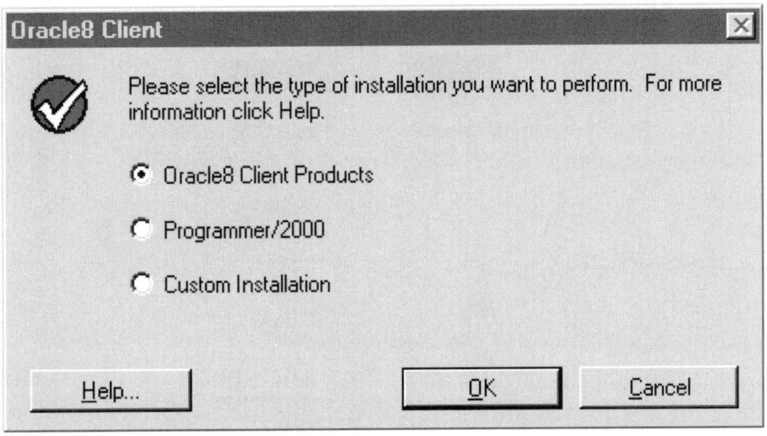

FIGURE 5-11. *Oracle documentation source selection*

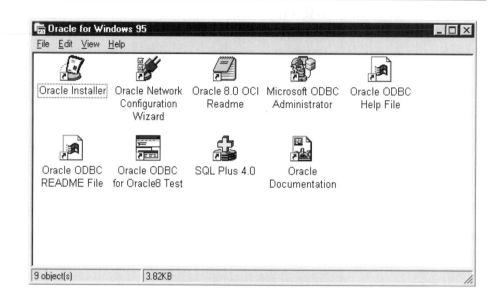

FIGURE 5-12. *Oracle for Windows 95 program group*

installing Oracle on another type of hardware using another operating system, the process might be somewhat different. Substitute that machine's equivalent command where we show UNIX commands. Hewlett-Packard (HP), Sun, Pyramid, Sequent, DEC Alpha, SCO, and Xenix are examples of popular UNIX systems. We will show you how to build a staging area, install the Oracle Server, then install an Oracle product other than the Server. We use a CD-ROM throughout all our discussions in this section; CD-ROM allows for the quickest and most flexible installations.

VIP
If you are not using CD-ROM and it is available on your hardware configuration, invest in a CD-ROM unit immediately.

Building the Staging Area

There are two kinds of staging areas: temporary and permanent. We recommend using the permanent staging area approach. It uses more disk space than the temporary staging area approach, but speeds up subsequent installation or upgrades. In situations where you cannot (or do not want) to dedicate ongoing disk space for a permanent staging area, use a temporary staging area instead. Once this permanent staging area is built, you can skip the step that builds it each time.

VIP

As of release 7.3.2, a temporary staging area consumes roughly 50MB (52,428,800 bytes) and a permanent staging area about 130MB (136,314,880 bytes).

Using release 7.3, the first step in building a permanent staging area is to create the temporary area, then build the permanent staging area from the installer program.

NOTE

With HP-UX 9.0 and 10.0, you must build a temporary staging area first, then start the installer (orainst), then build the permanent staging area from the temporary one.

The temporary area is usually built in a directory called *oracle_link*, and can be accomplished by doing the following:

1. Ask your system administrator (the person who is the keeper of your hardware) to mount the CD-ROM device and make it accessible. The following steps will show **/cdrom**, since this is where we have mounted the CD-ROM. The name you use depends on how the CD-ROM is mounted on your system.

2. Log onto your machine using the UNIX account of the owner of the Oracle software. This account name is usually (but does not have to be) "oracle."

3. Create the staging area directory by entering the command **cd /oracle** followed by **mkdir oracle_link**.

NOTE
The directory name "/oracle" is used as an example; it is not required, and you can use any location for the staging area you wish.

4. Proceed to the installation directory on the CD-ROM by entering the command **cd /cdrom/ORAINST**.

5. Enter the command **./START.SH**. When Oracle asks for the name of the link directory, enter the name **/oracle/oracle_link**. Oracle then builds the staging area. The work takes between five and twenty minutes, depending on the size of the computer you are using. Once this is completed, the temporary staging area is ready, and you can install the Server or any other products.

VIP
The temporary staging area does not contain a copy of the software being installed. Oracle installs and upgrades from a temporary area require the CD-ROM to be placed in the CD-ROM drive beforehand.

Starting the Installer

The Oracle installer is referred to as "orainst" across all computer types. In UNIX, the installer is started by changing to the installer directory by entering the command **cd $ORACLE_HOME/orainst** then typing the command **./orainst**. The section "Installer Environment" will guide you through answering some of the questions with which you will be presented. First a word about the look and feel of orainst.

It's a Friendly Little Thing

Oracle has re-architected the installer for release 7.3.2, and you may want to browse the text on the screen shown in Figure 5-13 if you have performed an installation with an earlier release. The preamble.txt shown provides useful information for all, targeted especially at people who have used the installer with a pre-7.3 version of Oracle.

We find that orainst is remarkably friendly and easy to work with. Let's look at the screen in Figure 5-14 and the four buttons on it: Help, Back, Cancel, and OK. These same four buttons appear on most orainst screens; some contain more. You move between the buttons with TAB and select a button using ENTER. The OK button accepts whatever Oracle has displayed on the screen. The Help button accesses orainst online help. The Back button backs up one step in the installer process, letting you revisit the screen in which you previously selected OK. It is remarkable how useful the Back button can be when you have answered a question, then wondered to yourself if this was what you actually wanted. The Cancel button terminates your orainst session and allows you to quit the installer at any time.

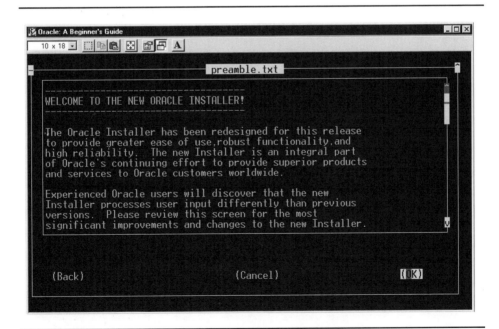

FIGURE 5-13.   *Information preamble.txt screen*

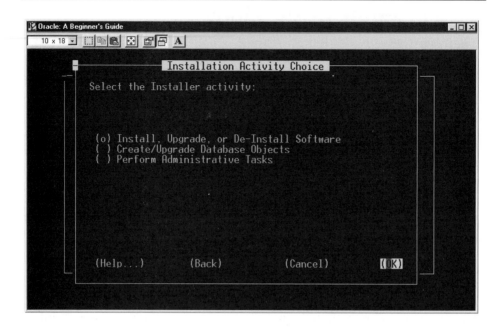

FIGURE 5-14. *Installation Activity Choice*

After suggesting that the installer is friendly, you may find yourself presented with some questions you have never had to answer before. We will now look at the issues orainst wants to settle through its series of questions and answers.

Installer Environment

When orainst starts, it asks you to provide details about the installation. In most cases, it suggests a response; however, if this is the very first time you are running the installer on your computer, you may have to enter each answer. Figure 5-12, the very first screen you see when you run orainst is an example of an information screen. You move around the screen using the TAB key, and press ENTER to select a response.

NOTE

When the cursor sits in the response area (the one line text box with the value presented by orainst), you press ENTER *there to accept the displayed item. You need not TAB to the OK button to carry on.*

Let's delve into some of the specifics: the next four sections discuss question and answer boxes in the order they are presented by orainst.

VIP

The series of dialog boxes and answers we suggest are an example of the interaction with the installation program. The nature of the boxes you interact with and the order in which they are presented may be different than what we show in the next few sections.

Installation Activity Choice

As shown in Figure 5-14, Oracle needs to know the nature of the installation activity you are about to perform. Now, let's look at the options displayed in more detail:

1. Install, Upgrade, or De-Install Software is used to:

   ■ Install a brand-new product

   ■ Upgrade software

   ■ Install new products

   ■ Install online documentation

   ■ Install or upgrade software to Parallel Server nodes

   ■ Build an Oracle7 staging area

- De-install products
- Migrate from V6 to Oracle7

2. Create/Upgrade Database Objects is used to:

   - Create new database objects
   - Create or upgrade database objects after upgrading products

3. Perform Administrative Tasks is used to:

   - Perform administrative tasks such as defining a terminal
   - Relink executables

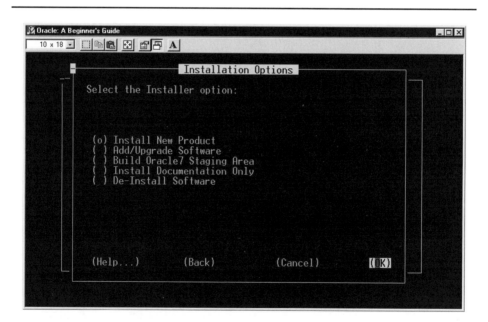

FIGURE 5-15. *Installation Options screen*

Installation Options

As just shown in Figure 5-15, next Oracle wants to know what you wish the installer to do during this session. Let's look at the selections displayed in more detail:

1. Install New Product is used to

   ■ Install a new version of a product

   ■ Install a later version of a product while keeping the earlier version as well

2. Add/Upgrade Software is used to

   ■ Add new products to an existing database

   ■ Upgrade an existing database to a new minor release

VIP

When we say minor release, we mean one where the third digit (e.g., the "3" in "8.0.3") were to change, as in going from release "8.0.3" to "8.0.4."

3. Build Oracle7 Staging Area is used to copy from a distribution CD to a temporary or permanent staging area from where the software will be installed. A staging area allows you to load your software into a designated directory, independent of the actual installation. You can complete the installation at a later time. A staging area can be designated as either permanent or temporary; however, a permanent staging area remains on your system indefinitely, while a temporary staging area is not usable after installation until reloaded.

4. Install Documentation Only is used to

   ■ Install online documentation without installing any product

   ■ Install documentation some time after a product installation

5. De-Install Product is used to remove an existing product before a product upgrade in an existing ORACLE_HOME.

Home Locator

This is where you specify the home directory for the Oracle software. The files you end up creating that make up the database need not be in the same location; most of the time you end up placing them elsewhere. Figure 5-16 shows the Home Locator dialog screen. Accept the text displayed or enter a different directory name, then press ENTER.

NOTE
The installer dialog boxes may keep referring to an OFA installation, standing for Optimal Flexible Architecture. This is an industry-standard feature dealing with a specific layout for the directory structure of a software installation; details may be obtained by obtaining a white paper from Oracle through their Web site at http://www.oracle.com and many other locations on the Internet.

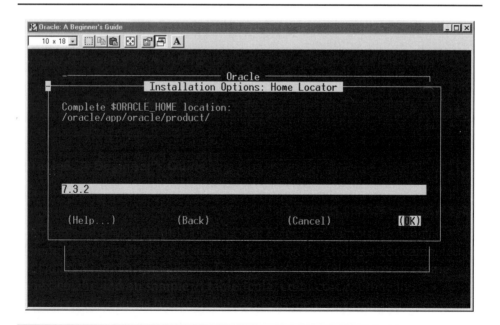

FIGURE 5-16. *Home Locator*

As you can see from the screen, orainst needs to establish the location of the Oracle software home directory. In most cases, it will be located in /oracle/app/oracle/product/7.3.2, but it depends on how the Oracle UNIX account has been configured. When Figure 5-16 appeared on our computer, the text "7.3.2" was already there. You may have to check with your system administrator to ensure that the value orainst presents is correct and, if it isn't, what the correct value should be.

DB Objects

Oracle then asks if you want to create the database objects associated with the operation of your soon-to-be-installed software. The main object components are the tablespaces, and other structures comprising a database. The relationship between database objects and a database is like the relationship between a document and a word processor—you cannot have database objects without a database within which they are stored. With the cursor highlighting "No," press ENTER to move on, as shown in Figure 5-17.

NOTE
The dialog involved and the details on the questions asked by the installer to create database objects are beyond the scope of this introductory chapter.

Logging and Status

The screen shown in Figure 5-18 now appears with a list of log files that will be written during the installation session. Four log files are created automatically during installation. During an initial installation, the Oracle-recommended log file names are supplied as defaults. If this is not an initial installation and any of the log files already exist, those filenames appear on the Logging and Status screen as defaults, as shown in Figure 5-18.

The most important of the four log files to be specified is the Installer Log. Periodically, if and when something goes wrong, you will be instructed to browse the file where you asked the Installer Log to be written.

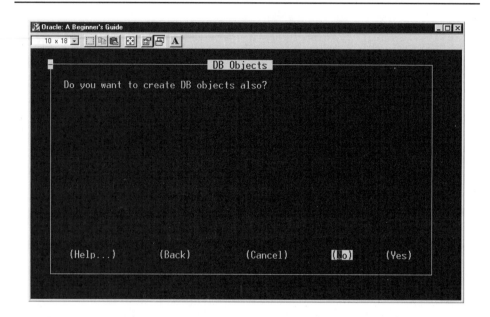

FIGURE 5-17. *DB Objects*

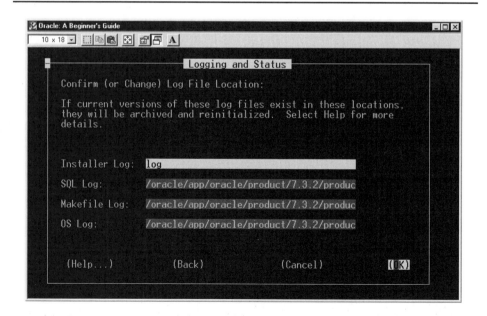

FIGURE 5-18. *Logging and Status file names*

Install Source and Staging Area

As this dialog box appears, there are two choices displayed. Since we have just gone through the process of building a staging area, we chose the Install from Staging Area option.

VIP

To move between options in an installer dialog box, move to the option selection area with the TAB *key, then between choices with the* ARROW *keys. Select the desired option with the spacebar.*

As the OK option is highlighted, press ENTER to continue to a screen where you specify the type of staging area in use—in our case, we select Permanent.

NOTE

This is a point in the installation where you will have to pay special attention to which option you select. Most of the time, Oracle will highlight "Temporary" by default and this will have to be changed before moving on.

Oracle then asks for the location of the permanent staging area. Specify what is suggested, if correct; otherwise re-enter the correct value, and then press ENTER.

ORACLE_SID

Oracle uses a system identifier (commonly called the *SID*) to identify each database. Enter whatever text (try one to four letters) you wish as an identifier. Choose a name that may be meaningful to the purpose for which the database is being created. For example, a production database could be called "prd" and a test database could be called "tst".

NLS

This screen is where you specify the language(s) you wish to use as the database operates. *NLS* stands for National Language Support, and Oracle runs with dozens of character sets and languages, including French, Spanish, German, Chinese, and Russian, to name a few. Most of the time you will leave the All Languages option highlighted and press ENTER to continue.

Relink All Executables

This screen is where you specify linking options. As this screen appears, the No option is usually highlighted. Leave as is and press ENTER. Linking is a process whereby Oracle takes a series of computer programs, libraries, and object code (e.g., Oracle has already taken a C program called oracle.c and compiled it into object code oracle.o) and creates what's called an executable.

Root Install Script File

This screen allows you to specify the name for a script to be run by root when the installation session terminates. The *root* user in UNIX is the custodian of the system, and an account from where someone does the UNIX administration. In most cases, you select the Create new root.sh option, and press ENTER. You are then asked to specify where the previous copy of root.sh will be saved.

NOTE
If this is not your first installer session, Oracle would have created a root.sh from a previous run, and the copy it produced is the one that will be saved in your specified name and location.

On the next information screen, Oracle informs you of the name and location of the saved root script.

Documentation Options

Oracle then presents three documentation selection dialog boxes:

NOTE

We recommend that you do not install any of these online docs; use a desktop (i.e. Windows 95-based documentation CD) to load this material as the interface is much more intuitive on the PC).

1. Online Help Load is where you specify whether you wish to install the electronic help files for the Server.

2. UNIX documentation is where you tell the installer whether to copy electronic UNIX documentation.

3. Product Documentation Library CD-ROM Install is where you specify whether to copy the product documentation during the installer session.

Software Asset Manager

The next screen, shown in Figure 5-19, is where you specify what products you want to install during the current session.

There are essentially four areas on this screen of importance:

1. The "From" area, which lists the available products in the permanent staging area. This box is populated when the Software Asset Manager appears.

2. The "Products installed" area lists what has already been installed; if this is a first-time installation, the area will be blank.

3. The line of buttons on the bottom from Help to Exit.

4. The Install/Remove buttons are highlighted, then selected after one or more products is chosen.

VIP

If the "Products available" box is empty, move to the "From" button, press ENTER, *and traverse the directory tree looking for the "unix.prd" file that contains the list of the products in the staging area. This is shown in Figure 5-20.*

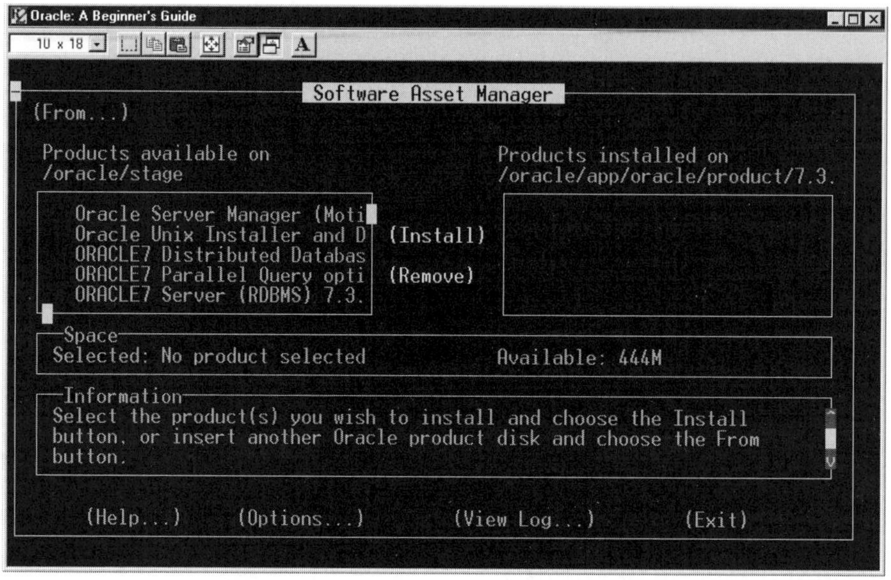

FIGURE 5-19. *Software Asset Manager*

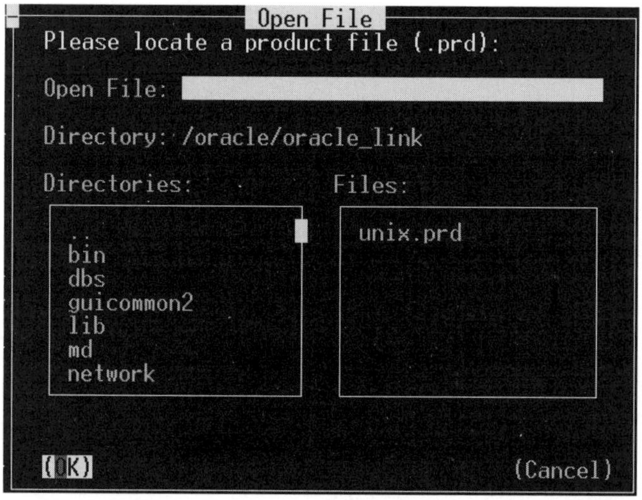

FIGURE 5-20. *Open File dialog box*

Move to the Files box, press the spacebar to highlight "unix.prd" and then press ENTER to continue.

SELECTING PRODUCTS TO INSTALL   Move the cursor to the "Products available" window, and move up and down with the ARROW keys. Select a product by pressing the spacebar and, if one is selected, it is de-selected as well with spacebar.

NOTE
There are dependencies between products and if you choose one that depends on others you have not chosen, Oracle will install the dependent products automatically.

COMPLETING THE INSTALLATION   After the products are selected, TAB to the Install button, and press ENTER to begin (finally!) the installation. As Oracle does its work, it will run through a series of dialog boxes.

- ■ **Hostname**   The network name for the server upon which you are doing the installation. Consult with your server administrator and then enter the proper name including the network domain. The Official Hostname dialog box is shown in Figure 5-21.

- ■ **TCP Service Port**   This is for the Administration Server; Oracle suggests the value "8888", which you can accept by pressing ENTER. In UNIX, a port is a conduit of sorts into the operating system: think of the port 8888 as an address through which TCP/IP connect requests are passed on to the operating system for processing.

- ■ **Administration server password**   Enter a password (we suggest **manager** for now) and re-enter when asked on the confirmation screen. This password is used at some later time to perform secure operations with the server handling remote connections via port 8888. These operations include starting and stopping the administration server.

- ■ **Group name for the DBA user**   The text "dba" is usually placed there, so accept as is. The UNIX dba group is a grouping of accounts allowed to start and stop an Oracle database and perform other Oracle-related activities.

- **OSOPER group name**   Accept the suggested text as well. This OSOPER group inherits the privilege to perform special activities as the group name just specified for the DBA user.

- **ORACLE_SID**   Confirm the text displayed on the next screen.

After all these dialog boxes are displayed, the installation commences. You will be presented with an information box with information about the administration server and how it will be launched when the installation completes. There should be no errors encountered, and the screen shown in Figure 5-22 will be displayed as the installer completes its work; press ENTER to acknowledge the information.

You are now returned to the Software Asset Manager. Move to Exit and then press ENTER to leave the installer.

Installing Oracle Products— Nondesktop

This activity is similar to installing the Universal Server as covered in the previous main section. Product installation is selected from the Installation Activity Choice screen by choosing the "Install, Upgrade, or De-install

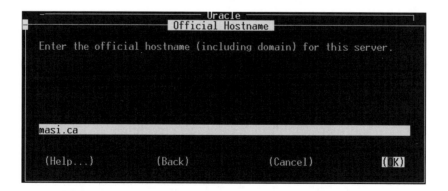

FIGURE 5-21.   *Official Hostname dialog box*

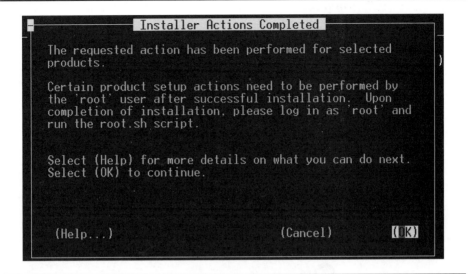

FIGURE 5-22. *Installation Complete information screen*

Software" option. When presented with the "Installation Options" screen, you select the "Add/Upgrade Software" option.

NOTE
Remember, move around the installer dialog boxes using the TAB key, move between options using the ARROW keys, and select an option using the spacebar.

After answering the series of questions asked by orainst, and after you have chosen one or more products to install from the Software Asset Manager screen, you begin the installation by selecting Install. Once product installation begins, after selecting Install, orainst looks at the version number of the installed product and the version of the product on the CD-ROM. You are informed of the results of the product version comparison, and you are asked whether you wish to continue. This confirmation screen is shown in Figure 5-23.

FIGURE 5-23. *Reinstallation Action confirmation*

Orainst may inform you, for example, that the installed version of PL/SQL is 2.3.2.0.0, and that you have chosen a CD-ROM containing the same version. The choice to continue is yours. If you decide to install a product, carry on by selecting Yes. After the product is installed, you are informed of the completed installation and returned to the Software Asset Manager screen. You are also informed if there were any problems with the installation, and you should then refer to the installation log file whose name you may have chosen on the Installation Log File screen discussed in an earlier section. When your requested product installation completes, orainst displays the Install Completed information box. Read the advice in that box, then select OK to return to the Software Asset Manager window. Leave the installer by moving to Exit using the TAB key, then pressing ENTER to quit orainst. Our experience dictates that most product installations proceed without a glitch; we have found orainst in the nondesktop environment stable and relatively easy to use.

Installing Personal Oracle— Desktop

We are going to have a look at two different installations of Oracle in desktop. For the first, we will be using CD-ROM, which is called drive d on the machine we use. Substitute the drive letter from your machine where appropriate. Oracle has moved to CD-ROM as its standard distribution medium; if you don't have one, it's probably time to get one. The second installation featured uses 60-day trial software downloaded from the Internet. The following configuration is required to run Personal Oracle in Windows 95:

- A 486 or stronger processor—Pentium preferred

- 295 megabytes (or 309,329,920 bytes) when downloaded from the Internet, or 50 megabytes (or 52,428,800 bytes) when installed from a CD-ROM

- 16 megabytes of memory (though 32 is recommended)

- Microsoft Windows 95

Oracle bundles their desktop products together in ways that are as varied as the names of the products in some bundles. In this section, we will look first at Personal Oracle with a release 7.2 runtime database, then look at their 7.3 offering on the World Wide Web.

Pre-installation Activity

Some readers may have upgraded from Windows 3.x to the Windows 95 operating system, bringing a previous installation of Personal Oracle up with the migration. Personal Oracle for Windows 3.x used the directory ORAWIN for the location of the Oracle software by default. Personal Oracle for Windows 95 uses the directory ORAWIN95 as its home, which may conflict with the setting registered with Windows 3.x. This issue will have to be dealt with before you proceed with the installation of Personal Oracle for Windows 95.

NOTE
The database files used with a Windows 3.x installation are not compatible with those used in Windows 95.

If you are upgrading from a Personal Oracle database in Windows 3.x to Windows 95, you need to:

1. Perform a full database export using the Windows 3.x software.

2. De-install the Windows 3.x version of Personal Oracle and all its products.

3. Complete the upgrade to Windows 95.

4. Install Personal Oracle for Windows 95 and all the tools required from a tools CD that is Windows 95-compatible.

5. Start the Personal Oracle Windows 95 database.

6. Import the data extracted in the first step so that the database in Windows 95 is an exact copy of the Windows 3.x database.

Installing Personal Oracle from a 90-day Trial CD

The installation we feature in this section is from a CD entitled *Oracle Workgroup /2000* (90-day trial part # C10623-2-CD also referred to as CD-ROM Version 4.3 on the jacket). There are many different bundles of Personal Oracle7 on the street; this one is used to give you a taste of what's in store. The bundle includes Personal Oracle for Windows 95 as well as a handful of other configurations for Workgroup Server, Objects for OLE, and Power Objects. There is no starter database in the Windows 95 folder on this CD: when the installation finishes, it is assumed you will be accessing a database on a remote file server. If you install the product from a different CD or after downloading it from the Web, the steps and screen shots may not be exactly the same as what you find in the next few sections.

Now, let's perform the installation:

1. Select Run from the Start Menu, then Browse to bring up the Explorer-like dialog box. Proceed to the CD, then the Po7Win95\Win95 folder as shown Figure 5-24.

2. Double click on setup.exe, and then click on Open in the Browse dialog box, then OK in the Run dialog box to start installation.

3. Oracle starts some setup work, then brings up the 90-day license period information box. Read the conditions, then click on OK. Read the welcome box, and follow any directions applicable to your computer. Click on OK to proceed, or Cancel to quit.

4. Oracle asks for confirmation of your name (or if this is a new Oracle installation you will be asked to enter the name) and the location of Oracle Home.

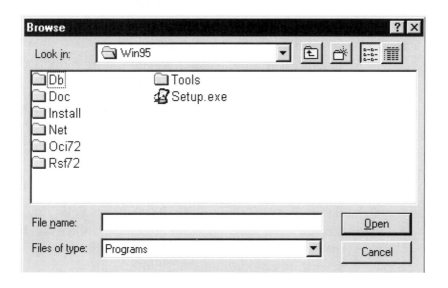

FIGURE 5-24. *Browse dialog box where setup.exe is found and selected*

VIP
*Some readers may be upgrading from a
Windows 3.x version of Personal Oracle and
may be asked to stipulate a different Oracle
Home, as shown in Figure 5-25. After entering
a new value for Oracle Home, you will carry
on with the next step.*

5. You will be asked if you want the installer to automatically update
your Windows 95 search path to include the folder where the
Personal Oracle executables reside. Click on OK to allow the
installer to do the update automatically.

6. The next screen you see is shown in Figure 5-26. The options
presented are:

■ The Application Developer option installs the software
necessary to access a local Personal Oracle database or one
residing on a remote server.

■ The Runtime (Database Only) option installs a starter local
database with most of the features you may already be used to
on a larger mini-computer such as HP or IBM.

■ The Custom option allows you to pick and choose what you
wish to install during this session. This option is selected and
will be used for this sample installation activity.

7. Click beside the Custom option, then OK to display the Software Asset
Manager listing the products on the CD. This is shown in Figure 5-27.

8. Highlight the products to install, using the CTRL-left-click to choose
multiple products. Products with the "+" sign beside them can be
expanded into a subset of products by clicking on the plus sign.

9. For the purpose of this exercise, select Online Help, Oracle7
DBMS, Oracle7 Utilities, Personal Oracle7 Navigator, and
SQL*Plus. After they are all highlighted, click Install to carry on.

10. When asked about creating the Starter Database, ensure Yes
is selected (as it will more than likely already be) and click
OK to continue.

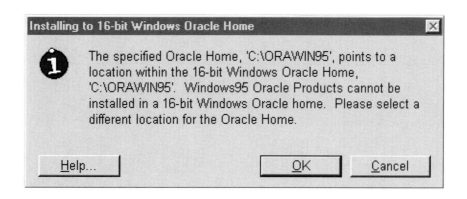

FIGURE 5-25.   *Alternate 32-bit ORACLE_HOME specification*

Oracle then proceeds through a series of tasks and displays information about what it is doing and what directories are being loaded. You may be presented with a series of dialog boxes asking for confirmation of the character set for the starter database as well as checking with you about some DLLs found on your hard drive. When the installer is finished, it will

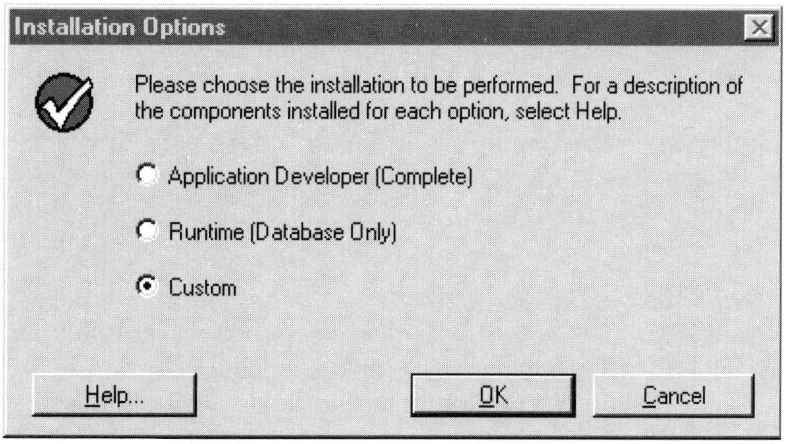

FIGURE 5-26.   *Selection of installation options*

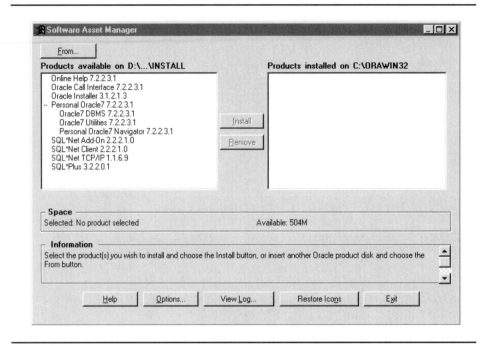

FIGURE 5-27. *Software Asset Manager*

return you to the Software Asset Manager. Notice how the products we selected are displayed in the "Products installed" section of this screen. Click Exit to return to your desktop. There will be two program groups created as shown in Figure 5-28.

Before moving on to a product installation, let's spend a moment looking at the Personal Oracle7 Navigator from where many administrators work with the starter database.

Personal Oracle7 Navigator
As Navigator is invoked, you will see the screen shown in Figure 5-29. The Personal Oracle7 Navigator is an application that you can use to access, create, modify, and delete projects, database objects, and database connections. It functions in much the same way as the Windows 95 Explorer.

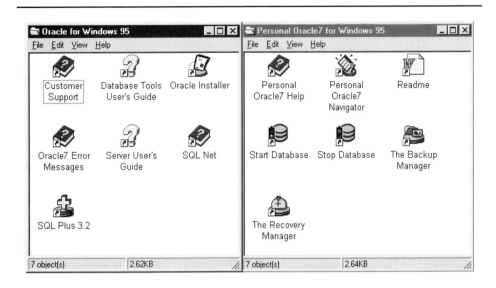

FIGURE 5-28. *Program Groups created in Windows 95*

The look, feel, and functionality of the navigator is familiar with
pull-down menus activated by the right mouse button and Windows 95

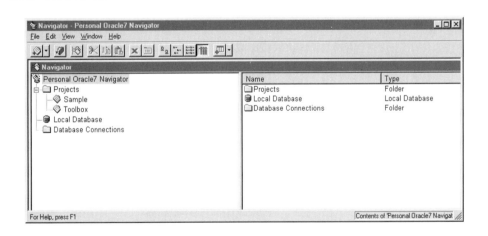

FIGURE 5-29. *Personal Oracle7 Navigator*

terminology throughout. Objects underneath the local database icon allow you to define and change many of the database objects defined in Chapter 4.

Installing Personal Oracle Downloaded from the Web

Many readers are able to get product easily from Oracle's Web site; their home page can be found at the address *http://www.oracle.com.* The look and feel of their site changes often, as do the pages belonging to so many vendors. Figure 5-30 shows the location of a fully functional copy of Personal Oracle for Windows 95.

There are two ways to download the product as shown:

I. In three parts - *runme.bat* is a batch file used to extract the software from the compressed files; the other two components are *po7w9501.exe* and *po7w9502.exe* as shown in the Explorer shown in Figure 5-31.

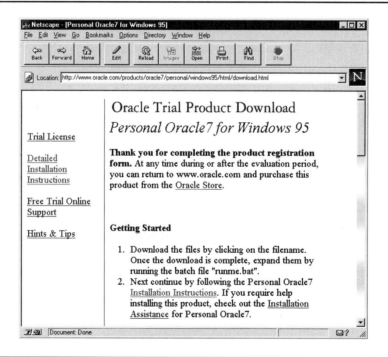

FIGURE 5-30. *Location of Personal Oracle on the Web*

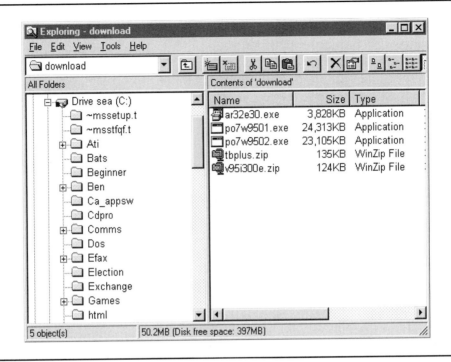

FIGURE 5-31. *Compressed files and batch file available on the Web*

VIP
To ensure the download was complete, the byte count of the files should be exactly as shown in Figure 5-31. The download for this chapter took 4$^{1/2}$ hours using a USR Sportster 28.8 Fax Modem.

   2. In 34 parts - the batch file *runme.bat* is used to extract the files from the archive; the other 33 parts are *po7w9501.exe to po7w9533.exe* where the software resides.

NOTE
If you are confident of the stability of your network connection to your Internet provider, use the three file approach. If you are not sure, use the other method.

Oracle provides a rich online installation help facility, as shown in Figure 5-32. The hotlinks on the Installation Guide page provide access to discussions and assistance with the most common tasks associated with an installation in Windows 95.

Don't forget to get the correct *runme.bat* batch file—it depends on which download method you choose. The next listing shows the batch file for the two file approach.

```
REM
REM     This is the file "runme.bat".  It contains the DOS commands needed
REM     to properly create the staging area on your hard drive.
REM
REM     IMPORTANT:  If you are viewing this as a page in your World Wide
REM     Web browser, you need to set up your Web browser to save files with
REM     extension ".BAT" to disk, or you could copy the contents of this page
REM     into a file and run it from the directory where you've downloaded
REM     the *.EXE files.
REM
REM     DOWNLOAD FILE SIZE(S):
REM
REM        PO7W9501.EXE                    24,895,881 bytes
REM        PO7W9502.EXE                    23,658,566 bytes
PO7W9501 -d -n
PO7W9502 -d -n
```

The installation is accomplished after running the batch file that places the files in the proper location with the proper names, then doing the following:

1. From the Start Menu, choose Run, then proceed to the WIN95 folder underneath where the downloaded files were extracted. Double-click on *setup.exe* to start the process.

2. Click on OK after reading the complete license agreement, noting the terms of the 60-day trial.

3. When presented with the company name and Oracle home dialog box, fill in the values desired or, if some are placed there for you, accept the text displayed or modify. Click OK.

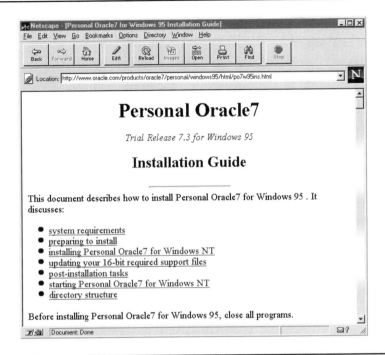

FIGURE 5-32. *Online help facility*

4. You are then asked to specify the type of installation you wish to perform. Though the choices are different, the screen resembles that shown for Oracle8 in Figure 5-3. When installing Oracle8, we chose Custom Installation; for this section, we will look at the Runtime (Database Only).

5. Select the Runtime radio button, then click OK. The installer proceeds to copy an assortment of files to the folder selected as Oracle home. The work proceeds, and Oracle updates the file copy and analyzing dependencies information box as it proceeds. It will create a Personal Oracle7 for Windows 95 group as it does its work, and copies the starter database into the correct location as one of its last steps.

6. When presented with the Information box regarding release 7.2 to 7.3 migration, read the text and click OK to complete the installation.

After the installation completes, you will find two program groups, as shown in Figure 5-33.

NOTE

If you find SQL*Plus 3.2 and Navigator shortcuts in either file folder, they can be sent to the Recycle Bin for deletion. In the next section, we will pick these two products off the download area after selecting the Custom choice in the dialog box similar to that shown in Figure 5-3.

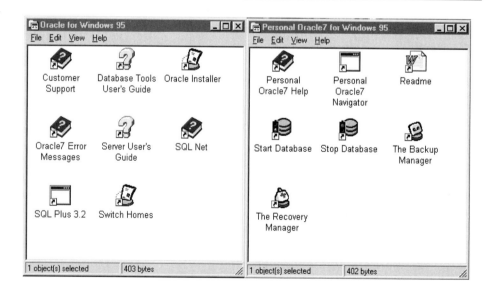

FIGURE 5-33. *Program groups after installation completes*

To install these components, do the following:

1. From the Start Menu, choose Run, then proceed to the WIN95 folder underneath where the downloaded files were extracted. Double click on *setup.exe* to start the process.

2. Click on OK after reading the complete license agreement, noting the terms of the 60-day trial.

3. When presented with the company name and Oracle home dialog box, fill in the values desired or, if some are placed there for you, accept the text displayed or modify. Click OK.

4. Select Custom from the next dialog box, to be presented with the screen shown in Figure 5-34.

5. Click on Oracle Navigator, then CTRL click on SQL*Plus to highlight these two products.

6. Click Install to copy these two components to complete the exercise.

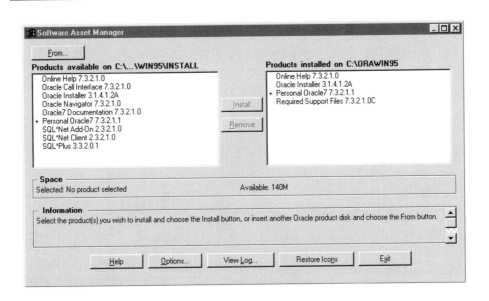

FIGURE 5-34. *Software Asset Manager*

7. Click Exit and do the subsequent confirmation to return to your Windows desktop.

You now have Personal Oracle for Windows 95 on your PC—enjoy! To close this section, inspect Table 5-1 for free installation support contact information. Readers new to Oracle and their desktop implementation may find this assistance helpful as they get started.

Installing Oracle Products— Desktop

All installation work on the desktop is done with the mouse and an assortment of dialog boxes, lists, and buttons.

VIP

We recommend installing products on the desktop by using the installation program on the CD in which the products are distributed. Sometimes, a version of orainst on one's hard drive does not recognize products on a CD.

Resource	Region	Contact Information
World Wide Web		*http://www.oracle.com/support/ support.html*
CompuServe	U.S. & Canada	1.800.524.3388
	Outside U.S. & Canada	+1.614.529.1349
Bulletin Board	U.S. & Canada	407.888.1234
	Outside U.S. & Canada	+1.407.888.1234
Fax Service	U.S. & Canada	415.506.8438
	Outside U.S. & Canada	+1.415.506.8438

TABLE 5-1.   *Free 60-day Trial Installation Help Contact Information*

To install an Oracle tool follow these instructions (the first four steps are identical to those listed in the last section where we discussed installing Personal Oracle):

1. Select Run from the Start Menu, then Browse to bring up the Explorer-like dialog box. Proceed to the CD, then the INSTALL folder, as shown Figure 5-35.

2. Double click on setup.exe, and then click on Open in the Browse dialog box, then OK in the Run dialog box to start installation.

3. Oracle starts some setup work, then brings up the Language dialog box. English is the highlighted language; if you want to use something else, pick anything from Arabic to Turkish in the drop-down list.

4. Oracle asks for confirmation or entry of your name and the location of Oracle Home.

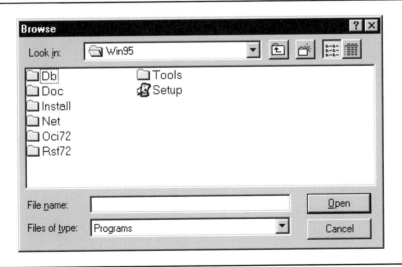

FIGURE 5-35. *Browse dialog box where setup.exe is selected*

5. Oracle then displays the Software Asset Manager, as shown in Figure 5-36. If the Products Available area is empty, click on From to bring up a Browse dialog box from which you can proceed to a folder on your hard drive or a CD containing the desired programs.

VIP

If you browse looking for the location of Oracle products, you will be searching for a file in an INSTALL directory named "windows.prd".

6. Highlight the product(s) you wish to install, then click on Install to proceed. Note as well the "+" sign beside some product names in the Products Available area of Figure 5-36. Clicking on that plus sign expands these products to their component parts which can be installed separately. The Developer/2000 Forms 4.5, for example, expands into Cue Card Sound Files, Demos, Designer, Online Documentation, Quick Tour, and Runtime.

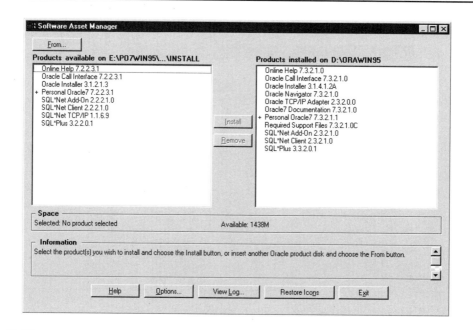

FIGURE 5-36. *Software Asset Manager*

From here on, the dialog boxes and information boxes Oracle displays depend on the tool you chose to install.

NOTE
Some products require other vendors' files before the installer can complete its work. If asked any questions about system support files, answer Yes after reading the displayed information.

Most tools will ask you to select a folder within which the product should be installed. Oracle suggests a name, and most of the time you simply accept the default location by pressing ENTER or clicking on OK. When the installer completes its work, return to the dialog box from which you came by clicking Exit in the Asset Manager.

What's Next

This completes the "Startup" section of this book. You now know about Oracle the company and Oracle the software. The fun has only just begun. In the next section, we will guide you through working with a number of Oracle products, and we'll offer some suggestions for using them effectively. The Developer Basics section starts with an introduction to the Structured Query Language (SQL): knowledge of this product is fundamental to what has become (after reading this Startup section) your expanding knowledge of what Oracle is, why the company is where it is today (at the top), how to install the software, and the types of objects in every Oracle database. Get yourself a cup of coffee—you could be here for a while.

CHAPTER

6

SQL 101

n this chapter, we teach you the basics of SQL. This could be the most important chapter of this book since, if you understand SQL, you understand a relational database. Back when we started working with Oracle, this was the tool of choice for writing all the reports. Then came along another tool called RPT. If you have ever used RPT, you will understand why some people thought it had limited use.

Today, you have lots of excellent choices for report writers. But if you just need to punch it, crunch it, and get it out the door, use SQL*Plus. SQL*Plus is Oracle's offering of a tool that can be used to manipulate Oracle data and prepare reports on the contents of that data. With Oracle's enhancements to the core SQL language, you have a great reporting tool. We have found that many of the reports we generate every day could be accomplished with SQL*Plus alone.

VIP

*SQL (Structured Query Language) is used by Oracle for all interaction with the database. SQL*Plus (one of many Oracle tools) is based on SQL, but it has some Oracle-specific features that can be used for writing reports and controlling the way screen and paper output is formatted.*

Some people don't use SQL*Plus for many of these tasks, for the same reason that some people find it easier to add up numbers with pencil and paper instead of a calculator. We are of the "keep it simple" camp—make it happen quick. So, SQL*Plus is our first choice for all reports. Only when our needs exceed the ability of SQL*Plus do we look for a better tool.

With this in mind, let's see what SQL*Plus can do. In this chapter, we will not try to teach you every nuance or detail about SQL*Plus; we will teach you what it takes to get at the information you need quickly. We will also teach you how to present this information in the best possible light. We will do this using a step-by-step process. First, we will teach you the two basic types of SQL statements. Next, we will create tables and populate those tables with data. Then, we will write some reports against those tables. This chapter will cover the following topics:

- DDL and DML: What they are and some practical examples of using them
- How to log into SQL*Plus
- The most common setup parameters
- How to retrieve data from the database
- How to format data using SQL*Plus
- How to update and delete data stored in the database
- How to create a table and insert data into a table
- How to alter a table

Terminology

The following definitions will arm you with the technical jargon to make it through this chapter:

- *DDL*, or Data Definition Language, is the SQL construct used to define data in the database. When you define that data, entries are made in Oracle's data dictionary. Common DDL keywords are **create**, **revoke**, **grant**, and **alter**.

- *DML*, or Data Manipulation Language, is the SQL construct used to manipulate the data in the database (rather than the definition of the data, done by DDL). Common DML keywords are **select**, **insert**, **update**, and **delete**.

- With Oracle, we use the word *commit* to indicate that data has been saved back to the database. Think of your favorite word processor. Each time you save your work, Oracle would refer to that action as committing your work.

- A *constraint* is a mechanism used to protect the relationship between data within an Oracle table or the correspondence between data in two different tables. Logic that insists that as a new employee is entered in the human resources application, his or her state of residence must be one of the 50 states in the U.S. is an example of a constraint.

■ An *object* in the Oracle8 database is a thing of significance within which information is stored. We commonly speak of object types—tables and views being the two most common.

■ If you try to get information out of an Oracle database using a program such as SQL*Plus, then this action is called a *query*.

■ *Functions* are operations performed on data that alter the data's characteristics. For example, forcing the text "Abbeflantro" to uppercase using the SQL keyword **upper** is an example of performing a function on the text.

■ *Rollback* is the activity Oracle goes through when a session changes some data in the database, then for some reason decides not to commit the change. This is the act of restoring the information to the state it was in prior to the **update** initiated by the user.

Two Types of SQL Statements

SQL statements fall into two major categories: DDL (Data Definition Language) and DML (Data Manipulation Language). Let's take a closer look at their differences and similarities.

DDL

Data Definition Language allows you to perform the following tasks:

■ Create a database object

■ Drop a database object

■ Alter a database object

■ Grant privileges on a database object

■ Revoke privileges on a database object

It's important to understand that when you issue a DDL SQL statement, Oracle commits the current transaction before and after every DDL statement. So, if you were inserting records into the database and you issued a DDL statement like **create table**, then the data from the **insert** command would be committed to the database. Table 6-1 is a partial list of DDL statements.

VIP
Statements that fall into the category of DDL are autocommit; this means that when Oracle8 informs you with a message like "Revoke succeeded", the command is complete and cannot be rolled back.

In summary, SQL commands that **alter**, **drop**, **create**, and **grant** are the most frequently used examples of the Data Definition Language. Just as the name implies, DDL is the SQL statements that help define and create tables and privileges.

SQL Command	Purpose
alter procedure	Recompiles a stored procedure
alter table	Adds a column, redefines a column, changes storage allocation
analyze	Gathers performance statistics for database objects to be fed to the cost-based optimizer
alter table add constraint	Adds a constraint to an existing table
create table	Creates a table
create index	Creates an index
drop index	Drops an index
drop table	Drops a table from the database
grant	Grants privileges or roles to a user or another role
truncate	Deletes all the rows from a table
revoke	Removes privileges from a user or database role

TABLE 6-1.   *Partial List of DDL Statements*

VIP
Data Definition Language is the set of SQL commands that create and define objects in the database, storing their definitions in the data dictionary.

DML

Data Manipulation Language allows you to **insert**, **update**, **delete**, and **select** data in the database. Just as the name implies, DML allows you to work with the contents of your database. Table 6-2 is a partial list of DML statements.

In summary, DML statements are SQL commands that allow you to manipulate the data in the database. The most common SQL statements are **insert**, **update**, **delete** and **select**.

VIP
Data Manipulation Language is the set of statements that allow you to manipulate the data in the database.

Now that we understand the two major types of SQL statements, let's get our feet wet. We will start by logging into SQL*Plus. From there, we will try some of the more common DDL and DML statements.

SQL Command	Purpose
insert	Add rows of data to a table
delete	Delete rows of data from a table
update	Change data in a table
select	Retrieve rows of data from a table/view
commit work	Make changes permanent (write to disk) for the current transaction(s)
rollback	Undo all changes since the last commit

TABLE 6-2. *Partial List of DML Statements*

SQL*Plus: Getting In

The easiest way to learn about SQL is by using SQL*Plus. So, let's begin by
logging into SQL*Plus. For these examples, picture an Oracle username of
polly whose password is **gone**. Enter SQL*Plus in one of two ways:

- Double-click the SQL PLUS 4.0 icon in the Oracle8 for Windows
  NT folder. You are prompted for a username and password in a
  Connect dialog box.

- From a DOS window,

  1. Enter the command **sqlplus polly/gone**. Oracle8 will open up a
     separate DOS window and display the herald as shown in the
     next listing:

     ```
     SQL*Plus: Release 4.0.3.0.0 - Production on Sun May 11 12:20:12 1999
     Copyright (c) Oracle Corporation 1979, 1994, 1996.  All rights reserved.
     Connected to:
     Oracle8 Server Release 8.0.3.0.1 - Production
     With the distributed, heterogeneous, replication, objects
     and parallel query options
     PL/SQL Release 3.0.3.0.1 - Production
     SQL>
     ```

  2. Log into SQL*Plus passing just the username, as in **sqlplus polly**,
     and you are prompted for the account password.

  3. Log into SQL*Plus passing no parameters, as in **sqlplus**, and you
     are prompted for the account and password.

After entering SQL*Plus, you should see the SQL*Plus prompt: SQL>.

create Statement

The first phase of any database always starts with DDL statements, since it
is through DDL that you create your database objects. First, we will create
four tables: customer, state, X, and Y:

```
SQL> create table customer(
  2        last_name  varchar2(30) not null,
  3        state_cd   varchar(2),
```

```
    4       sales       number)
    5   tablespace custspace
    6   storage(initial 25k next 25k minextents 1);
Table created.
SQL> create table state (
    2       state_cd   varchar(2) not null,
    3       state_name varchar2(30));
Table created.
SQL> create table x (
    2       col        varchar2(30));
Table created.
SQL> create table y (
    2       col        varchar2(30));
Table created.
```

NOTE

In listings, numbers after the SQL> prompt string should not be entered by you. When you press ENTER to go to the next line, SQL*Plus puts those numbers there. The column definitions are bounded by a set of parentheses.

Data Typess

By examining the **create table** scripts above, a few items become obvious. Not only do you have to give each table a name (e.g., customer), you must also list all the columns or fields (e.g., last_name, state_cd, and sales) associated with the table. You also have to tell the database what type of information that table will hold. For example, the column sales holds numeric information. An Oracle database can hold many different types of data. Table 6-3 is a partial list of the most common data types.

NOTE

Oracle8 offers an enhanced set of data types to handle very large objects, as well as a more robust mechanism to store numeric data. The large object data types are rolled together and referred to as LOBs (large objects).

Data Type	Description
char(size)	Stores fixed-length character data, with a maximum size of 2,000
nchar(size)	Same as the char data type, except the maximum length is determined by the character set of the database (e.g., Eastern European, Korean, or American English)
varchar2(size)	Stores variable-length character data, with a maximum size of 4,000
nvarchar2(size)	Same as the varchar2 with the same caveat listed for the nchar data type
varchar	Currently the same as char
number(l,d)	Stores numeric data, where "l" stands for length and "d" for the number of decimal digits
blob	A binary large object, where maximum size is 4 GB (gigabytes)
raw(size)	Raw binary data with a maximum length of 2,000 bytes
date	Stores dates from January 1, 4712 B.C. to December 31, 4712 A.D.
long	Stores variable-length character data up to 2GB (gigabytes)

TABLE 6-3. *Partial List of Data Types*

VIP
When defining numeric columns with a length and number of decimal digits, the length defines the total number of digits, including integer and decimal. For example, the largest number that can be stored in number(4,2) is 99.99.

Remember that an Oracle database is made up of tables and that those tables are defined by the columns or fields within the table. Those columns or fields have an attribute that tells what kind of data they can hold. The type of data they hold tells the database what it can do to the contents—this is especially relevant in the sections in this chapter entitled "Using Functions with the Number Data Type," "Using Functions with the Character Data Type," and "Using Functions with the Date Data Type." For example, the number type tells Oracle it can add, subtract, multiply, or divide the contents.

What Is Null and Not Null?

If you look closely at the customer table, you will see the qualifier "not null" next to the last_name column. This means the database will not accept a row of data for that customer table unless the columns so defined have data in them. In other words, not null columns are mandatory fields. In the customer table, this means the last_name and state_cd fields must contain a value in order to insert a row of data into the table.

VIP

*Another way of thinking of not null is to use the word "mandatory." A **not null** column means data for that column can never be empty.*

WHAT'S A NULL VALUE?   A common question people ask is "What is a null value?" Null is a column that contains no data. Think of it as a character string with a length of 0. Many times, people will load null into a column value if it is unknown. The most common mistake people make is to load null into a numeric column. The problem is 1+null is null. So, if you accidentally load null values into a numeric field, you can very quickly cause your reports to add up incorrectly.

VIP

Never use null to represent a value of zero in a numeric field. If you might perform arithmetic on a numeric column, give it a value of zero instead.

On the customer table **create** statement, notice the storage clause used to size the table. As well, we have used the **tablespace** clause to place the table in a certain tablespace in the database. The storage clause is discussed in more detail in *Tuning Oracle* (Corey, Abbey, and Dechichio, Osborne/McGraw-Hill/Oracle Press, 1995).

At the end of each line, you see a semicolon (;). This tells Oracle that you have finished entering the SQL statement and to begin execution.

describe

One of the nicest enhancements that Oracle has added to its implementation of SQL is the **describe** command. This command gives you a quick summary of the table and all its columns. For example, the command **describe customer** yields the following output:

```
Name                              Null?     Type
--------------------------------  --------  ----
last_name                         not null  varchar2(50)
state_cd                          not null  char(2)
sales                                       number
```

> **NOTE**
> The **describe** command can be shortened to
> **desc** in SQL*Plus.

insert

Now that we have created some tables, let's use DML. We will start with the customer table. The statements **insert into customer values ('Teplow','MA', 23445.67);** and **insert into customer values ('Abbey','CA',6969.96);** create two rows in the customer table. Oracle responds with the following message for each set of column information created by the insert command:

```
1 row created.
```

The row created message is returned once for each successful **insert**; the message informs you of the number of rows created. If there are many **insert** statements in a program, the output would resemble the following:

```
SQL> insert into customer values ('Porter','CA', 6989.99);
1 row created.
SQL> insert into customer values ('Martin','CA',2345.45);
1 row created.
SQL> insert into customer values ('Laursen','CA',34.34);
1 row created.
SQL> insert into customer values ('Bambi','CA',1234.55);
1 row created.
SQL> insert into customer values ('McGraw','NJ', 123.45);
1 row created.
```

insert with Columns Specified

Next, we insert data into the state table, using a slight variation on the **insert** command: we will specify the column names into which the data is inserted. This is very useful on a very large table, for which you might not have all the data for every column in the table on the insert. A good example of not having all the data up front is a budget system where you won't have the actual dollars spent data until the end of the month. Let's take a look at a program with this variation of the **insert** command that allows you to selectively load columns in a table:

```
SQL> insert into state (state_name, state_cd)
   2 values ('Massachusetts','MA');
1 row created.
SQL> insert into state (state_name, state_cd)
   2 values ('California','CA');
1 row created.
SQL> insert into state (state_name, state_cd)
   2 values ('NewJersey','NJ');
1 row created.
```

Let's finish up our inserts by loading data into tableX and tableY.

```
SQL> insert into X values ('1');
1 row created.
SQL> insert into X values ('2');
1 row created.
SQL> insert into X values ('3');
1 row created.
SQL> insert into Y values ('3');
1 row created.
SQL> insert into Y values ('4');
1 row created.
SQL> insert into Y values ('5');
1 row created.
```

select

The **select** command is how you retrieve data from an Oracle database. Simply put, you are telling the database which information you have selected to retrieve. This is the most common SQL statement you will see. The **select** command has four basic parts:

1. The word **select** followed by what you want to see (i.e., the names of the columns in the tables mentioned in the next part). This is mandatory.

2. The word **from** followed by where you get it from (i.e., the names of one or more tables where the data resides). This is mandatory.

3. The word **where** followed by any selection criteria (i.e., conditions that restrict the data that the statement retrieves). This is optional.

4. The words **order by** followed by the sort criteria (i.e., a list of column names from part one that control how the data is presented). This is optional.

Let's issue our first **select** statement against a data dictionary view called user_tables:

```
SQL> select * from user_tables;
PERSON                                  USER_DATA
      10          40          1       255              10240
      10240               1       121                50          1
           1 YES N 1              1      N ENABLED
                 NO              N      NO
```

Let's discuss what has just happened. Based on our criteria, the text **select *** tells Oracle to retrieve all the columns in the view. This is a special and very popular form of the **select** command.

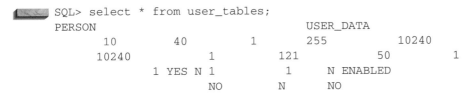

VIP
*To see all the columns from a table, use the asterisk (*) with the **select** statement.*

In this chapter (and you may have noticed this elsewhere), we refer to the Oracle feature called a view. Think of a view as a subset of one or more tables. A view is a special database object that can be created to restrict access to certain columns or rows of data in a table. A view acts like a table in all other aspects (i.e., in most cases, you can **update** or **insert** data using a view rather than a table). A good example of why you might use a view is to allow managers to see only their own employees' payroll records.

VIP

A view is a special database object that can be created to restrict access to certain columns or rows of data within a table.

select with Columns Specified

Rather than using the asterisk as we did in the previous section, we can specify one or more columns after the **select** keyword. The asterisk instructs Oracle to display all the columns from a table. Let's now issue this same **select** statement but specify a column we want to see:

```
SQL> select table_name from user_tables;
TABLE_NAME
------------------------------
CUSTOMER
STATE
X
Y
4 rows selected.
```

where

Up to now, you have seen how the **select** command can be used to bring back all the columns (**select ***) or a subset of the columns (**select column1, column3**). What if you want to see only certain rows of your data? You do this with a **where** clause. For example, if you want to see all the customers with a state_cd of MA, you would issue the command **select last_name, state_cd, sales from customer where state_cd = 'MA';**. The output would resemble the following:

```
LAST_NAME                                         ST     SALES
------------------------------------------------- --  ----------
Teplow                                            MA    23445.67
```

where Clause with and/or

A **where** clause instructs Oracle to search the data in a table and return only those rows that meet your criteria. In the example above, we asked Oracle to bring back only those rows that have state_cd equal to MA. This was accomplished by **where state_cd = 'MA';**.

Sometimes you want to bring back rows that meet multiple criteria. For example, you might be interested in the rows with a state_cd of CA and sales greater than 6,000. The statement **select * from customer where state_cd = 'CA' and sales > 6000;** produces the following output:

```
LAST_NAME                       ST      SALES
------------------------------  --  ----------
Porter                          CA     6989.99
Abbey                           CA     6969.96
```

In the above example, we wanted back rows that met all the criteria. What if you wanted to retrieve rows that met either criterion? Let's look at the statement **select * from customer where state_cd = 'CA' or sales > 6000;**. This produces the following output:

```
LAST_NAME                       ST      SALES
------------------------------  --  ----------
Porter                          CA     6989.99
Martin                          CA     2345.45
Laursen                         CA       34.34
Bambi                           CA     1234.55
Teplow                          MA    23445.67
Abbey                           CA     6969.96
```

Notice how Teplow is displayed since his sales are greater than 6000, even though he is not from the state_cd CA. The **and** and **or** are known as logical operators. They are used to tell the query how the where conditions affect each other. The concept of logic as it applies to how Oracle evaluates multiple conditions could be a book in itself. Let's take the time to delve into some of the evaluation techniques. Table 6-4 explains how Oracle deals with **and** and **or** when they appear together in the same **where** clause.

The logic involved with multiple **and** and **or** words (referred to as compound conditions) can become confusing unless you look at each statement separately and walk slowly through its logic. For example, let's examine the statement **select last_name from customer where state_cd =**

Operator	Reason
or	Returns TRUE when either one of the conditions is true
and	Returns TRUE only when both conditions are true

TABLE 6-4. *Logical Operators and/or*

'MA' and state_cd = 'CA';. With the two conditions connected by the **and** keyword, both conditions must be true for the compound condition to be true.

VIP

*Compound conditions connected by the **and** keyword must all evaluate to TRUE for the whole statement to be true.*

Using the statement **select last_name from customer where state_cd = 'MA' and state_cd = 'CA';**, let's look at a row whose state_cd value is MA. The first condition evaluates to TRUE (since MA equals MA), and the second condition evaluates to FALSE (since CA is not equal to MA). The logic of the statement says that only rows whose state_cd is MA and CA at the same time can be displayed. Of course this is impossible, and thus the condition fails, since TRUE+FALSE=FALSE. We deliberately created this **select** statement to show how complicated your **where** clauses can become in relatively no time.

where Clause with NOT

Oracle also supports the ability to search for negative criteria. For example, you might want to see all the customers who are not in state_cd MA. The **statement select * from customer where state_cd != 'MA';** (the characters != mean "not equal" to SQL*Plus) would yield the output

```
LAST_NAME                                        ST     SALES
------------------------------------------------ -- ----------
Porter                                           CA    6989.99
McGraw                                           NJ     123.45
Martin                                           CA    2345.45
```

```
Laursen                                        CA       34.34
Bambi                                          CA     1234.55
Abbey                                          CA     6969.96
```

where Clause with a Range Search

Oracle also supports range searches. For example, you might want to see all the customers with sales between 1 and 10,000. This would be done using the statement **select * from customer where sales between 1 and 10000;**, and the output would resemble the following:

```
LAST_NAME                                      ST     SALES
--------------------------------------------   --   ----------
Porter                                         CA     6989.99
McGraw                                         NJ      123.45
Martin                                         CA     2345.45
Bambi                                          CA     1234.55
Laursen                                        CA       34.34
Abbey                                          CA     6969.96
```

where Clause with a Search List

Oracle also supports the concept of searching for items within a list. For example, you might want to see all the customers with a state code of NJ or CA. The statement **select * from customer where state_cd in ('NJ','CA');** would show the following:

```
LAST_NAME                                      ST     SALES
--------------------------------------------   --   ----------
Porter                                         CA     6989.99
McGraw                                         NJ      123.45
Martin                                         CA     2345.45
Laursen                                        CA       34.34
Bambi                                          CA     1234.55
Abbey                                          CA     6969.96
```

where Clause with a Pattern Search

Oracle also supports pattern searching through the **like** command. For example, you could tell Oracle to retrieve all the last names that begin with the letter M by issuing the statement **select * from customer where last_name like 'M%';**. The output would resemble the following:

Operator	Purpose	Example
=	Test for equality	select * from state where state_cd = 'MA';
!=	Test for inequality	select * from state where state_cd != 'MA';
^=	Same as !=	select * from state where state_cd ^= 'MA';
<>	Same as !=	select * from state where state_cd <> 'MA';
<	Less than	select * from customer where sales < 100;
>	Greater than	select * from customer where sales > 100;
<=	Less than or equal to	select * from customer where sales <= 10000;
>=	Greater than or equal to	select * from customer where sales >= 10000;
in	Equal to any member in parentheses	select * from customer where state_cd in ('MA','NJ');
not in	Not equal to any member in parentheses	select * from customer where state_cd not in ('MA','NJ');
between A and B	Greater than or equal to A and less than or equal to B	select * from customer where sales between 1 and 50;
not between A and B	Not greater than or equal to A and not less than or equal to B	select * from customer where sales not between 1 and 50;
like '%tin%'	Contains given text (e.g., 'tin'),	select * from customer where last_name like '%tin%';

TABLE 6-5.   *Common Comparison Operators*

sorted by state descending (i.e., Vermont before Mississippi) and ascending by last_name.

VIP
*When no order (i.e., descending or ascending) is specified in an **order by**, Oracle sorts ascending.*

Number Data Type

These fields contain only numeric data. Let's see what you can do to the columns of this type in a **select** statement. Table 6-6 highlights the most popular arithmetic operations and how they are worded in SQL*Plus.

As you can see in Table 6-6, you can certainly perform all the standard arithmetic operations: add, subtract, multiply, and divide. With Oracle, your ability to manipulate the contents goes far beyond the standard list. In addition to the operators mentioned, there is an extensive list of functions. Before we present that list, let's talk about what a function is.

Using Functions with the Number Data Type

A function manipulates the contents of a column in a SQL statement. When using a function in a SQL statement, the column value upon which the function is performed is changed as the column value is displayed. Displaying a number column's absolute value is a good example of a function; a column that contains the number –321 has an absolute value of 321. In SQL*Plus, absolute value is indicated by placing parentheses around the column name, and the word "abs" in front, e.g., abs(ytd_sales). Thus, a SQL statement worded **select abs(ytd_sales) from customer;** would display the value 321 when a ytd_sales column contained the value –321 or +321.

Operator	Operation Performed	Example
+	Addition	select ytd_sales + current_sales from customer;
-	Subtraction	select ytd_sales - current_sales from customer where state_cd = 'NJ';
*	Multiplication	select ytd_sales * commission from customer;
/	Division	select ytd_sales / 12 from customer;

TABLE 6-6. *Arithmetic Operators*

Table 6-7 shows some popular functions performed on number data type columns, how they are worded in SQL*Plus, and the value they display. Notice that the **select** statements in Table 6-7 use a table called dual. This table is owned by SYS and is used in situations where correct SQL syntax (i.e., must contain a **from** portion) must be used and there is no other table in the database used in the statement.

Table 6-7 presents an extensive list of functions that can be performed on number data. This is only a partial list; to access SQL*Plus online help, enter the command **help functions**.

Function	Returns	Example	Displays
ceil(n)	Nearest whole integer greater than or equal to number	select ceil(10.6) from dual;	11
floor(n),	Largest integer equal to or less than n	select floor(10.6) from dual;	10
mod(m,n)	Remainder of m divided by n. If n=0, then m is returned	select mod(7,5) from dual;	2
power(m,n)	Number m raised to the power of n	select power(3,2) from dual;	9
round(n,m)	Result rounded to m places to the right of the decimal point	select round(1234.5678,2) from dual;	1234.57
sign(n)	If n = 0, returns 0; if n > 0, returns 1; If n < 0, returns -1	select sign(12) from dual;	1
sqrt(n)	Square root of n	select sqrt(25) from dual;	5

TABLE 6-7. *Common Functions on Number Data*

NOTE

With Oracle8 on Windows NT, the SQL*Plus help facility is in the Oracle documentation, and you will be informed as shown in the next listing.

```
SQL> help functions
SQL*Plus Help Files are included in Oracle Documentation.
You have to read SQL*Plus Help Files from Oracle Documentation.
SQL>
```

If you try to perform a numeric function on nonnumeric data, you will receive an Oracle error. For example, the statement **select floor('ABC')** **from dual;** will cause the following error since the data ABC is not numeric:

```
ERROR:
ORA-01722: invalid number
```

There is a whole different set of functions you perform with character data. Let's take a look at what Oracle can do with a character string.

Character Data Type

These are fields that are entered as char, varchar, or varchar2 in the **create table** statement. The character data type can be used to represent all the letters, numbers, and special characters on your keyboard. There is a whole complete set of functions you can use with the character data type.

Using Functions with the Character Data Type

Table 6-8 lists the most common functions you will perform with the character data type.

Function	Return	Example	Displays
initcap(char)	Changes the first character of each character string to uppercase	select initcap('mr. teplow') from dual;	Mr. Teplow
lower(char), Makes the entire string lowercase	select lower('Mr. Frank Townson') from dual;	mr. frank townson	
replace(char, str1, str2)	Character string with every occurrence of str1 being replaced with str2	select replace('Scott', 'S', 'Boy') from dual;	Boycott
soundex(char)	Phonetic representation of char. Commonly used to do fuzzy name searches. You can compare words that are spelled differently but sound alike	select last_name from employee where soundex(last_name) = soundex('SMYTHE');	SMITH
substr(char,m,n)	Picks off part of the character string char starting in position m for n characters	select substr('ABCDEF',2,1) from dual;	B
length(char)	Length of char	select length ('Anderson') from dual;	8

TABLE 6-8. *Common Functions on Character Data*

The concatenation operator deserves special attention before moving onto the discussion of the date data type. This is quite useful when you want to join two character fields together. It is called an operator, though we include it in this section on functions. Two vertical bars (||) indicate concatenation. The statement **select 'ABC' || 'DEF' from dual;** returns the text ABCDEF. Think of a form letter. The statement **select 'Dear ' || last_name || ':' from customer;** would return the text "Dear John:" for the row whose last_name was John.

Date Data Type

Date is the third most common type of data you find in an Oracle database. When we created the customer table, we could have easily included an additional column called sale_date, as in the following:

```
SQL> create table customer
  2 (last_name   varchar2(30) not null,
  3  state_cd    varchar2(2),
  4  sales       number,
  5  sale_date   date);
Table created.
```

In Oracle, the date data type really contains two values: the date and the time. This is critical to remember when comparing two dates, since Oracle always stores a time with the date. The default date format in Oracle is DD-MON-YY where DD is the day, MON is the month, and YY is the two-digit year.

NOTE

Oracle supplies a century-specific date format mask DD-MON-RR, which is designed to preserve century digits when entering a two-character year. Please consult the Oracle8 Server SQL Reference for details under the date data type.

VIP

To ensure preservation of the four-digit year as we move towards the 21st century, it is wise to use the DD-MON-YYYY date format as much as possible.

Using Functions with the Date Data Type

Oracle has provided you a list of extensive functions to help you manipulate the date data type. For example, suppose you want to send out a reminder to a customer on the last day of the month for an unpaid invoice. If you want to print the letter and send it when appropriate, you would perform the function last_day to place the correct date in the reminder's header. Table 6-9 shows the most common date functions.

Special Formats with the Date Data Type

You can use a number of formats with dates. These formats are used to change the display format of a date. Table 6-10 shows some date formats and their output.

Function	Returns	Example	Displays
sysdate	Current date and time	select sysdate from dual;	28-FEB-99 on February 28, 1999.
last_day	Last day of the month	select last_day(sysdate) from dual;	31-MAR-99 on March 12, 1999
add_months(d,n)	Adds or subtracts n months from date d	select add_months (sysdate,2) from dual;	18-MAY-99 on March 18, 1999
months_between (f,s)	Difference in months between date f and date s	select months_between (sysdate, '12-MAR-99') from dual;	13 in April 1998
next_day(d,day)	Date that is the specified day of the week after d	select next_day (sysdate,'Monday') from dual;	05-JAN-98 on December 30, 1997

TABLE 6-9. *Common Functions on Date Data*

Format	Returns	Example	Displays
Y or YY or YYY	Last one, two, or three digits of year	select to_char(sysdate, 'YYY') from dual;	999 for all dates in 1999
SYEAR or YEAR	Year spelled out; using the S places a minus sign before B.C. dates	select to_char(sysdate, 'SYEAR') from dual;	-1112 in the year 1112 B.C.
Q	Quarter of year (January through March = 1)	select to_char (sysdate, 'Q') from dual;	2 for all dates in June
MM	Month (01-12; Dec = 12)	select to_char(sysdate, 'MM') from dual;	12 for all dates in December
RM	Roman numeral month	select to_char(sysdate, 'RM') from dual;	IV for all dates in April
Month	Name of month as a nine-character name	select to_char(sysdate, 'Month') from dual;	May followed by 6 spaces for all dates in May
WW	Week of year	select to_char(sysdate, 'WW') from dual;	24 on June 13, 1998
W	Week of the month	select to_char(sysdate, 'W') from dual;	1 on October 1, 1995
DDD	Day of the year: January 1 is 001, February 1 is 032, etc.	select to_char(sysdate, 'DDD') from dual;	363 on December 29, 1999
DD	Day of the month	select to_char(sysdate, 'DD') from dual;	04 on October 4 in any year
D	Day of the week (1-7)	select to_char(sysdate, 'D') from dual;	1 on March 14, 1999

TABLE 6-10.   *Common Formats Using Date Data*

Format	Returns	Example	Displays
DY	Abbreviated name of day	select to_char(sysdate, 'DY') from dual;	SUN on March 28, 1999
HH or HH12	Hour of day (1-12)	select to_char(sysdate, 'HH') from dual;	02 when it is 2 hours, and 8 minutes past midnight
HH24	Hour of day using 24-hour clock	select to_char(sysdate, 'HH24') from dual;	14 when it is 2 hours and 8 minutes past noon
MI	Minutes (0-59)	select to_char(sysdate, 'MI') from dual;	17 when it is 4:17 in the afternoon
SS	Seconds (0-59)	select to_char(sysdate,'SS') from dual;	22 when the time is 11:03:22

TABLE 6-10. *Common Formats Using Date Data* (continued)

VIP
Be careful about using the format MM for minutes (you should use MI for minutes). MM is used for month; it will work if you try to use it for minutes, but the results will be wrong. This is a common pitfall; just ask Mark!

Date Arithmetic

Just as soon as you start working with the date data type, you will ask the question "How many days ago did we change the oil in the car?" Date arithmetic allows you to find this answer. When you add two to a date column, Oracle knows that you mean two days. Say the column sale_date contains 03-MAR-98; in this case, the SQL statement **select sale_date+10 from customer;** would return 13-MAR-98. Let's look at two more examples with date arithmetic.

VIP
Date arithmetic can be one of the most frustrating operations in SQL*Plus. Oracle is very stringent with the rules on date formats upon which arithmetic can be performed.

The statement **select last_name, sale_date+10 from customer;** tells Oracle to add ten days to the value in the sale_date column. A sale_date containing 17-MAR-98 would display as 27-MAR-98. Oracle takes care of arithmetic that spans month or year boundaries. For example, the statement **select to_char(sysdate+14) from dual;** will return 06-JAN-99 on 23-DEC-98.

Converting from One Column Type to Another

Many times, you may want to convert a data column from one data type to another (e.g., number to date, character to number). Oracle has three main conversion functions:

- **to_char** converts any data type to character data type. The statement **select to_char(8897) from dual;** returns a character data type answer containing the characters 8897.

- **to_number** converts a valid set of numeric character data (e.g., character data 8897) to number data type. The statement **select to_number('8897') from dual;** returns a number data type answer containing the number 8897.

- **to_date** converts character data of the proper format to date data type. This is the conversion that provides the most problems. The statement **select to_date('12-DEC-99') from dual;** succeeds, since 12-DEC-99 is a valid date format. However, problems arise if you pass the statement **select to_date('bad date') from dual;** to Oracle.

VIP
Using the to_date conversion mechanism can generate a wide assortment of Oracle errors when it receives bad date format data.

Update, Delete, and Alter

You will probably use these three SQL commands the most after **select**. Many SQL programs you write will have a mixture of these statements (i.e., **update**, **delete**, and **insert**) coupled with statements starting with the **select** keyword.

update

Sometimes it is necessary to update data stored within a table. You do this via the **update** command. The command has three parts:

- The word **update** followed by the table you want to change. This is mandatory.

- The word **set** followed by one or more columns you want to change. This is mandatory.

- The word **where** followed by selection criteria. This is optional.

For example, say you want to change all the sales figures to 0 in the customer table. You would issue the SQL statement **update customer set sales = 0;** and Oracle would respond with the number of rows updated. If you want to change only those customers from state_cd of MA to 0, you could use the SQL statement **update customer set sales = 0 where state_cd = 'MA';**. As you can see, the **update** command is a very powerful tool at your disposal.

delete

The **delete** command is used when you want to remove one or more rows of data from a table. The command has two parts:

- The words **delete from** followed by the table name you want to remove data from. This is mandatory.

- The word **where** followed by the criteria for the delete. This is optional.

Let's take a closer look at the **delete** command. If you want to remove all the customer records, you could issue the SQL statement **delete from**

customer;. If you just want to delete records with customers from state_cd CA, you would use the SQL statement **delete from customer where state_cd = 'CA';**.

alter

After a table is created, you sometimes realize you need to add an additional column. You do this with the **alter table** command. For example, the statement **alter table customer add (sale_date date);** would successfully add the sale_date column to the customer table if it did not exist. Most of the time, you will use **alter** to add a column to a table. The statement **alter table x modify (col1 date);** is used to change the data type for a column that already exists in a table.

VIP

*Oracle8 is very strict with its rules about column contents when you wish to change the data type for a column if the column contains data when the **alter** is issued.*

You are allowed to stack the columns in the **alter table** statement. The command **alter table x modify (col1 date, col5 number(3,1));** is just as valid as two separate **alter** statements.

VIP

*There are some strict rules governing what types of **alter table** statements are valid under what conditions. If you enter an invalid alter table statement, Oracle informs you and tells you why it is not valid.*

Joining Two Tables Together

In the real world, much of the data you need is in more than one table. Many times, you need to go to multiple tables. For example, let's say that in the customer table you only store the state code; then, if you want the state name, you would need to join the customer table to the state table. You do this by joining the tables together. By definition, relational databases such as Oracle allow you to relate (or join) two or more tables based on common fields. Most often, these fields are what we refer to as key fields.

There are two types of keys: primary and foreign. A primary key is what makes a row of data unique within a table. In the state table, state_cd is the primary key. The customer table also contains state_cd, which in this case is a foreign key. One table's foreign key is used to get information out of another (foreign) table. With this in mind, let's take a look at two tables, X and Y first mentioned in the "create Statement" section of this chapter. The SQL statement **select * from x;** returns these rows:

```
col
---
1
2
3
```

The statement **select * from y;** returns these rows:

```
col
----
3
4
5
```

Let's see what happens when you join the two tables together. Oracle allows you to give tables an alternate name, called an alias. In this case, we are going to give tableX the alias right and tableY the alias left. Then, we can use the alternate names with the columns to keep things clear. The statement **select right.col, left.col from x right, y left where right.col = left.col;** yields the following output:

```
col col
--- ---
3    3
```

Notice the col column values in both tables were compared, and the SQL statement required both tables to match on their respective col column values. The only column value that matches both tableX and tableY is the row with the number 3 in the col column value. Hence, only one row is selected as the tables are joined.

Formatting the Output

Up to now, we have learned how to **create** and **alter** tables, **insert** data into the tables, **update** and **delete** from the tables, and convert from one data type to another. Now we'll learn how to put it all together and write a great report. In SQL*Plus, you can set many parameters to control how SQL*Plus output is displayed. You can see all the current settings by issuing the SQL*Plus command **show all**. The output from this command resembles the following:

```
feedback ON for 6 or more rows
heading ON
linesize 80
numwidth 10
trimsp OFF
autotrace off
spool ON
user is "SYSTEM"
space 1
worksize DEFAULT
lines will be wrapped
pagesize 14
showmode OFF
pause is OFF
ttitle OFF and is the 1st few ...
btitle OFF and is the 1st few ...
define "&" (hex 26)
escape OFF
concat "." (hex 2e)
sqlprompt "SQL> "
underline "-" (hex 2d)
null ""
verify ON
message ON
sqlcode 0
tab ON
scan ON
dclsep OFF
termout ON
echo OFF
sqlcase MIXED
headsep "|" (hex 7c)
maxdata 32767
```

```
time OFF
cmdsep OFF
xisql OFF
sqlterminator ";" (hex 3b)
sqlprefix "#" (hex 23)
release 39512
sqlnumber ON
autocommit OFF
newpage 1
long 80
document ON
trimout ON
timing OFF
qbidebug OFF
numformat ""
synonym OFF
suffix "SQL"
flush ON
sqlcontinue "SQL>"
pno 1
lno 15
buffer SQL
embedded OFF
arraysize 15
crt ""
copycommit 0
compatibility version NATIVE
recsep WRAP
recsepchar " " (hex 20)
blockterminator "." (hex 2e)
copytypecheck is ON
longchunksize 80
serveroutput OFF
flagger OFF
```

As you can see, there are many parameters you can set to alter your environment. We are going to change the major ones.

Page and Line Size

The **set linesize** command tells Oracle how wide the page is. The most common settings are 80 and 132. To set the line size to 80, enter the command **set linesize 80**. The **set pagesize** command tells Oracle how long the page is. The most common settings are 55 and 60. To make it easier to

LAST_NAME	ST	SALES
McGraw	NJ	123.45
Martin	CA	2345.45

You could also tell Oracle to look for all the last names that contain the characters "tin" by entering the command **select * from customer where last_name like '%tin%';**. It would return the following data:

LAST_NAME	ST	SALES
Martin	CA	2345.45

where Clause: Common Operators

As you can see from these many examples, Oracle has a very powerful set when it comes to restricting the rows retrieved. Table 6-5 is a partial list of operators you can use in the **where** clause.

order by

Let's take another look at the contents of the customer table. This time, we will request the list sorted by last_name in descending alphabetical order. The command **select * from customer order by last_name desc;** gives the following results:

LAST_NAME	ST	SALES
Teplow	MA	23445.67
Porter	CA	6989.99
McGraw	NJ	123.45
Martin	CA	2345.45
Laursen	CA	34.34
Bambi	CA	1234.55
Abbey	CA	6969.96
7 rows selected.		

As you can see, Oracle brought the list back in descending sorted order. We could have easily sorted the list in ascending order by issuing the command **select * from customer order by last_name;**. We could have also done a multilevel sort by issuing the command **select * from customer order by state_cd desc, last_name;**. This command would list customers see the page breaks, you can set this parameter to 30 using the command **set pagesize 30**.

Page Titles

You can also tell Oracle how you want the page title to show up. The **ttitle** command includes many options. We usually stick with the default settings: the text shown in the title is centered on the line, and the date and page number are printed on every page. To place the title on two lines, use the vertical bar character (|) to get SQL*Plus to issue two lines. The command **ttitle 'Database Technologies | Customer Report'** tells SQL*Plus to center the text "Database Technologies" on the first title line, then to skip to line two and center the text "Customer Report."

Page Footers

The **btitle** command is used to place something on the bottom of every page. We recommend putting the program name there. Then, when users want you to change a report, all they need to tell you is the name on the bottom. This can help avoid a lot of confusion. The command **btitle '--- sample.sql ---'** tells SQL*Plus to center the text "--- sample.sql ---" at the bottom of every page. You can use the word **left** or **right** to place the text in **btitle** elsewhere than the center of the page; if no placement word is included in btitle, Oracle places the text in the center.

Writing SQL*Plus Output to a File

The **spool** command tells Oracle to save SQL*Plus output to a datafile. To use the spool command, you include the name of the output file. On Windows NT, for example, this can be done by entering the command **spool c:\report\out.lis**. Most operating systems append the text **.lst** to the end of the name you specify. For example, the command **spool report** will produce a file called report.lst.

VIP

*SQL*Plus adds an extension to the filename mentioned in the spool command. This extension can differ among operating systems.*

Say we have issued the commands **set linesize 70**, **set pagesize 23** and formatted the sales column using the command **col sales format 99999999**. We want to save the output of the SQL statement **select * from customer;** to a file. The output from that command is shown in Figure 6-1; this output would be captured in the filename specified with the spool statement. Notice that there are no decimal digits in the sales since the column was formatted using 99999999.

To stop spooling, issue the command **spool off** or **spool out**. The latter closes the output file and prints it as well.

Formatting Columns in the Output

Most times, you need to format the actual column data. You do this through the column command. Let's issue two additional formatting commands, then reissue the query on the customer table.

The command **column last_name format a8 wrap heading 'Last | Name'** tells SQL*Plus that there should be only eight characters displayed in the last_name column. The 8 places a length on the display width of last_name, and the a tells SQL*Plus that it will be only character data. The

```
D:\ORANT\BIN\PLUS40.exe                                    _ □ ×
Sun May 11                                          page    1
                    Database Technologies
                      Customer Report

LAST_NAME            ST    SALES
-------------------- --   ---------
Teplow               MA    23466
Abbey                CA     6978
Porter               CA     6990
Martin               CA     2345
Laursen              CA       34
Bambi                CA     1235
McGraw               NJ      123


               --- sample.sql ---

7 rows selected.

SQL> _
```

FIGURE 6-1. *Sample formatted output*

wrap portion tells SQL*Plus that if a last_name shows up that is longer than 8 characters, the extra characters should spill onto the next line. The heading portion tells SQL*Plus to print the heading "Last Name" on the report, split over two lines.

The command **column state_cd format a8 heading 'State|Code'** tells SQL*Plus to reserve 8 positions for display of the state_cd and put the two-line heading "State Code" at the top of the state code column. Now the identical SQL statement **select * from customer;** will produce the output shown in Figure 6-2.

Hey—pretty slick! Now let's format the number field. The format clause indicates the number of places to use to display each number and where to insert the commas. The statement **column sales format 999,999,999,999.00 heading 'Sales'** tells SQL*Plus to print up to 12 integer digits and 2 decimal digits, using the commas to separate the thousands. The enhanced report output is shown in Figure 6-3.

```
 D:\ORANT\BIN\PLUS40.exe                                        _ □ ×
Sun May 11                                              page    1
                      Database Technologies
                        Customer Report

Last      State
Name      Code        SALES
--------  --------   ----------
Teplow    MA           23466
Abbey     CA            6978
Porter    CA            6990
Martin    CA            2345
Laursen   CA              34
Bambi     CA            1235
McGraw    NJ             123

                   --- sample.sql ---

7 rows selected.

SQL>
```

FIGURE 6-2.   *Output with two-column formatting commands*

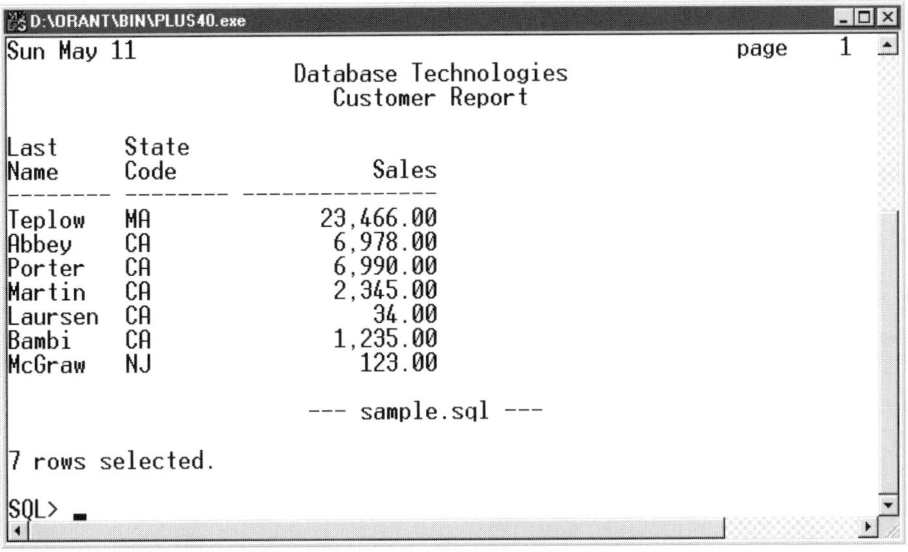

```
D:\ORANT\BIN\PLUS40.exe                                          _ □ ×
Sun May 11                                               page   1
                          Database Technologies
                            Customer Report

Last       State
Name       Code                    Sales
--------   --------   ----------------
Teplow     MA               23,466.00
Abbey      CA                6,978.00
Porter     CA                6,990.00
Martin     CA                2,345.00
Laursen    CA                   34.00
Bambi      CA                1,235.00
McGraw     NJ                  123.00

                   --- sample.sql ---

7 rows selected.

SQL> _
```

FIGURE 6-3. *Output with all columns formatted*

Break Logic

Now let's add some break logic. Refer to the "Sample Report #2" section of Chapter 9 where we explain control break logic. One of the things SQL*Plus makes easy is dealing with breaking. As soon as you issue the break command, SQL*Plus is smart enough to manage all break logic for you.

Let's look at the SQL query **select state_cd, last_name, sales from customer order by state_cd, last_name;**, with the column format command **col sales format 999999.00**. Without using break logic, the output from this query is shown in Figure 6-4.

Let's issue the command **break on state_cd**, and the same query output changes to what is shown in Figure 6-5. Notice how the state_cd CA prints in line 1, is suppressed in lines 2 through 5 (since the state_cd has not changed from line 1), then prints again in lines 6 and 7 with different values.

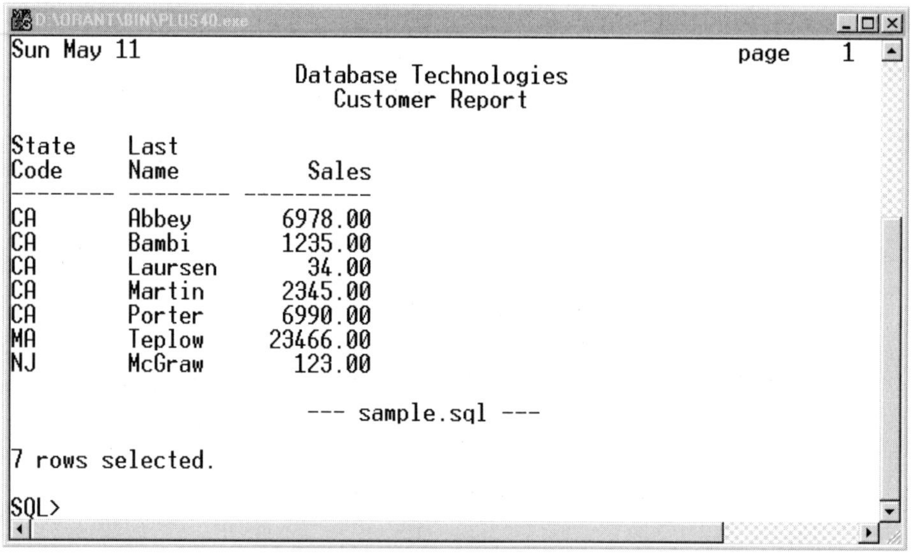

```
Sun May 11                                          page     1
                      Database Technologies
                        Customer Report

State    Last
Code     Name           Sales
-------- -------- -----------
CA       Abbey       6978.00
CA       Bambi       1235.00
CA       Laursen       34.00
CA       Martin      2345.00
CA       Porter      6990.00
MA       Teplow     23466.00
NJ       McGraw       123.00

                   --- sample.sql ---

7 rows selected.

SQL>
```

FIGURE 6-4. *Output without break logic*

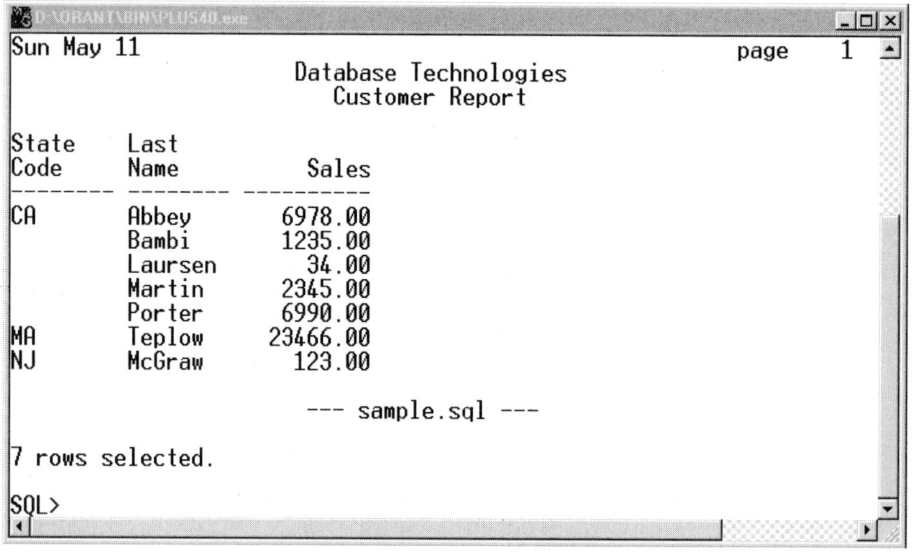

```
Sun May 11                                          page     1
                      Database Technologies
                        Customer Report

State    Last
Code     Name           Sales
-------- -------- -----------
CA       Abbey       6978.00
         Bambi       1235.00
         Laursen       34.00
         Martin      2345.00
         Porter      6990.00
MA       Teplow     23466.00
NJ       McGraw       123.00

                   --- sample.sql ---

7 rows selected.

SQL>
```

FIGURE 6-5. *Break report output*

VIP

To implement break logic in SQL*Plus, you must order the query by the same column on which the break command is issued.

To illustrate this point, the command **break on state_cd** followed by the query **select state_cd,last_name,sales from customer order by last_name;** would produce the output shown in Figure 6-6.

Notice how ordering the query results by last_name has interfered with the desired output; the three CA states print first, then one NJ, followed by another CA entry.

Break and Skip

Let's take this one step further. Often when implementing break logic, we want to leave one or more blank lines before displaying the new break column value. This is done with the skip command. Let's reformat the sales column with the command **col sales format $999,999,999.99 heading**

```
Sun May 11                                              page      1
                         Database Technologies
                            Customer Report

State      Last
Code       Name            Sales
------     ------      -----------
CA         Abbey           6978.00
           Bambi           1235.00
           Laursen           34.00
           Martin          2345.00
NJ         McGraw           123.00
CA         Porter          6990.00
MA         Teplow         23466.00

                      --- sample.sql ---

7 rows selected.

SQL>
```

FIGURE 6-6. *Output with break on state_cd and ordered by last_name*

'YTD | Sales' and reissue the break with **break on state_cd skip 1**. Now, the statement **select state_cd,last_name,sales from customer order by state_cd,last_name;** produces the output shown in Figure 6-7.

Notice how Oracle suppresses printing of the state_cd every time. You could have easily told Oracle to compute total sales at each break. We discuss this in the next section.

Computing Column Values at Break

You just need to tell SQL*Plus what you want added up, using the **compute sum** command. Let's now issue the commands necessary to complete the formatting of the break and to compute the YTD totals.

The command **compute sum of sales on report** forces a report total at the end of the output. The word **report** is used here to trigger the sum of a number field to be displayed at the end of a report. The command **compute sum of sales on state_cd** forces totals to be printed for a state when a new state code is printed.

```
Sun May 11                                              page    1
                        Database Technologies
                          Customer Report

State    Last               YTD
Code     Name              Sales
-------  --------  ------------------
CA       Abbey           $6,978.00
         Bambi           $1,235.00
         Laursen            $34.00
         Martin          $2,345.00
         Porter          $6,990.00

MA       Teplow         $23,466.00

NJ       McGraw            $123.00




                --- sample.sql ---

7 rows selected.

SQL>
```

FIGURE 6-7.   *Break report output with one line after break*

To print the report total, we need to reset the break conditions with the command **break on report skip 1 on state_cd skip 1**. We change the SQL statement to sort the data by state_cd. Ordering the data by the same column mentioned in the break statement is necessary for break reporting.

NOTE
You may have to increase the page size to get the output from this section to print on one page. Do so by entering the command **set pagesize 28**.

The SQL statement is now **select state_cd, last_name, sales from customer order by state_cd, last_name;**. Figure 6-8 shows the break output after reformatting the sales column with the statement **col sales format $999,999,999.00 heading 'YTD|Sales'**.

```
D:\ORANT\BIN\PLUS40.exe                                              _ □ x

Sun May 11                                                 page    1
                           Database Technologies
                             Customer Report

State     Last                   YTD
Code      Name                  Sales
--------  --------  ------------------
CA        Abbey            $6,978.00
          Bambi            $1,235.00
          Laursen             $34.00
          Martin           $2,345.00
          Porter           $6,990.00
********            ------------------
sum                       $17,582.00

MA        Teplow          $23,466.00
********            ------------------
sum                       $23,466.00

NJ        McGraw             $123.00
********            ------------------
sum                          $123.00

                    ------------------
sum                       $41,171.00


                    --- sample.sql ---

7 rows selected.
SQL>
```

FIGURE 6-8. *Break report output with totals by state_cd and at end of report*

Break Logic and Compute Sum Using Two Tables

Finally, let's utilize what we've learned in this chapter to show a final report. Recall the earlier "Joining Two Tables Together" section where we discussed joins: you select data from more than one table and match column values from one against the other. Now, rather than printing the state_cd, let's print the state name instead.

We need the state_name column from the state table, and we can join the state table to the customer table via state_cd. The select statement becomes **select state_name, last_name, sales from state a,customer b where a.state_cd = b.state_cd order by state_name, last_name;**. And since we are using the state_name column, we have to restate the break conditions to SQL*Plus using **break on report skip 1 on state_name skip 1**. We also need to define the compute sum statements for state_name and the report with **compute sum of sales on state_name** and **compute sum of sales on report**. We are now ready to issue the query joining the two tables, and the output produced is shown in Figure 6-9.

```
 D:\ORANT\BIN\PLUS40.exe                                    _ □ ×

Sun May 11                                           page    1
                       Database Technologies
                         Customer Report

                   Last              YTD
STATE_NAME         Name            Sales
-----------------  --------  ----------------
California         Abbey          $6,978.00
                   Bambi          $1,235.00
                   Laursen           $34.00
                   Martin         $2,345.00
                   Porter         $6,990.00
******************          ----------------
sum                           $17,582.00

Massachusetts      Teplow        $23,466.00
******************          ----------------
sum                           $23,466.00

New Jersey         McGraw           $123.00
******************          ----------------
sum                              $123.00

                            ----------------
sum                           $41,171.00


                   --- sample.sql ---

7 rows selected.

SQL>
```

FIGURE 6-9.   *Final report output*

What's Next

Now, that was a chapter! You've come a long way! You are well on your way to becoming familiar with the power of SQL and Oracle's SQL*Plus. Not a bad report writer, you say. No argument here. We have been using SQL*Plus since day one. It's a workhorse and always will be. As you experiment with its features, you will be amazed at how much you can do with it.

With this first chapter on developer basics, you now have a solid groundwork with SQL. Follow the next few chapters as we discuss more tools you need to be familiar with as you jump into Oracle at the deep end. We'll be back . . . .

CHAPTER

7

PL/SQL

rogrammers need to be able to assemble a set of data and process the results of a query one row at a time. Imagine arriving at the supermarket checkout counter with a cartload of groceries and insisting the checkout person pass everything over the bar code scanner at once. That person would have absolutely no control over what is being processed—it's all or nothing. Without the ability to manipulate data row by row, the programmer, depending on the application's requirements, could be likened to that poor checkout person—in other words, you could be that checkout person. With version 6, Oracle implemented a procedural processing language referred to as PL/SQL (pronounced "pea ell sequel") that will make your job a great deal easier. PL/SQL has programming constructs that resemble most programming languages.

VIP
The skills you will acquire or already have will not be lost when you move from some flavor of Oracle7 to Oracle8. The version number of PL/SQL increases with Oracle8, but all you learn from this chapter or already have under your belt still works under version 8.

There are two versions of PL/SQL: one is part of the database engine, the other is a separate engine embedded in a number of Oracle tools. We call them database PL/SQL and tool PL/SQL. They are very similar: both use the same programming constructs, syntax, and logic mechanisms. Tool PL/SQL has additional syntax designed to support the requirements of the tools. For example, to place a push button on a form to navigate to the bottom of the screen, the movement would be coded using PL/SQL in an Oracle Forms system. This chapter will deal with database PL/SQL. The extra constructs and some of the extra syntax used in tool PL/SQL in Oracle Forms are covered in Chapter 8.

In this chapter, you will learn about the following:

■ Where Oracle uses PL/SQL

■ PL/SQL character set

■ Variables and PL/SQL reserved words

■ Common data types

- Components of PL/SQL

- Cursors

- Coding conventions

- The look and feel of PL/SQL

- Dealing with compilation errors

In the middle of some PL/SQL code examples in this chapter, we will use three dots (...) to indicate omissions. These dots are not part of the code; they indicate portions of code unnecessary to the point at hand.

Terminology

The following definitions will arm you with the technical jargon to make it through this chapter:

- An *executable* is the name of a program written using one of the assortment of computer programming languages. When you type the name of an executable, the program runs. For example, when you use SQL*Plus, you enter the command **sqlplus**.

- A *character set* describes the range of characters that a computer language supports and displays in reports. Most programming languages, including PL/SQL, can display just about any character set as text.

- *Arithmetic operators* are symbols used to define mathematical operations with data. Common operators are +, -, *, and / .

- *Relational operators* define states of comparison or choice, such as comparing two dates to see their relationship to one another. Common operators are >, <, and <> .

- *Variables* are programmer-defined names to hold items of information.

- *Reserved words* have special meaning to PL/SQL. They are reserved for use by Oracle and cannot be used as variable names. For example, the word "declare" means something special to PL/SQL and cannot be used as a variable name.

■ A *data type* defines the class of a piece of information (data). In everyday terminology, we are used to classifying information as numeric or character. The character data type contains all representable characters from a specific alphabet. The numeric data type contains the decimal digits 0 through 9.

■ A *loop* is a construct in a computer program where a segment of code is executed repeatedly.

■ An *exit condition* is the part of a loop where a test is performed on data and, if the test evaluates to TRUE, the loop terminates.

■ *Control structures* influence the flow of processing in a computer program. If there were two different ways to process data, the mechanism used to decide which processing route to follow is a control structure.

■ A *stored object* is a PL/SQL code segment saved in the database and used by developers and end users as Oracle systems operate. We spoke about the procedural capabilities of Oracle in Chapter 1 in the "Procedural Component" section.

Why Do I Need to Know PL/SQL?

When we first started using PL/SQL, we looked around on the disk for an executable called plsql. We did not find one, so then we tried writing PL/SQL blocks in SQL*Plus. Lo and behold—there it was! If you have access to Oracle Forms or its predecessor SQL*Forms version 3, that is the best way to learn PL/SQL and hone your skills. When using Oracle stored procedures, database triggers, packages, and functions, all the coding is done using PL/SQL. You will not get very far with Oracle without knowing PL/SQL. It is the basis of all the programming you may end up doing in the following Oracle tools:

■ Oracle Forms

■ Oracle Reports

■ SQL*Plus

■ Oracle Graphics

If you want to become fluent with the Oracle product set, PL/SQL must become part of your skill set. If you have any programming experience with ADA, PL/SQL will seem very familiar. We will cover some introductory concepts and programming constructs in this chapter. As you become more familiar with PL/SQL, you will be able to take advantage of its rich features.

PL/SQL Character Set

As with all other programming languages, there is a set of characters you use in PL/SQL. Just about any character you can enter from the keyboard is a PL/SQL character, yet there are rules about using some characters in some situations. In this section, you will learn details on:

- Characters you may use when programming in PL/SQL

- Arithmetic operators

- Relational operators

- Miscellaneous symbols

Characters Supported

When programming in PL/SQL, you are limited to the following characters:

- All uppercase and lowercase letters

- Digits 0 through 9

- Symbols ( ) + - * / < > = ! ~ ; : . ' @ % , " # $ ^ & _ | { } ? [ ]

Some of these characters are for code; others serve as arithmetic operators (division, addition, exponents, etc.) and relational operators (equal and not equal). For example, in a communications application, the developer may use a variable named "area_code" to store a client's calling area. The choice "area_code" of the characters a r e a _ c o d e conform to the rules outlined in the "Variables" section of this chapter.

Arithmetic Operators

The following table shows the common arithmetic operators used in PL/SQL. If you are familiar with other high-level programming languages, this will not be new to you.

Operator	Meaning	Operator	Meaning
+	addition	-	subtraction
*	multiplication	/	division
**	exponentiation		

Relational Operators

The next table shows the PL/SQL relational operators. If you have experience with any other programming languages, then you have seen these symbols before.

Operator	Meaning	Operator	Meaning
<>	not equal	!=	not equal
^=	not equal	<	less than
>	greater than	=	equal

Miscellaneous Symbols

To support programming in PL/SQL, the following symbols are used. This table shows a partial list of symbols; they are the most commonly used symbols and the ones you must know to start using PL/SQL.

Symbol	Meaning	Example
()	list separators	and NAME in ('Jones','Roy','Abramson')
;	end-of-statement	procedure_name (arg1,arg2);
.	item separator (in the example, it separates an account name from a table name)	select * from account.table_name;
'	character string enclosure	if var1 = 'SANDRA' ...

:=	assignment	rec_read := rec_read + 1;
||	concatenation	full_name := 'Nahtan' || ' ' || 'Yebba';
--	comment delimiter	-- This is a comment
/* and */	comment delimiters	/* This too is a comment */

Variables

Variables are names used in PL/SQL to process items of data. The programmer selects names to use for these variables based on the following rules:

- Variables must start with a letter (A-Z).

- Variables can be optionally followed by one or more letters, numbers (0-9), or the special characters $, #, or _.

- Variables must be no longer than thirty characters.

- There can be no spaces embedded in the variable name.

With these three rules in hand, let's look at some examples. Table 7-1 shows sample variable names and determines their validity.

Variable Name	Valid?	Reason
23_skidoo	No	Must start with a letter
nature_trail	Yes	
nature-trail	No	Only special characters are $ # or _
love boat	No	Cannot contain any whitespace
a_very_insignificant_variable_name	No	Longer than 30 characters
me_____and$$$$$you	Yes	
lots_of_$$$$$$	Yes	
23	No	Must start with a letter

TABLE 7-1. *Valid and Invalid Variable Names*

Reserved Words

Think of a reserved word as being copyrighted by PL/SQL. When choosing names for variables, you cannot use these reserved words. For example, the word "loop" means something to PL/SQL, and the following segment of code would be invalid.

```
declare
    employee varchar2(30);
    loop number;
```

You are not permitted to use a reserved word as a variable name. We do not recommend it, but if you want to, you may join two reserved words together (e.g., loop_varchar2) to build a variable name. A complete list of PL/SQL reserved words can be found by entering the command **help command** while logged into SQL*Plus. SQL*Plus is discussed in Chapters 6 and 12 of this book.

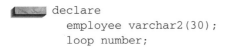

NOTE

You or your database administrator must have installed SQL*Plus online help for this command to succeed. If Oracle responds with "HELP not accessible," help is not set up.

Common Data Types

So far, we have discussed the characters that can be used when programming in PL/SQL, naming variables, and reserved words. Now we move on to the data itself. A PL/SQL program is written to manipulate and display many different types of data. Oracle, like all computer software, has data types (e.g., characters) divided into a number of sub-types. For example, some of the sub-types of the number datatype are integer (i.e., no decimal digits allowed) and decimal (i.e., number with one or more decimal digits). PL/SQL supports a wide range of data types. This section provides an overview of what you will run across most often and find most useful in your code. In this section, you will learn details on the following data types:

- varchar2
- number
- date
- Boolean

varchar2

This is a variable-length, alphanumeric data type. In PL/SQL, it can have a length of up to 32,767 bytes. The definition in the declare section is terminated by the semicolon (;), and all varchar2 definitions are done to resemble

```
variable_name varchar2(max_length);
```

where the length in parentheses must be a positive integer, as in

```
vc_field varchar2(10);
```

It may be initialized (i.e., set to its initial value) at the same time by using the syntax

```
vc_field varchar2(10) := 'STARTVALUE';
```

number

This data type can be used to represent all numeric data. The format of the declaration is

```
num_field number(precision,scale)
```

where *precision* can be from 1 to 38 characters, and *scale* represents the number of positions specified by precision that are for decimal digits. Keep in mind that the declaration

```
num_field (12,2)
```

describes a variable that can have up to ten integer digits (precision[12] - scale [2]) and up to two decimal digits.

date

This data type is used to store fixed-length date values. The declaration takes no qualifiers and is done as

```
date_field date;
```

By default, Oracle displays dates in the format DD-MON-YY; thus September 26, 1984 is displayed as 26-SEP-84. When programming with dates in PL/SQL, you must use this format.

VIP

Oracle has a date format mask DD-MON-RR that is to be used for preservation of dates entered with a four-character year. Please consult the SQL*Plus documentation set for details on using this mask to ensure Oracle does not drop the century digits as it stores dates.

Boolean

This data type is a switch that holds the status TRUE or FALSE. When you use this data type, you test its status and then can do one thing if it is true, something else if false. For example, say you were trying to see if a corporation had distributed a 10K form for its 1998 fiscal year. Using a boolean variable, it would be set to TRUE if the form had been filed.

PL/SQL Components

We now move on to a discussion of how PL/SQL is put together. Using the knowledge from the previous few sections, we can start to formulate some living and breathing code examples. PL/SQL offers the standard set of procedural techniques that developers have been using since the dawn of computers: logic, looping, and error handling mechanisms.

In this section, you will learn details on the following topics:

- Exceptions
- Control structures, including program control, if logic structures, and looping structures
- "Do nothing" construct
- declare section

Exceptions

This is the PL/SQL method of dealing with error conditions. In a real-world application, you may not find the information you are looking for when you attempt to retrieve data. Oracle carries on processing until it completes successfully or encounters an error condition. Table 7-2 lists common

Exception	Explanation
no_data_found	If a **select** statement attempts to retrieve data based on its conditions, this exception is raised when no rows satisfy the select criteria.
too_many_rows	Since each implicit cursor is capable of retrieving only one row, this exception detects the existence of more than one row. (See the "Implicit Cursors" section later in this chapter, where we define and discuss implicit cursors.)
dup_val_on_index	This exception detects an attempt to create an entry in an index whose key column values already exist. For example, suppose a billing application is keyed on the invoice number. If a program tries to create a duplicate invoice number, this exception would be raised.
value_error	This exception indicates that there has been an assignment operation where the target field is not long enough to hold the value being placed in it. For example, if the text ABCDEFGH is assigned to a variable defined as "varchar2(6)", then this exception is raised.

TABLE 7-2. *Most Common Exceptions in PL/SQL*

PL/SQL exceptions; by testing for these exceptions, you can detect errors that your PL/SQL programs raise.

Control Structures

Control structures are the heart of any programming language. Since most systems are written to handle a number of different situations, the way different conditions are detected and dealt with is the biggest part of program control. This section provides you with details on the following topics:

- Program control

- Three types of the **if** logic structure

- Four types of looping structures

Program Control

Program control is governed by the status of the variables it uses and the data it reads and writes from the database. As an example, picture yourself going to the DMV (Department of Motor Vehicles) to renew your car registration. When you enter the building, you are presented with the instructions "Sticker renewals in Room 12-G." Once you find 12-G, you receive these instructions: "Cash/certified check ONLY in lines 1 and 2. All payment types accepted in lines 3 to 15." Your decision-making process begins with the question "Why am I here?" The program control for this decision-making example is shown in Table 7-3.

if Logic Structures

When writing computer programs, situations present themselves in which you must test a condition; when it evaluates to TRUE you do one thing, when it evaluates to FALSE you do something different. PL/SQL has three **if** logic structures that allow you to test true/false conditions. In most computer programs, many lines of code will test the value of a variable and, based on its value, perform one or more operations. In everyday life, we are continually bombarded with decision-making; this is how you code decision-making with PL/SQL.

Process or Decision to Make	Next Step	
1. Here for driver's license transactions	YES=5	NO=2
2. Here for car sticker renewal	YES=7	NO=3
3. Here for driving test	YES=6	NO=4
4. Oops, in the wrong building!		13
5. Go to room 12-A and carry on desired transaction		13
6. Go to room 12-B and carry on desired transaction		13
7. Go to room 12-G		8
8. Paying by cash or certified check	YES=10	NO=9
9. Paying by check or credit card	YES=11	NO=12
10. Do cash or certified check transaction		13
11. Do check or credit card transaction		13
12. They don't take play money!		13
13. Leave building		

TABLE 7-3. *Program Control Decision-Making*

IF-THEN   This construct tests a simple condition. If the condition evaluates to TRUE, one or more lines of code are executed. If the condition evaluates to FALSE, program control is passed to the next statement after the test. The following code illustrates implementing this logic in PL/SQL.

```
if var1 > 10 then
    var2 := var1 + 20;
end if;
```

The test (in this case, >) is a relational operator we spoke about in the "PL/SQL Character Set" section of this chapter. The statement could have been coded using the following instead, with the same results.

```
if not(var1 <= 10) then
    var2 := var1 + 20;
end if;
```

You may code nested **if-then** statements as shown in the following.

```
if var1 > 10 then
    if var2 < var1 then
      var2 := var1 + 20;
    end if;
end if;
```

Notice the two **end if** parts in the previous code—one for each **if**. This leads us into two rules about implementing **if** logic in PL/SQL.

GUIDELINE 1
*Each **if** statement is followed by its own **then**. There is no semicolon (;) terminator on the line that starts with **if**.*

GUIDELINE 2
*Each **if** statement block is terminated by a matching **end if**.*

IF-THEN-ELSE This construct is similar to **if** except that when the condition evaluates to FALSE, one or more statements following the **else** are executed. The following code illustrates implementing this logic in PL/SQL.

```
if var1 > 10 then
    var2 := var1 + 20;
else
    var2 := var1 * var1;
end if;
```

Note that the same logic can be expressed the other way—adding 20 to var1 with the **else** and squaring var1 with the **if** branch of the statement.

```
if var1 <= 10 then
    var2 := var1 * var1;
else
    var2 := var1 + 20;
end if;
```

The statements can be nested, as shown in the following listing.

```
if var1 > 10 then
    var2 := var1 + 20;
else
    if var1 between 7 and 8 then
       var2 = 2* var1;
    else
       var2 := var1 * var1;
    end if;
end if;
```

This leads us to two more rules about implementing **if** logic in PL/SQL.

GUIDELINE 3
*There can be one and only one **else** with every*
***if** statement.*

GUIDELINE 4
There is no semicolon (;) terminator on the
*line starting with **else**.*

IF-THEN-ELSIF   This format is an alternative to using the nested
if-then-else construct. The code in the previous listing could be reworded
to read

```
if var1 > 10 then
    var2 := var1 + 20;
elsif var1 between 7 and 8 then
    var2 = 2* var1;
else
    var2 := var1 * var1;
end if;
```

This leads us into one final rule about implementing **if** logic in PL/SQL.

GUIDELINE 5
*There is no matching **end if** with each **elsif**.*

In this code segment, the **end if** appears to go with its preceding **elsif**:

```
if var1 > 10 then
    var2 := var1 + 20;
elsif var1 between 7 and 8 then
    var2 = 2* var1;
end if;
```

In fact, the **end if** belongs to the **if** that starts the whole block rather than the **elsif** keyword. Notice how the previous listings indent portions of the PL/SQL code to indicate to which conditions they belong.

NOTE

We recommend you use the indentation convention—it is easier to follow and understand the flow of logic and control.

Examine the following two listings, which illustrate no indentation and indentation.

```
/* Code segment 1 - hard to follow. */
if var1 < 5 then var2 := 'Y'; elsif
var1 = 5 then
var2 := 'N';
else var2 := null; end if;
/*                                    */
/* Code segment 2 - easier to follow. */
if var1 < 5 then
    var2 :=  'Y';    --Statement is controlled by
                     --first test on var1 being true
elsif var1 = 5 then
    var2 := 'N';     --Statement is controlled by
                     --second test on var1 being true
else
    var2 := null;    --Statement is controlled by second
                     --test on var1 being false
end if;
```

Using the DMV example from above, let's word the logic using PL/SQL.

```
create or replace procedure license_transaction(the_act in varchar2) as
begin
    if the_act = 'DLT' then
```

```
        12a;
    elsif the_act = 'DT' then
        12b;
    else
        12g;
    end if;
end;
/
```

Looping

Looping provides the ability to execute a process over and over again until complete. In a real-life situation, think of looping when you unload your groceries from your car—there are two loops in this activity. The first is the repetitive action of picking up one or more grocery bags and walking in your front door. The second is the repetitive whine that comes from your lethargic 16-year-old: "Why is it always me who has to help?" In general, looping is based on the logic shown in Table 7-4.

One of the problems with coding loops is making sure there is code to allow them to terminate when an exit condition has been satisfied. Unfortunately, all too many times, developers write endless loops (we have never done that, of course, but we know many who have). The best way to sum up looping and the major problems programmers may have with it is to quote from an online technology dictionary we once saw:

Definition of LOOP: See "Definition of LOOP."

Implementing loops in PL/SQL is discussed in the next few sections.

Process or Decision to Make	Next Step	
1. Set condition to enter loop (i.e., done_loop=N)	2	
2. End loop condition is true (i.e., done_loop=Y)	YES=6	NO=3
3. Process data	5	5
4. There is more data to process	YES=2	NO=5
5. Set exit condition (i.e., done_loop=Y)	2	2
6. Done processing		

TABLE 7-4. *Looping Logic*

LOOP-EXIT-END LOOP   This construct contains three parts. Study the commented code below to see how this is used.

```
cnt := 1;                 --Initialize the loop counter before
                          --        loop starts
loop                      --Part 1: Loop keyword starts the loop
   cnt := cnt + 1;        --Part 2: Incrementing the loop counter
   if cnt > 100 then      --        Testing cnt for exit
                          --        condition
       exit;              --        End loop condition met,
                          --        so get out
   end if;                --        "end-if" to match previous "if"
   ...
   ...
end loop;                 --Part 3: End loop keywords to end the
   ...                    --        loop
   ...
   ...
```

LOOP-EXIT WHEN-END LOOP   This is similar to the previous example, except the exit condition is detected differently.

```
cnt := 1;                 --Initialize the loop counter before
                          --        loop starts
loop                      --Part 1: Loop keyword starts the loop
   cnt := cnt + 1;        --Part 2: Incrementing the loop counter
   exit when cnt > 100    --        Test for exit condition by
   ...                    --        examining "cnt"
   ...
   ...
end loop;                 --Part 3: End loop keywords to end
   ...                    --        the loop
   ...
```

WHILE-LOOP-END LOOP   With this construct, the exit condition is manually set somewhere inside the loop. The test for exit condition is accomplished by the comparison in the **while** part of the loop.

```
cnt := 1;                 --Initialize the loop counter before
                          --loop starts
while cnt <= 100 loop     --Part 1: The "while" checks exit
   ...                    --condition every time before executing
   ...                    --loop
   ...                    --Part 2: Code executed inside the loop
```

```
     . . .
     cnt := cnt + 1;        --         Incrementing counter to arrive
     . . .                  --         at exit condition
end loop;                   --Part 3: End loop keywords to end the loop
     . . .
```

FOR-IN-LOOP-END LOOP   The final construct we examine allows
repetitive execution of a loop a predefined number of times. There are three
parts to the loop:

■ The **for in** portion, in which the variable to track the looping is
defined

■ The one or more statements within the loop that are executed until
the variable controlling the loop reaches the exit condition value

■ The **end loop** portion that terminates the loop

The following shows an example of how this loop mechanism can
be used:

```
for cnt in 1 .. 3 loop
   insert into tab1 values ('Still in loop',cnt);
end loop;
```

"Do Nothing" or "Null" Construct

Sometimes, especially when using **if** logic, you end up testing a condition;
when that condition is TRUE, you do nothing; when otherwise, you
perform some operation. This is handled in PL/SQL in the following way:

```
if cnt >= 90 then
   null;
else
   insert into tab1 values ('Still less than 90',cnt);
end if;
```

The **null** keyword denotes performing no operation.

The Declare Section

This part of PL/SQL blocks is where you define your variables. If you are
familiar with COBOL, this is similar to working storage. You will see the

common data types we discussed previously, plus the cursor variable type, which we cover in the next section. The following code is an example of a procedure's declare section.

```
create or replace procedure samp (parm1 in varchar2,
                                  parm2 in varchar2) as
-- This is the DECLARE section; when coding a stored object
-- the DECLARE is implied, and need not be mentioned
    accum1 number;
    accum2 number;
    h_date date := sysdate;   --Notice variables can be
                              --initialized here too.
    status_flag varchar2(1);
    mess_text varchar2(80);
    temp_buffer varchar2(1);
    cursor my_cursor is
      select ' '
        from person
       where last_name = parm1
         and sal_stat = parm2;
  begin
    ...
    ...
  end;
/
```

Cursors

PL/SQL uses cursors for management of SQL select statements. Cursors are chunks of memory allocated to process these statements. Sometimes you define the cursor manually, and other times you let PL/SQL define the cursor. A cursor is defined like any other PL/SQL variable and must conform to the same naming conventions. In this section, you will learn about both explicit and implicit PL/SQL cursors. Using explicit cursors, you must declare the cursor, open it before using it, and close it when it is no longer needed. Using implicit cursors, you do none of these; you simply code your select statement and let PL/SQL handle the cursor on its behalf.

Explicit Cursors

This technique defines a cursor as part of the **declare** section. The SQL statement defined must contain only **select** statements—there can be no

insert, **update**, or **delete** keywords used. In this section, you will learn how to do the following:

- Name your explicit cursors
- Prepare (or open) an explicit cursor for use
- Fetch data using an explicit cursor
- Release the cursor's memory when done with it

The listing at the end of the previous section shows explicit cursor definition. When using explicit cursors, you always code four components:

- The cursor is defined in the **declare** section of your PL/SQL block.
- The cursor is opened after the initial **begin** in the PL/SQL block.
- The cursor is fetched into one or more variables. There must be the same number of receiving variables in the **fetch** as there are columns in the cursor's **select** list. For example, look at the following cursor definition:

```
declare cursor mycur is
   select first_name, last_name, ssn
     from person
    where pin = passed_pin;
```

- The cursor is closed after you are done using it.

The following listing puts these four parts together.

```
   ...
   ...
declare
   fname          varchar2(10),
   lname          varchar2(30),
   ssec_num       varchar2(8),
   cursor mycur is
     select first_name, last_name, ssn
       from person
      where pin = pin_in;
begin;
   open mycur;
   fetch mycur into fname, lname, ssec_num;
```

```
  while mycur%found loop
    if ssec_num is null then
        insert into e_msg values (pin_in,'No SSNUM');
    else
        insert into e_tab values (pin_in,sysdate);
    end if;
    fetch mycur into fname, lname, ssec_num;
  end loop;
  close mycur;
end;
...
...
/
```

Note the following points about explicit cursors:

■ The success or failure of the cursor (we call it "mycur" here) is determined by testing either "%found" or "%notfound." The cursor returns success if it retrieves a row from the database based on its selection criteria. This test must be done before the cursor is closed.

```
if mycur%found then
    ...
end if;
if mycur%notfound then
    ...
    ...
end if;
...
...
fetch mycur into temp_buffer;
close mycur;
--This will not work since the cursor has been closed.
if mycur%found then
    ...
    ...
end if;
```

■ If a cursor is repeatedly fetched in a loop construct, a running total of the number of rows retrieved so far can be found in the "%rowcount" system variable.

```
while counter < 100 loop
   fetch mycur into temp_buffer;
   if mycur%rowcount <= 50 then
      ...
   else
      ...
   end if;
counter := counter+1;
end loop;
```

■ All cursors must be fetched into one or more variables (depending on the number of columns in the cursor's select list). The following is not legal:

```
open mycur;
fetch mycur;
if mycur%found then
   ...
```

■ The target variable(s) of the cursor must match the columns in the table being selected in data type:

```
-- This is correct
--
declare
  cursor mycur is
    select pin,          /* pin is numeric         */
           last_name     /* last_name is character */
      from person
     where pin = pin_in;
    field1 varchar2(10);
    field2 number;
begin
  open mycur;
  fetch mycur into field2, field1;
  ...
-- This is incorrect
--
declare
  cursor mycur is
    select pin,          /* pin is numeric              */
           last_name     /* last_name is character data */
      from person
     where pin = pin_in;
```

```
       field1 varchar2(10);
       field2 number;
    begin
     open mycur;
     fetch mycur into field1, field2;
     ...
```

You will receive an error if you try to open a cursor that is already open or close a cursor that has already been closed. You can check the status of a cursor using "%isopen", which evaluates to either TRUE or FALSE.

```
...
...
if mycur%isopen = 'TRUE' then
   null;
else
   open mycur;
end if;
```

If a PL/SQL block uses more than one cursor, each cursor must have a unique name.

Implicit Cursors

The following code segment uses implicit cursors. You place your **select** statement inline and PL/SQL handles cursor definition implicitly. There is no declaration of implicit cursors in the declare section.

```
...
begin
  if counter >= 20 then
     select last_name
       into lname from person
      where pin = pin_in;
     ...
  else
     ...
  end if;
end;
/
```

Note the following points that pertain to using implicit cursors:

■ There must be an **into** with each implicit cursor.

```
--This is incorrect
if this_value > 0 then
   select count(*) from person;
end if;
--This is OK
if this_value > 0 then
   select count(*) into cnter from person;
end if;
```

■ As with explicit cursors, the variables that receive data with the **into** keyword must be the same data type as the column(s) in the table.

■ Implicit cursors expect only one row to be returned. You must examine some of the exceptions, as discussed in Table 7-2. The most common ones to look out for are "no_data_found" and "too_many_rows."

```
...
if counter >= 10 then
   begin
     select age into person where pin = pin_value;
     exception
       when too_many_rows then
             insert into tabA values (pin_value, sysdate);
       when no_data_found then
             null;
   end;
end if;
...
...
/
```

Which Approach to Use

We find using explicit cursors more efficient and recommend you use them for the following reasons:

■ The success or failure is found by examining the PL/SQL system variable "%found" or "%notfound". Code segments that use explicit cursors simply test one of these variables to detect success or failure of a select statement using an explicit cursor.

■ Since the explicit cursor is manually defined in the **declare** section, the PL/SQL block can be more structured (the definitions are done in one place, and the code that uses the cursor is in another).

■ The best programmers use them!

PL/SQL Tables

Interesting enough, when looking at relational database theory, query results assembled by a join of two or more tables is a table itself. Often one needs to loop through a set of data using PL/SQL and compare values against a set of lookup values. PL/SQL allows one to load these lookup tables into memory, thereby reducing the I/O operations required to reference the lookup table values.

In many places throughout this book we have spoken of data types—character, alphanumeric, and numeric, to name a few. PL/SQL tables are declared with a user-defined data type **table**. Inspect the following code to see how a table of states of the union would be loaded for lookup purposes.

```
set serveroutput on size 100000
declare
   state_rec person%rowtype; -- state_rec has same makeup
                              -- as a row from the STATE table
 type just_names is table of state.name%type
        index by binary_integer; -- the local just_names
                                 -- table contains
   i binary_integer := 0;       -- "rows" with the same
                                 -- makeup as each row in STATE
   nametab just_names;
   begin
      for state_rec in    -- notice how the rows are
                          -- fetched" from STATE by this query
                          -- embedded in the FOR loop
        (select name from state) loop
      i := i+1;
      nametab(i) := state_rec.name;
      dbms_output.put_line (nametab(i));
    end loop;
```

```
   end;
/
```

The output for the first few rows of names read from the STATE table would be

```
Alaska
Alabama
Arkansas
```

NOTE
PL/SQL tables are supported with release 2.3 of PL/SQL, but not by earlier versions.

The Look of PL/SQL

PL/SQL is a mixture of SQL*Plus and procedural code. Comment text is delimited by the slash-asterisk combination (/* comment */) or two dashes (--), as in the following:

```
begin
   declare tfield varchar2(20);
   begin
       select desc
         into tfield
         from prod              /*  PROD is a central lookup */
         where pnum = 'FR4512';  /*  table owned by PLANNING  */
   end;
end;
/
```

or

```
begin
   declare tfield varchar2(20);
   begin
       select desc
         into tfield
         from prod              --PROD is a central lookup
         where pnum = 'FR4512';  --table owned by PLANNING
   end;
end;
/
```

Inspect the following PL/SQL code segment and study the comments. They will illustrate how the pieces of PL/SQL go together.

```
create or replace procedure do_trav
                (class_in in varchar2) as
   cursor mycur is          --This is the start of a PL/SQL block
      select count(*)        --Local variables and explicit
        from person          --cursors are defined here
      where class_code = class_in;
      cnt number;
   begin                        --This inner "begin" is start of the
      open mycur;               --code executed when the PL/SQL is
      fetch mycur into cnt;  --invoked.
      while mycur%found loop
         if cnt > 100 then                 --"If" procedural logic
            insert into trav_audit (class_in,cnt)
                  values (classin,cnt);   --An implicit cursor
         else
            update trav_audit       --Inline update statement
                  set cnt = cnt+1 where classin = class_in;
         end if;                --"If" statement ends with "end-if"
         fetch mycur into cnt;
      end loop;
   end;                         --Each "begin" terminated by
end;                            --matching "end" keyword
/                               --"/" terminates the PL/SQL block
```

Compilation Errors

When a PL/SQL block is passed to Oracle for compilation, you may be informed of some errors. As we indicate in the previous listing, the slash (/) terminates the PL/SQL block and passes the code to Oracle. Inspect the following error-ridden compilation. Note that the errors raised by a PL/SQL compilation are not displayed until you code the statement **sho errors**.

```
create or replace procedure temp (count in number) as
   begin
      declare cursor mycur is
        select count(*) from emp;
      begin;
        open mycur;
        fetch mycur;
      end;
```

```
 end;
/
Warning: Procedure created with compilation errors.
SQL> sho errors
Errors for PROCEDURE TEMP:
LINE/COL ERROR
-------- -----------------------------------------------------
1/17     PLS-00103: Encountered the symbol "COUNT" when
         expecting one of the following:
         <an identifier> <a double-quoted string>
         Replacing "COUNT" with "<an identifier>".
5/8      PLS-00103: Encountered the symbol ";" when
         expecting one of the following:
         begin declare exit for goto if loop mod null
         pragma raise
         return select update while <an identifier> etc.
         exit was inserted before ";" to continue.
7/16     PLS-00103: Encountered the symbol ";" when
         expecting one of the following:
         . into
         Resuming parse at line 7, column 16.
```

As your experience with PL/SQL increases, you will become quite adept at debugging your code based on the output of this **sho errors** command.

Code Examples

We will now present three simple requirements and show how to do them using PL/SQL. The comments embedded in these examples illustrate some of the points we have made throughout this chapter.

Example #1

Let's see how to figure out a person's date of birth by using his or her social security number. The code is commented to illustrate how PL/SQL works. We are using an implicit PL/SQL cursor.

```
create or replace procedure get_dob (ss_num varchar2,
                                dob out date) as
  begin                          -- Start of program
    select birth_date            -- Implicit cursor
      into dob                   -- DOB and BIRTH_DATE must
      from person                --      be same data type
```

```
       where soc_sec_num = ss_num;
     exception when no_data_found then
        error_notify (ss_num);           -- Call another procedure
  end;
end;
/
```

Let's study a few concepts based on the code in this listing:

- The line that defines the procedure has two variables enclosed in parentheses. The first contains the value of the social security number of the person whose date of birth we require. The second will receive the date and pass it back to the user that invoked the procedure.

- Notice the semicolon (;) terminators are missing on the **begin** and the **create or replace procedure as** lines of code. These two lines never have a semicolon.

- The success or failure of a cursor is determined using the "%found" and "%notfound" words.

- The cursor is closed after it is used. You must examine the success or failure of a cursor before closing it.

Example #2

This example shows how to accomplish exactly the same result as above, but using a function instead of a procedure. A function can receive as many variables as possible, but returns only one value, as you will see in the listing. The code is similar, but reads differently from the procedure.

```
create or replace function get_dob (ss_num varchar2) return
                    date is
   birthd date;              --Local date field to hold birth date
   begin
     begin
       select dob
         into birthd      --"into" mandatory for implicit cursor
         from person
       where soc_sec_num = ss_num;
       exception
         when no_data_found
```

```
        begin
          error_notify (ss_num);       -- Call another procedure
          birthd := trunc(sysdate);
        end;
      when others then null;
  end;
  return birthd;
 end;
end;                         --Termination of outer block
/                            --"/" terminates PL/SQL block
```

Let's study a few concepts based on the code in this listing:

- Since we are using an implicit cursor, we do not define it in the **declare** section of the procedure.

- The error situation "no_data_found" is the implicit cursor method of doing what "%found" or "%notfound" does with explicit cursors.

- The "when_others" error check is a bucket that traps all other types of errors and returns control to the code that invoked the procedure.

Example #3

As area codes are split into pieces, some numbers stay with the old code, and some are moved to the new. Let's look at a procedure that loops through a list of the first three numbers of a phone number for a specified area code and changes the area code for those exchanges that do not have a row in STATIC_EXC (exchanges with a row in this table are to keep the old area code).

```
create or replace procedure
          ac_switch (oac number,
                     nac number) as
  l_pref_3           number(3);      -- Implicit DECLARE
  l_change_sw        number(3);
  l_change_it        varchar2(1);
  cursor mycur is
    select distinct pref_3
      from phone_nbr
     where are_code = oac;
  begin                              -- Main processing
    open mycur;                      -- Open before fetch
    fetch mycur into l_pref_3;
```

```
        while mycur%found loop            -- Start of loop
          change_it := 'N';
          begin                           -- "begin" of select
            select ''                     -- with exception block
              into l_change_sw
              from static_exc
             where area_code = oac
               and pref_3 = l_pref_3;
            exception
              when no_data_found then     -- Check success of select
                   l_change_it := 'Y';
          end;                            -- Close of select/exception
          if l_change_it = 'Y' then
            update phone_nbr
               set area_code = nac
             where area_code = oac
               and pref_3 = l_pref_3;
          end if;
          fetch mycur into l_pref_3;
        end loop;                         -- End of loop
      end;                                -- End of Main processing
    end;                                  -- End of Procedure
    /
```

Let's study a few concepts based on the code in this listing:

- Note the use of the word **distinct** when the cursor is declared. Some readers may be familiar with the keyword **unique** as well; it cannot be used in PL/SQL, only SQL*Plus.

- The cursor is opened before data is fetched; note how there is one receiving field with the **fetch into**, the same as the one sending field mentioned in the cursor.

- The **select** statement that references STATIC_EXC is enclosed in its own inner **begin end** block. This is done when you need to check one or more exceptions in an implicit cursor.

What's Next

Starting with version 6, Oracle made a commitment to PL/SQL, and it has evolved into the standard programming language in all Oracle tools. We have discussed the basics of PL/SQL and shown you some bottom-line functionality and features to get you started. Work with PL/SQL, and in little or no time, you will find yourself comfortable with a remarkably powerful programming language. As you read on and look at Oracle Forms and Oracle Reports, you will see how tool PL/SQL is used.

CHAPTER

8

Oracle Forms

n this chapter, we will further round out your knowledge of developer basics. Using Oracle Forms, programmers create data entry and query screens with a mouse-driven user interface.

NOTE

We feature version 4.5 of Oracle Forms; this is an established product, popular in the development community and what readers are familiar with. There is widespread acceptance of release 4.5 as a solid application development environment, and a subsequent version of this work will feature 5.0.

There is a gamut of GUI (graphical user interface) products on the market; Oracle Forms, part of the Developer 2000 suite of products, is Oracle's offering. When you are done reading this chapter, you will know about the following topics:

■ What Oracle Forms is and what it can do for you

■ Hardware required to run Oracle Forms

■ How to install Oracle Forms

■ How to prepare your PC for running Oracle Forms

■ Setting preferences in Oracle Forms

■ How to build a few basic Oracle Forms screens

■ Screen formatting in Oracle Forms

■ How to use Oracle Forms Runtime

TIP

Learn the procedures and concepts presented in each sample exercise in this chapter one at a time. Before moving on to the next exercise, practice what you have learned. While the forms we build are simple, they illustrate fundamental Oracle Forms concepts.

Terminology

The following definitions will arm you with the technical jargon you need to make it through this chapter.

■ *ODBC*, or Open Database Connectivity, software allows communication between one vendor's data source (e.g., Oracle Server) and another vendor's tools (e.g., Powersoft's PowerBuilder). Using ODBC, you can use an Oracle Forms-based data entry screen to manipulate data stored in a non-Oracle database.

■ *OLE2*, or Object Linking and Embedding version 2, allows dynamic sharing of objects between two OLE2-compliant software programs. Using Microsoft Word 6 for Windows (OLE2-compliant), you can embed a Microsoft Excel (OLE2-compliant) spreadsheet in a document; when the contents of the spreadsheet change, the OLE2 link gives Word immediate access to the changes.

■ *Inheritance* allows the creation of objects in Oracle Forms that take on the look and feel and processing associated with other objects. Using inheritance, changes made to the referenced object affect the objects that have inherited its properties.

■ *WYSIWYG* stands for "what you see is what you get." In all GUI products, the look of your information on the screen is exactly the way printed output will look. For example, if you bold text in a WYSIWYG word processor, the text is bolded on the screen.

■ A *block* is a container for items in Oracle Forms. Blocks can be related to tables in the database.

■ *Interface items* are objects in Oracle Forms with which the operator interacts. Enterable fields, push buttons, check boxes, and radio buttons are all interface items.

■ Oracle Forms uses *locking* to preserve the integrity of data. Locking ensures that more than one user is not allowed to modify the same item of information at the same time.

■ When working with Microsoft Windows 3.x, the *control box* is in the upper-left corner of the screen. Double-clicking on a control box closes the window to which it belongs.

What Is Oracle Forms?

Oracle Forms version 4.5 is part of Developer 2000, an integrated software development and runtime environment with a Microsoft Windows look and feel. All Developer 2000 tools are integrated, and all run primarily against an Oracle7 database.

Oracle Forms is a feature-rich application building tool that produces production-quality screens utilizing data stored in a database. You can embed graphics, sound, video, word processing documents, and spreadsheets through the use of OLE2. You can embed objects from Excel or 1-2-3 for Windows in your Oracle Forms screens. Oracle Forms can also share data with other Developer 2000 tools through a special module. Its predecessor, SQL*Forms 3.0, bundled with version 6 of Oracle, was a character-based screen environment. Oracle has emphasized programmer productivity with Developer 2000: the Designer is a fully mouse-driven interface, with the ability to do most of the development without a great deal of coding. In this chapter, we will discuss the two main components of Oracle Forms: Oracle Forms Designer and Oracle Forms Runtime.

Hardware Requirements to Run Oracle Forms

The following minimum configuration is required to use Oracle Forms. The list is exactly the same as the one presented in Chapter 9, where we discuss Oracle Reports.

- A 386 or stronger central processing unit (CPU), though a 486 or Pentium is preferred

- At least 60 megabytes (or 61,440,000 bytes) of available disk space

- A 40MHz or faster processor—speeds of 66 or better are preferable

- At least 8MB (megabytes) of extended memory for Oracle Forms Runtime and 16MB for Oracle Forms Designer

- MS-DOS or PC-DOS versions 5 or 6, or DR-DOS version 6 or higher

- MS Windows 3.1 or Windows 95

We recommend that you install a CD-ROM drive on your machine, if you do not already have one. Oracle is moving toward this format as its default distribution medium mostly because the huge amounts of data that fit easily on a fraction of a CD-ROM (each holds 600MB, or 638,976,000 bytes) could easily take up a very large number of 3.5-inch diskettes. When Personal Oracle7 was in its beta, or testing stage, one of our clients had over 86MB of Oracle and Oracle-support software on a 486 PC. Had they installed from diskette, that could have easily been over 60 diskettes!

How to Install Oracle Forms

As with the rest of the Oracle products for Windows, installation is done from the Oracle installer (referred to as orainst in Chapter 5). To begin installation, click on the Oracle Installer icon in the Oracle group of the Windows Program Manager. You will be presented with the Oracle Installer startup screen, shown in Figure 8-1.

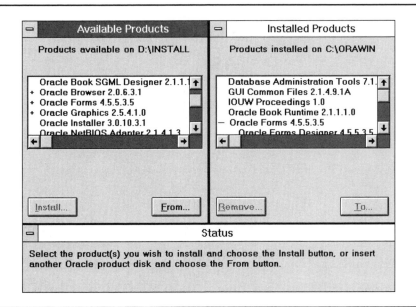

FIGURE 8-1. *Oracle installer startup screen*

Notice the two boxes on the screen in Figure 8-1, called Available Products and Installed Products. If Oracle Forms is not one of the available products, scroll through the list until it appears. Once in view, there may be a plus (+) sign beside the Oracle Forms name. This indicates that there are components that can be installed together or separately. Click on the plus (+) sign to expand the component list, as shown in Figure 8-2. While that component list is displayed, you may install each Oracle Forms component separately.

When you are ready to start installing, click on Install. During the installation process that follows, you will be asked to designate a directory for the product. Oracle suggests placing it in \orawin\forms45. Unless you are already using that directory for something else, accept it as is. After selecting the directory for the installation, the installer goes about its work setting up Oracle Forms. When the installation terminates (be patient—it can take upwards of 20 minutes, or longer if you are installing from diskette), you will see the product in the Installed Products list on the right of the installer screen. You are now ready to use Oracle Forms. The

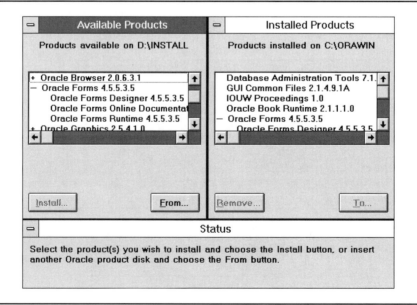

FIGURE 8-2. *Oracle Forms component list expansion*

installer will also create a CDE2 Demos program group. Many of the forms Oracle provides as demos contain code that illustrates how to use the many new features of Oracle Forms 4.5. When orainst finishes, double-click on the installer's control box to return to the Windows Program Manager.

NOTE
Even though the products are called part of Developer 2000, the program groups created when they are installed are called CDE2 Tools and CDE2 Demos.

Preparing Your PC to Run Oracle Forms

The following must be done before running Oracle Forms:

■ You must have access to a local or remote Oracle7 database. To access a remote database, you or your database administrator must have installed SQL*Net and been able to successfully connect to the database.

■ You must have already loaded your network software if you are accessing a remote database. If you are using a local Personal Oracle7 database, this is not necessary.

Oracle Forms Designer

Oracle Forms Designer is where the building of the application takes place. Four components make up the interface to Oracle Forms Designer: the Object Navigator, the property sheet, the layout editor, and the PL/SQL editor. The most important of the four is the Object Navigator. This navigator is shared by all of the Developer 2000 tools (e.g., Oracle Reports, discussed in Chapter 9). Learning to utilize its functions will allow for a smooth transition to the other tools.

The single property sheet is a new idea in Oracle Forms 4.5 (Oracle Forms 4.0 had a separate sheet for each object type). Object attributes can be added, modified, or removed using the Oracle Forms 4.5 property sheet.

The layout editor is now fully WYSIWYG. This is where you place all of the objects for the particular screen that is being developed. The PL/SQL editor is where all PL/SQL code can be added, modified, removed, and compiled. All work is done in the PL/SQL editor regardless of the type of PL/SQL object you are working with (i.e., a trigger, a stored procedure, or a library).

Before we dive into Oracle Forms, let's look at the assortment of buttons and tools you will be using in this chapter. Oracle Forms calls the collection of buttons along the top of its screen the toolbar and the collection of tools down the side of its screen the tool palette. Figure 8-3 shows the various buttons that we will be using throughout this chapter. There are many more buttons and tools you can use with Oracle Forms Designer than we will discuss in this chapter. We will only touch on the ones we will be using.

Object Navigator

The Object Navigator is used primarily to move quickly between the other three interfaces. Its other purpose is drag-and-drop application

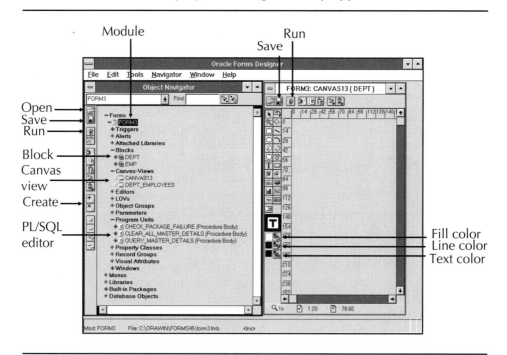

FIGURE 8-3. *Oracle Forms buttons*

development. Utilizing the Object Navigator, you can access objects and libraries both on disk and in the database. By dragging these objects into your Oracle Forms Designer workspace, you have added their functionality to your form.

Canvas-view

Canvas-views are where you design the look and feel of your screens; this is what the client or user is going to interact with. If the layout of a canvas (screen) is pleasing to the eye, you are halfway there. While working with canvas-views, you can control the application's color, size, font, data access, and style. Think of a canvas-view as a layout editor where you paint your application's objects, with the entire screen as your canvas. Figure 8-4 shows a canvas-view.

You create a new canvas-view in the Object Navigator by highlighting Canvas-Views and clicking on the Create tool on the Object Navigator tool palette. You control what type of canvas it will be in the canvas-view property sheet. The property sheet can be reached in the Object Navigator

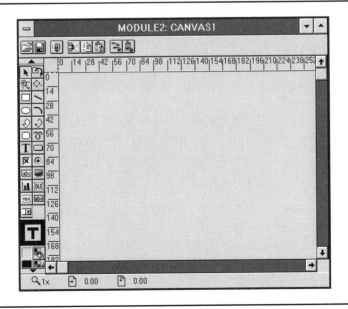

FIGURE 8-4. *A typical canvas view*

by highlighting Canvas-Views and then choosing Tools from the main menu and then Properties.

Property Sheet

The property sheet is where you set object attributes. There are a lot of different looks that you can achieve, and most of them are determined by individual tastes. It is very important to carefully plan out what the screens are going to look like at the beginning of a project, especially when several developers are involved. Figure 8-5 shows a property sheet for the module MODULE1. Here you define characteristics of modules, such as the module's title and whether buttons used in the module should have a raised 3-D visual effect. The nature of the characteristics you define using a property sheet depends on what type of object is being designed (i.e., property sheet for a module, a canvas-view, or a block).

As you move through the entries on most property sheets, you will find three ways to change properties:

- Some properties are set by typing information into the text entry box that is highlighted when the property is selected. The Name property shown in Figure 8-5 is set this way.

- Some properties are set by clicking on the down arrow that appears when the property is highlighted. A drop-down menu appears from which the property characteristics are chosen. The Class property shown in Figure 8-5 is set this way.

- Some properties are set by clicking on a More button that appears when the property is highlighted. A dialog box appears within which the property characteristics are set. The Coordinate property shown in Figure 8-5 is set this way.

VIP

When you type in an entry for a property (e.g., the name of a canvas-view), press ENTER to update the value beside the property in the property sheet. Leave the property sheet by double-clicking on the control box.

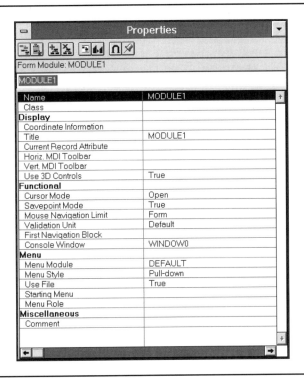

FIGURE 8-5.   *Property sheet*

PL/SQL Editor

The PL/SQL editor is where the application will take on its specialized functionality. You can control exactly what the program can and cannot do based on the work you do in this editor. This is where all of the form's triggers and procedures are edited and compiled. It is also where database procedures can be accessed, modified, and compiled. The PL/SQL editor is accessed by double-clicking on the PL/SQL Editor button on the Object Navigator. A PL/SQL editor screen is shown in Figure 8-6.

NOTE
If there is a plus (+) sign beside Program Units on the Object Navigator, double-click on it to display any defined program units and their PL/SQL editor buttons.

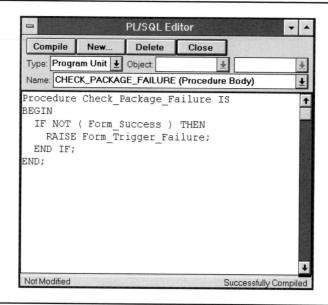

FIGURE 8-6. PL/SQL editor screen

Now that we have had a look at the tools we will be using in this chapter's exercises, as well as the Object Navigator, canvas-views, property sheet, and PL/SQL, let's discuss setting options in Oracle Forms. You can customize the look and feel of Oracle Forms according to your preferences by setting options.

Setting Options

The first area to look at is setting options. This is where you set aspects of Oracle Reports Designer to suit your individual tastes. The menu at the top of the Designer screen is where you start:

    1. Click on Tools on the menu at the top of the screen. This menu is available anywhere from any Oracle Forms screen.

2. Click on Options to open the dialog box shown in Figure 8-7. There are two folders in this box, one to set Designer options, the other to set Runtime. Figure 8-7 shows the default settings for Designer Options when the dialog box appears for the first time. Figure 8-8 shows the Runtime options folder. In Figure 8-7, notice how Generate Before Run, Run Module Asynchronously, and File are selected. These offer the most flexibility in Oracle Forms, and are usually left as is.

NOTE
We recommend using the Designer and Runtime option defaults. They reflect the most common preferences, and can be changed anytime by visiting this dialog box.

3. Click on OK to return to the Object Navigator.

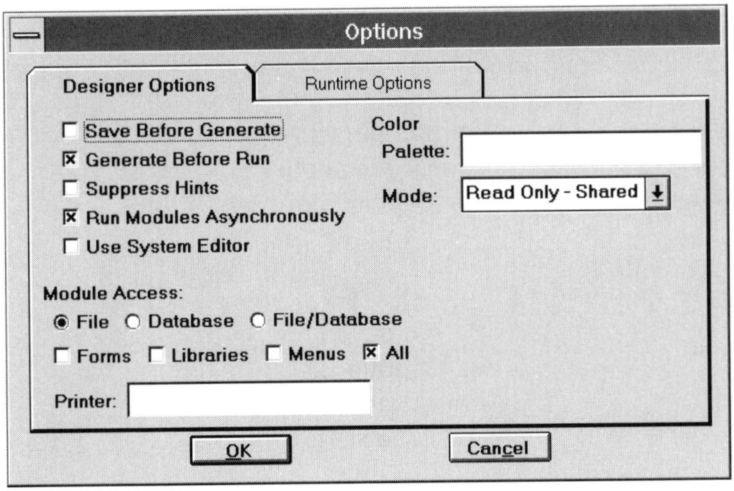

FIGURE 8-7. *Designer options folder*

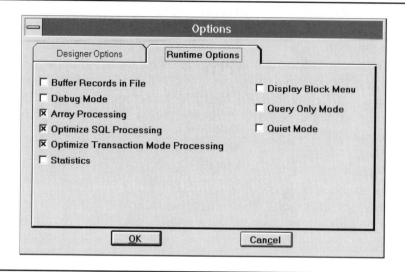

FIGURE 8-8. *Runtime options folder*

NOTE
The default settings in the Options dialog box will suit your needs most of the time. When you run Oracle Forms programs right from the Designer, you may wish to visit the Options dialog box and make some changes in the Runtime Options folder.

Working with Oracle Forms Files

In this section, you will learn how to do the following:

■ Create and save a new form

■ Open an existing form

■ Change the name of a form

After double-clicking on the Oracle Forms Designer icon in the Windows Program Manager, Oracle Forms Designer will appear. The form name MODULE1 will be highlighted in the Object Navigator. At this point, you can open an existing form or begin working on a new one.

Creating a New Form

After loading Oracle Forms Designer, you are ready to begin creating an application. By default, Designer starts with a new form ready to go (with the name MODULE1). If you have done some work on a form in the Designer, and wish to start a new form, select New on the File menu at the top of the screen. Alternatively, you can highlight the text Forms at the top of the Object Navigator, and double-click on the Create tool on the Object Navigator tool palette.

TIP

After loading Oracle Forms, if you immediately open an existing form, the MODULE1 form created by default is removed automatically.

Opening an Existing Form

To open a form that already exists, select Open on the File menu at the top of the screen. The Open dialog box appears, as shown in Figure 8-9. Alternatively, you may click on the Open tool on the Object Navigator tool palette. Double-click on a filename, or click on a filename to highlight it, then click on OK to open the report. The title of the form in the Object Navigator will change to show the name of the form you have opened.

TIP

The quickest way to open a form is to use the shortcut key CTRL-O. This brings up the same dialog box shown in Figure 8-9.

Saving a Form

To save a form you have been working with, select Save on the File menu at the top of the screen, or click on the Save tool on the Object Navigator tool palette. If this is the first time you are saving a form, Oracle Forms displays the Save As dialog box shown in Figure 8-10. Enter a filename for the report, then click on the OK button to complete the save. The name of

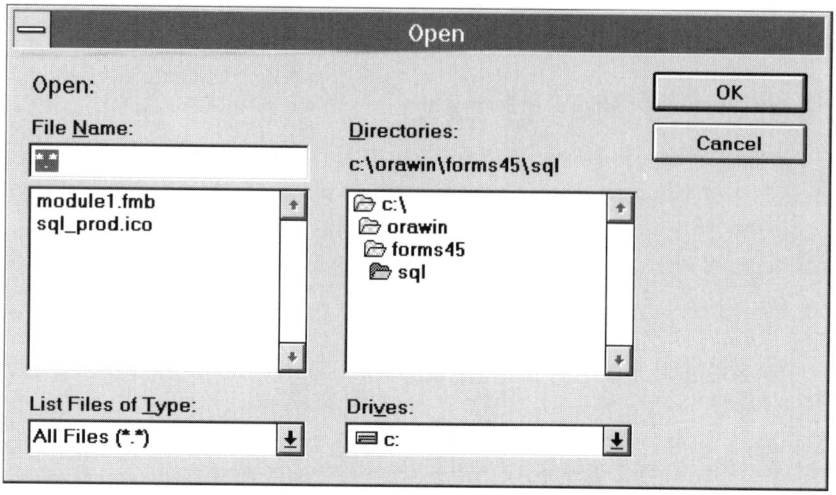

FIGURE 8-9. *Open dialog box*

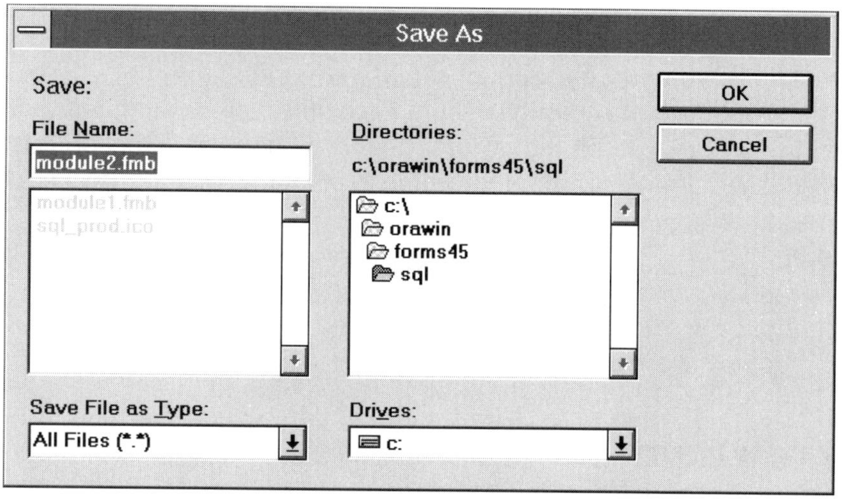

FIGURE 8-10. *Save As dialog box*

the file you enter must conform to DOS file naming conventions. If Oracle Forms knows the name of the form you are working with (i.e., you have saved it previously in the same session), it saves the form without opening the Save As dialog box.

TIP
The quickest way to save a form is to use the shortcut key CTRL-S. If Oracle does not know the name of the report you are saving, it will open up the dialog box shown in Figure 8-10.

Changing the Name of a Form

If you wish to change the name of a form, select Save As on the File menu at the top of the screen. Oracle Forms brings up the dialog box shown in Figure 8-10. Enter a new filename, then click on the OK button to complete the save using the new name.

The Right Mouse Button

The right mouse button has special meaning for Oracle Forms. It allows quick access to the layout editor (also referred to as canvas-view), PL/SQL editor, and property sheets. For example, when you click on the right button while the mouse cursor is on the Object Navigator, a menu appears, as shown in Figure 8-11.

In addition, clicking the right button while the mouse cursor is on a canvas-view shows the menu in Figure 8-12. Notice how the available options in these menus are context-sensitive: the Cut, Copy, and Layout Editor options are inactive.

NOTE
If you have your mouse defined with the right button as the primary one, you would use the left button to accomplish what we discuss in this section. Most mouse software allows you to redefine the two mouse buttons.

Let's now move on to discuss the quickest way to start building forms with Oracle Forms Designer.

Cut	Ctrl+X
Copy	Ctrl+C
Paste	Ctrl+V
Properties...	
Layout Editor...	
PL/SQL Editor...	
Help	

FIGURE 8-11. *Right mouse button menu on Object navigator*

Default Block Facility

When you're just beginning to use Oracle Forms, there are some quick ways to get your hands dirty (i.e., define a form and do some programming). Within the New Block function, you have the ability to create a default block. All items used in Oracle Forms, whether they come from a table in the database or not, must be in a block. To define a new block, select New Block from the Tools menu at the top of the screen. A

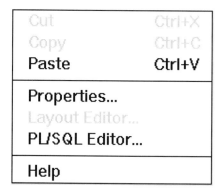

FIGURE 8-12. *Right mouse button on canvas-view*

dialog box is brought up, as shown in Figure 8-13. There are four areas of control in this dialog box:

- **General folder**   Here is where you specify a name for the block, a table (if any) of the block references, and a canvas-view the block belongs to.

- **Items folder**   Here is where fields can be selected and their basic attributes can be defined, such as Label, Width, and Object Type. The Type is chosen from a drop-down list shown in Figure 8-14. The list contains Windows-specific types, such as Radio Group and Check Box.

- **Layout folder**   Here is where you define whether the fields should be Tabular (for multi-record blocks) or Form (for single-record blocks). You also set the orientation of the records (vertical or horizontal), the space left between fields, and the number of records to display. This is where you set some of the familiar dialog box features in Windows, such as whether the block should have a scroll bar and whether Oracle Forms should create an additional block with VCR-style buttons for executing standard navigation and query functions.

- **Master/Detail folder**   Here is where you define relationships between blocks (we will go into detail about these relationships in Exercises #2 and #3 in this chapter).

Hands-On Experience

Enough said! Let's build a few simple forms from scratch to illustrate how to develop screens with Oracle Forms. For these forms, we are accessing a Personal Oracle7 database using some of the tables delivered with the software, belonging to the Oracle user *scott* whose password is *tiger*.

Exercise #1

In this exercise, we will start from the beginning and work through some important steps in creating a new form. We will show you how to do the following:

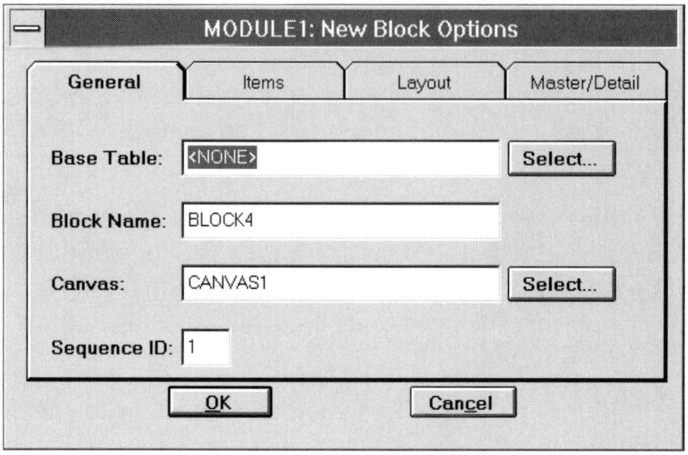

FIGURE 8-13. *New Block Options dialog box*

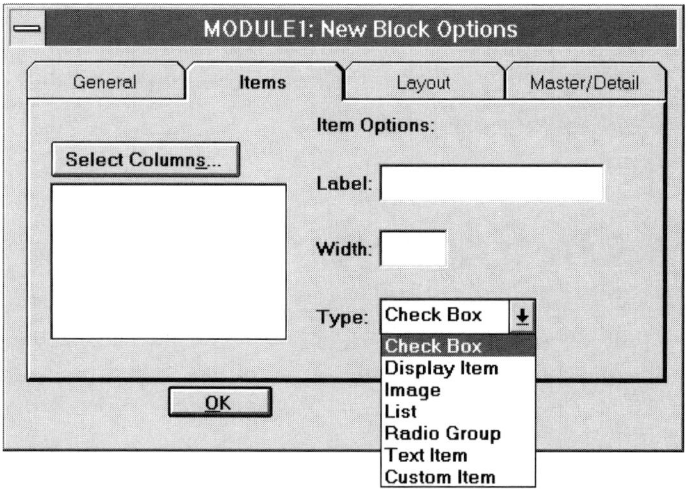

FIGURE 8-14. *Object Type drop-down list*

- Create a window

- Create a content canvas-view

- Create a default block, then customize some of the item attributes

- Save and run the form

When Oracle Forms starts up, it automatically creates a new form and window to start working with. Let's get started by performing the following steps:

1. Click on Windows in the Object Navigator. The plus (+) sign in front of the Windows branch indicates that there are lower levels that can be expanded. Click on the plus sign to expose WINDOW0.

2. Change the name of the new window by highlighting the name WINDOW0, and changing it to EMPLOYEE. You have just created your first window (fun, eh?).

3. Create a canvas-view on which to put your first block. Double-click on the plus sign beside Canvas-Views on the Object Navigator. Oracle Forms creates the initial canvas-view and calls it CANVAS1. Again, you want to change this name to something more meaningful, so click once on the highlighted name and change it to EMPLOYEE. By utilizing these same names, you are quickly able to determine where all of the objects are located.

4. You are now ready to create your first block. Select New Block on the Tools menu at the top of the screen. This brings up the New Block Options dialog box we first saw in Figure 8-13.

TIP
The New Block Options dialog box can also be brought up by clicking on Blocks in the Object Navigator, then clicking on the Create tool on the Object Navigator's tool palette.

5. Click on the General tab, then enter **emp** in the Base Table text box. Tab to the Block Name text box, and emp should appear in the Block Name text box. Since there is only one canvas-view defined, Oracle Forms places the text EMPLOYEE in the Canvas text box.

6. Click on the Items tab, then click on the Select Columns button. You will be asked to connect to the Personal Oracle7 database. Enter the user name **scott** and the password **tiger**.

7. When connected, Oracle Forms will bring up all the columns in the emp table with a plus sign in front of each. To deselect a column (i.e., not use it in the block) in the Items folder, double-click in its name or, while the column is highlighted, click on the Include check box to make the "x" disappear. Set the width for the hiredate column to 40 and change its Label to Hired. Set the width for the sal column to 40, and change its Label to Salary.

8. Click on the Layout tab. Click on the arrow beside Style, and choose Form from the drop-down list that appears.

9. Accept the block you have just defined by clicking on the OK button. Your canvas-view looks like the screen in Figure 8-15.

VIP
Sometimes your canvas-view does not appear when you close the New Block dialog box. If this happens, double-click on the Canvas-View button on the Object Navigator to bring up the screen shown in Figure 8-15.

10. Save the form by pressing CTRL-S to open the Save As dialog box. Enter the name **form1**, then click on OK.

NOTE
When we discussed Designer Options earlier in the "Setting Options" section, we accepted a Designer default by telling Oracle Forms to Generate Before Run. This is why we do not have to generate here.

11. Press CTRL-R to run the form. When the form appears, select Execute from the Query menu, then select Execute on the menu at the top of the screen to bring up data, as shown in Figure 8-16. Click on the control box in the Oracle Forms 4.5 (Runform) window to return to the Designer.

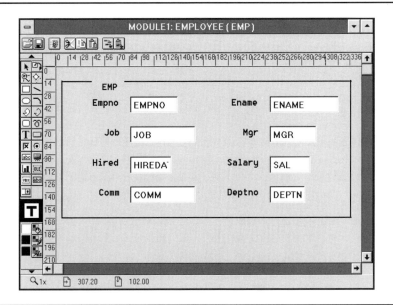

FIGURE 8-15. *Completed employee canvas-view*

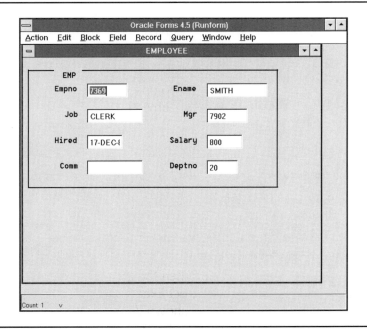

FIGURE 8-16. Emp table record displayed in employee window

Pretty nice form, if you don't say so yourself! Before moving on, let's look at two items. The first is a display problem you may have noticed in Figure 8-16. See how the entire date in the hiredate column is not showing? To fix this, follow these steps:

1. Position yourself on the canvas-view EMPLOYEE, then click on the display area for hiredate.

2. Click on the handle (six handles surround the field when it is selected) on the right side of the field, and stretch it a bit to the right. When you release the mouse button, the field will be resized to accommodate all of the data in hiredate.

3. Save the form by pressing CTRL-S, then look at the changes by pressing CTRL-R. Click on the control box in the Oracle Runform window to return to the Designer.

Let's also look at a quick way to customize item attributes on a canvas-view.

1. Navigate to the EMPLOYEE canvas-view by clicking in its window if it is still visible, or double-clicking on its button in the Object Navigator.

2. Hold down CTRL and click on each field on the canvas. Each field shows six handles after all fields are selected.

3. Place the cursor on the canvas-view, and press the right mouse button. Choose Properties from the menu that appears.

4. Select Background Color property, and change it to Green.

5. Close the property sheet by double-clicking on its control box.

6. Save the form by pressing CTRL-S.

The next time you run the form, its background color will be green. This completes our first exercise.

Exercise #2

In this exercise, you will learn what a master-detail relationship is, when to use it, and how to create it. A master-detail relationship is an association between two base table blocks; the parent is called a master block, and there is a detail block whose records are associated with the parent's. The master-detail relationship in Oracle Forms ensures that the detail block displays only those records that are associated with the current record in the master block and coordinates querying between the two blocks. In Chapter 1, we showed how Oracle Reports handles this master/detail relationship.

The primary reason for a master-detail relationship is to enable the users of your application to access multiple detail records of information linked by a common master record. A good example of this is an invoice. The record of the customer in the customer master file is the master record. The order placed consists of many items—the detail record. The two pieces of information are linked together to give the users greater visibility and usability of the information. Oracle Forms provides this unique feature to make developing applications easier. Since Oracle Forms allows definition of this link between the two types of records as a standard feature, the developer is able to concentrate on other areas of the application. Now we will create this type of relationship with Oracle Forms:

1. Click on the Forms Designer icon in the CDE2 Tools group of the Windows Program Manager. When the Designer is done loading, follow steps 1 through 10 from the previous section ("Exercise #1") to create your first block.

NOTE
*Alternately, you can open the previous form, click on File and then Save As to change its name, and save it under the name **form2** (or whatever name you choose).*

2. Let's now create the second block. Position yourself on the Object Navigator by selecting Object Navigator from the Window menu at the top of the screen, then click on Block. With the Block text highlighted, click on the Create tool on the Object Navigator tool palette to open the New Block Options dialog box.

3. Enter **dept** in the Base Table text box in the New Block Options General folder, then TAB to the block name (notice Oracle Forms puts the table name as the block name). Click on the Items tab, then click on Select Columns. When Oracle displays all the columns in the dept table, they all have the plus (+) sign beside them.

4. Click on the Master/Detail tab, then enter the block name **emp** in the Master Block text box.

5. Enter the text **emp.deptno = dept.deptno** in the Join Condition text box. The dialog box now looks like Figure 8-17.

6. Click on OK to accept the setup for the new dept block. Save the form by pressing CTRL-S.

7. Press CTRL-R to run the form. When the form appears, select Execute from the Query menu at the top of the screen. Figure 8-18 shows the screen after the query executes.

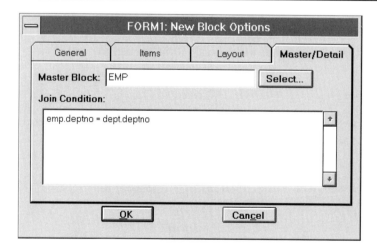

FIGURE 8-17. *Master/Detail folder showing link between master and detail block columns*

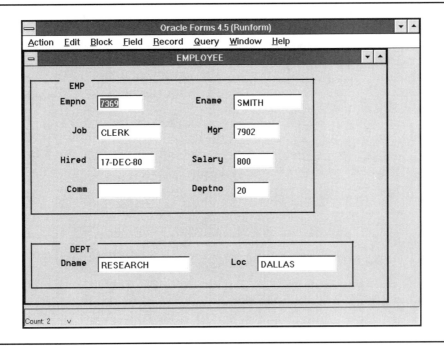

FIGURE 8-18. *Master/detail form first record*

8. Select Next from the Record menu at the top of the screen. Notice that when the data scrolls to the next record in the top block, the bottom block scrolls as well. Figure 8-19 shows the second row from the emp and dept tables.

9. Double-click on the Oracle Forms 4.5 (Runform) control box to return to the Designer. Press CTRL-W to close the form.

You are then positioned on the Object Navigator once again. Double-click on the Oracle Forms Designer control box to return to the Windows Program Manager. We have now built a master/detail form, something you will do time and time again with Oracle Forms.

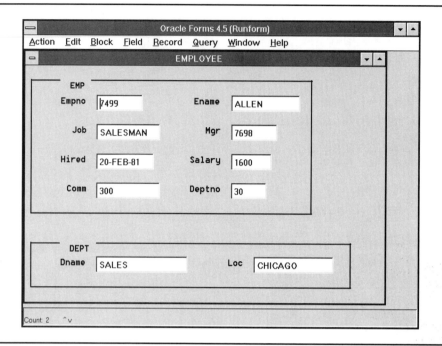

FIGURE 8-19. *Master/detail form second record*

Exercise #3

In this exercise, we will create another master/detail form, using the dept table as the master and emp as the detail. We will use a different layout, so that multiple rows from the detail table are displayed at one time. In this exercise, we will show you how to format the detail block using a nondefault layout. We will also place a scroll bar in the detail block. Let's get started:

1. Double-click on the Forms Designer icon in the Windows Program Manager to start the Designer. Select New from the File menu at the top of the screen, then Form on the menu that opens up to the right.

2. Click on Block on the Object Navigator, then click on the Create tool on the Object Navigator tool palette to bring up the New Block Options dialog box. Enter **dept** for the Base Table and **dept** for the Block Name in the General folder.

3. Click on the Items tab, then click on Select Columns. When Oracle Forms retrieves the column names from dept, click on OK. You are now done creating the master block.

4. Click on the Layout tab, then select Form from the drop-down list beside Style.

5. If you haven't already, return to the Object Navigator. Click on Block, then click on the Create tool on the Object Navigator tool palette to start the detail block.

6. Enter **emp** for the Base Table and **emp** for the Block Name in the General folder.

7. Click on the Items tab, then click on Select Columns. Oracle Forms retrieves the column names from dept.

8. Click on the Layout tab. The Style should be set to Tabular, and the Orientation to Vertical. If either of these values is incorrect, change them using each one's drop-down list. Change the Records to **6** and Spacing to **8**.

9. Click on Integrity Constraints and Scrollbar in the Layout folder, and Oracle Forms fills their boxes with an "x."

10. Click on the Master/Detail tab, and then the Select button to bring up the dialog box shown in Figure 8-20. Select the single constraint displayed by clicking on OK. This returns you to the Master/Detail folder. Click on OK to complete defining the new block.

11. Save the report by clicking on the Save tool on the Object Navigator's tool palette. Enter the name **form3**, then click on OK in the Save dialog box.

12. Run the form by clicking on the Run tool on the tool palette (you will find this tool on most tool palettes and toolbars, not just on the Object Navigator). When the screen appears, notice that there is more than one emp record for the displayed dept information. This is shown in Figure 8-21.

13. Select Next from the Record menu at the top of the screen to get to the next record, and the contents of both blocks change together. The new record is shown in Figure 8-22.

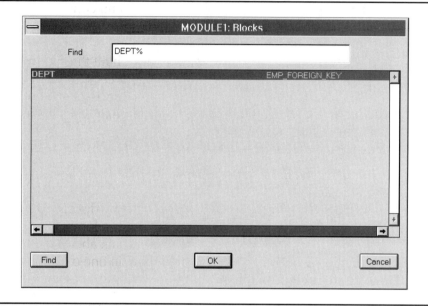

FIGURE 8-20. *Blocks dialog box where the link between blocks is chosen*

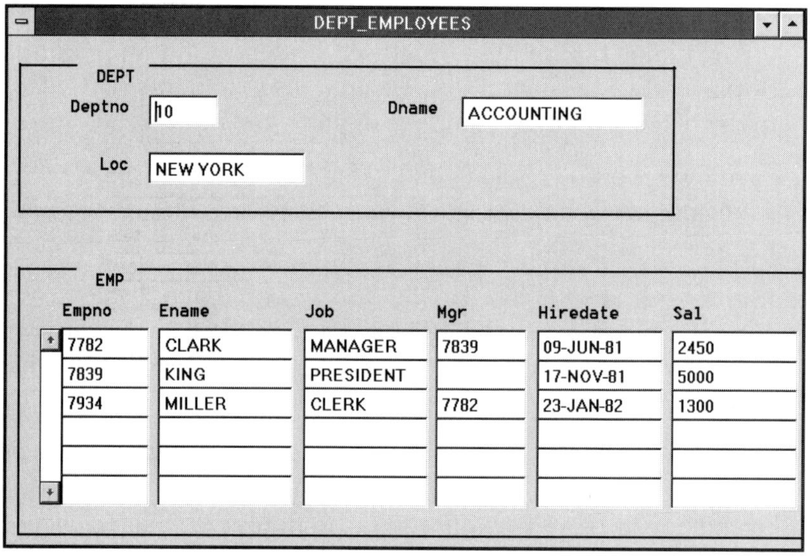

FIGURE 8-21. *Master/detail with multiple detail rows displayed together*

14. Double-click on the Oracle Forms 4.5 (Runform) control box to return to the Designer.

This completes our hands-on exercises. We have built three forms, saved, run, modified them, and modified them again. Let's move on to screen formatting. Since Oracle Forms runs on PCs, the assortment of colors, fonts, graphics, and fill you have become familiar with can be used here as well.

Screen Formatting

We will now round out the chapter on Oracle Forms by discussing screen presentation issues. Forms should be designed to have a look that is pleasing to the eye as well as being functional. Let's talk about color and fonts, and then move on to how to embed a graphic in one of your forms.

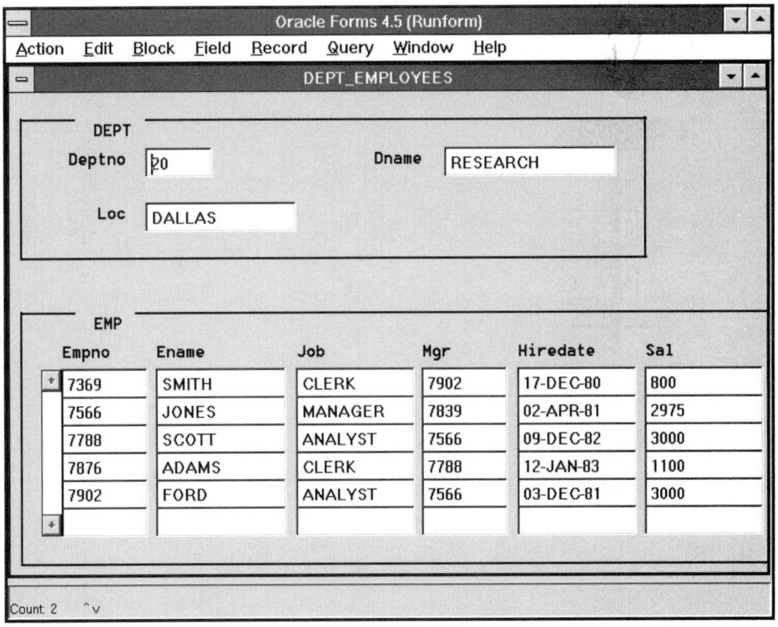

	Oracle Forms 4.5 (Runform)	▼ ▲
Action Edit Block Field Record Query Window Help		

| | DEPT_EMPLOYEES | ▼ ▲ |

DEPT

Deptno 20   Dname RESEARCH

Loc DALLAS

EMP

Empno	Ename	Job	Mgr	Hiredate	Sal
7369	SMITH	CLERK	7902	17-DEC-80	800
7566	JONES	MANAGER	7839	02-APR-81	2975
7788	SCOTT	ANALYST	7566	09-DEC-82	3000
7876	ADAMS	CLERK	7788	12-JAN-83	1100
7902	FORD	ANALYST	7566	03-DEC-81	3000

Count: 2   ^ v

FIGURE 8-22. *Second row in multiple detail window*

Color, fonts, and graphics are just a few of the options that a developer can use to ensure usability and acceptance of an Oracle Forms application.

Color

There are three areas of color that can be controlled: fill, line, and text. Fill is the color of the background, and it is represented by the Fill Color tool on the canvas-view tool palette. The line color is represented by the Line Color tool on the tool palette; this sets the color of the outer edge of any geometric shape. Text is the color of the alphanumeric characters, and it is represented by the Text Color tool on the tool palette. To set the color for one of these items, click on its tool on the tool palette, then move around the color selection palette, as shown in Figure 8-23.

NOTE
The boxes beside the three tools for choosing colors indicate the current color choice. In addition, the "T" button above the three color tools in Figure 8-24 show the current color scheme.

Fonts

Fonts are available for all fields and labels. Fonts vary from computer to computer, and they are one of the most difficult options to control. The best fonts to use are the standard Windows fonts, or, if the application will span

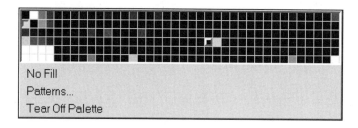

FIGURE 8-23. *Color selection palette*

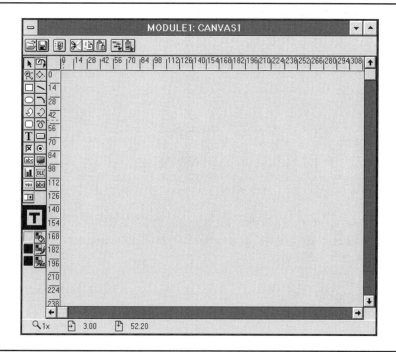

FIGURE 8-24. *The "T" button showing the current color scheme*

multiple platforms, one of the more common ones, such as MS Sans Serif. When the selected font is not available on a particular system, the system defaults to a different font, which may not be that similar. For instance, on all Windows computers, the TTF font Times New Roman is very popular. If this book were read into a Motif environment, it might default to MS Sans Serif.

It is important to realize that proportional fonts are much more pleasing to the eye than fixed fonts, such as Courier. With proportional fonts, thin letters such as "I" take less space than wider letters such as "G". The text in this paragraph uses proportional fonts. Using fixed fonts, all letters, regardless of their width, take up the same amount of horizontal space. To change the font of an item:

1. Select the item to change by clicking on it.

2. Select Font from the Format menu at the top of the screen.

3. Scroll through the Font dialog box, select the desired font, and select any desired attributes, such as bold and italic.

4. Click on OK to choose the selection you have made. When you return to the canvas-view, the font for the selected item changes.

VIP
*Experience dictates you should use underline
and bold sparingly. They may look nice during
design but can be a nuisance when a screen
goes to production.*

When you need to use special fonts and text attributes, keep in mind that all attributes may not be supported by the computer configuration on all your clients' machines.

Graphics

Graphics are pictures that are typically used for splash or logo screens. A splash screen is a window that comes up briefly while the application is loading. It can be used to announce the entrance to an application or as a distraction as processing occurs in the background. For instance, if there is a need to do extra setup or security checks that take several seconds to complete, a developer may want to include a splash screen to let end users know that processing is occurring or to distract them from the time it takes to complete that processing. Another use of graphics is the inclusion of the company logo. To use a graphic in your form, follow these steps:

1. Position yourself on a canvas-view by double-clicking on the Canvas-View button on the Object Navigator.

2. Select Import from the Edit menu at the top of the screen. When the Import (for Drawings) or Import Image (for Images) dialog box appears, enter the filename of the image or drawing to import, or use the browser to select the file to import.

3. Click on OK to import the image or drawing.

VIP
*When you select Import from the Edit menu, if
the Image and Drawing choices are not active,
click anywhere in the Canvas-Views editor,
and repeat the operation. The active options
on this menu depend on the active object
when Edit is selected.*

We now move on to Oracle Forms Runtime, leaving you with one last
point that, unfortunately, should restrict just how fancy you may get with
screen design. As with all fun things in life, enjoy these options (colors,
fonts, and graphics) in moderation. Too much of any of the available screen
formatting techniques will cause unpleasant side effects. Remember, you
are not the only one who will have to stare at your application for long
periods of time. It may be a good idea to get a second opinion on the
aesthetics of your screen design.

Oracle Forms Runtime

This part of Oracle Forms is used to run menus and screens. It is invoked by
clicking on the Forms Runtime icon in the CDE2 Tools program group.
When you are presented with the Runtime welcome screen, do the
following to run a report:

1. Press CTRL-R to bring up the Open dialog box. Enter the name of the
   form to run, or browse and then select the one you want.

2. Once you have selected a report (e.g., form1), click on OK.

3. Enter your user name and password when asked to connect to the
   Personal Oracle7 database.

4. Go about whatever you need to do with the form, then exit Oracle
   Forms 4.5 (Runtime) by double-clicking on its control box.

After developers code Oracle Forms programs, the source code is
compiled and becomes part of the set of application code delivered to the

end user. The end user invokes Forms Runtime within an application to work with the network of system screens and menus.

What's Next

Oracle Forms 4.5 has reinforced Oracle's position as one of the major players in the GUI data entry environment. We have shown you some basics and have hopefully tickled your fancy, and now you can't wait to try bigger and better things, right? Our next chapter discusses another component of Oracle's Developer 2000 suite of products, Oracle Reports. A lot of the techniques you have picked up in this chapter can be applied to Oracle Reports, since, as you will soon see, it has the same look and feel and operator interface as Oracle Forms.

CHAPTER

9

Oracle Reports

n this chapter, we will discuss the Developer 2000 tool called Oracle Reports. Programmers familiar with some ad hoc query tools on the market will find the look and feel of Oracle Reports very familiar. Version 2.0 of this tool was a major rewrite of its predecessor, SQL*Reportwriter. The version we feature in this chapter, version 2.5, has a sophisticated programmer interface and has been significantly enhanced for ease of use.

NOTE
Even though Oracle is perched to release Reports 3.0, we feature version 2.5 here since it is more familiar to application developers. As Oracle8 and Oracle Reports 3.0 become more popular, this chapter will reflect that move by featuring Reports 3.0.

When you are done reading this chapter, you will know about the following:

- Oracle Reports and what it can do for you

- Hardware required to run Oracle Reports

- How to install Oracle Reports

- How to prepare your PC to run Oracle Reports (Oracle Reports runs on computers other than PCs, but we will concentrate on PCs in this chapter)

- How Oracle Reports processes queries

- Where to set preferences in Oracle Reports

- How to work with Oracle Reports files

- How to build a two-query report

- How to create and display a computed field

- Basic output formatting using Oracle Reports

- How to build a single-query matrix report

- How to use Oracle Reports Runtime

NOTE
Learn the procedures and concepts presented in each sample report in this chapter one at a time. Before moving on to the next exercise, practice what you have learned so far. While the reports we build are simple, they illustrate fundamental Oracle Reports concepts.

Sample Data

You can run the following SQL program to create and populate the tables used in the exercises in this chapter. The user name and password that the program asks you to enter are the same ones through which you connect to the database to run the following program:

```
rem *  ------------------------------------------------------------
rem *   Script to set up tables used in Chapter 9 from
rem *   Oracle8: A Beginner's Guide ISBN 0-07-882122-3
rem *  ------------------------------------------------------------
set echo on
drop table person;
drop table clssn;
drop table bonus;
drop table factory;
drop table commission;
create table person (
    pin             number(6),
    last_name       varchar2(20),
    first_name      varchar2(20),
    hire_date       date,
    salary          number(8,2),
    clssn           varchar2(5));
create table clssn (
    clssn           varchar2(5),
    descr           varchar2(20));
create table bonus (
    emp_id          number(4),
    emp_class       varchar2(2),
    fac_id          varchar2(3),
    bonus_amt       number);
create table factory (
    fac_id          varchar2(3),
```

```
      descr             varchar2(20),
      prov              varchar2(2));
create table commission (
    sales_id            number(3),
    qtr                 varchar2(1),
    comm_amt            number(8,2));
insert into person values
    (100110,'SAUNDERS','HELEN','12-DEC-87',77000,'1');
insert into person values
    (100120,'FONG','LYDIA','11-MAY-88',55000,'3');
insert into person values
    (100130,'WILLIAMS','FRANK','09-DEC-82',43000,'4');
insert into person values
    (100140,'COHEN','NANCY','14-AUG-93',44000,'4');
insert into person values
    (100150,'STEWART','BORIS','11-NOV-91',48000,'4');
insert into person values
    (100160,'REDMOND','KENNETH','01-FEB-92',32000,'5');
insert into person values
    (100170,'SMYTHE','ROLLY','11-JUL-83',33000,'5');
insert into person values
    (100180,'FRANKS','HENRY','31-JUL-83',55000,'3');
insert into person values
    (100190,'GREENBERG','JOE','30-MAR-86',21000,'6');
insert into person values
    (100200,'LEVIS','SANDRA','06-DEC-89',18000,'7');
insert into person values
    (100210,'APPOLLO','BILL','12-APR-89',44000,'4');
insert into person values
    (100210,'JENKINS','SALLY','12-DEC-87',44000,'4');
insert into clssn values ('1','Manager');
insert into clssn values ('2','Chief');
insert into clssn values ('3','Leader');
insert into clssn values ('4','Analyst');
insert into clssn values ('5','Clerk');
insert into clssn values ('6','Trainee');
insert into clssn values ('7','Part time');
insert into bonus values (123,null,'AE',2000);
insert into bonus values (124,null,'AF',2200);
insert into bonus values (125,null,'AH',1200);
insert into bonus values (126,null,'AH',1200);
insert into bonus values (127,null,'AF',1200);
insert into bonus values (128,null,'AT',1500);
insert into bonus values (129,null,'AT',1100);
insert into bonus values (130,null,'AU',1400);
```

```
insert into bonus values (131,null,'AE',200);
insert into bonus values (132,null,'AF',220);
insert into bonus values (133,null,'AG',120);
insert into bonus values (134,null,'AG',200);
insert into bonus values (135,null,'AG',200);
insert into bonus values (136,null,'AU',1400);
insert into bonus values (137,null,'AH',100);
insert into bonus values (138,null,'AU',1400);
insert into factory values ('AE','Northeast','ON');
insert into factory values ('AF','Northwest','MN');
insert into factory values ('AH','Southeast','ON');
insert into factory values ('AT','Central','MN');
insert into factory values ('AU','South','CA');
insert into commission values (10,1,140);
insert into commission values (10,2,10);
insert into commission values (10,3,null);
insert into commission values (10,4,810);
insert into commission values (20,1,1200);
insert into commission values (20,2,200);
insert into commission values (20,3,500);
insert into commission values (20,4,100);
insert into commission values (30,1,40);
insert into commission values (30,2,19);
insert into commission values (30,3,340);
insert into commission values (30,4,null);
```

Terminology

The following definitions will arm you with the technical jargon you need to make it through this chapter.

- *Comma insertion* is used to format numeric data for display purposes. It places commas in large numbers to make them more readable to the user (e.g., the number 83892029 is displayed as 83,892,029).

- *Zero suppression* replaces leading zeros with spaces in numeric data for display purposes. Using zero suppression, the number 00003487 would be displayed as   3487 (i.e., with four blanks in front of the number where the zeros used to be).

- Asking Oracle to convert PL/SQL code into executable format is referred to as *compiling* PL/SQL. While coding PL/SQL in Oracle

Reports, you'll come across many dialog boxes with which you can ask Oracle to compile your PL/SQL before dissolving the box.

- *Binary* is a format used by computers to store executable programs. In the DOS world, the programs winword.exe (used to invoke Word 6 for Windows) or control.exe (used to run the Windows main program group control panel option) are examples of binary files.

- Asking Oracle to convert your report definition to binary format is called *generating* a report.

- You may wish to have a suggested layout for the report output, based on the report type and number of fields being displayed. This is referred to as using Oracle Reports' *default layout feature*.

What Is Oracle Reports?

Oracle Reports is a feature-rich reporting tool that produces production-quality output using data sources such as the Oracle database. Developers are able to embed graphics, sound, video, and a wide assortment of visual aids in screen and hard-copy (printed) output. Its predecessor, SQL*Reportwriter, which was bundled with version 6 of Oracle, was a character-based reporting environment. In Oracle Reports, the designer interface is mouse-driven.

In this chapter, we will discuss the two most frequently used components of Oracle Reports, Oracle Reports Designer and Oracle Reports Runtime. Because all Developer 2000 tools are integrated and run against an Oracle database, Oracle Reports can share data with other Developer 2000 tools. They all have a Microsoft Windows look and feel.

Hardware Requirements to Run Oracle Reports

The following minimum configuration is required to use Oracle Reports:

- A 386 or stronger central processing unit (CPU), although a 486 or Pentium is preferred

- At least 60 megabytes (or 61,440,000 bytes) of available disk space

- A 40MHz or faster processor—speeds of 66 or better are preferable

- At least 8MB (megabytes) of extended memory

- MS-DOS or PC-DOS version 5 or 6, or DR-DOS version 6 or higher

- Microsoft Windows 3.x or Windows 95

We recommend that you install a CD-ROM drive on your machine, if you do not already have one. Oracle, like many other software manufacturers, is moving toward this format as its default distribution medium primarily because the huge amounts of data that fit easily on a fraction of a CD-ROM (each holds 600MB, or 638,976,000 bytes) could easily take up a very large number of 3.5-inch diskettes. When Personal Oracle7 was in its beta, or testing, stage one of our clients had over 86MB of Oracle and Oracle-support software on a 486 PC. Had they installed from diskette, that could have easily been over 60 diskettes!

Installing Oracle Reports

As with the rest of the Oracle products for Windows, installation is done from the Oracle installer (referred to as orainst in Chapter 5). To begin installation, click on the Oracle Installer icon in the Oracle group of Program Manager. You will be presented with the Oracle Installer startup screen shown in Figure 9-1. Notice that there are two boxes side-by-side on the screen: Available Products and Installed Products. If Oracle Reports is not one of the available products, scroll through the list until it appears. Once in view, there may be a plus (+) sign beside the product name. This indicates that components of the product can be installed together or separately. Double-click on the product name to expand the component list, as shown in Figure 9-1. While that component list is displayed, each one may be installed separately. We recommend you install all three components of Oracle Reports. If the component list is expanded, select all three by holding down CTRL and clicking on Designer, Runtime, and Online Documentation. If the component list is not expanded, simply click on Oracle Reports.

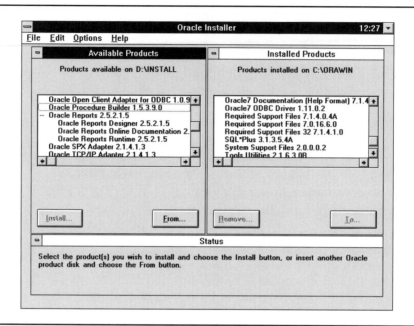

FIGURE 9-1. *Oracle installer startup screen, showing the Oracle Reports component list in the Available Products box*

NOTE

To expand a product list, double-click on the product name. To collapse a list when product components have been expanded, click on the product name with the "-" sign beside it. When a product can be expanded, there is a "+" sign beside its name.

During the installation process, you will be asked to designate a directory for the product. Oracle suggests placing it in \orawin\reports25. Unless you are already using that directory for something else, accept it as is. When the installation terminates (be patient—it can take upwards of 30 minutes), you will see the product in the Installed Products box on the right side of the Oracle Installer screen. To leave the installer, double-click on the control button. You are now ready to use Oracle Reports. When you return to the Program Manager, you will see the Oracle Reports-specific

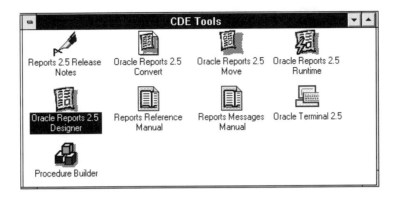

FIGURE 9-2. *Oracle Reports icons*

icons in the CDE2 Tools program group as shown in Figure 9-2. (This is the suite of tools currently referred to by Oracle as Developer 2000.) The installation also produces a CDE2 Documentation program group separate from CDE2 Tools.

Preparing Your PC to Run Oracle Reports

Those of you familiar with Windows-based products have probably installed one of them before. Oracle Reports, just like the rest of these products, has requirements for its operating environment to allow it to run properly. The following must be done before running Oracle Reports.

- You must have access to a local or remote Oracle7 database. To access a remote database, you or your database administrator must have installed SQL*Net and been able to successfully connect to the database.

- You must have already loaded your network software if you are accessing a remote database. If you are using a local Personal Oracle7 database, this is not necessary.

How Oracle Reports Processes Queries

Oracle Reports can be a very complex product, yet you can design useful and sophisticated output with little or no programming. A network of nested **select** statements can produce the desired results in a short time period. Nested **select** statements are a series of SQL statements in which column values from a high-level query (called the parent query) are passed down for further processing to a lower-level query (referred to as the child query). A query that is a child of a higher-level query can in turn be the parent of a query of a lower level. Table 9-1 shows an example of how Oracle Reports handles this processing. The information in the Type column indicates a parent (P) or child (C) query.

There is a significant difference in the way these queries are worded; usually when more than one table is referred to in a SQL statement, you place both table names in the **from** line of that statement. The parts of SQL statements are discussed in Chapter 6 and Chapter 12. Asking SQL to process a statement using more than one table is called a join operation. The column values in the tables are compared against one another using a join condition. Rows whose column values match one another appear as

Query Name	Query Text	Type	Column Values
Q_1	select oname, location, province from offices	P	Passes oname to Q_2 Passes location to Q_3
Q_2	select oname, leader_name, leader_rank from leaders	C P	Receives oname from Q_1 Passes leader_rank to Q_4
Q_3	select location, desc_e, desc_f from locations	C	Receives location from Q_3
Q_4	select leader_rank, rank_weight, rank_desc from ranking	C	Receives leader_rank from Q_2

TABLE 9-1. *Parent/Child Query Example*

the results of the query. Most join conditions are done using equality as the relational operator, though conditions using other operators (such as >, <, or <>) are possible. The following listing shows how a common join condition is worded.

```
select oname,location,province,
       desc_e,desc_f        /* The columns come from both tables.*/
  from offices,locations     /* For a row to be fetched, its      */
 where offices.location =    /* location column values must be    */
       locations.location;   /* the same in both tables.          */
```

In Table 9-1, notice how the SQL text in Q_2 mentions the column oname but does not equate it to the value passed from its parent query (Q_1). As well, Q_3 does not equate location to the value it receives from its parent (Q_1). Finally, Q_4 does not explicitly equate leader_rank to the value it receives from its parent (Q_2). Thus, when a row is selected from Q_1, it passes down its oname column value to Q_2 and its location column value to Q_3. Also, when a row is selected in Q_2, it passes its leader_rank column value to Q4.

Oracle Reports Designer

This component is where the developer defines new reports and enhances existing ones. It is invoked by double-clicking on the Reports Designer icon in the CDE2 Tools program group. Before we dive into Oracle Reports, let's take a look at the assortment of buttons and tools you will be using in this chapter.

Oracle Reports calls the buttons along the top of its screen the toolbar and the tools down the side of its screen the tool palette. Figure 9-3 shows the Data Model button in the Object Navigator. Figure 9-4 shows the various tools and buttons in the Data Model. Figure 9-5 shows the Run tool on the Layout toolbar. There are many more buttons and tools you can use with Oracle Reports Designer than we will discuss in this chapter. We will only touch on the ones that we will be using.

The Object Navigator

The Object Navigator is shown in Figure 9-6. You access all objects used in your reports from this central navigator. Oracle Reports uses the term

Data Model

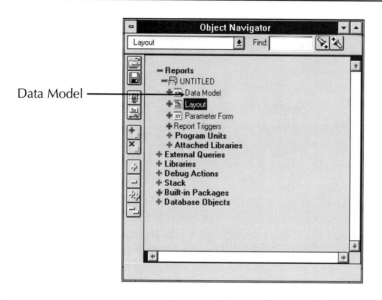

FIGURE 9-3. *Data Model button on the Object Navigator*

Run   Default Layout

Query

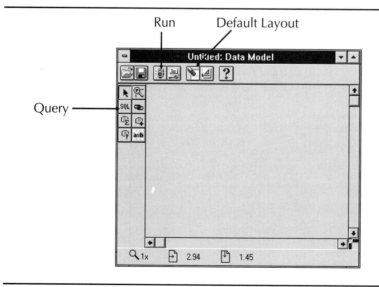

FIGURE 9-4. *Data Model tools*

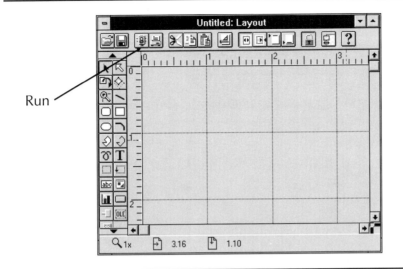

Run

FIGURE 9-5.   *Run tool on the Layout toolbar*

object to refer to a report's component parts. Some of these parts (shown in Figure 9-6) are discussed in sections of this chapter (specifically the Data Model).

Oracle Reports uses the "+" and "-" signs in the Object Navigator, similar to the installer we talked about earlier. To expand an object in the Object Navigator, click on its "+" sign; when an object is expanded, click on its "-" sign to collapse the expanded list.

Setting Preferences

By setting preferences, you can tell Oracle Reports about your work habits and how you would prefer Oracle Reports to behave. You can store Oracle Reports programs in the database or in DOS files on your PC; in Preferences, you tell Oracle Reports which you want to use during each session. Once preferences have been set, some of the dialog boxes will not appear, since you have specified the way you want Oracle Reports to

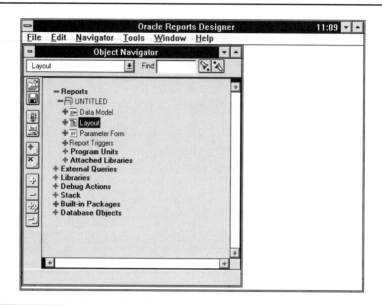

FIGURE 9-6. *Object Navigator*

behave. For example, to tell Oracle Reports to save all report programs to files, do the following:

1. Click on Tools on the menu at the top of the screen, then Tools Option to bring up the Tools Option dialog box. There are three folders in this box; if the Preferences folder is not showing, click on its tab to bring it to the front of the screen.

2. In the Object Access area, click on the Storage Type drop-down arrow. Click on File from the drop-down menu that appears to return to the Preferences folder. If this is the first time you have set preferences, the options already selected (e.g., Suppress Define Property Sheets) are Oracle Reports defaults.

3. Click on Save Preferences, then click OK as shown in Figure 9-7 to complete the activity.

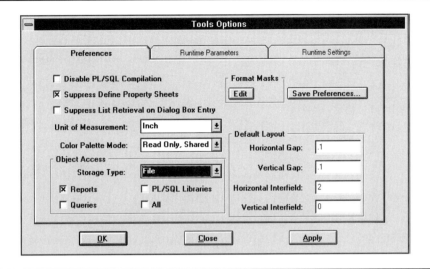

FIGURE 9-7. *Preferences object access selected*

You are then returned to the Object Navigator or wherever you were before setting the object access preference. Other preferences you can choose include the following:

- You can format masks for numeric data, utilizing comma insertion and zero suppression. Using this feature, you can tell Oracle Reports to display the number 012730 as 12,730.

- You can adjust the horizontal and vertical space between fields on a default layout. Some people find the amount of space left between fields too little; this space can be changed and saved for future reference.

- You can instruct Oracle Reports about when you want PL/SQL to be compiled. You can choose to compile whenever you leave a dialog box in which you have written some PL/SQL code, or you can tell Oracle Reports to compile only when generating a report.

How to Work with Oracle Reports Files

Now that you have told Oracle Reports to save report files to your hard disk, let's cover working with these report definition files. In this section, you will learn how to do the following:

- Create a new report
- Save a new report
- Open an existing report

Once Oracle Reports Designer is finished loading, you will see the Oracle Reports Object Navigator discussed previously. You can either start working with a new report or open an existing one.

Creating a New Report

If the object navigator shows the UNTITLED report, simply start designing the new report by double-clicking on the Data Model button on the Object Navigator. If you have been working on a report and wish to start a new one, do the following.

1. Select New from the File menu.

2. When the menu opens up to the right, click on Report.

Oracle Reports creates the new report and calls it UNTITLED. The Object Navigator now shows both reports.

TIP
The quickest way to start a new report is to use the shortcut key CTRL-E. If your work needs to be saved before the new report definition begins, Oracle will prompt you to save before starting a new report.

Opening an Existing Report

You can open an existing report by doing the following.

1. Select Open from the File menu.

2. When Oracle Reports brings up the Open Report dialog box, double-click on the filename to open, or click once to highlight a name, then click on the OK button to open the report.

After opening the report, Oracle Reports changes the Object Navigator to display the report you have just opened.

TIP
The quickest way to open a report is to use the shortcut key CTRL-O. This opens the Open Report dialog box.

Saving a Report

You can save a report by doing the following:

1. Select Save from the File menu.

2. When Oracle Reports brings up the Save Report dialog box, enter a filename for the report.

3. Click on the OK button to complete the action. The name of the file you enter must conform to DOS file-naming conventions.

TIP
The quickest way to save a report is to use the shortcut key CTRL-S. If Oracle does not know the name of the report you are saving, it will open up the Save Report dialog box and ask you for the name.

Changing the Name of a Report

If you wish to change the name of a report, do the following.

1. Select Save As from the File menu.

2. After Oracle Reports brings up the Save As dialog box, enter a new filename for the report.

3. Click on the OK button to complete the action. The name of the file you enter must conform to DOS file-naming conventions.

Two Main Designer Components

You will spend most of your time in the Designer using either the Data Model screen or the Layout screen. Using the Data Model screen, you define the data you will use in the report and its relationships with other data in the report. It is shown in Figure 9-8. You invoke the Data Model screen by double-clicking on the Data Model button on the Object Navigator.

Access the Layout screen by double-clicking on the Layout button on the Object Navigator. The Layout screen, as shown in Figure 9-9, is where you define the look of your report. You cut and paste objects on this screen to fine-tune the placement of information on your report output.

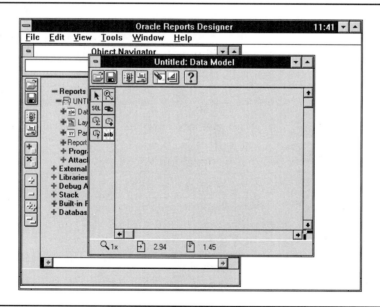

FIGURE 9-8. *Reports Data Model screen*

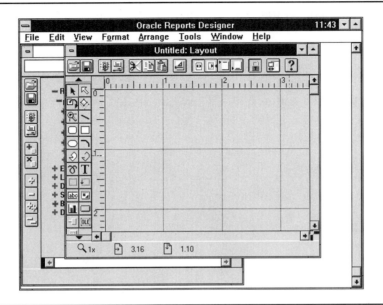

FIGURE 9-9.   *Reports Layout screen*

Moving Between the Screens

When the Data Model screen is active, you move to the Layout screen by double-clicking on the Layout button on the Object Navigator. You move to the Data Model screen by double-clicking on the Data Model button on the Object Navigator.

TIP
You can tile or cascade the two screens by selecting Tile or Cascade from the Window menu. Then, you can move back and forth between the two simply by clicking somewhere in the one you wish to work with.

Sample Report #1

This first example illustrates the simplest form of Oracle Reports output: displaying a few columns in a table, nothing fancy. We use the person and clssn tables shown in Table 9-2. The information in the Matches column indicates if the clssn column in person relates to the clssn column in clssn. We will use these columns to create a *link condition*. This condition instructs Oracle Reports on how to link two queries together; once defined, Oracle Reports processes the queries using the parent/child technique, which we discussed earlier in the "How Oracle Reports Processes Queries" section.

Exercise #1

You are required to print a list showing everyone's pin and full name. The output will resemble the following:

```
Pin        Full name
101210     SALLY JENKINS
```

In this section we will show you how to:

■ Create a query and define the query selection criteria

■ Pick tables and columns for query selection from a Personal Oracle7 database

■ Define a computed field and where it is displayed

Person Table		Matches
pin	number(6)	
last_name	varchar2(20)	
first_name	varchar2(20)	
clssn	varchar2(5)	clssn in CLSSN
Clssn Table		Matches
clssn	varchar2(5)	clssn in PERSON
descr	varchar2(20)	

TABLE 9-2.   *Tables Used in Sample Report #3*

■ Customize headings on a report using the Default Layout dialog box

■ Run a report

To program this report, do the following.

I. In the Object Navigator, double-click on the Data Model button to open the Data Model screen, if it isn't already open.

2. In the Data Model screen, click on the Query tool.

3. The cursor changes to a large plus (+) sign. Drag the cursor into the workspace. Click to create a query box, as shown in Figure 9-10.

4. Double-click on query Q_1 to bring up the Query dialog box shown in Figure 9-11. It is now time to define the query used for this report. The query dialog box has two folders. To define the query, if the General folder is obscured, click on its tab to bring it to the front of the box.

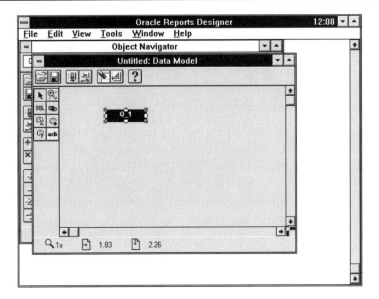

FIGURE 9-10.   *Data model showing a first query*

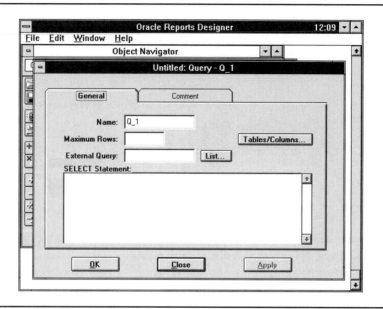

FIGURE 9-11. *Query dialog box*

5. Click on Tables/Columns. Oracle Reports asks you to connect to the database to bring up a list of available tables and columns. Enter your user name and password. Leave the Database blank, since you are accessing a local Personal Oracle7 database. Click on Connect to log into the database.

6. Once connected, you will see the Table and Column Names dialog box, as shown in Figure 9-12. As the screen appears, Tables and Views are already selected in Object Types, as is Current user in User types. Click on PERSON in the Database Objects box. If the person table name is not in the table name list, you may have to scroll down to make it appear.

7. Hold down CTRL, and click on first_name, last_name, and pin, as shown in Figure 9-12.

8. Click on Select-from, then click on Close. The table and column names you have just selected are transferred back to the Query dialog box as if you had entered them manually.

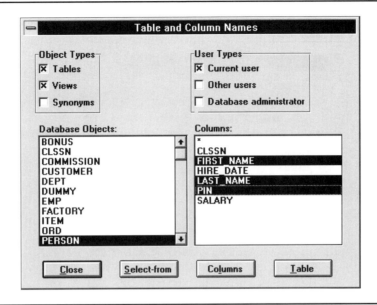

FIGURE 9-12. *Tables and columns selected*

9. Click on Apply, then click on Close to return to the data model shown in Figure 9-13.

NOTE
If you know the names of the table and columns you will be using in your query, you may proceed to the SELECT Statement text box in the Query dialog box and type in your query. After typing the query text, enter your user name and password, then click on Connect to log into Personal Oracle7. After Oracle verifies your query text, click on Close to return to the Data Model screen.

10. Click on the Formula Column tool to define a formula field. The cursor changes to a large plus (+) sign. Drag the cursor into the workspace and click somewhere in the group G_1 box. A field

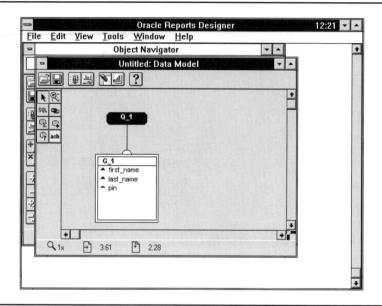

FIGURE 9-13. *Data model showing Q_1 and G_1*

called CF_1 appears when the button is released, as shown in Figure 9-14.

11. Double-click on the CF_1 field to bring up the Formula Column dialog box, as shown in Figure 9-15. The Formula Column dialog box has two folders. To define the formula, if the General folder is obscured, click on its tab to bring it to the front of the box.

12. Click on the Datatype drop-down arrow. Select Char.

13. In the Width box, enter **30**.

14. Click on Edit to bring up the Program Unit definition box. Enter the formula text **return (:first_name||' '||:last_name);** as shown in Figure 9-16.

NOTE

When the Program Unit definition box appears, you may have to shunt the windows around on the screen to make its data entry area appear.

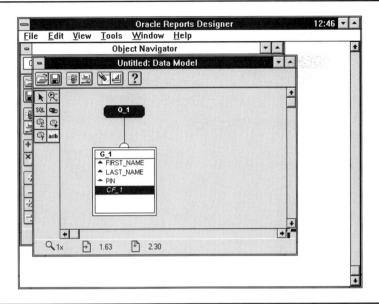

FIGURE 9-14.   *Data model with a computed field*

15. Click on Compile, then click on Close to return to the Formula
Column dialog box.

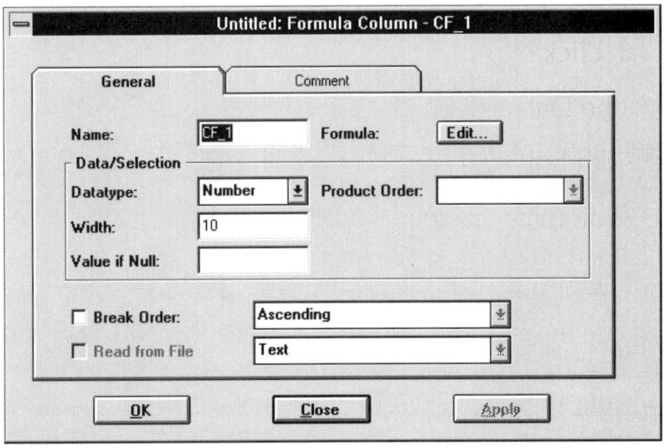

FIGURE 9-15.   *Formula column dialog box*

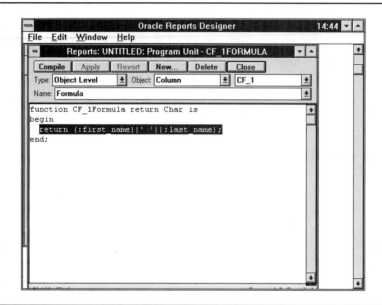

FIGURE 9-16. *Formula Program Unit dialog box*

16. Click on Apply, then click on Close to return to the Data Model screen. The formula field you have just defined shows up as CF_1.

NOTE
You may find that when you compile the formula you have entered in the Program Unit definition box, Oracle Reports returns you to the Data Model screen. You must move to the Formula Column box and click on Apply and then Close before continuing.

17. Click on the Default Layout tool. When presented with the six style options as shown in Figure 9-17, notice that the Tabular option is selected. If the Data/Selection folder is at the front of this box, click on the Style folder's tab to bring it to the front.

18. Click on the Data/Selection tab, then click on FIRST_NAME and LAST_NAME. The text changes from white on black to black on gray; this indicates the fields will not display on the report.

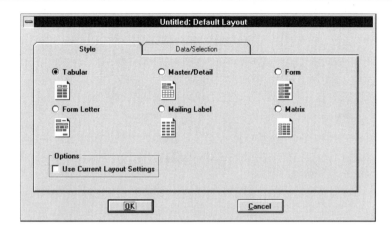

FIGURE 9-17. *Default Layout style selection*

19. Highlight the value in the Label column for CF_1 and change it to the text **Full Name**.

20. Click on OK. You are presented with the Oracle Reports Layout screen. Since we have defined the layout using the Default Layout dialog box, there is no work to be done here.

21. Save the report by pressing CTRL-S.

VIP
We recommend that you save your work every few minutes. Good habits you may have learned while word processing should also be practiced with Oracle Reports.

22. Enter the name **reports1** for the report, then click on OK to complete the save.

23. Click on the Run tool.

24. Click on Run Report in the Runtime Parameter Form to bring up the report output on the Previewer window, as shown in Figure 9-18.

25. Click on Close to close the Previewer window.

26. Press CTRL-W to close the report and return to an empty Object Navigator.

Congratulations! You have just used Oracle Reports 2.5 to build a simple report, reading data from a Personal Oracle7 database.

Exercise #2

We need to modify the report output to capitalize the first name and last name of each person and sort the data by last name. The output will resemble the following:

```
Pin          Full name
101210       Sally Jenkins
```

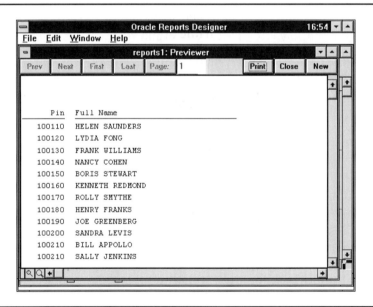

FIGURE 9-18. *Report output on the Previewer window*

In this section we will show you details on how to:

- Open an existing report
- Modify an existing query
- Sort the rows returned from a query
- Format data in a computed field

The following modifications to the initial report will accomplish this:

1. Press CTRL-O to open the Open Report dialog box. Double-click on reports1 to open the report.

2. Double-click on the Data Model button to display the Data Model screen.

3. Double-click on query Q_1, and when the Query dialog box appears, add the text **order by last_name** at the end of the existing query.

4. Click on Apply, then click on Close to record the change to query Q_1.

5. Double-click on field CF_1. In the Formula Column dialog box, click on Edit.

6. In the Program Unit definition box, change the line starting with "return" to **return initcap((:first_name||' '||:last_name));** as shown in Figure 9-19.

7. Click on Compile, then click on Close to return to the Formula Column dialog box.

8. Click on Apply, then click on Close to return to the Data Model screen.

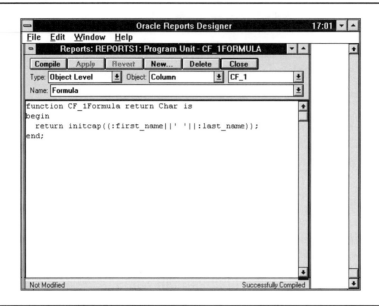

FIGURE 9-19. *Capitalizing the full name*

VIP
You may find that when you compile the formula you have entered in the Program Unit definition box, Oracle Reports returns you to the Data Model screen. You must move to the Formula Column box and click on Apply, then click on Close before continuing.

9. Save the report by pressing CTRL-S. Oracle Reports does not open a dialog box when you save the report, since it already knows the name (reports1).

10. Click on the Run tool.

11. Click on Run Report in the Runtime Parameter Form to bring up the report output on the Previewer window, as shown in Figure 9-20.

12. Click on Close to close the Previewer window.

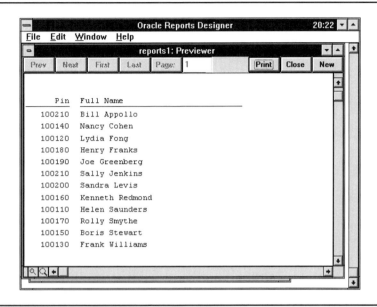

FIGURE 9-20.   *Report output on the Previewer window*

Exercise #3

We need to further enhance the report output to list each person's classification. The output will resemble the following:

```
Pin           Full name                    Classification
101210        Sally Jenkins                Analyst
```

In this section we will show you details on how to:

- Create a second query

- Add a column to an existing query

- Define the link condition between two queries

- Suppress double display of the linking column

NOTE
We assume that you are working uninterrupted from the previous exercise. If, for some reason, you are not yet connected to the database, Personal Oracle7 will ask you to reconnect with the user name and password during this exercise.

Program this by doing the following:

1. At this point, you should be looking at the Data Model screen. If you are not, double-click on the Data Model button on the Object Navigator.

2. Click on the Query tool.

3. The cursor changes to a large plus (+) sign. Drag the cursor into the workspace. Click to create the query box called Q_2.

4. Double-click on query Q_2 to open the Query dialog box, General tab. Enter the query text **select clssn,descr from clssn** in the SELECT Statement text box to define the query.

5. Click on Apply, then click on Close to return to the Data Model screen shown in Figure 9-21.

6. Double-click on query Q_1 to return to the query dialog box, and add the text **,clssn** (be sure to enter the comma before **clssn**) to the query after the text **pin** in the SELECT Statement text box. It now looks like Figure 9-22.

7. Click on Apply, then click on Close to return to the Data Model screen. Oracle Reports uses the name clssn1 in group G_1 for the clssn column in query Q_1.

8. Click on the Data Link tool.

9. Click on the clssn1 column in group G_1. While holding CTRL, drag the cursor to the clssn column in group G_2. Release the mouse. Oracle Reports draws the link shown in Figure 9-23.

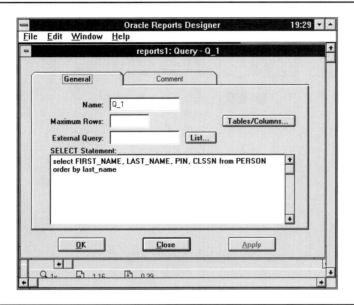

FIGURE 9-21. *Q_1 with new column added*

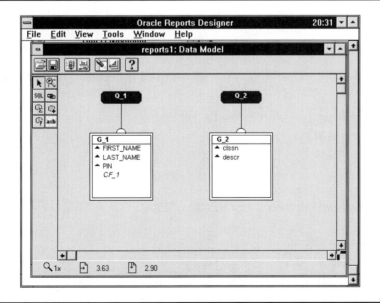

FIGURE 9-22. *Data model showing Q_1 and Q_2*

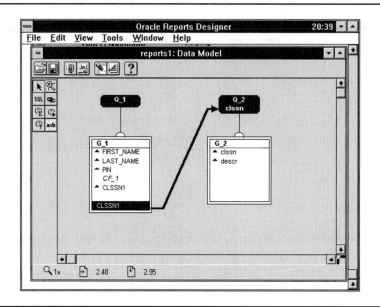

FIGURE 9-23. *Data model showing link condition*

10. Click on the Default Layout tool. When the Default Layout box appears, if the Data/Selection folder is obscured, click on its tab to bring it to the front of the screen.

11. Click on clssn and clssn1. The text changes from white on black to black on gray; this indicates the fields will not display on the report.

12. Highlight the value in the Label column for descr and change it to **Classification**.

NOTE
You may have to scroll down the list of columns to make the descr column appear.

13. Click on OK to accept the layout just entered. Oracle Reports may ask you if you want to replace the existing layout with the one you just entered. Click on OK to confirm this replacement, and you are presented with the Layout screen.

14. Save the report by pressing CTRL-S.

15. Click on the Run tool.

16. Click on Run Report in the Runtime Parameter Form to bring up the report output on the Previewer window, as shown in Figure 9-24.

17. Click on Close to close the Previewer window, then press CTRL-W to close the report.

Sample Report #2

In this example we will discuss:

■ Suppressing display of some column values

■ Changing field headings and display widths using the Default Layout dialog box

■ Splitting the makeup of an existing group

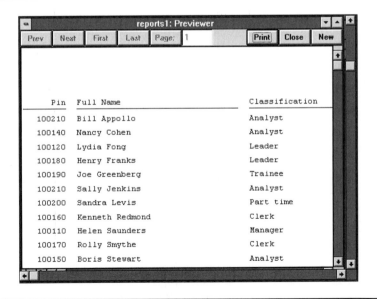

FIGURE 9-24. *Report output on the Previewer window*

■ Creating and displaying running totals

This exercise uses the Bonus table, shown in Table 9-3.

Exercise
We need to produce a listing of employees with bonuses sorted by factory. The output should resemble the following:

```
Factory    Emp ID       Bonus
   AE       123          2000
            131          200
   AF       124          2200
            127          1200
            132          220
   AG       133          120
            134          200
```

Notice how the factory is not repeated when successive employees are in the same factory. This is a concept called control break. Control breaking means that data is only printed on a report when there is a change in value. Control break works as illustrated in Table 9-4, using the factory values from the previous listing. In Table 9-4, the factory values should only be printed for rows 1, 3, and 6. By examining the previous listing, this appears to be the case.

If double bonuses were handed out to employee 124, the report would then resemble the following:

```
Factory           Emp ID              Bonus
   AE               123               4000
                    124               1000
                                      250
   AF               126               4000
```

Bonus Table

emp_id	number(4)
emp_class	varchar2(2)
fac_id	varchar2(3)
bonus_amt	number

TABLE 9-3.   *Table Used in Sample Report #2*

Row #	Current Factory	Previous Factory	Print Current
1	AE	undefined	Y
2	AE	AE	N
3	AF	AE	Y
4	AF	AF	N
5	AF	AF	N
6	AG	AF	Y
7	AG	AG	N

TABLE 9-4. *Control Break Column Suppression*

This can be accomplished by doing the following:

1. Position yourself back in the Object Navigator, click on the text "Reports", and then the Data Model button on the Object Navigator.

2. Click on the Query tool.

3. The cursor changes to a large plus (+) sign. Drag the cursor into the workspace. Click to create query box Q_1.

4. Double-click on query Q_1 to bring up the Query Definition dialog box.

5. Enter the query text **select fac_id,emp_id,bonus_amt from bonus order by fac_id** in the SELECT Statement text box.

6. Click on Apply. If you are not still connected to Personal Oracle7, enter the user name and password when Oracle asks you to connect. Leave the Database area blank, since you are using a local database.

7. Click on Close to return to the Data Model screen as shown in Figure 9-25.

8. Click on the Default Layout tool. When the Default Layout dialog box appears, if the Data/Selection folder obscures the Style folder, click on the Style tab to bring the Style folder to the front. When presented with the six style options, notice that the Tabular option is selected.

9. Click on the Data/Selection tab. Change the headings for the columns to **Factory**, **Emp ID**, and **Bonus**, and the display widths for Factory to **7** and for Bonus to **12**. Click on OK to go to the Layout screen.

10. Click on the Run tool. Click on Run Report in the Runtime Parameter Form to bring up the report output on the Previewer window, as shown in Figure 9-26. Notice how the values for fac_id repeat even if the next factory is the same as the previous.

11. Define another group to allow for control break suppression of a repeating fac_id. After returning to the Data Model screen, click on fac_id in group G_1 and drag it somewhere else on the data model. The act of moving fac_id out of group G_1 and placing it on its own in group G_2 is what causes it not to be repeated until its value changes. Notice how group G_2 is created when the mouse is released.

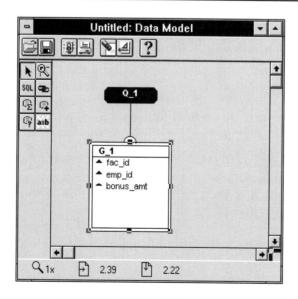

FIGURE 9-25. *Data model showing Q_1 and G_1*

12. Click on the Default Layout tool, then click on OK to go to the Layout screen. You need to go to the Default Layout dialog box (even though you do nothing there), so Oracle Reports can react to the creation of group G_1 and suppress repeating fac_id values until it changes.

13. Click on the Run tool. When presented with the Runtime Parameter Form, click on Run Report to produce the output shown in Figure 9-27. Notice how the fac_id value only shows at the start of the report and when its value changes.

14. Click on Close to close the Previewer window.

15. Press CTRL-S to save the new report, and when prompted, enter the name **reports2**.

16. Press CTRL-W to close the data model and return to the Object Navigator.

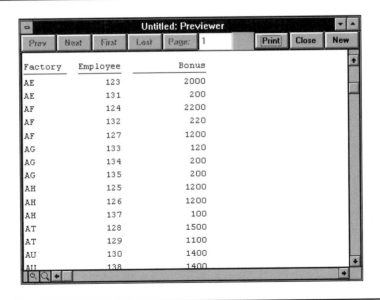

FIGURE 9-26.   *Report output in Previewer window*

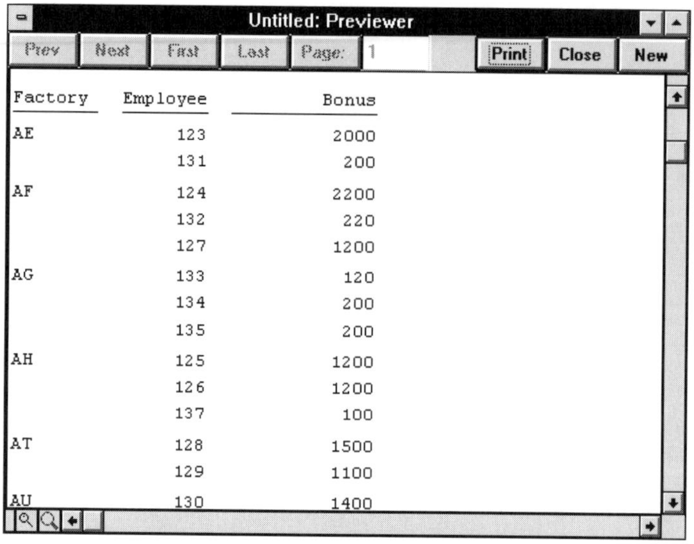

Untitled: Previewer							
Prev	Next	First	Last	Page: 1		Print	Close	New

Factory	Employee	Bonus
AE	123	2000
	131	200
AF	124	2200
	132	220
	127	1200
AG	133	120
	134	200
	135	200
AH	125	1200
	126	1200
	137	100
AT	128	1500
	129	1100
AU	130	1400

FIGURE 9-27. *Report output with fac_id control break suppression*

Sample Report #3

In this example we will:

- Define and show examples of matrix reports

- Show you how to break up a report group to allow for matrix reporting

- Show you how to define the matrix report cross-product group

- Show you how to modify the matrix report default layout

This example illustrates a feature of Oracle Reports called matrix reports. A matrix report uses values from columns selected in the report query as column and row headings. Using the data described in Table 9-5, the output from this type of report looks like the following.

COMM Table

qtr	number
sales_id	number
comm_amt	number(8,2)

TABLE 9-5.   *Table Used for Sample Report #3*

	1	2	3	4
10	200	300	400	70
20	150	40	600	
30		500	890	50

Notice how the sales_id column values are displayed down the page as row labels; the qtr column values display across the page as column headers; the actual comm_amt data populates the cells defined by the other two column values. The interesting thing about the matrix report is that if there is no data for the fourth quarter, the report display would change to this:

	1	2	3
10	200	300	400
20	150	40	600
30		500	890

Now, let's build this report.

1. Position yourself back at the Object Navigator, click on the text "Reports", then the Data Model button.

2. Click on the Query tool. The cursor changes to a large plus (+) sign. Drag the cursor into the workspace. Release the mouse, then double-click on query Q_1 to bring up the Query dialog box. Enter the query text **select qtr, sales_id, sum(comm_amt) from comm group by qtr, sales_id order by qtr, sales_id** in the SELECT Statement text box. Give the query a more descriptive name, changing the Name from Q_1 to Q_matrix.

3. Click on Apply, then click on Close to return to the data model.

4. Create groups G_2 and G_3 from group G_1. Click on qtr in group G_1 and drag it elsewhere in the data model to create group G_2. Click on sales_id in group G_1 and drag it elsewhere in the data model to create group G_3. Having these separate groups is required for matrix reporting. The resulting data model is shown in Figure 9-28.

5. Create the cross-product group (the secret behind matrix reporting). Oracle Reports uses the term "cross-product" to define a special group for matrix reporting. Click on the Cross Product tool and lasso the work area around groups G_2 and G_3. This creates group G_4 and the data model changes to that shown in Figure 9-29.

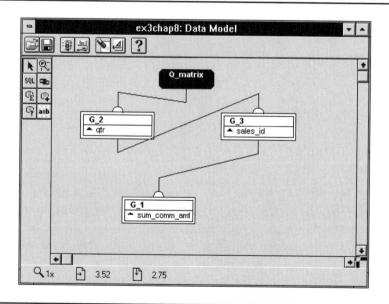

FIGURE 9-28.   *Data model showing groups G_1, G_2, and G_3*

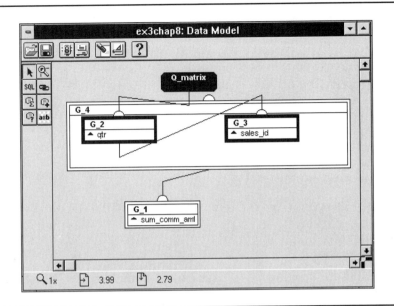

FIGURE 9-29. *Data model showing cross product group G4*

VIP

Before you lasso groups to create a cross-product group, you may have to move the groups around on the Data Model screen. The lasso you create cannot intersect any groups that are not in the cross-product group.

6. Click on the Default Layout button. When the Default Layout dialog box appears, click on Matrix in the Style folder.

7. Click on the Data/Selection tab. Blank out the labels for all three columns, and change the display width of comm_amt to **12**.

8. Notice the repeat direction for the first group is Matrix. Change the Repeat text beside the second group to Across. Having Across as the repeat function for this group immediately after the Matrix repeat group is another secret of matrix reporting. Accept this default layout by clicking on OK.

9. Click on the Run button. When presented with the Runtime Parameter Form, click on Run Report to produce the output shown in Figure 9-30. Notice there are no labels whatsoever on the report, and the column values from sales_id appear down the left side of the report. The qtr values appear across the top of the report as column headings.

10. Click on Close to close the Previewer window.

11. Press CTRL-S to save the report, and when prompted, enter the name **reports3**.

12. Press CTRL-W to close the report, then exit Oracle Reports by double-clicking on the control box, or selecting Files then Close from the menu at the top of the Oracle Reports screen.

This finishes the hands-on exercises using Oracle Reports Designer.

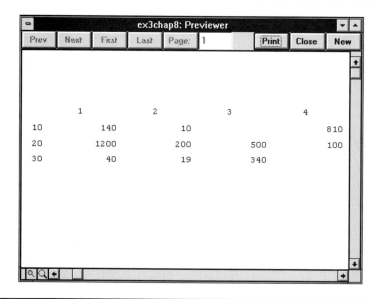

FIGURE 9-30. *Report output for matrix report*

Oracle Reports Runtime

This part of Oracle Reports is used to run reports. It is invoked by clicking on the Reports Runtime icon in the CDE2 Tools program group. When you are presented with the Runtime welcome screen, do the following to run a report:

1. Press CTRL-R to bring up the Open dialog box shown in Figure 9-31.

2. Once you have selected a report (e.g. **reports1**), click on OK.

3. Enter the user name and password when asked to connect to the Personal Oracle7 database.

4. When presented with the Runtime Parameter Form, click on Run Report. The next thing you will see is your report output.

5. Click on Close when done browsing the output.

This will leave you positioned at the Reports Runtime startup screen. After developers code Oracle Reports programs, the source code is compiled and becomes part of the set of application code delivered to the

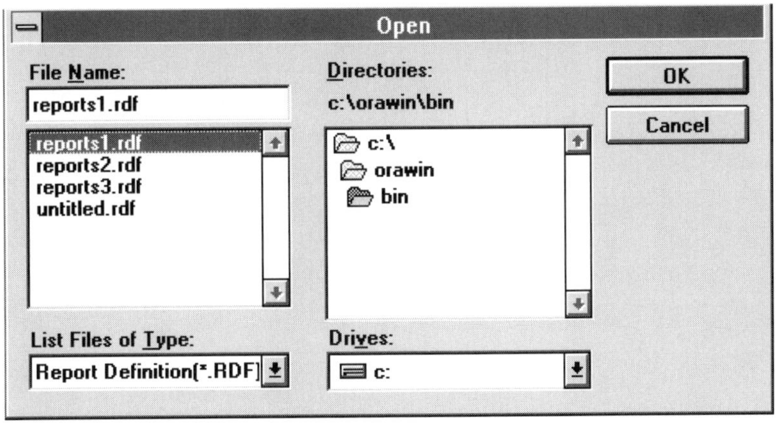

FIGURE 9-31. *Open report dialog box*

end user. The end user invokes Reports Runtime within an application to browse and print report output.

What's Next

We have just touched the surface with Oracle Reports. You can spend hours learning more about the tool's functionality, but in a relatively short period of time, you can teach yourself how to develop and deploy Oracle Reports to take advantage of its advanced features. For example, using the Parameter Screen Painter (we have not discussed this feature in this chapter), you can format the design of the dialog box Oracle Reports initiates when a report is invoked. You use the Parameter form to tell Oracle Reports where you want the output to be sent (printer or screen). Experiment with the features of Oracle Reports and make use of a very flexible and powerful reporting tool.

Our next chapter is about Oracle Loader. It rounds out this section on developer basics. One of the nice things about Oracle Loader is that, after you learn how to use it, you can take all your favorite data from one of your existing systems, move it into Oracle, and then write programs using the skills you have just acquired in this chapter and its predecessor ("Oracle Forms"). You've already come a long way.

CHAPTER
10

Loader

his chapter introduces Oracle Loader, the tool used to move data from another data source into the Oracle database. In this chapter we'll also offer some advice on using this tool effectively. When existing systems are converted to Oracle, Loader ensures that all the data is moved from an old system's format into Oracle's format. By the end of this chapter, you will know details on the following topics:

- Using Oracle Loader with Oracle8 for Windows NT

- How to run Oracle Loader and the parameters it requires

- The parts of an Oracle Loader control file

- The files written by Oracle Loader as it runs

Oracle Loader is pretty much the same regardless of the computer you are using. It behaves the same way whether you're running Oracle7 on a Macintosh or on an HP minicomputer, or Oracle8 in Windows NT.

Terminology

The following definitions will arm you with the technical jargon you need to make it through this chapter.

- A *text file* contains data that is made up of the numerals 0-9, the uppercase and lowercase characters A-Z, and the special characters ~[-]!@#$%^&*()_Ä +=|\?/>.<,"':;{[]}. You use text files to move data between different operating systems and computer types.

- A *control file* provides information to a program in the format of keywords and values. For example, when you're using Oracle Loader, the keyword bad= tells where to place the data that for some reason is not loaded into the Oracle database.

- A *record* is a row of information made up of all the data elements stored in an Oracle table. For example, in an inventory application,

each occurrence of a part_id and part_description is called a
record. The next table illustrates this concept:

Record #	Part id	Description
1	ABW34E	Thingimajigg
2	ABW45W	Whatchamicallit
3	ABW77H	Gitgatgiddle
4	ABW99K	Framazan

■ A *unique key* is used to uniquely identify each record in an
   Oracle table. There can be one and only one row with each unique
   key value.

In this chapter, as well as Chapter 15 where we discuss export and
import, we are going to feature the Oracle8 Windows NT character mode
interface rather than using the Data Manager.

VIP
*When the GUI interface is unavailable from
time to time, it may be necessary to run
Oracle Loader from a DOS window using the
command line rather than Data Manager.*

What Is Oracle Loader?

In this chapter, we will first look at Oracle Loader using the Oracle8 for
Windows NT interface. Then we will have a look at what's going on in the
background using Loader on a UNIX machine.

Oracle Loader reads files and places the data in the Oracle database
based on the instructions it receives from a control file. The control file tells
Oracle Loader where to place data, and it describes the kinds of data being
loaded into Oracle. It can filter records (i.e., not load records that do not
conform), load data into multiple tables at the same time, and generate a
unique key or manipulate data before placing it in an Oracle table.

Moving data out of your existing system into Oracle is a two-step process. First, you create a text file copy of your existing data using your current software, then you load the data from that text file into Oracle using Oracle Loader.

Sometimes Oracle Loader is called SQL*Loader; we use the two product names synonymously. Over the past few years, Oracle has taken the "SQL*" prefix off most of its products and replaced it with the company name. Since you may use Oracle Loader to move data into one or more tables, throughout this chapter we will also use the words "table" and "tables" interchangeably.

Running Oracle Loader—Oracle8

By the end of this section, you will know how to invoke Oracle Loader and the most common parameters supplied when Oracle Loader is invoked.

To invoke Oracle Loader, enter the command **sqlldr80**. If you do not include any parameters, you are given online help: the output will resemble what is shown in the following listing.

```
SQL*Loader: Release 8.0.3.0.1 - Production on Wed Apr 23 19:6:11 1999
Copyright (c) Oracle Corporation 1994, 1996.  All rights reserved.
Usage: SQLLOAD keyword=value [,keyword=value,...]
Valid Keywords:
       userid -- ORACLE username/password
      control -- Control file name
          log -- Log file name
          bad -- Bad file name
         data -- Data file name
      discard -- Discard file name
   discardmax -- Number of discards to allow         (Default all)
         skip -- Number of logical records to skip   (Default 0)
         load -- Number of logical records to load   (Default all)
       errors -- Number of errors to allow           (Default 50)
         rows -- Number of rows in conventional path bind array or between
                 direct path data saves
                    (Default: Conventional path 64, Direct path all)
     bindsize -- Size of conventional path bind array in bytes
                    (Default 65536)
       silent -- Suppress messages during run (header, feedback, errors,
                 discards, partitions)
```

```
         direct -- use direct path                        (Default FALSE)
       parfile -- parameter file: name of file that contains parameter
                    specifications
      parallel -- do parallel load                        (Default FALSE)
          file -- File to allocate extents from
skip_unusable_indexes -- disallow/allow unusable indexes or index
                         partitions   (Default FALSE)
skip_index_maintenance -- do not maintain indexes, mark affected
                          indexes as unusable  (Default FALSE)
commit_discontinued -- commit loaded rows when load is discontinued
                       (Default FALSE)
PLEASE NOTE: Command-line parameters may be specified either by
position or by keywords.  An example of the former case is 'sqlload
scott/tiger foo'; an example of the latter is 'sqlload control=foo
userid=scott/tiger'.  One may specify parameters by position before
but not after parameters specified by keywords.  For example,
'sqlload scott/tiger control=foo logfile=log' is allowed, but
'sqlload scott/tiger control=foo log' is not, even though the
        position of the parameter 'log' is correct.
```

There is a long list of parameters; however, most sessions will be started with commands similar to **sqlldr80 username control=cfile.ctl**. In the following sections, we will discuss userid and control plus a few more keywords from the previous listing which, if used, influence how Oracle Loader runs. Afterwards, we will present a few examples and show the command lines to accomplish the desired results.

NOTE
The keywords discussed in the next few sections have no specific order. If you provide keywords and values on the command line, they can be in any order.

Userid

Userid must be the user name and password for an account that owns the table being loaded or that has access to someone else's table for loading. If you omit the password, Oracle will prompt you for it as the session begins. Along with the control parameter, this is one of the two required inputs to Oracle Loader.

TIP
Let Oracle Loader prompt you for the password in order to protect your password confidentiality.

Normally, rather than include the keyword userid on the command line, you include an Oracle user name and let Oracle Loader prompt for the password. Thus, the command **sqlldr80 username** is the same as **sqlldr80 userid=username**; in both cases, you are prompted for the control filename, then the account password.

Control

Control names a file that maps the format of the input datafile to the Oracle table. The format of the control file is discussed in the "Oracle Loader Control File" section later in this chapter. If you do not include the control keyword when calling Oracle Loader, you are prompted, as in the following:

```
sqlload frieda
control = person
Password:
SQL*Loader: Release 8.0.3.1 - Production on Sat Mar 11 13:21:54 2000
Copyright (c) Oracle Corporation 1994, 1996.  All rights reserved.
```

TIP
Use the file extension .ctl for your Oracle Loader control files. It will be obvious that the control file is using this extension.

Parallel

Running Oracle Loader in parallel can speed up the time Oracle Loader takes to complete and, in situations where there are large amounts of input data, shrink runtimes dramatically. Invoking Oracle Loader with **parallel=true** runs multiple sessions, loading data simultaneously into the same table. When using this option, the target tables must have no indexes.

The parallel sessions' data is merged by Oracle in a number of temporary tables, then inserted as a single unit of data. This parameter defaults to false; a parallel session is started by coding **parallel=true** as Loader is invoked.

NOTE
Refer to the "Load Operations" piece in the "Parallelization" section of Chapter 19 for more details on running SQL*Loader in parallel.

Direct

When using a direct load, data is assembled in memory in the same format as Oracle data blocks, and the data block is copied directly into data blocks in the target datafile. This parameter defaults to false; to run a direct load, code **direct=true**. The direct load runs faster than conventional loads, especially when accompanied by **parallel=true**.

VIP
*If you choose **direct=true** for an Oracle Loader session, and for some reason the load aborts, any indexes on the target table will be left in direct load state and will have to be dropped and recreated.*

Skip

This parameter defaults to 0. If you code a positive integer value, Oracle Loader skips over the specified number of rows and starts loading with the record immediately after the specified number. This may prove useful in large loads. For example, you might browse the log file for a load that was supposed to move 1,000,000 rows into Oracle and find that the table has run out of space and received only 275,000 rows. Rather than redo the load from scratch, for the next session you could include the parameter **skip=275000**.

Load

This parameter defaults to all. If you code a positive integer value, Oracle will load that exact number of rows, then quit. You may want to use this if you want a subset of a very large amount of data moved into a development or test database for a system on its way to production.

Log and Bad

These two parameters are not normally mentioned on the command line. They inherit their filenames from the name of the control file used for the session. The command **sqlldr80 control=person.ctl** would log the session to **person.log** and write records that contain bad data into the file **person.bad**.

Discard

Sometimes you place one or more conditions on the input data; in this case, records that do not pass the condition(s) are discarded. If you include this parameter followed by a filename, these discarded records are written to the specified file. See the "Discard File" section later in this chapter, where we give an example of placing a condition on a load session.

Example #1

Pretend you want to invoke an Oracle Loader session using the parameters and parameter values from the following table. Say it's a large load, and you want to run multiple load sessions at the same time.

Component	Value
User name	frieda
Password	shoemaker
Control file	bruce
Load	all records
Parallel	yes
Direct	No

The command to accomplish the load as described in the previous table would be **sqlldr80 frieda/shoemaker control=bruce parallel=true**. Note that there is no filename extension on the file **bruce**, so Oracle Loader assumes the control filename is **bruce.ctl**. By excluding the parameters load and direct, they assume their defaults (i.e., all and false, respectively).

Example #2

This time we want to load an additional 1,000 records into a table. Records number 1 to 499 were loaded in a previous session. To speed things up, we wish to use the direct load path with parallel sessions.

Component	Value
User name	frieda
Password	shoemaker
Control file	bruce.crl
Skip	500
Direct	yes
Load	1000
Parallel	yes

The command to accomplish the load described in the previous table would be **sqlldr80 frieda/shoemaker control=bruce.crl parallel=true direct=true skip=500 load=1000**. Note the filename extension on the file **bruce** since it is not the Oracle Loader **.ctl** default.

Example #3

For this example, suppose you wanted to load records number 501 to 520 using the direct path load mechanism. This also illustrates how Oracle Loader prompts for missing components of a parameter (i.e., Oracle Loader expects a user name and password after the userid parameter, but we only supply the user name).

Component	Value
User name	frieda
Skip	500
Direct	yes
Load	20

Notice in this example that we will not supply a password or the name of the control file when invoking Oracle Loader. The command would be **sqlldr80 frieda direct=true load=20 skip=500**. Oracle will prompt for the missing parameters, as shown in the following listing:

```
control = bruce
Password:
SQL*Loader: Release 8.0.3.1 - Production on Thu Dec 29 18:08:43 2001
Copyright (c) Oracle Corporation 1994, 1996.  All rights reserved.
```

Notice that we enter **bruce** for the control filename, and Oracle Loader assumes its extension will be **.ctl**.

Oracle Loader Control File

We will now move on to building the control file. The control file sets up the environment for a Loader session: it tells Loader where to find the input datafile, which Oracle table the data should be loaded into, what, if any, restrictions to place on which data is loaded, and how to match the input data to the columns in the target table. When you're just getting started with Oracle Loader, the control file is the area that can cause the most problems. If the control file has errors, the Oracle Loader session stops immediately. Let's look at the four main parts of an Oracle Loader control file, as shown in Figure 10-1.

```
-- Notice this is how you embed
-- comments in a control file.
load data                                       -- Part 1
infile 'person.dat'                             -- Part 2
into table person                               -- Part 3
(first_name      position(01:14)    char,       -- Start of part 4
 surname         position(15:28)    char,
 clssn           position(29:36)    char,
 hire_date       position(37:42)    date 'YYMMDD')
```

FIGURE 10-1. *Sample control file*

We will now discuss the four parts shown in Figure 10-1, focusing on the format and the instructions each part gives to Oracle Loader.

Part 1: Load Data

The keywords *load data* start most Oracle Loader control files, regardless of the contents of the rest of the control file. They serve as a starting point for the rest of the control file, and nothing else. Think of these two keywords as the title page of a book.

Part 2: Infile

This line names the input file. Notice in Figure 10-1 how the input filename is enclosed in single quotes. Though the quotes are not mandatory here, they are required in some situations. For example, in UNIX, let's say the input file description line is infile $HOME/person.dat. The dollar sign causes the following error to be raised:

```
SQL*Loader: Release 8.0.3.1 - Production on Thu Dec 21 18:28:36 1999
Copyright (c) Oracle Corporation 1994, 1997.  All rights reserved.
SQL*Loader-350: Syntax error at line 2.
Illegal combination of non-alphanumeric characters
infile $HOME/person.dat
```

TIP
We recommend enclosing the input filename in single quotes. Get in the habit in case you find yourself working with Oracle Loader under circumstances where they are mandatory.

Part 3: Into Table

This line instructs Oracle Loader where to place the data as it is loaded into Oracle. There are four modifiers to the into table portion of the control file:

1. **Insert** is the default and expects the table to be empty when the load begins.

2. **Append** adds new rows to the table's existing contents.

3. **Replace** deletes the rows in the table and loads the new rows.

4. **Truncate** behaves the same as replace.

   Normally, you will not code the insert qualifier with Oracle Loader, since it is the default. The most common error you may encounter is when you try to load data into a table that contains rows, and you have not included append, replace, or truncate on the into table line. If this happens, Oracle Loader returns the following error:

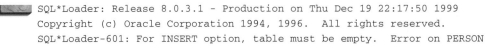

```
SQL*Loader: Release 8.0.3.1 - Production on Thu Dec 19 22:17:50 1999
Copyright (c) Oracle Corporation 1994, 1996.  All rights reserved.
SQL*Loader-601: For INSERT option, table must be empty.  Error on PERSON
```

Part 4: Column and Field Specifications

This section of the control file matches characters in the input file to the database columns of the target table. There are four parts to each line in this specification: the column name in the target table, the keyword position, the start and end character positions, and the data type of those characters in the input file. In Figure 10-1, the data in the input file starts in position 1 and goes to position 42, using every character in the input record. The position keyword followed by character number specifications becomes more meaningful when you wish to load parts of each line in the input file rather than the entire line. Picture the following column and field specifications in a control file:

```
(first_name position (01:14) char,
 surname     position (15:28) char,
 clssn       position (29:36) char,
 hire_date   position (40:46) date 'YYMMDD')
```

Whichever characters lie in positions 37 through 39 are ignored.

   Loading date fields into Oracle deserves special mention. Oracle dates default to the format DD-MON-YY, where DD stands for the day, MON for the three-character month name, and YY for the two-digit year. If the data in the input file is not in this format (and it usually isn't), you must tell Oracle how the dates appear in that file. Suppose the following four lines were fed into Oracle Loader:

```
BORIS        ABBEFLANTRO  AU2     830101
NANCY        BESDESMITH   MX      840926
```

```
FRANCIS        DEFWAYNO      DX       860422
NORMAN         NADROJIAN     CR5      860422
```

The column and position section of the control file would be

```
(first_name  position  (01:14)  char,
 surname     position  (15:28)  char,
 clssn       position  (29:36)  char,
 hire_date   position  (37:42)  date 'YYMMDD')
```

VIP
*The date format you specify in the control file
is the format of the data in the input file, **not**
the format you want Oracle to use for storage.*

Since there are rules for dates (e.g., the month 13 is impossible, as is the day 31 in the month of June), Oracle will reject data in the input file that violates these rules. Examine the errors returned while loading data into the created column in a table using the date format YYMMDD:

```
BORIS          ABBEFLANTRO   AU2      831501
NORMAN         NADROJIAN     MX       860422
NANCY          BESDESMITH    DX       840926
FRANCIS        DEFWAYNO      CR5      870229
Record 1: Rejected - Error on table STUFF, column CREATED.
ORA-01843: not a valid month
Record 4: Rejected - Error on table STUFF, column CREATED.
ORA-01847: day of month must be between 1 and last day of month
```

The first record is rejected because there is no month number 15 (83**15**01). The fourth record is rejected because there is no day number 29 in February, 1987 (8702**29**) : 1987 was not a leap year.

Oracle Loader Outputs

As Oracle Loader runs, it writes a number of files that are used to figure out how successful the load was. By default, Oracle Loader writes a log file and, based on the success or failure of the load and the parameters used when it is invoked, may write a bad and a discard file. Unless specified otherwise, these two extra files have the same name as the control file with the extensions **.bad** and **.dsc**, respectively.

Log File—Complete Load

The output shown in the following listing was produced by a session using the command sqlload control=person. Oracle Loader does not put the line numbers in the log file—we put them there for referencing in our discussion. The log file produced is called person.log.

```
 1  SQL*Loader: Release 8.0.3.1 - Production on Fri Mar 12 10:44:14 1998
 2  Copyright (c) Oracle Corporation 1994, 1997.  All rights reserved.
 3  Control File:   person.ctl
 4  Data File:      person.dat
 5  Bad File:      person.bad
 6   Discard File:  none specified
 7  (Allow all discards)
 8  Number to load: ALL
 9  Number to skip: 0
10  Errors allowed: 50
11  Bind array:     64 rows, maximum of 65536 bytes
12  Continuation:    none specified
13  Path used:      Conventional
14  Table PERSONNEL, loaded from every logical record.
15  Insert option in effect for this table: REPLACE
16  Column Name                    Position   Len  Term Encl Datatype
17  ------------------------------ ---------- ----- ---- ---- -------------
18  FIRST_NAME                          1:14    14             CHARACTER
19  SURNAME                            15:28    14             CHARACTER
20  CLSSN                              29:36     8             CHARACTER
21  HIRE_DATE                          37:42     6             DATE YYMMDD
22  Table PERSONNEL:
23  2609 Rows successfully loaded.
24  0 Rows not loaded due to data errors.
25  0 Rows not loaded because all WHEN clauses were failed.
26  0 Rows not loaded because all fields were null.
27  Space allocated for bind array:              3584 bytes(64 rows)
28  Space allocated for memory besides bind array:    52603 bytes
29  Total logical records skipped:          0
30  Total logical records read:          2609
31  Total logical records rejected:         0
32  Total logical records discarded:         0
33  Run began on Fri Mar 12 10:44:14 1996
34  Run ended on Fri Mar 12 10:44:16 1996
35  Elapsed time was:     00:00:02.12
36  CPU time was:         00:00:00.54
```

Lines 1 and 2 are the Oracle Loader herald displayed at the top of all log files. Lines 3 to 15 report on the parameters that were in effect as the session ran. Lines 16 to 21 report the column and table information as specified in the control file. Lines 22 to 26 show the number of rows loaded successfully as well as the number rejected. Lines 27 through 36 show the size of some of the Oracle Loader memory structures, start and stop times of the session, and the CPU time accumulated.

NOTE
The length of your Oracle Loader control file depends on the outcome of the session and the amount of table and column information displayed.

Log File—Incomplete Load

When one or more rows are rejected because of invalid data, Oracle Loader writes the bad rows to its bad file. The log file from an incomplete load is similar to the output shown earlier produced by a complete load, but with additional information.

Rejected Row Explanations

As Oracle Loader writes rejected rows to its bad file, it makes an entry in the session log file similar to the following:

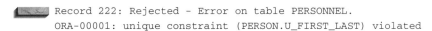

```
Record 222: Rejected - Error on table PERSONNEL.
ORA-00001: unique constraint (PERSON.U_FIRST_LAST) violated
```

The target table insists each first_name and surname combination must be unique; thus the data in record 222 is rejected, since it contains duplicate first_name and surname information. In the following listing, record 87 has no value in the first_name position in the input record, and the row is rejected:

```
Record 87: Rejected - Error on table PERSONNEL.
ORA-01400: mandatory (NOT NULL) column is missing or NULL during insert
```

Finally, record 1189 has been rejected, since the month number columns contain the number 14, which is not a valid month. The full date lies in columns 37 to 42 in the input data file; thus positions 39 and 40 are expected to contain a two-digit month number.

```
Record 1189: Rejected - Error on table PERSONNEL, column HIRE_DATE
ORA-01843: not a valid month
```

The log file displays the Oracle error number with some descriptive text to help you zero in on the reason.

Load Statistics

When one or more rows are rejected, the statistics change to reflect those numbers:

```
Table PERSONNEL:
   2903 Rows successfully loaded.
   3 Rows not loaded due to data errors.
   0 Rows not loaded because all WHEN clauses were failed.
   0 Rows not loaded because all fields were null.
```

VIP
You should verify that all the records in the input file were read by summing the numbers in the load statistics section of the log file. The result should equal the number of lines in the input file.

Bad File

This file is only written when one or more rows from the input file are rejected. In our example, we invoked Oracle Loader using the command **sqlload / control=person**. Thus, rejected rows, if any, are placed in a file called person.bad. The format of the rows in the bad file is the same as the input file. For example, record 1189 would be written to this bad file:

```
FWUFFEROO     DES          FE8        851429
```

There is no descriptive information in the bad file, so you must match the log file error messages with the bad file information.

VIP
If you use the same control file for successive Oracle Loader sessions, deal with the rows in each run's bad file before running the next session.

Here's a story of how not checking the bad file affected one of our clients. This client ran three Oracle Loader sessions using the same control file. The input to the three sessions was accrec1.dat, accrec2.dat, and accrec3.dat, each containing 11,000 records. The first run loaded 11,000 records successfully and created no bad file. The second run loaded 10,811 rows successfully and wrote 189 rows to the bad file. The client did not deal with the rows written to the bad file and instead ran the third session, which wrote a bad file containing 42 rows. The 189 rows written to the bad file by the second session were lost and were never loaded properly. When the client's employees started to use the data on their application, they wondered why information was missing!

Discard File

The control file shown in Figure 10-1 instructed Oracle Loader to attempt to load all records in the input file. In the following listing, the control file uses the when keyword to discard rows whose clssn column positions contain the text "CR4."

```
load data
infile 'person.dat'
into table personnel
when clssn <> 'CR4'
(first_name position (01:14) char,
 surname     position (15:28) char,
 clssn       position (29:36) char,
 hire_date   position (37:42) date 'YYMMDD')
```

The discard file is not created unless the **discard=** parameter is used when invoking Oracle Loader.

What's Next

We have introduced you to Oracle Loader and shown you how it is used to move data from text files into Oracle database tables. The material we covered here just skims the surface, but you now have enough information to use Oracle Loader for most load session requirements. Oracle Loader contains a wealth of additional functionality you can use for more sophisticated sessions. Experiment with Oracle Loader and investigate its power—you will use it from day one.

This chapter completes the Developer Basics section of this book, in which we have talked about SQL, PL/SQL, Oracle Forms, Oracle Reports, and Oracle Loader. Armed with the knowledge gained from this section, carry on.

CHAPTER
11

Application Tuning 101

his chapter is the first of four in the "Developer Bells and Whistles" section of this book. In the "Developer Basics" section (Chapters 6 through 10), we provided you with a foundation. Now, it's time to move on.

Most corporations and individuals purchase software to help them carry on their day-to-day activities. All of us expect systems written using this software to operate efficiently—we expect them to ingest gobs of information and do exactly what we want them to do quickly. Realistically, we can only expect them to do this if the applications are tuned. Tuning is a process whereby applications are optimized to run as quickly as possible and use as few computer resources as possible.

Oracle, like all other vendors, provides tools with which to write custom applications. In this book, we discuss some of the tools Oracle provides for this purpose: SQL*Plus (Chapters 6 and 12), Oracle Forms (Chapter 8), Oracle Reports (Chapter 9), and PL/SQL (Chapter 7). Developers (also called programmers) who write code with these Oracle products will want to write code that uses the Oracle8 Server efficiently. All too often, when a new computer system is installed, the users complain about how slow the system is and how long it takes to get responses to queries on its screens. By the end of this chapter, you will have some basics on the following:

- Why applications should be tuned

- The two main components in the tuning process

- How Oracle stores data

- How Oracle processes SQL statements

- The shared pool or shared SQL area

- Writing SQL statements to use the shared pool

- Using indexes to access data more efficiently

- Taking advantage of parallel processing

- Ways to reduce wait situations

Why Tune Oracle Systems?

As new applications come on board, we hear constant complaining about how poorly they perform. As applications are written, you should attend to their performance and make it as important a component as the programming itself. There are many short- and long-term benefits to tuning applications:

■ Well-tuned applications require less attention down the road.

■ Your end users will be happier with the system's performance and its ability to process more data in less time.

■ Applications that have been tuned make more efficient use of resources on your computer.

There is only a finite amount of computing power on any computer. This is especially crucial in a multiuser system when more than one person is using the system simultaneously. The throughput of your systems will be better with tuned applications. Throughput is a measurement of the amount of data your systems are capable of processing in a given time period. The more time you spend tuning applications, the more information they will be able to ingest and send back to you as reports, graphs, and onscreen query results.

Tuning applications can be a time-consuming and frustrating exercise, but using the ideas and guidelines in this chapter, you will get the most bang for your buck. In Chapter 13, we discuss more technical details of the tuning process.

Terminology

The following definitions will arm you with the technical jargon to make it through this chapter:

■ A *query* is a request for information from the database. For example, when you press the green key (commonly the one that tells the machine which account you wish to work with) on the automatic teller machine, you are requesting a balance from your checking account.

■ *Query results* are the data that satisfy a query. The account balance displaying on the ATM screen is an example of query results.

■ *Disk access* is the act of reading information from the database files on disk.

■ A *wait situation* arises when a user process is "standing by" while resources or data it requires are being tied up by other user processes.

■ A *view* is a subset of one or more tables' data assembled in memory to satisfy the results of a SQL statement. One example of a view is a list of all employees in the western region of a company; the table on which that view is built contains all the employees regardless of their location.

■ A *synonym* is a name stored in the data dictionary used to refer to tables and views. Think of a synonym as a nickname for tables and views.

■ A *public synonym* is created by the DBA (database administrator), pointing at an object somewhere in the database. Any user can refer to that object using the public synonym.

■ A *data dictionary* is maintained by Oracle containing information relevant to the database. It is used by Oracle to find out who is allowed to log into the database, what datafiles are associated with the database, and other information required to permit your systems to operate. As well, Oracle stores information about what the data in the database looks like. For example, Oracle's data dictionary defines the fact that a North American area code is three numbers (i.e., no letters or special characters) and that the states and provinces are two letters (no numbers or special characters).

■ An *object* is an umbrella definition encompassing all data source names stored in Oracle's data dictionary. Objects are usually tables, but they can also be views or synonyms.

■ A *cache* is a portion of memory that Oracle reserves to do a specific job as the database operates. The caches contain data that has been read from the database, information about the SQL statements that have been processed, and other information required to run the instance.

■ An *execution plan* is the "map" that Oracle builds to get at the data that satisfies a user's query. The plan is built using statistics about the data that reside in the data dictionary. When Oracle builds an execution plan, it looks for the shortest and least costly route—somewhat like using the ABCFHI route rather than the ABDEGHI route, as shown in Figure 11-1.

■ A *block* is the smallest unit of storage that Oracle uses. The block size of the database is set when the database is created and can range from 2K (2,048 bytes) up to 16K (16,384 bytes). Oracle maintains a list in memory of free data blocks and places new information created by your applications in them.

■ The operation that reads data from and writes data to disk is called *I/O* (input/output).

■ Oracle assigns a *rowid* to data as it places it in data blocks. The rowid uniquely identifies each row in the database.

■ An *index* is a structure separate from a table that contains one or more column values from a table plus the rowids of the rows with those values.

■ A *select list* is the group of columns mentioned in the SQL statement, following the **select** keyword up to the list of objects referenced in the **from** portion of the statement. In the following SQL statement, the boldfaced text is called the select list:

```
select last_name, first_name, date_of_birth
  from person
 where pin = 100720;
```

■ A *secure database operation* is an Oracle database operation usually restricted to DBA users. Creating a tablespace, creating new users, and managing rollback segments are examples of secure database operations.

■ A *system privilege* is given to users and allows them to perform secure database operations. For example, the system privilege **select any table** allows the recipient to select data in any object anywhere in the database.

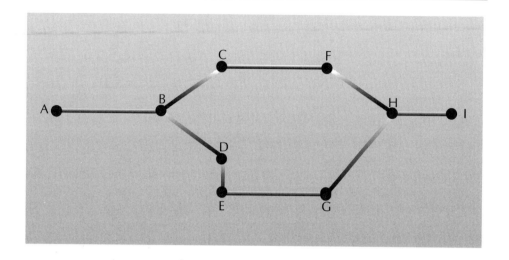

FIGURE 11-1. *Two paths to get from A to I*

Main Components in the Tuning Process

Tuning Oracle applications is much the same exercise regardless of the size of a computer on which Oracle is running. Tuning zeros in on a computer's main components and ensures they are being used efficiently. All computers are made up of the following components:

- The central processing unit (CPU) is responsible for all operations the computer will undertake. You often hear of a 386, a 486, and a Pentium in the microcomputer world, or DEC Alpha in the minicomputer environment. These are processor class names that have become part of computer lingo. The faster the processor, the faster the computer.

VIP

With the advent of computers with more than one CPU, parallel processing alone has taken a giant leap towards speeding execution of applications.

■ Secondary storage devices such as hard drives, floppy disk drives, and CD-ROMs are used to save information that applications create as they operate.

■ Computer memory is where programs operate and commonly requested data waits in anticipation of the next request for information.

■ The other peripherals that complete the requirements are a computer monitor and a keyboard.

VIP

The two main components in the tuning process are reading information from memory and reducing I/O operations.

The next section of this chapter will discuss the roles that reading information from memory and reducing I/O operations play in the tuning process.

Memory

Since all computers contain a finite amount of memory, making optimal use of memory is a contributing factor to tuning. In this section, we will discuss the basics on the following:

■ How all data is routed through memory

■ The communication lines from the database to the users

■ The shared SQL area

■ The key to efficient use of memory

As Oracle runs, it receives requests for data from users. The data sits in an assortment of datafiles on disk. The flow of information among users, memory, and the database is outlined in Figure 11-2.

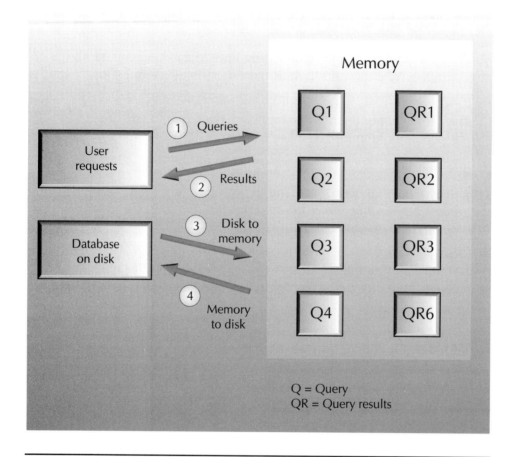

FIGURE 11-2. *Flow of information among database, memory, and users*

Notice the four communication lines:

■ User to memory (UM): Requests for data initiated by applications are assembled in memory, where Oracle decides the most efficient way to get to the desired data.

■ Memory to user (MU): Results of queries are transferred from memory to the user session that made the request.

■ Disk to memory (DM): As requests are received, data that satisfies the request is transferred to memory.

■ Memory to disk (MD): Data that has been changed or created is written to disk.

There is no direct communication between the database and the users. All reads, writes, and changes to data pass through Oracle memory structures. This stresses the importance of using memory efficiently.

VIP
Oracle keeps the results of previously executed queries in memory until the space they occupy is required for results to more recent queries.

Oracle maintains a shared SQL area in memory, also referred to as the shared pool. All SQL statements are executed from this pool. When a SQL statement is passed to Oracle, before loading a SQL statement into this pool, Oracle searches this pool for an identical statement. If it finds a match, the new statement is discarded and the one already in the pool is executed in its place. We'll refer to the preparation for execution and placement in the shared pool as the preparation phase.

When an SQL statement is passed to Oracle for execution, it must first be placed in the shared pool. Oracle executes SQL statements after loading them into the shared pool.

VIP
Oracle keeps prepared SQL statements in the shared pool. These statements are executed when an identical request is received from a user.

How the Communication Lines Are Used to Process Queries

Let's look at the way Oracle would process five queries from user processes using the four communication lines UM, MU, DM, and MD introduced in Figure 11-2. The indicator PR stands for "prepare SQL statement" in Tables 11-1 and 11-2.

The memory shown in Figure 11-2 is the shared pool; it contains prepared SQL statements Q1, Q2, Q3, and Q4 as well as query results QR1, QR2, QR3, and QR6, which are still in memory. The Processing column values in the table show the communication lines from Figure 11-2 that are used to process each query and return its results.

The processing for queries Q1, Q2, and Q3 are the most desirable, since there is no disk access. Next desirable is processing Q6; even though the SQL statement has to be prepared, there is no disk access. Q4 requires disk access; even though the prepared statement is still in memory, its

Query	Processing	Reason
Q1	UM MU	This can be satisfied in memory since the prepared SQL statement Q1 as well as its query results QR1 still reside there.
Q2	UM MU	This too can be satisfied in memory since the prepared SQL statement Q2 as well as its query results QR2 still reside there.
Q3	UM MU	This too can be satisfied in memory since the prepared SQL statement Q3 as well as its query results QR3 still reside there.
Q4	UM MD DM MU	The prepared SQL statement Q4 still resides in the shared pool. The results to that query the last time it was executed have been removed from memory. Hence, the new request must read data from disk, put it in memory, then pass it back to the user.
Q5	UM PR MD DM MU	There is no prepared SQL statement in memory. Hence, this request needs to prepare the SQL statement, read data from disk, put it in memory, then pass it back to the user. This is the least desirable of all processing situations since the SQL statements need to be prepared, then data must be read from disk.
Q6	UM PR MU	There is no matching prepared SQL statement, though the query results QR6 are still in memory.

TABLE 11-1. *Query Processing Using Memory*

Query	Processing	Reason
Q1	UM MU	This can be satisfied in memory since the prepared SQL statement Q1 as well as its query results QR1 still reside there.
Q2	UM MU	This too can be satisfied in memory since the prepared SQL statement Q2 as well as its query results QR2 still reside there.
Q3	UM MU	This too can be satisfied in memory since the prepared SQL statement Q3 as well as its query results QR3 still reside there.
Q4	UM MD DM MU	The prepared SQL statement Q4 still resides in the shared pool. The results to that query the last time it was executed have been removed from memory. Hence, the new request must read data from disk, put it in memory, then pass it back to the user.
Q5	UM PR MD DM MU	There is no prepared SQL statement in memory. Hence, this request needs to prepare the SQL statement, read data from disk, put it in memory, then pass it back to the user. This is the least desirable of all processing situations since the SQL statements need to be prepared, then data must be read from disk.
Q6	UM PR MU	There is no matching prepared SQL statement, though the query results QR6 are still in memory.

TABLE 11-2. *Processing Query Using an Index*

query results are not in memory. Oracle prepares the statement issued by Q5 and must retrieve its results from disk.

VIP
Access to data in memory is quicker than access to data on disk. It is desirable to get as much information as possible from memory.

VIP
If you can write SQL statements that match those sitting in the pool, the preparation phase can be skipped. Avoiding the preparation phase is the single most important area to attend to when tuning Oracle applications.

Disk Access

Reading information from disk is referred to as disk access. Minimizing disk access is important given the operations the computer performs when reading from disk. It takes time to position the reader above the exact spot on the disk where the data resides, and the time to transfer the data to memory can become quite significant. In this section, we will discuss the basics on the following:

- How Oracle stores data

- How Oracle accesses your data

- How to minimize disk access

We mentioned in the previous section how all data is transferred from disk to memory before being made available to users. I/O is required to make this transfer. Oracle places data in blocks in the datafiles that make up the database. When a data block is too full to hold any more data, Oracle places its data in the other blocks in the datafile. Each row in a data block can be identified by its address or rowid. Oracle fetches data for your queries using one of the two methods discussed in the next few sections. We now discuss using indexes to help minimize disk access. When we show you how Oracle processes data with and without an index, you will begin to see their advantages when attending to application tuning.

Processing with an Index

If an index exists, and a SQL statement is worded in a way to take advantage of the index, the index is searched first. Oracle reads the index and processes according to the steps shown in Table 11-2.

VIP
The number of I/O operations to process a query using an index can be significantly lower than the number required to process a query without an index.

Think of an index as an address book: the rows of data are the names in that book, and the rowids are the street addresses. If you know that the Jacobs live at 234 Rideau, you can proceed directly to the location of their house. If you know the Jacobs live on Rideau but you don't have their address, you would have to go from house to house until you found them. Oracle goes through the same exercise when using indexes. Indexes provide rapid access to your data.

Figure 11-3 shows a very simple example. Suppose the column values shown for tableA are in the column named ID. IndexA contains ID column values plus the location of the first column with that ID value (i.e., the first row with ID=15 can be found in location 005).

The user passes a SQL statement to Oracle on tableA looking for the data in the row with ID=15. Oracle reads entries in indexA to find where it should look in the table data to find the desired row. If Oracle read indexA from start to finish, it would encounter the address for ID=15 in the fourth entry in the index and proceed to get the data from the row at address 005. If indexA did not exist, Oracle would read tableA and find the ID=15 in the fifth row in the table. This example shows how Oracle would need to perform one additional I/O if indexA did not exist.

Processing Without an Index

When no index exists that can be used to satisfy a query, Oracle does a full table scan. It reads every row in a table and evaluates column values against the selection criterion. It discards rows that do not qualify and includes rows that do. Oracle reads every row in the table, processing according to the steps in Table 11-3.

and there are 80,000 rows in the table. Oracle has packed 40 book records into each data block. Thus, data blocks numbered 0001 to 2000 contain book information. Suppose Oracle has placed a book with ISBN 882122-3 in data block number 0807. If the table has an index, fetching that book's data would require two I/O operations—the first to read the index entry and get the rowid of where the 882122-3 row is stored, and the second to retrieve the book's publisher and year in print. If there is no index, Oracle would have to read the table's data starting with data block 0001 until it reached a data block with the desired ISBN (data block 0807). Thus, without an index, fetching the book's data would require 807 I/O operations!

Using Statements in the Shared Pool

As we stated near the start of this chapter, using memory efficiently is a large contributor to the application-tuning process. Coupled with using indexes (which results in minimizing disk access), you are well on your way to tuning applications. In this section, we will discuss some of the basics on the following:

- How Oracle processes SQL statements
- How to word SQL statements to reuse ones already in the pool
- How to implement coding conventions
- How to store code in the database

Process	Next Step	
1. Are there more rows in the table?	YES=2	NO=4
2. Do the column values in this row match the selection criterion?	YES=3	NO=1
3. Mark the data for inclusion in the query results.	1	
4. Display query results.		

TABLE 11-3. *Processing Without an Index*

Steps in SQL Statement Processing

When Oracle receives a SQL statement, it runs an internal routine to compute the statement's value. To illustrate computing a value, let's run a very simple routine using the U.S. cities shown in Table 11-4.

Notice that each city/state combination has been assigned a six-digit ID. Let's pretend the ID is the same as the identifier that Oracle assigns to every table as it is created. Now we will look at some SQL statements that use these city names as table names, and we'll figure out the value of each statement. You can see how the statement

```
select col1, col2, col3, col4
   from PORTLAND              /* OR in this case */
 where col5 > col6;
```

is not the same as

```
select col1, col2, col3, col4
   from PORTLAND              /* ME in this case */
 where col5 > col6;
```

The value of the city coded in the former statement is 978219, and the one in the latter is 446721. Similarly, in the next three statements, the first two statements are the same, but the second and third are not:

```
select col1, col2, col3, col4
   from SPRINGFIELD           /* MA in this case */
 where col5 > col6;
select col1, col2, col3, col4
   from SPRINGFIELD           /* MA in this case */
 where col5 > col6;
select col1, col2, col3, col4
   from SPRINGFIELD           /* MO in this case */
 where col5 > col6;
```

The value of the city coded in the first two statements is 893417, and the value in the third statement is 662198.

VIP

Using the same name for objects in a SQL statement is not enough; the names must evaluate to the same object in the database.

City	State	ID
Portland	ME	446721
Portland	OR	978219
Springfield	MA	893417
Springfield	MO	662198

TABLE 11-4. *U.S. Cities, States, and Identifiers*

Table 11-5 gives a thumbnail sketch of how a statement is evaluated when sent for processing. The computing of a statement's value is shown as the first step.

Ideally, statements should be processed using steps 1, 2, 3, and 8. Statements passed to Oracle that do not pass the tests in both steps 2 and 3 are processed using steps 1, 2, 3, 4, 5, 6, 7, and 8. Wording SQL statements in such a way to take the 1-2-3-8 path is more efficient than taking the 1-through-8 path.

Wording SQL Statements to Reuse Ones in the Pool

In this section, we will discuss adopting coding conventions and storing code in the database.

When SQL statements are passed to Oracle for processing, the secret is to reuse a statement already in the pool rather than forcing Oracle to prepare each new statement as it is received. We stated previously that Oracle reuses statements in the shared pool if it receives one identical to one already in the pool. In the next two sections, we discuss standardizing the format of the code you write and using centralized code stored in the Oracle data dictionary.

Coding Conventions

We will present one of many possible schemes for coding SQL statements. Adopt this method if you like the looks of it.

Process	Next Step	
1. Compute the value of statement.	2	2
2. Is there a statement in the pool with the same value?	YES=3	NO=4
3. Is there a statement in the pool that matches character by character?	YES=8	NO=4
4. Prepare the SQL statement for execution.	5	
5. Make room for the new statement in the pool.	6	
6. Place the statement in the shared pool.	7	
7. Update the map of the pool showing statement values and location in the pool.	8	
8. Execute the prepared SQL statement.	8	

TABLE 11-5.   *Simplified Steps for Parsing a SQL Statement*

NOTE
Establishing and USING a coding convention is more important than the actual style you decide to use.

Once you have a convention in place, you can start coding SQL statements to take advantage of ones already in the shared pool. To get the most out of this discussion, you should have read Chapter 6 and/or Chapter 12.

The **select** statement in SQL is made up of five parts. Using the following code, let's review the components of a statement.

```
select col1, col2, sum(col3)    /* Part 1 */
    from fiscal_year            /* Part 2 */
  where col1 > col2             /* Part 3 */
    and col1 > 10               /* Part 3 */
  group by col1, col2           /* Part 4 */
  order by col1;                /* Part 5 */
```

These are the five component parts of a SQL statement:

- The **select** keyword that starts the statement followed by the list of columns being displayed in the query results

- One or more tables from which the data is obtained

- One or more conditions that determine which values are desired

- The **group by** keyword followed by one or more column names on which some summarizing is to be done as the data is fetched

- The **order by** keyword followed by a list of one or more columns that determine the sorting method for the desired rows

The guidelines we now present help ensure that SQL statements you code can find a match against one already prepared and sitting in the shared pool.

FORMATTING THE PARTS OF THE SQL STATEMENT   Rather than letting the statement spill haphazardly onto the next line at column 80, do the following:

```
select col1, col2, sum(col3)
   from fiscal_year
 where col1 > col2
   and col1 > 10
 group by col1, col2
 order by col1;
```

NOTE
*You could take a plastic ruler and line it up with the **select** keyword to ensure that all other lines' keywords align with the letter "t" from **select**. The | (vertical line) in the next listing represents that ruler.*

```
select|col1, col2, sum(col3)
   from|fiscal_year
 where|col1 > col2
   and|col1 > 10
 group|by col1, col2
 order|by col1;
```

GUIDELINE 1

*Use a separate line for each part of the SQL statement. Align the first keyword in each line to end in the same column as the **select** keyword on the first line.*

UPPERCASE OR LOWERCASE?   Lowercase code is easier on the eyes than either mixed case or all uppercase. Some installations decide to use uppercase for all SQL special words and lowercase for all others. The problem is that developers forget which is which. You could easily end up with the following two statements:

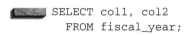
```
SELECT col1, col2
    FROM fiscal_year;
```

and

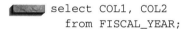
```
select COL1, COL2
    from FISCAL_YEAR;
```

Both statements are written by developers trying to ensure they conform to the uppercase and lowercase convention. Using mixed case, it's just too easy to forget which is which.

GUIDELINE 2

Use lowercase characters in all SQL statements.

COMMAS EMBEDDED IN THE STATEMENT   We find the code easier to read leaving a space after the comma. For example, we find the first code easier to read than the second in the following:

```
select col1, col2, sum(col3)
```

```
select col1,col2,sum(col3)
```

GUIDELINE 3
Put commas right beside the text they follow,
and leave one space afterwards.

COMMAS AS THE LAST CHARACTER ON A LINE   In come cases, developers like to place the trailing comma on one line as the first character in the next line:

```
select col1, col2
      ,col3
```

We prefer to see it the following way:

```
select col1, col2,
       col3
```

GUIDELINE 4
When a comma is the last character on a line,
put it on that line rather than skipping to the
next line and then inserting the comma.

FORMATTING CONTINUATION LINES   When the same part of a SQL statement continues onto the next line, line them up as in the following listing:

```
select col1, col2, sum(col3), col4, col5, sum(col6),
       col7, col8, col9, col10, col11, col 12, col13
```

GUIDELINE 5
Start lines in column 8 that belong to the same
part as the previous line.

FORMATTING THE STATEMENT QUALIFIERS   When formatting the **where** and **and** part of the SQL statement (also referred to as the predicate), the placement of each **and** should resemble

```
where
    and
    and
    and
    and
```

GUIDELINE 6

*When you have the **where** followed by one or more lines that start with **and**, start the former in column 2 and the latter in column 4.*

FORMATTING PARENTHESES   Syntax requires the use of parentheses in many SQL statements. The most common spot is where a function (e.g., finding the largest value with **max** or taking the first three characters of a 10-character string with substr) is used is a column in a select list as in

```
select col1, col2, sum(col3)
```

GUIDELINE 7

Leave no spaces on either side of parentheses when they appear in SQL statements.

STATEMENT TERMINATOR   This statement terminator is the signal to Oracle that you are done coding your statement, and wish to begin processing. You may use the semicolon (;) or the forward slash (/).

GUIDELINE 8

Use the semicolon (;) terminator for SQL*Plus statements. When your programs contain a mixture of SQL*Plus and PL/SQL, you must terminate a group of PL/SQL statements with a slash (/). Reserve using the slash for that purpose.

FORMATTING OPERATORS   When you compare column values in your SQL statements, you most commonly use the equal sign (=). Other operators, such as <> for not equal or > for greater than, are coded like the equal sign.

GUIDELINE 9
Leave a space on either side of operators used anywhere in SQL statements.

SQL statements are easier to read with spaces, as shown in the following example:

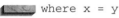

```
where x = y
  and d = c
  and j = p
```

rather than

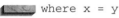

```
where x=y
  and d=c
  and j=p
```

VIP
Design your coding conventions (or use the ones we've recommended) and stick to them. Passing statements for processing that are identical to ones already in the pool helps tune your applications.

EXAMPLES   Theory is all fine and dandy, plus a whole bunch of guidelines as we have outlined. Seeing them put into practice will crystallize the theory we speak about in the previous section. Let's look at two more complex examples; they are commented to highlight the implementation of the guidelines we have presented.

```
rem *************** Example #1 *******************

rem * The decode in the column list starts back in column 8 so the code
rem * in parentheses within the decode is not broken onto two lines.
rem * There is a single space left after each comma as well as
rem * no space before the opening parenthesis in the decode.
select fy_code, prd.prod_num, prd.sdesc_e, proj_num, prj.sdesc_e,
       comm_amt, comm_amt*1.10,
       decode(fiscal, 'Y', 'multi', 'single'), bud_class
  from prod prd, project prj, bud_mast bud, commitment
 where prd.prod_num = prj.prod_num
   and bud.rpt_cat = prd.rpt_cat
 order by fy_code, prd.prod_num;


rem *************** Example #2 *******************

select max('&1'), max('&2'), max(sysdate), max('DETAIL'), max(a.sr),
       b.sdesc_e,
       /*  Note how the parentheses have no spaces on either side  */
       /*  and there is one space after each comma but nothing     */
       /*  before.                                                 */
       nvl(round(sum(nvl(a.comm_amt, 0)), 0), 0),
       nvl(round(sum(nvl(a.precomm_amt, 0)), 0), 0),
       nvl(round(sum(nvl(a.budget_orig, 0)), 0), 0),
       nvl(round(sum(nvl(a.budget_rev,0)), 0), 0),
       nvl(round(sum(nvl(a.exp_accr, 0)), 0),0),
       nvl(round(sum(nvl(a.exp_accr_comm, 0)), 0), 0),
       nvl(round(sum(nvl(a.free_bal, 0)), 0), 0),
       nvl(round(sum(nvl(a.adj_bal, 0)), 0), 0)
  from fms_financials a, fms_control_obj b
 where b.cobj_type = 'SR'        /* The first word in each line ends in  */
   and b.cobj_code = a.sr        /* column 8.                            */
   and b.fy_code = '&2'
   and a.repname = '&1'          /* All the where and and lines line     */
   and a.fy_code = '&2'          /* up with one another.                 */
   and a.qualifier = 'SRDETAIL'
 group by a.sr, b.sdesc_e;
```

Storing Code in the Database

Oracle provides the ability to store segments of code in the database. As your applications operate, this code is read from the database and passed to the shared pool for processing like any other SQL statement.

VIP
*Code read from the database will almost
always match a code segment already
prepared and resident in the shared pool.*

Suppose you work at a library and you want to be able to generate an electronic reminder to the front desk every morning that identifies the borrower, book title, and author of books more than seven days overdue. You may have a number of applications that can initiate these reminders by clicking on an Overdue Note button on a lending information screen. Each of those screens may have its own code behind the scenes handling overdue notice generation, or each screen may invoke a routine similar to the following:

```
create or replace procedure overdue_notice (borrower_ident char) as
   l_book_name      varchar2(40);
   l_book_ident     number;
   l_due_date       date
   -- Get any overdue book numbers for current person
   cursor mycur is
     select book_name, book_ident, due_date
       from overdue_notes
      where borrower_id = borrower_ident;
   begin
     open mycur;
     fetch mycur into l_book_name, l_book_ident, l_due_date;
     while mycur%found loop
        -- Create an overdue notice
        insert into overdue_notes
           values (book_ident, book_name, borrower_ident,
                   book_title, was_due, sysdate, user);
        fetch mycur into l_book_name, l_book_ident, l_due_date;
     end loop;
   end;
 /
```

The following SQL text places the PL/SQL in the database:

```
create or replace
```

NOTE
*Use the **create or replace** syntax when storing objects in the Oracle8 database to avoid having to drop the procedure, package, or function before creation.*

VIP
Design your applications to take advantage of code stored in the database. Look at all your business processes and centralize common procedures. Study existing applications and convert their centralized processing routines into code segments stored in the database.

IMPLEMENTING STORED PROCEDURES   In conjunction with the DBA you work with, there are some things to do before you can store procedures in the database and start using them. It is not simply a matter of deciding to use stored procedures. You must consult with your DBA or the implementation may not work for the reasons outlined below:

- Stored procedures occupy space in the system tablespace in your database. You may have to work with the DBA to ensure the space in this tablespace is sufficient. The DBA may have allocated space for this system tablespace before stored procedures were investigated.

- You must give other users privileges to execute your procedures by issuing a command similar to **grant execute on overdue_notice to public;**.

- The DBA must create a public synonym for your stored procedure; for example, **create public synonym overdue_notice for polly.overdue_notice;**.

CALLING STORED PROCEDURES   Stored procedures can be executed from a PL/SQL block (we discuss PL/SQL blocks in Chapter 7), as in

```
-- other PL/SQL statements followed by
if sysdate - :due_back >= 6 then
   overdue_notice (borr_ident);
end if;
```

Stored procedures can be executed from SQL*Plus (we discuss SQL*Plus in Chapter 6 and Chapter 12), as in

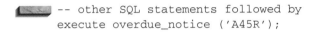

```
-- other SQL statements followed by
execute overdue_notice ('A45R');
```

NOTE
When calling procedures, packages, and functions, one must pass the correct number of parameters with the appropriate data type to the stored object.

Triggers, Functions, and Packages

Besides stored procedures, Oracle provides for three other kinds of centralized code that is stored and read from the database: triggers, functions, and packages.

- ■ Triggers are associated with tables and run transparently when predefined events happen to the data in the table. For example, you may use a database trigger to log the fact that an accounts receivable clerk has lowered the amount owing on an outstanding account.

- ■ Functions accept a number of parameters and pass a single value back to the calling program. For example, the validation of a ZIP code could be done with a function. The routine would be invoked with a ZIP code, and the function could pass back true or false depending on whether the ZIP code is valid.

VIP
You can embed your own functions in SQL statements in the same way you use Oracle8 SQL functions on number, date, or character data.

Look at the next listing to see how a user-defined function is set up and then used in an SQL statement:

```
SQL> create or replace function is_yorn (in_char varchar2) return boolean is
  2    if in_char = 'Y' then
  3       return true;
  4    else
  5       return false;
  6    end;
  7  /
Function created.
SQL> select last_name, first_name, cdesc_e, c_inc_date
  2    from person a, cstat b
  3   where a.c_code = b.c_code
  4     and is_yorn(a.status) = 'Y'
  5     and a.pin = 100782;
LAST_NAME                FIRST_NAME            CDESC_E       INC_DATE
------------------------ -------------------- ------------- -----------
Phipps                   Susan                 Indet.        05-JUL-1998
```

- Packages are single program units that contain procedures and functions. By grouping them together, the developer defines a set of routines that are commonly invoked together or one after another.

Refer to *Tuning Oracle* (Corey, Abbey, and Dechichio; Osborne/McGraw-Hill/Oracle Press, 1995), in particular Chapter 7 ("Application Tuning"), where writing generic code using procedures, triggers, functions, and packages is discussed in more detail.

Parallel Processing

With the advent of bigger and more powerful computers, multi-CPU machines have begun appearing that leverage the Oracle8 Parallel Query feature, also called *PQO*. Oracle8 can parallelize many operations using PQO; in Chapter 10, we spoke of running Oracle Loader in parallel. The Oracle8 Server can parallelize sorts, joins, table scans, table population, and index creation operations. PQO is ideal in the following situations:

- Processing queries that access a large amount of data by scanning very large tables (normally in excess of 1,000,000 rows).

- Processing queries that join more than one very large table; the gain using parallelization is especially evident when tables with millions of rows are accessed together to assemble query results.

- Processing that involves creation of large indexes, bulk loads, summarization operations, and copying large amounts of data between Oracle8 objects.

- Processing queries on machines that fall into the SMP (symmetric multiprocessor) or MPP (massively parallel processors) category, and clusters (more than one computer working together and accessing the same set of disks and a central database).

- Processing queries whose data resides in many datafiles on many different disk drives.

- Processing on machines where the CPU is typically underutilized or on intermittently used CPUs; classically, these CPUs check in with an average utilization of less than 40 percent.

- Processing queries alongside sufficient memory to support additional memory-intensive processes such as sorts.

It is the responsibility of the application developer to approach the DBA and work closely with other resources to identify operations that can be processed in parallel.

 VIP
There must be more than one CPU on a machine to enable the benefits of parallel processing. When looking at parallelization, do not experiment with the feature on a single-CPU machine since it will degrade performance.

Determining How Much to Parallelize

It is the DBA's responsibility to set up an Oracle8 instance to leverage the power of PQO. Since the application developer knows system data better than most DBAs, you must work with the DBA to define a degree of parallelization for objects to fully utilize PQO. Oracle will compute a default degree of parallelization based on the number of disks upon which a table's data resides. Before deciding how much to parallelize, the developer and DBA need to do the following:

- Look at the nature of the way the user community accesses a system's data. Typically, when queries retrieve information from the same set of tables and when multiple user processes are running concurrently, you reduce the degree of parallelization.

- Decide the nature of the systems that access the Oracle8 database. Ask questions and figure out the balance between decision support system (DSS) access and OLTP (online systems) access. These two genres of systems have different processing requirements, and thus their different goals may influence how much parallelization it makes sense to implement.

- Look at implementing parallel aware features of the Oracle8 cost-based optimizer (affectionately called *CBO*). We discuss CBO in Chapter 13, and look at ways the DBA and the application developer can work together to leverage Oracle8 enhancements that instruct the optimizer to be more parallel aware.

Let's cap this chapter about application tuning by looking at ways to reduce waits for data and resources. Waits normally involve one of two situations that are caused by:

- User processes queuing behind one another as they look for precious sort space and CPU time

- User processes tying up records in the Oracle8 database that are required by other user processes to allow them to go about their work

Reducing Wait Situations

The Oracle Server technology supports just about all its suite of tools. Installations continue to use a wide assortment of front-end tools to work with data stored in Oracle's data repository. Reducing wait situations is an attainable goal regardless of the hodgepodge of tools one uses to get at Oracle.

VIP

Enhance the speed of your online applications by minimizing the frequency and length of wait situations.

The next few sections outline a few ways to decrease the time spent waiting for resources in use by other users.

COMMIT Your Work Often

Regardless of what tool you use with Oracle, save your work often. If a user works with an Oracle Forms–based application, either commit programmatically or enliven a *Save* key on data entry screens. In SQL*Plus, after each *insert*, *update*, and *delete*, after each statement, issue a **commit** (or the more popular **commit work** one sees in PL/SQL).When you save your work often, you release all the resources (locks, latches, redo space, etc.) required until you complete your transaction. Reducing resources frees them up for other users and reduces their wait times. Interestingly enough, the other all-important feature of saving your work often is that you run less risk of losing work you have so carefully completed!

Let Oracle Do Its Own Locking

Oracle will issue the least restrictive lock it requires to accomplish a task you have asked it to perform. Don't lock manually with the SQL *lock* verb. Oracle does a fine job on its own. Its lock manager does the best job when left on its own. With the emergence of *tpo* (the transaction processing option) in version 6, the default lock became share update. With *share update* locks, different transactions can update different rows in the same Oracle data block concurrently.

Close Down Unused Application Windows

Terminal inactivity robs valuable resources from other users who may need them to go about their work. When users allow their terminals to sit and not do anything, they are still tying up a bottom-line amount of shared memory required to support their session, even though they are not doing anything. Freeing up that memory by leaving an unattended session will reduce wait time for resources with other users.

Use Multitasking Sparingly

It is tempting to open up multiple sessions in many windows when using a GUI front end. It is not unheard of when users find themselves in a deadly embrace with themselves. That is, they have multiple windows open attempting to update the same data that sits uncommitted on another window. If you practice good housekeeping with your Windows applications, you will reduce your own wait times.

 VIP
In cooperation with your database administrator, investigate the occurrences of wait situations as your applications operate using the v$waitstat data dictionary view belonging to SYS.

What's Next

After reading this chapter, you've come a long way! Perhaps you (as we were one time) are just getting started on the road to application tuning. We have provided you with some bottom-line theory and pointed you in the right direction to get started. Even though the points we make are the basics of application tuning, they are applicable to all developers regardless of how long they have been using Oracle.

In Chapter 12, we will cover some advanced SQL concepts, and we'll show you some more complex examples. The SQL language is a powerful programming environment; after reading Chapter 12, you will be well on your way to exploiting some of its remarkable functionality.

CHAPTER
12

Advanced SQL

his chapter will teach you the finer points of SQL as a programming language. The Oracle8 base product contains version 4.0 of SQL*Plus. Readers familiar with releases prior to 4.0 will not find too many differences. Version 3.0 first appeared with Oracle7 in 1992/93, and SQL*Plus has been pretty much the same product ever since with a few enhancements. Our experience has shown that SQL is a very flexible programming tool once you master some of its more advanced features: for example, one of our favorite tricks is using SQL to write SQL. We will show you how to use this feature, plus a number of others that will put you on the fast track to becoming a skilled SQL developer. Here is a list of the major items we will discuss:

- Grouping results from a SQL statement
- Using subqueries (query within a query)
- Using SQL*Plus to generate SQL and create datafiles for other programs
- Using **decode** and **new_value**
- Defining variables in SQL*Plus
- Passing values into SQL*Plus
- Advanced **repheader** features
- Set theory in SQL*Plus
- Structured programming
- Using an editor in SQL*Plus
- Handling nulls in SQL*Plus

This chapter is intended to teach you more about Oracle8 and its SQL implementation, and when you are finished with it, you will be able to create very sophisticated reports. You will also be able to determine when it is appropriate to use SQL*Plus or when it makes more sense to use a different tool, like Oracle Reports.

Terminology

The following definitions will arm you with the technical jargon you need to make it through this chapter:

- A *command file* contains a series of commands that are read by a program such as SQL*Plus. The work accomplished by a command file is the same as if you had typed each command interactively one after the other.

- *Functions* perform operations on data that alter the display or data type of the data. For example, reformatting the date 11-DEC-99 to be displayed as December 11, 1999 is done by using a function.

Functions That Group Results

These functions allow you to group sets of data together for the purpose of getting summary information. When you group rows together, think of this as an operation that lumps similar types of information together as the information is retrieved from the database. Table 12-1 lists the most common group functions, using the customer table we introduced in Chapter 6.

Function	Returns	Example
avg(column_name), The average value of all the values in column_name	select avg(sales) from customer;	
count(*)	The number of rows in a table	select count(*) from customer;
max(column_name), The maximum value stored in column_name	select max(sales) from customer;	
min(column_name)	The minimum value stored in column_name	select min(sales) from customer;

TABLE 12-1. *Most Common Group by Functions*

After looking at the most common group functions, let's move on and look at how they can be applied. A large number of the queries you write in SQL*Plus perform group functions as the data is retrieved from the database. Mastering the use of functions is fundamental to your understanding of the power of SQL and SQL*Plus.

Using the group by Clause

We discussed in Chapter 1 how the relational database model works with sets of rows. These sets can also be thought of as a group. You may use the functions described in Table 12-1 with or without the **group by** clause. When you don't mention the **group by** clause in a query, such as **select max(sales) from customer;**, you are telling the database that you want to treat all the rows in the table as one group. For example, you might want to know the average sales of all your customers or the total sales for all customers. The query **select avg(sales) from customer;** gives you the average, and **select sum(sales) from customer;** gives you the total sales for all customers. This is useful, but many times you are really interested in looking at your data in predetermined classes or groups. For example, to know the average sales by state, we use the query **select state_cd, avg(sales) from customer group by state_cd;**. Most people understand the purpose of the **group by** statement at first but have trouble implementing it. You must ensure that the **group by** clause references the correct number of columns in each SQL statement.

VIP

*When using **group by**, whatever columns are not mentioned in the **group by** portion of the query must have a group function on them.*

Let's review when omitting the function can cause problems. If we issue the statement **select last_name, state_cd, sum(sales) from customer group by last_name;**, the following error is returned:

```
ERROR at line 1:
ORA-00979: not a GROUP BY expression
```

Since the column state_cd is not included in the **group by** clause, it must have a group function on it. In other words, we must use a function such as **max()**, **min()**, **sum()**, **count()**, or **avg()**. If you can't find a group function you want to use on a particular column, then move that column to the **group by** clause.

Using the having Clause

Just as you have search conditions (e.g., where state_cd = 'MA') for individual rows of a query, you can use the **having** clause to specify a search condition for a group of rows. For example, suppose you only wanted to see the states with more than 300 customers. Using the **having** clause, the query would be **select state_cd, avg(sales) from customer group by state_cd having count(state_cd) > 300;**.

VIP
*The **having** clause allows you to specify a search condition for a group of rows. The traditional **where** search condition works with an individual row, not a group of rows.*

Query within a Query

Another powerful ability of SQL is having a query within a query; which is also known as using a subquery. The format of using a subquery is

```
{main query text} where {condition}
          ({sub query text});
```

For example, the main query in the following data looks at the customer table, the subquery at state:

```
select last_name,sales
   from customer
 where state_cd =
         (select max(state_cd)
            from state);
```

Note that the subquery is enclosed in parentheses. In addition, the condition in the **where** clause is resolved based on the results of a query. In other words, your **where** clause contains a SQL statement itself. Say you only want to see the sales of customers that exceed the average of all sales for the whole company. You would enter the query **select state_cd, sales from customer where sales > (select avg(sales) from customer);**. As you can see, the ability to have a query within a query is very powerful. You are enabled to build SQL statements that return data based on the information stored in the database. As your database changes, the query stays the same. Suppose you had determined beforehand that the average sales figure was $12,800 and you had worded the previous query **select state_cd, sales from customer where sales > 12800;**. You'd be in trouble if the average sales figure changed—you would have to change the query.

VIP

Using subqueries allows you to write SQL statements that can stay the same as your data changes (which it always does!).

Running SQL statements with embedded subqueries can affect performance. You will find, as your experience with subqueries increases, that you will need to work closely with your DBA to optimize statements with subquery processing.

Creating Datafiles for Other Programs

One of the most common programs we see people write is one that will feed data from an Oracle8 database into a spreadsheet. Let's use SQL*Plus to do this. Most spreadsheets require data in which each item is separated by a comma. Character-type data needs to be enclosed in single or double quotes. If we need single quotes, the following code will do this for us:

```
SQL*Plus: Release 4.0.3.0.0 - Production on Sun May 11 12:20:12 1999
Copyright (c) Oracle Corporation 1979, 1994, 1996.  All rights reserved.
Connected to:
Oracle8 Server Release 8.0.3.0.1 - Production
With the distributed, heterogeneous, replication, objects
and parallel query options
PL/SQL Release 3.0.3.0.1 - Production
rem * Make spreadsheet data program
SQL> set heading off
```

```
SQL> set pagesize 0
SQL> set feedback off
SQL> set echo off
SQL> spool out.dat
SQL> /* Notice you need to select four single quotes to */
SQL> /* put a single quote in the output data file     */
SQL> select ''''||last_name||''''||','||''''||
  2      state_cd||''''||','||''''||sales
  3      from customer;
SQL> spool off
```

VIP
Since the single quote means something special to Oracle8 (i.e., it starts and ends a literal), you must select four of them together if you want the single quote character in your query results.

If we need double quotes, the following will work:

```
SQL*Plus: Release 4.0.3.0.0 - Production on Sun May 11 12:20:12 1999
Copyright (c) Oracle Corporation 1979, 1994, 1996.  All rights reserved.
Connected to:
Oracle8 Server Release 8.0.3.0.1 - Production
With the distributed, heterogeneous, replication, objects
and parallel query options
PL/SQL Release 3.0.3.0.1 - Production
SQL> set heading off
SQL> set pagesize 0
SQL> set feedback off
SQL> set trimspool on
SQL> set echo off
SQL> spool out.dat
SQL> /* Notice how you place a double quote between two single */
SQL> /* to place a double quote in the output data file        */
SQL> select '"'||last_name||'","'||state_cd||'",'||sales
  2   from customer;
SQL> spool off
```

The output would be

```
'Teplow','MA',23445.67
'Abbey','CA',6969.96
```

```
'Porter','CA',6989.99
'Martin','CA',2345.45
'Laursen','CA',34.34
'Bambi','CA',1234.55
'McGraw','NJ',123.45
```

with single quotes, or

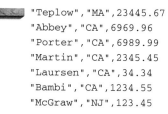

```
"Teplow","MA",23445.67
"Abbey","CA",6969.96
"Porter","CA",6989.99
"Martin","CA",2345.45
"Laursen","CA",34.34
"Bambi","CA",1234.55
"McGraw","NJ",123.45
```

with double quotes. Table 12-2 discusses the lines in the program to make the spreadsheet data.

Component	Meaning
set heading off	Since you are creating a datafile, you do not want headings.
set pagesize 0	You do not want page breaks, so you set this to zero for datafile output.
set linesize 80	You set this to the size of the longest line in your output datafile.
set trimspool on	Tells Oracle8 to trim trailing blanks off spooled output.
set feedback off	Suppresses SQL*Plus from telling you how many rows are retrieved to satisfy the query.
set echo off	Tells SQL*Plus not to echo the SQL statement as it is run.
spool out.dat	Tells Oracle8 to send the results of the query to a file named out.dat.
spool off	Tells Oracle8 to close the output datafile.

TABLE 12-2. *Discussion of Lines of Code from a Spreadsheet Data Creation Program*

NOTE
*The **set trimspool on** command only works in SQL*Plus with a version number greater than or equal to 3.2 (that is with Oracle8, 7.3, and 7.2). You have always been able to trim blanks from screen output; this is how it is done as data is written to a file.*

As you can see from Table 12-2, SQL*Plus is a very flexible tool. It is also a very easy tool to create datafiles with. Getting data into and out of an Oracle8 database is typically very easy from the Oracle side.

SQL Creating SQL

There is no reason why you cannot get SQL to create SQL programs. In fact, this is a technique most DBAs find very useful. The following SQL code will generate a SQL file called out.sql that will contain SQL statements:

```
SQL*Plus: Release 4.0.3.0.0 - Production on Sun May 11 12:20:12 1999
Copyright (c) Oracle Corporation 1979, 1994, 1996.  All rights reserved.
Connected to:
Oracle8 Server Release 8.0.3.0.1 - Production
With the distributed, heterogeneous, replication, objects
and parallel query options
PL/SQL Release 3.0.3.0.1 - Production
SQL> set heading off
SQL> set pagesize 0
SQL> set feedback off
SQL> set echo off
SQL> spool out.sql
SQL> select 'set pagesize 55' from dual;
SQL> select 'grant select on  '||table_name||'  to public;'
  2     from user_tables;
SQL> spool off
```

As you can see, we have a program that creates another SQL program. The first **select** references the dual table. This is a table owned by Oracle user SYS that contains only one row. We use it in this case to load a setup

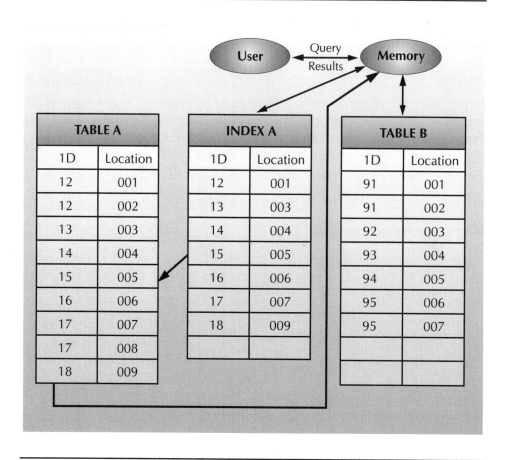

FIGURE 11-3. *Tables with and without an index*

I/Os Required with and Without an Index

Now that we have discussed processing with and without an index, let's examine a real-life example. Let's say a table holds the following information:

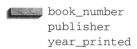

book_number	varchar2(20)
publisher	varchar2(40)
year_printed	varchar2(4)

command for the output file called out.sql; we then follow up with the **grant** statements. You have all the elements you need to generate numerous SQL programs from SQL programs. Let's say this code was run from an Oracle account that owned a customer and state table. The contents of out.sql would be

```
set pagesize 55
grant select on CUSTOMER to public;
grant select on STATE to public;
```

The decode Statement

The **decode** statement is how you implement if-then logic in SQL*Plus. (We discussed how this is done in PL/SQL in Chapter 7.) One of the most powerful functions within SQL*Plus is the **decode** statement. Most people shy away from it due to its ugly syntax. As soon as you add other functions onto the columns, you can very quickly get what we call "ugly SQL." Like a small dog, its bark is far worse than its bite. With that in mind, let's take a look at the format for a **decode** statement:

```
decode (column_name,comparison,action,comparison, action,. . .
      else action)
```

The **decode** statement compares the column contents to the comparison field. If they are equal, then **decode** does the action. If they are not equal, **decode** goes on to the next comparison. If none of the comparisons match, then the else action is performed.

Suppose we want to write a query that would categorize our customers by region, so that customers on the east side of the Mississippi come under the heading East and customers on the west side of the Mississippi come under the heading West. Let's take a look at how to do this with **decode**:

```
column region format a20 heading 'Region'
column sales  format 999,999,999,999,999.99
compute sum of sales on report
compute sum of sales on region
break on report on region
select decode(state_cd, 'MA', 'East',
                        'NJ', 'East',
                        'CA', 'West',
```

```
                         'Middle of River'),sales
from customer
order by 1;
```

The logic expressed by this listing is as follows:

```
if state_cd = 'MA' then
    display 'East'
elsif state_cd = 'NJ' then
    display 'East'
elsif state_cd = 'CA' then
    display 'West'
else
    display 'Middle of River');
```

This example demonstrates the power of using **decode**. Unlike a subquery (or a **select** within a **select**), which will abort if no rows are found, the **decode** statement has the else clause, which can handle exceptions. The bottom line is that the **decode** function is very powerful and can be used to implement logic in SQL*Plus.

Defining Variables in SQL*Plus

In SQL*Plus, it is possible to define variables that can then be used further on in the same program. Think of a variable as a table column with one row of data. Like a table column, a variable has a type (number or character), and, like a table column, it contains data. Think of a variable as a single row of data from a table with one column. The key thing to remember is that a command file can have one or more SQL queries within it. By using the SQL*Plus **define** statement, we are able to define a variable that can be referenced in all SQL statements in the command file. So let's see how you define variables, using the following code as an example:

```
define rpt_cd = "MA"
select sales from customer where state_cd = '&rpt_cd';
```

VIP
Though not mandatory, enclose the text assigned to variables in double quotes. This allows you to embed spaces in the value.

We have assigned the variable named "rpt_cd" the value MA. Thus, when issuing a query, we can prefix the variable name with an ampersand (&) and enclose it in single quotes. To view all variables that have been defined, enter the word **define** by itself. Say we have defined the three variables "rpt_cd," "sales_amt," and "cust_start." The command define would present the following output:

```
DEFINE RPT_CD          = "MA" (CHAR)
DEFINE SALES_AMT       = "18000" (CHAR)
DEFINE CUST_START      = "A" (CHAR)
```

To see the value of one variable, enter **define** followed by the name of the variable. If you entered **define sales_amt**, you would be told

```
DEFINE SALES_AMT       = "18000" (CHAR)
```

NOTE
All variables, regardless of the data type assigned, are character data.

If for some reason you wish to clear the value of a variable, enter the word **undefine** followed by the variable name. If you issue the command **undefine sales_amt**, then the command **define sales_amt**, you are informed the variable has been cleared as shown in the next listing:

```
symbol sales_amt is UNDEFINED
```

NOTE
*The **define** and **undefine** words may be abbreviated to **def** and **undef**.*

Substitution Variables in SQL*Plus

Many times when we are running a query, we do not know beforehand what value the user wants to use in the report. When the report is started, you want to type in a value to be used for the report. You do this by placing an ampersand (&) in front of the section of code you want replaced. For example, let's have Oracle8 prompt us for the value of "rpt_cd." The

SQL statement would be **select sales from customer where state_cd = '&rpt_cd';**. When this statement is executed, Oracle8 asks you to supply the value for "rpt_cd." Then the query runs based on the report code you supply. This way, you are able to build a report without knowing the user's specific needs.

Many times you want to avoid being prompted multiple times for a variable you use more than once. An easy way to do that is by using double ampersands. This tells Oracle8 to ask for the variable once and issue a **define** command on it. For example, the **statement select state_cd, avg(&&rptcol), max(&&rptcol) from customer group by state_cd;** will prompt for the value of "rptcol" only once (the three dots at the end of the old and new lines represent code not relevant to the listing):

```
Enter value for rptcol: sales
old   1: select state_cd, avg(&&rptcol), max(&&rptcol) . . .
new   1: select state_cd, avg(sales), max(sales) from . . .
ST AVG(SALES) MAX(SALES)
-- ---------- ----------
CA   3514.858    6989.99
MA   23445.67   23445.67
NJ    123.45     123.45
```

VIP

*When a variable has been defined with the && convention, you must **undefine** the variable if you want to give it a different value.*

We all know that presentation is everything. The default prompt would not be acceptable for the typical end user we encounter. You use the **prompt** and **accept** command to give us a more descriptive prompt. Examine the following:

```
clear screen
prompt ******************************************
prompt Enter "ALL" to see all your tables
prompt Or Enter a Partial table name
accept tname prompt "Enter ALL/Partial Tablename....:"
select table_name
  from user_tables
 where table_name like '%&tname%'
    or upper('&tname') = 'ALL';
```

When this is run, the following output is produced for the same user who owns a customer and a state table:

```
*******************************************
Enter "ALL" to see all your tables
Or Enter a Partial table name
Enter ALL/Partial Tablename....:ALL
old    3:   where table_name like '%&tname%'
new    3:   where table_name like '%ALL%'
old    4:          or upper('&tname') = 'ALL')
new    4:          or upper('ALL') = 'ALL')
TABLE_NAME
------------------------------
CUSTOMER
STATE
```

As you can see, Oracle8 generates the prompt statements and places the input you give it into a variable called "tname," then uses the value of "tname" in the **where** clause. You should also pay special attention to the use of the word "ALL." It has a special meaning in this case. If you enter ALL at the prompt, then the condition upper('&tname') = 'ALL' becomes 'ALL' = 'ALL', which is true. Thus every row is retrieved. If you do not enter ALL, then the database will only retrieve the table names that meet the entered criteria. This is a very powerful technique. Also notice the **clear screen** command that clears the screen before displaying the first prompt. This is used to make the prompt present better on the screen.

Sometimes you want to prompt the user for inputs and then pass those directly to SQL on the command line. This is also a very easy thing to do. If you name the variables in your program "&1," "&2," and so on, Oracle8 will take data passed into it on the command line and assign it to the variable "&1," "&2," and so on. For example, suppose we have a SQL program named test.sql containing the following:

```
select state_cd, sales from customer
  where sales > &1
    and state_cd = '&2';
```

If we wish to report on all data where the sales are greater than $1,000 and the state is CA, we could call the above program with the command

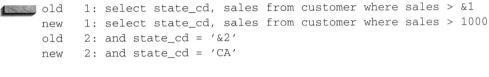

```
sqlplus username/password @test 1000 CA
```

and the output would be

```
old   1: select state_cd, sales from customer where sales > &1
new   1: select state_cd, sales from customer where sales > 1000
old   2: and state_cd = '&2'
new   2: and state_cd = 'CA'

ST     SALES
--  ----------
CA    6969.96
CA    6989.99
CA    2345.45
CA    1234.55
```

NOTE

*Oracle8 displays old and new lines as it substitutes values for variables. This display can be suppressed with the SQL*Plus command **set verify off**, which can be abbreviated to **set ver off**.*

If you are already in SQL*Plus, you use the start command to run a program, and pass variables after the name of the program. The **start** command tells Oracle8 to get the command file, load it, and then execute it (using any parameters that you enter with the start command).

```
start test.sql 1000 CA
```

As you can see, SQL*Plus has numerous capabilities when it comes to passing parameters. By passing values to SQL*Plus as you invoke a program, you can write one SQL query and have it satisfy a number of users' needs. In addition, you can very easily interface it with other programs.

NOTE
*Most operating systems allow using the @ sign rather than the word **start**. What's the difference between the two, you ask? Four keystrokes!*

Changes with SQL*Plus 4.0

In this section, we cover a few new features of SQL*Plus 4.0 delivered with Oracle8. Report header and footer commands are the most noticeable change, so let's look at these and a few other differences before delving more into writing SQL*Plus reports. Most of the changes with SQL*Plus 4.0 are designed to reflect new data types, as discussed in Chapter 4, and some of the techniques for handling very large objects.

Header and Footer Commands

We looked at the **ttitle** and **btitle** commands in Chapter 6 when we wrote the Database Technologies customer report. The command **repheader** places and formats a specified report header at the top of each report, or lists the current **repheader** definition. Its corollary is the **repfooter** command, which places and formats a specified report footer at the bottom of each report, or lists the current **repfooter** definition.

Storing the SQL*Plus Environment

Often, developers or DBAs prefer to set up their own environment in SQL*Plus. Using the new command **store**, you can save attributes of the current SQL*Plus environment in a host operating system file (a command file). Then, the next time you log into SQL*Plus, you can run that command file to restore the environment, as shown below.

```
SQL*Plus: Release 4.0.3.0.0 - Production on Sun May 11 12:20:12 1999
Copyright (c) Oracle Corporation 1979, 1994, 1996.  All rights reserved.
Connected to:
Oracle8 Server Release 8.0.3.0.1 - Production
With the distributed, heterogeneous, replication, objects
and parallel query options
PL/SQL Release 3.0.3.0.1 - Production
```

```
SQL> -- Restore the environment so painstakingly set up; note that the
SQL> -- filename ends in the ".cmd" text which is nonstandard and
SQL> -- must be included.
@D:\ORANT\DATABASE\resenv.cmd
```

set autotrace

The **set** command now has an **autotrace** clause. The **autotrace** clause displays a report on the execution of successful SQL DML statements (**select**, **insert**, **update** or **delete**). The report can include execution statistics and the query execution path. We will discuss **autotrace** in Chapter 13 while looking at the **explain plan** command.

serveroutput

While using PL/SQL as featured in Chapter 7, you can display text to the terminal using the **put_line** command that is part of the dbms_utility package owned by SYS. To enliven output from **put_line**, the **set serveroutput** command now has a **format** clause. You can use **wrapped**, **word_wrapped**, or **truncated** with the **format** clause.

repheader—the Whole Header and Nothing but the Header

Up to now, you have only seen examples where we use the default behavior of the **repheader** command. As you know, the **repheader** command is used to print a title at the top of each page. In Chapter 6, we showed you the default behavior of **ttitle**, because from experience we have found this to be sufficient for the majority of your needs. However, there comes a time when you want more. Perhaps you need a clerk's name in the heading, or page numbers on the left. Regardless, there is much more you can do with the **repheader** command, at which Table 12-3 takes a closer look.

NOTE
The bold formatting command may not work on all operating systems.

Option	Meaning
col n	Indents to position n of the current line.
skip n	Skips to the start of a new line; if you enter 0, then it goes to the beginning of the line.
left, right, center	Left align, right align, or center align.
bold	Displays data in boldface.
format char	Specifies the format model to be used (similar to the format command with col).
sql.lno	The current line number.
sql.pno	The current page number.
sql.user	The name of the user logged into SQL*Plus.

TABLE 12-3. *Advanced Formatting for repheader*

The best way to understand these advanced formatting features is to use them. So let's do a more sophisticated **repheader** command:

```
set linesize 62
repheader left 'Michael Abbey Systems International Inc.' -
skip center -
'An Oracle Systems Consulting Company' -
right 'Page: ' format 999 sql.pno -
skip center bold 'Customer Report'
```

The title would then show up on any report as

```
Michael Abbey Systems International Inc.
          An Oracle Systems Consulting Company   Page:   1
              Customer Report
```

The hyphen (-) in **repheader** represents a line continuation, and the **skip** word instructs **repheader** to skip the specified number of lines (or one line, if a number is omitted). As you can see, you can get pretty sophisticated with this command.

VIP

Oracle8 documentation suggests using the **repheader** *command to format an SQL*Plus report title rather than* **ttitle***, and the same with* **repfooter***. Use whichever you wish, though the default* **ttitle** *is more rich than the* **repheader** *default.*

column—the Whole Column and Nothing but the Column

As you have seen from previous examples, the **column** command controls how your data is displayed. Just like the **ttitle** command, you have lots of options with **column**. We will now present a summary of the extra formatting commands for number and then character data.

NOTE

The **column** *command can be abbreviated to* **col** *and the* **format** *command to* **form***.*

Formatting Number Data

The **format** command determines how the information from the database will be displayed. Table 12-4 highlights the most useful formats for number data.

The next listing shows some of these formats in action:

```
SQL> column sales    format 999,999,999.99
SQL> select sales from customer;
Michael Abbey Systems International Inc.
     An Oracle Systems Consulting Company              Page:    1
                        Customer Report

          SALES
     --------------
        23,445.67
         6,969.96
         6,989.99
```

Format character	Example	Description
9	format 999999	Determines the display width based on the number of digits entered. When you have a number overflow, it will display "######'. You will not see any leading zeros.
0	09999	Displays leading zeros.
	99990	When value is zero, it displays a zero instead of a blank space.
$	$99999	Places a dollar sign in front of the number.
B	B99999	Displays a zero as a blank.
MI	99999MI	Displays a minus sign when the value is negative.
PR	99999PR	Places <> around a negative number.
,	99,999	Places a comma in the position specified.
.	999.999	Places a decimal point where specified and rounds appropriately.

TABLE 12-4. *Common Number Formats Used with column Command*

```
        2,345.45
          34.34
        1,234.55
         123.45
7 rows selected.

SQL> column sales        format $099999
SQL> select sales from customer;
Michael Abbey Systems International Inc.
     An Oracle Systems Consulting Company        Page:    1
                        Customer Report
SALES
--------
 $023446
 $006970
 $006990
 $002345
```

```
$000034
$001235
$000123
7 rows selected.
SQL>
```

Formatting Character Data

Character data can be harder to deal with. For example, say you want
to print a report in which the number of characters across a page is 80.
The report lists names and salaries. Some of the names (e.g., Alexander
Springhurst, at a length of 21 characters) are longer than others (e.g., Sue
Ray, at a length of 7 characters). If you allocate the necessary space to
accommodate short names, the long names could be broken over multiple
lines and become hard to read.

Wrapping and Truncating Character Data

The following three words can be used to format character data and are
useful when a report needs to display character data that is longer than the
width of the column display you have set.

■ **wrap:** This command tells SQL*Plus to display the specified number
of characters, then go to the next line and continue. Using our long
name example, if the full_name column were formatted using the
column expression column **full_name format a18 wrap**, the name
would appear as

```
Name              City
----------------- ----------------
Alexander Springhu  Winnipeg
rst
```

■ **word_wrap:** This command tells SQL*Plus to display the specified
number of characters, but move a word to the next line rather than
split the word into pieces. Using the column expression column
full_name **format a18 word_wrap**, the name would appear as

```
Name              City
----------------- ----------------
Alexander         Winnipeg
Springhurst
```

- **truncate:** This command tells SQL*Plus to display the specified number of characters, and ignore the rest. Using the column expression **column full_name format a18 truncate**, the name would appear as

```
Name                City
------------------  ----------------
Alexander Springhu  Winnipeg
```

Justify left, center, or right

This controls the centering of the column heading (not the data in the column). By default, a number column heading is right-justified, and a character is left-justified. The following listing illustrates how these affect a column heading display format using the statement **select state_name from state;**:

```
column state_name justify right
         STATE_NAME
------------------
Massachusetts
California
NewJersey
col state_name justify center
     STATE_NAME
------------------
Massachusetts
California
NewJersey
```

new_value

You can create a variable that will hold data from a column using **new_value**. Once a variable is defined, you can then place its value into a **repheader** command. This is useful when you want to create a master/detail report with a value from the report appearing in the heading. To place a value in the heading, you must always reference a column from your query (in our example the column state_cd) in the **break** command, with the **skip page** option. For example, using the SQL statement **select**

state_cd, last_name, sales from customer order by 1;, examine the following output:

```
column state_cd new_value rpt_cd
repheader left 'STATE CD: ' rpt_cd skip 1
break on state_cd skip page
STATE CD: CA
ST LAST_NAM SALES
-- -------- ------------

CA Abbey          6,970
   Porter         6,990
   Martin         2,345
   Bambi          1,235
   Laursen           34

STATE CD: MA
ST LAST_NAM SALES
-- -------- ------------

MA Teplow        23,446

STATE CD: NJ
ST LAST_NAM SALES
-- -------- ------------

NJ McGraw           123

7 rows selected.
```

You could also use this technique to put today's date in the heading. Examine the following code to see how today's date is put in a report title using **new_value**:

```
column today new_value today_date
select to_char(sysdate,'HH24:MM:SS DD-Mon-YYYY') today
  from dual;
repheader center 'Michael Abbey Systems International Inc.' -
      skip left today_date -
      right 'Page: ' format 999 sql.pno skip
select sales from customer;
```

When this is run, the date appears on line two of the title (format resembling 18:12:13 26-Mar-99), with the page number on the left side of the same line.

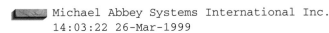

```
Michael Abbey Systems International Inc.
14:03:22 26-Mar-1999                              Page:    1
       SALES
    ----------
    23445.67
     6969.96
     6989.99
     2345.45
       34.34
     1234.55
      123.45
```

SQL*Plus Set Theory

The nice thing about a relational database is that you write SQL queries that
act upon sets of data versus a single row of data. Not having to issue a read
makes it very, very powerful. SQL by design has a very strong relationship
to math theory. There is a series of set functions that work very nicely with
an Oracle8 database using SQL*Plus. We will discuss these set operators in
the next few sections, using tables x and y (both have a single column of
character data type). The next listing shows the contents of these tables:

```
select * from x;

COL
---
1
2
3
4
5
6
6 rows selected.
select * from y;
COL
---
5
6
7
3 rows selected.
```

union

Using this operator in SQL*Plus returns all the rows in both tables with no duplicates. In the previous listing, both the tables have columns with the value of 5 and 6. The query **select * from x union select * from y;** returns the following results as expected:

```
COL
---
1
2
3
4
5
6
7
7 rows selected.
```

intersect

Using this operator in SQL*Plus returns all the rows in one table that also reside in the other. Using tables x and y, the column values 5 and 6 are in both tables. The query **select * from x intersect select * from y;** returns the following results as expected:

```
COL
---
5
6
```

minus

Using this operator in SQL*Plus returns all the rows in the first table minus the rows in that table that are also in the second table. Using tables x and y, the column values 5 and 6 are in both tables. The query **select * from x minus select * from y;** returns the following results, as expected:

```
COL
---
1
2
3
4
```

VIP

When using these set operators with Oracle8, the data types of the column(s) in both tables must be the same.

The following error occurs if the data types differ (using table z, whose single column is number data type):

```
select * from x union select * from z
       *
ERROR at line 1:
ORA-01790: expression must have same datatype as corresponding expression
```

Structured Code Techniques

SQL is a programming language like any other: to do it right requires care. The first thing we recommend you do is have a SQL script with common setup information and the most common column definitions. Look at the following example:

```
rem ****************
rem * setup.sql
rem ****************
rem This script contains common setup information and
rem formatting information I use for many sql scripts
rem Michael Corey    05/23/98    Created
rem Michael Abbey    10/23/98    Changed pagesize to 60,
rem                              to add additional
rem                              5 lines for new printer.
rem Standard set-up
set echo off
set pagesize 60
set linesize 80
rem ***********************************
rem * common column format statements
rem ***********************************
column bytes heading 'Bytes' format 999,999,999.99
column kbytes heading 'K Bytes' format 999,999,999.99
column less1 heading 'Under 1|Minute' format 999,990
column sales heading 'Sales|Ytd' format 999,999,999,999,999.99
state_cd heading 'St|Cd' format a2
state_name heading 'State|Name' format a20 truncate
```

```
column sum(sales) heading 'Sales|Ytd' format 999,999,999,999,999.99
column sum(bytes) heading 'Bytes'      format 999,999,999.99
column table_name heading 'Table|Name' format a20 wrap
rem ********************
rem * End of script
rem ********************
```

This command file holds the most common setup items (i.e., **pagesize** and **linesize**) and the most common column format statements. The next step is to write your SQL query and invoke the preceding program to format and set up the report. This is done in the following listing:

```
SQL*Plus: Release 4.0.3.0.0 - Production on Sun May 11 12:20:12 1999
Copyright (c) Oracle Corporation 1979, 1994, 1996.  All rights reserved.
Connected to:
Oracle8 Server Release 8.0.3.0.1 - Production
With the distributed, heterogeneous, replication, objects
and parallel query options
PL/SQL Release 3.0.3.0.1 - Production
SQL> rem *****************************************
SQL> rem *    customer.sql
SQL> rem *****************************************
SQL> rem * This report gives a complete customer listing
SQL> rem * Mike Corey  10/23/98
SQL> rem * Call in standard setup residing in central repository
SQL> @D:\ORANT\DATABASE\setup.sql
SQL> rem * Set the report title and page footer
SQL> repheader center 'Database Technologies Inc.' skip -
     center 'Customer Report'
SQL> repfooter center '*** customer.sql ***'
```

By using a standard setup file, you merely execute it first. This sets up the environment. Then your program (i.e., customer.sql) contains the query to get the data, any **break** logic (the **break** statement), any totals you want to display, and the **repheader** and **repfooter** commands the report uses (we discussed **btitle** in the "Page Footers" section of Chapter 6; **repfooter** behaves the same as **btitle**). You don't spend a lot of time formatting the data; instead, you spend your efforts on the program logic needed to accomplish the task.

Notice that the **btitle** name is the name of the command file. The reason for this is when an end user calls you up about a report, you can easily tell what the source code is. In real life, many SQL statements you use for your reports will tend to be slight variations of each other. By putting the report title in the footer of the report, you can zero in on which report needs attention. This technique is illustrated in the next listing:

```
SQL> repfooter skip 2 center '**** my_report.sql ****'
```

Command Line Editing

When you are working with SQL*Plus, it becomes apparent very quickly that Oracle8 holds the last command executed in a buffer. To access that buffer, you merely have to enter a slash (/) and hit the ENTER key. This action will cause the last SQL query entered to run again. If you ever leave two semicolons at the end of your command file, you learn very quickly that the query ran twice.

Many times when building these command files, if you are like most of us, you have fat-fingered the typing and need to make a minor change. We find in these cases that it's much easier to use the command line editor you get with SQL*Plus than retyping the whole line. Even though this editor is very crude, it has always served a very useful purpose. You can make changes very quickly to the SQL buffer and then execute a SQL statement once again. Table 12-5 takes a look at the core commands.

Editor Command	Purpose
(a)ppend	Add text to the end of the current line.
(c)hange /old/new/	Replace old text with new text in the current line.
(c)hange /text/	Remove the text from the current line.
del	Delete the current line.
(i)nput text	Add a line after the current line.
(l)ist	Show all the lines in the buffer.
(l)ist n	Show line number n in the buffer.
(l)ist m n	Show line numbers starting with line m and ending with line n.

TABLE 12-5. *SQL*Plus Line Editing Commands*

The key to this editor is knowing what the current line is: the only line that you are able to change. With that in mind, let's try a few things. Let's look at our query by entering the command list:

```
1    select state_cd, last_name, sales
2    from customer
3*   order by 1
```

The asterisk tells us what the current line is. So let's change the current line to line one. From now on, we will use the abbreviated form of the command (presented in parentheses in Table 12-5). Type the command **l 1** (the letter "l" followed by the number one), and SQL*Plus lists line one:

```
1*   select state_cd, last_name, sales
```

Now the current line is set at line one. Let's change state_cd to customer.state_cd. You enter the command **c/state_cd/customer.state_cd/** and SQL*Plus responds with

```
1*   select customer.state_cd, last_name, sales
```

Now let's list the entire query again using the command **l**:

```
1    select customer.state_cd, last_name, sales
2    from customer
3*   order by 1
```

Let's remove the **order by** statement. Since we are pointing to line three, we just enter the delete command **d** and then list our query with the command **l**:

```
1    select customer.state_cd, last_name, sales
2*   from customer
```

Notice how SQL*Plus leaves the current line as line two after doing the delete we requested. With the edited command in the SQL buffer, we can run it again using the command **r** or by typing the slash (/) character. Either produces the following query output:

```
ST LAST_NAME
-- ------------------------------
MA Teplow
CA Abbey
```

```
CA Porter
CA Martin
CA Laursen
CA Bambi
NJ McGraw
```

Your last SQL query is kept in the buffer until you exit SQL*Plus.

Arrrghh! We Need a Real Editor

As we said, this command line editor is great for simple tasks. But it only allows you to edit the SQL query itself. Many times, a lot of formatting and setup is required to make a simple SQL query into a usable report. That job is best done with a full editor. There is a command in SQL*Plus that lets you define your favorite editor for use directly from SQL*Plus. The command is formatted as **define _editor="editor_name"** where editor_name is the name of the program that runs your favorite editor. In UNIX, that text may be vi, in VMS it may be edt.

You can set up any editor of your choice. To use the editor you define in this manner, type the command **edit** or abbreviate it to **ed**. Oracle8 will then issue the command you have used in the **define _editor** command.

NOTE

*The SQL Worksheet in Oracle Enterprise Manager can be used for many activities we discuss here with SQL*Plus. Most of the formatting commands only work in SQL*Plus.*

Nulls in SQL*Plus

The ever elusive "null" character deserves even more special attention as you move up to Oracle8. When a column value in a table is not known, one says "it is null." With Oracle8, the length of a column that contains a null value is zero, though Oracle8 quickly points out that this may not always be the case in future releases.

Problems with Nulls in Comparison Operations

The only way to allow true preservation of null data is using the keywords **is null** and **is not null** as shown in the next listing.

```
select count(*)
  from mytab
 where cola is null;
select count(*)
  from mytab
 where cola is not null;
```

The query **select count(*), comm_amt from comm group by comm_amt;** returns the following output:

```
COUNT(*)   COMM_AMT
--------- ---------
       12      1200
        7      1700
        8
```

You can quickly get into trouble when using other constructs for **null** comparisons. Picture a table whose comm_amt column contains the following data:

Column Value	Number of Rows
null	8
1200	12
1700	7

Now the fun begins: let's try issuing the SQL statement **select count(*) from comm where comm_amt < 1700;**, and the result is a count of 12. This result is determined from the not null values in the comm_amt column containing the value 1200. Note how the rows whose value is null are not counted. Oracle does not know the value of the comm_amt column whose value is null; null is meaningless and indeterminate and hence the null column value rows are not returned. This leads into the next discussion about how to do comparisons using null column values.

Using NVL for Null Comparisons

The **nvl** function is the solution to the null column value comparison problem. Picture the following enhanced statement to retrieve bona-fide counts from our comm table:

```
SQL> select count(*),nvl(comm_amt,0) from comm group by nvl(comm_amt,0);
  COUNT(*) NVL(COMM_AMT,0)
--------- ---------------
        8               0
       12            1200
        7            1700
```

The **nvl** function substituted the value "0" into all rows whose comm_amt column value was null. Using this newfound functionality, let's issue our previous query to find out how many rows have a comm_amt value less than 1700.

```
SQL> select count(*) from comm where nvl(comm_amt,0) < 1700;
  COUNT(*)
---------
       20
```

Let's finish off this brief discussion of nulls by looking at the right and the wrong way to do character string comparisons against null column values. Your ability to deal with null column values will lead to a better comprehension of Oracle8 data stored as null values.

The Null=Null Comparison Anomaly

By not using the **is null** and **is not null** syntax, you can easily get yourself into more trouble. Picture the following statements, commented to illustrate the point each makes:

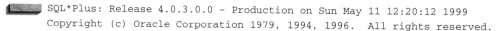

```
SQL*Plus: Release 4.0.3.0.0 - Production on Sun May 11 12:20:12 1999
Copyright (c) Oracle Corporation 1979, 1994, 1996.  All rights reserved.
```

```
Connected to:
Oracle8 Server Release 8.0.3.0.1 - Production
With the distributed, heterogeneous, replication, objects
and parallel query options
PL/SQL Release 3.0.3.0.1 - Production
SQL>
SQL> -- Oracle8 cannot resolve the equality condition since the ''
SQL> -- represents a zero length character string BUT NOT a null value
SQL>
SQL> select 12 from dual where null = '';
no rows selected
SQL>
SQL> -- One would think that Oracle8 would allow equality comparison
SQL> -- between two '' strings, but not so! Watch out!
SQL>
SQL> select 12 from dual where '' = '';
no rows selected
SQL> -- Even though the comparison is coded correctly with the null
SQL> --  keyword,
SQL> -- the null on the left side of the = is meaningless as is the one
SQL> --  on
SQL> -- the right; 2 meaningless values can't be compared against one
SQL> --  another
SQL> select 12 from dual where null = null;
no rows selected
SQL>
SQL> -- This in the only way to do it properly to get the desired results
SQL>
SQL> select 12 from dual where null is null;
        12
---------
        12
SQL>
SQL> -- Let's do the same sort of thing using the nvl function
SQL>
SQL> select 12 from dual where nvl(null,'X') = nvl(null,'X');
        12
---------
        12
SQL>
```

VIP

Many developers and DBAs find the way Oracle handles null values frustrating; obviously there is nothing anyone can do about it other than familiarize yourself with the convention, and be prepared with that knowledge if any query results are suspicious.

What's Next

What we have given you in this chapter are all the pieces to become really productive with SQL and SQL*Plus. We did not intend for this book to be the complete guide to programming in SQL; rather, it's a guide to the most useful techniques and commands. Armed with our introductory chapter on SQL, you now have an understanding of how to word queries and how to format SQL*Plus report output. Remember, SQL is the foundation of Oracle. The better you know it, the better you will be able to use Oracle.

In the next chapter, we will discuss some advanced concepts about application tuning. You will be able to add some more SQL skills to your repertoire as we look at ways to write efficient SQL queries and take advantage of its truly remarkable features.

CHAPTER
13

Advanced Application
Tuning

n Chapter 11, we discussed the two most important concepts in application tuning: writing SQL statements that match ones resident in the shared pool, and minimizing reads from disk by using indexes. In this chapter, we will take it to the next step. Each component part in the application tuning exercise can seem rather insignificant on its own, but rolled together into a tuning methodology, each component in the tuning process is a worthwhile contributor.

Tuning applications should begin with the programmer and the very first line of code, and continue throughout the system lifecycle. There are always many different ways to do something with a given requirement—the good way, and all the others. It is not enough just to know how to use Oracle. Tuning your applications will enable you to get the best performance out of Oracle. When your applications are tuned, they use fewer resources, which has a ripple affect. Efforts to tune the Oracle software could be wasted without your taking the time to tune applications. In this chapter, we will highlight the following issues that pertain to application tuning:

- The twin optimization approach used to process SQL statements
- The three phases in SQL statement processing
- Naming variables in Oracle tools
- Data access path chosen by Oracle
- Primary key constraints
- Looking at the contents of the shared pool
- Explain plan and autotrace
- The tkprof facility
- Oracle Trace

We will discuss ways to maximize your available resources and focus on the areas of tuning your applications that will benefit you the most.

Terminology

The following definitions will arm you with the technical jargon you need to make it through this chapter:

- An *access path* is the method Oracle determines to get at your data. It chooses this path based on a number of evaluation processes over which we have no control.

- The *execution plan* is a roadmap to the data involved in every SQL statement, and it is built by Oracle based on a set of predefined optimization techniques.

- *Locks* are internal mechanisms Oracle maintains to ensure the integrity of your data. For example, when a user starts to change the information in a personnel record, Oracle issues a lock to ensure that no one else can make changes until the first user is finished.

- The *environment* is a section of memory allocated to each session on a computer. This memory contains session-specific information, such as the user's name, the system identifier of the user's database, and a list of directories to search for programs when the user issues a command.

- *ORACLE_HOME* is the location on one of your disks (a directory) under which the Oracle software resides. It is defined at installation time, and it becomes part of the environment as Oracle operates.

- When you inspect a series of characters (e.g., the text ahdjek9kk) for the occurrence of one or more characters (e.g., k9), the characters you are looking for are referred to as the *lookup string*.

- The *optimizer* is a set of internal Oracle routines that decides the most efficient access path to your data. These routines are run when Oracle is trying to arrive at the most efficient way to access data to satisfy a SQL statement.

- A *unique* or *primary key* refers to one or more column values in a table that can uniquely identify each row in a table. Picture a primary key as one's social insurance number, used by the Canadian government to identify each resident of Canada (even though a study once found over 700 people had the same social insurance number—guess the Department of Employment and Immigration was not using Oracle then!). For one or more columns to be a primary key, the values cannot be duplicated anywhere else in the table's data.

- A *host character* is placed in a SQL*Plus program to drop back to the operating system to issue a command. Execution of the SQL script is suspended until the operating system command completes. You are then returned to SQL*Plus.

Optimization

Advanced application tuning requires an understanding of how Oracle optimizes SQL statements. Oracle uses one of two approaches to accomplish this. With the rule-based approach, Oracle ranks data access path efficiency based on a set of rules. With the cost-based approach, which is the Oracle8 default, Oracle examines the data in one or more tables in the SQL statement and selects the access path that will cost the least (i.e., use the least resources and take the least amount of time).

NOTE

Armed with the material we cover in this chapter about the cost-based optimizer (or CBO), we recommend using CBO after gathering statistics on your data using the approach we outline.

VIP
If you are running a version of the Oracle Applications (e.g., Financials, HR, or Assets), continue to use the rule-based optimization approach. Very few, if any, routines in the Applications have been tuned using cost-based approaches; the rule-based approach works best with these systems.

By the end of this section, you will understand the advantages of each approach and have a good feel for which one you should use.

Cost-Based Approach

When using the cost-based approach, Oracle optimizes a SQL statement to cost the least. "C," "B," and "O" were once some of the three most dreaded letters to come out of a technically-savvy Oracle software individual. Cost-based optimization involves weighing a number of factors that can affect the performance of a SQL statement, and arriving at the execution plan that "costs" the least. In this context, cost is a measurement of many factors including the amount of computer resources (e.g., I/O and CPU consumption) and the time to complete execution. As database administrators transition their Oracle environments to using CBO, there are a number of issues that can spring up. Let's highlight some of those issues and allow you to get the best bang for your buck out of this approach.

In some ways CBO is magic (or seems to be); in other ways, it isn't. When you go out and decide what groceries to buy for you and your family, you weigh factors such as cost, appearance, and your like or dislike of certain commodities. For CBO to work its magic, it needs information such as the number of rows in each table, the distribution of keys within a table's primary key column(s), and the number of data blocks allocated to and occupied by the table's rows. The trick to getting this information is deciding how often it should be collected, and ensuring that when the statistics are collected, no errors are encountered. Let's look at the three (actually there are four, with one cluster-related object we are not covering) data dictionary views whose contents are populated by the statistic collection keyword **analyze**. Below are the important columns for CBO; since they are part of Oracle's data dictionary, they are never updated manually.

USER_TABLES

```
num_rows        number
blocks          number
chain_cnt       number
avg_row_len     number
degree          varchar2(10)   -- of parallelism
sample_size     number          -- size of sample when estimating statistics
last_analyzed   date
partitioned     varchar2(3)    -- may optimize differently if partitioned
```

USER_INDEXES

```
distinct_keys             number
avg_leaf_blocks_per_key   number          -- this and the next give CBO an idea
avg_data_blocks_per_key   number          -- of index entry distribution
status                    varchar2(8)
num_rows                  number
sample_size               number          -- if index stats were estimated
last_analyzed             date
degree                    varchar2(40)
partitioned               varchar2(3)
```

USER_TAB_COLUMNS

```
num_distinct    number
low_value       raw(32)    -- column value in second lowest index entry
high_value      raw(32)    -- column value in second highest index entry
num_nulls       number     -- Oracle8 keeps statistics on NULLs (also 7.3)
last_analyzed   date
sample_size     number     -- is analysis estimated rather than computed
```

Gathering Statistics in SQL*Plus

There are many ways to collect statistics for CBO, many of which most readers may be familiar with. I recommend estimating statistics on tables, and computing statistics for indexes. The lock requested for computing statistics is very restrictive and, if it cannot be acquired, the statement will fail with error ORA-00054 as shown next.

```
ORA-00054    resource busy and acquire with NOWAIT specified
Cause:       The NOWAIT keyword forced a return to the command
             prompt because a resource was unavailable for a LOCK
             TABLE or SELECT FOR UPDATE command.
Action:      Try the command after a few minutes or enter the
             command without the NOWAIT keyword.
```

Let's now examine the **analyze** command using a few examples. We recommend estimating statistics on tables according to the following:

1. Estimate statistics for all tables using a sample percentage of rows.

2. Sample using 20% of the rows in the table; Oracle randomly selects the rows to include in the sample.

Thus, a few **analyze** statements for a handful of tables resembles

```
analyze table lumberjack estimate statistics sample 20 percent;
analyze table mountie estimate statistics sample 20 percent;
analyze table suspenders estimate statistics sample 20 percent;
```

We recommend computing statistics for all indexes; the following listing shows a few index collection SQL statements.

```
analyze index lumberjack_pk compute statistics;
analyze index mountie_pk compute statistics;
analyze index suspenders_pk compute statistics;
```

Let's look at two SQL statements whose output can be captured and passed to Oracle to analyze tables and indexes in any user's schema.

```
SQL*Plus: Release 4.0.3.0.0 - Production on Mon May 12 20:43:31 1999
Copyright (c) Oracle Corporation 1979, 1994, 1996.  All rights reserved.
Connected to:
Oracle8 Server Release 8.0.3.0.1 - Production
With the distributed, heterogeneous, replication, objects
and parallel query options
PL/SQL Release 3.0.3.0.1 - Production
SQL>
```

```
SQL> -- Tweak the SQL*Plus environment by suppressing headings,
SQL> -- feedback about number of rows fetched, and echoing of commands
SQL> -- to the screen.
SQL> set pages 0 feed off echo off
SQL> -- Capture output to ana_all.sql
SQL> spool ana_all.sql
SQL> prompt set echo on feed on
SQL> spool ana_all
SQL> select 'analyze table '||owner||'.'||table||
  2    ' estimate statistics sample 20%;'
  3    from all_tables
  4    where owner = upper('&1');
SQL>
SQL> select 'analyze index '||owner||'.'||
  2    index_name||' compute statistics;'
  3    from all_indexes
  4    where owner = upper('&1');
SQL> spool off
```

When this program terminates, you are left with a series of SQL statements written to the file "ana_all.sql". Run this in SQL*Plus to collect statistics for the schema defined by the substitution variable passed to the program.

Gathering Statistics Using PL/SQL Procedures

Two packages belonging to SYS can be used to analyze objects. Table 13-1 shows the expected parameters and their meanings for the

Parameter	Default Value
Owner of objects to analyze	None—must be supplied
Method for collection	None—must be *estimate* or *compute*
Rows in sample	Optional—defaults to null
Percent of rows in sample	Optional—defaults to null

TABLE 13-1. *Inputs to the analyze_schema Procedure*

"dbms_utility.analyze_schema" procedure. This procedure is used to analyze all the objects in a schema in one pass.

To estimate statistics for the MALLIA schema, using a 20 percent sample, the procedure would be invoked from SQL*Plus using the syntax:

```
execute dbms_utility.analyze_schema ('MALLIA','ESTIMATE',null,20);
```

Some DBAs find "dbms_ddl.analyze_object" more flexible. It offers a more detailed collection mechanism than analyze_schema. Table 13-2 shows the parameters passed to analyze_schema and their meanings.

To compute statistics for the index shauna_2 owned by MALLIA, using a 20 percent sample, the procedure would be invoked from SQL*Plus using the syntax:

```
execute dbms_ddl.analyze_object ('INDEX','SHAUNA_2','COMPUTE');
```

VIP
We prefer the analyze_object approach if you use PL/SQL to collect statistics; when using analyze_schema and an Oracle error is encountered, all the work done prior to raising the error is lost.

Parameter	Default Value
Type of object	None—must be table or index
Owner of object to analyze	None
Method for collection	None—must be *estimate* or *compute*
Rows in sample	Optional—defaults to null
Percent of rows in sample	Optional—defaults to null

TABLE 13-2.   *Inputs to the analyze_object Procedure*

Controlling Usage of CBO

DBAs can control how CBO is used using one of the following approaches:

1. By the instance (i.e., for all SQL statements passed to Oracle for processing)—the init.ora entry **optimizer_mode** sets the default optimization approach. Common values are **all_rows**, **first_rows**, and **choose**. Classically, reporting-based applications that work with complete sets of rows as they operate are the best candidates for the first. Screen-based systems where users retrieve a set of rows but most of the time only work with the first set of those rows are candidates for the second approach. The **choose** keyword causes Oracle to behave according to the following logic:

   ■ If there are no statistics available for all tables involved in an SQL statement, Oracle will use the rule-based approach.

   ■ If at least one table involved in an SQL statement has statistics, Oracle will estimate statistics on the fly for the other objects using the **all_rows** goal.

2. By the session—while using SQL*Plus, the **alter session** command is passed to Oracle and the optimizer runs according to the specified approach until either the session ends or another **alter session optimizer_goal** statement is encountered. The next listing illustrates this convention.

```
SQL*Plus: Release 4.0.3.0.0 - Production on Mon May 12 20:43:31 1999
Copyright (c) Oracle Corporation 1979, 1994, 1996.  All rights reserved.
Connected to:
Oracle8 Server Release 8.0.3.0.1 - Production
With the distributed, heterogeneous, replication, objects
and parallel query options
PL/SQL Release 3.0.3.0.1 - Production
SQL> alter session set optimizer_goal = ALL_ROWS;
Session altered.
... ...
... ... Whole bunch of SQL statements
... ...
SQL> alter session set optimizer_goal = CHOOSE;
Session altered.
SQL>
```

3. By the statement—developers embed hints to the SQL statements they are formatting, using one of two conventions.

- with the /* beginning and */ ending comment block indicators as in

```
select /*+ choose */ name, address ....
```

- with the – comment leaders as in

```
select --+ choose
    name, address ....
```

These two conventions are identical to one another except that one uses the double-dash facility, which causes any text on the same line to be treated as part of the comment. The funny thing about hints is that they are simply comments, so if one makes a coding error, Oracle gives no notification or syntax error.

Methodology for Statistic Collection

Let's look at a few guidelines about statistic collection that will enable collection and storage of valid, current statistics for CBO. Regardless of how you prefer to collect statistics, intervention may be required from time to time to ensure the operation completes successfully.

GUIDELINE #1
Inspect the listing file produced by the
analysis program.

All too many times, we hear of installations painstakingly collecting statistics on objects and not ensuring the job runs successfully. If one or more objects contain archaic stats, they could adversely contribute to the selection of a non-optimal execution plan. To assist the process that inspects the listing produced by the analysis job, we suggest doing the following:

1. When building the script that collects statistics, use the semicolon terminator for each statement. This offers more flexibility than the forward slash (/) terminator, as you will see in the next step. In other words, use the convention shown in bold in the next listing rather than that shown in italics.

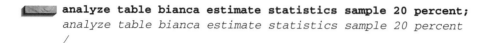

```
analyze table bianca estimate statistics sample 20 percent;
analyze table bianca estimate statistics sample 20 percent
/
```

2. Using some text searching software (the example we show uses a freeware **tsearch** program in Windows NT), search the output listing looking for the **analyze** keyword on any lines that are not terminated by the semicolon as illustrated in the following listing. The command **tsearch analyze -e ";" d:\orant\database\ana_all.lst > fail.sql** produced the following output (the **-e ";"** tells **tsearch** to exclude lines found with the text "analyze" and a semicolon):

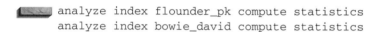

```
analyze index flounder_pk compute statistics
analyze index bowie_david compute statistics
```

Then the output trapped in fail.sql can be run in SQL*Plus to analyze objects whose statistic collection failed the first time.

GUIDELINE #2

*Use the SQL*Plus method of statistic collection.*

When using SQL*Plus, you end up passing statements to Oracle for each object in the schema individually. The success or failure of one statement has no effect on other statements. When using the analyze_schema procedure, it can be all or nothing.

GUIDELINE #3

Use an automated notification mechanism to ensure one intervenes when required to ensure all the desired objects have been successfully analyzed.

Whether you use a host-based e-mail facility (such as UNIX *elm*), a gateway from your server to your office mail system, or run the collection program on a client and then hook output dissemination to the client-based network transport, you must send output from the statistic collection to two or more locations. Do not take for granted that the analyze job ran with 100 percent successful completion.

Rule-Based Approach

Oracle ranks access paths on a weight of 1 to 15, and then chooses the access path with the lowest rank. Think of ranking as going into a grocery store and inspecting the Granny Smith apples. As you pick them up, you turn them over, look for bruises, and examine the color of the skin. Ones you like the most are ranked with the number "1," those you prefer the least are ranked with the number "15." Just like the rule-based approach to optimizing, the rank number affects whether the apple is chosen or discarded in favor of one with a better (or lower) rank.

When retrieving data, Oracle can find the location of a desired row fastest if it knows its rowid (each row can be uniquely identified by its rowid). The rowid provides immediate access to data; it identifies its exact location. Picture the rowid as the address of each piece of data stored in the Oracle database.

Access path rankings are determined by the available indexes and how the SQL statement is worded. Let's look at the most common rule-based access path weights and their meaning. For the next few sections, we will refer to the part of the SQL statement using **where** and one or more **and** as the where/and part of the statement.

VIP

The lower the rank of the access path chosen to satisfy a query, the faster and more efficient the processing.

Rule-Based Access Path Rank 1

This path is available when the **where** keyword equates the rowid to a single value. For example, the statement

```
select *
  from fin_mast
 where rowid = '008A4.0002.009D';
```

would be ranked using this weight. In the SQL statements that you write for your applications, you never know rowids, so this path is not explicitly used very often. However, if you are using Oracle tools such as Oracle Forms and you retrieve a row of information onto a screen, its rowid is fetched as well. When you update the row and save the information back to the database, Oracle Forms passes a SQL statement to Oracle using this rowid construct. You may have seen this if you have ever received an Oracle error from Oracle Forms (yes, Oracle errors do happen):

```
Oracle error occurred while executing KEY-COMMIT trigger:
update tabA set name=:nam,address=:addr ........ where
rowid=:rowid
```

Oracle knows the rowid of the record on the screen you are attempting to update, and uses this access path to perform the update.

Rule-Based Access Path Rank 4

This path is available when all columns in a unique or primary key are referenced by your SQL statement in equality conditions. Let's look at the following table:

Column	Part of Primary Key
street_name	Y
house_number	Y
city	N

The SQL statement

```
select *
   from street_master
 where street_name = 'ROBSON'
   and house_number = '2802';
```

could take advantage of this access path; all the columns in the primary key are mentioned in the where/and and they are compared using equality. The SQL statement

```
select *
   from street_master
 where street_name = 'ROBSON'
   and house_number >= '2802';
```

could not take advantage of this access path, since the comparison condition performed on the house_number column is not equality (there is a greater than or equal to comparison). Likewise, the statement

```
select *
   from street_master
 where street_name = 'ROBSON';
```

does not use all the primary key columns in the where/and and cannot be ranked with this weight.

Rule-Based Access Path Rank 8

If the statement's **where** clause mentions all the columns in a composite index and performs equality comparisons, this access path will be used. Remember, a composite index is one built on more than one column in a table.

Rule-Based Access Path Rank 9

This access path is used if the where/and portion of the SQL statement uses one or more single-column indexes. If more than one single-column index is used, the conditions must be connected with and. For example, consider the fin_mast table indexed on fin_id. The following SQL statement uses this access path:

```
select max_out
   from fin_mast
 where fin_id = '1234M';
```

If there is also an index on the fin_rel column of the same table, the following statement will not use this access path, since the conditions are connected using **or,** not **and**.

```
select max_out
   from fin_mast
 where fin_id = '1234M'
     or fin_rel is not null;
```

Rule-Based Access Path Rank 15

The full table scan is used for any SQL statement that does not satisfy the criteria for other weighted access paths. Each record in the table is read sequentially; those that qualify for all selection criteria are chosen, those that do not are discarded.

The rule-based access path weights not discussed in this section are beyond the scope of this book.

Why CBO Over Rule-based Optimization

Whether you are a database administrator for an OLTP system or a data warehouse administrator for a decision support system, fluency with the cost-based optimizer is mandatory. In the early days of CBO, installations reported that their SQL queries were taking longer than they used to using the rule-based approach. We believe that if you systematically analyze your objects and find a robust way to ensure the work is accomplished as planned, CBO will work well for you. If you don't think it is, speak with Oracle about your problems and, if you have your "house in order," you will find most of the time that CBO works as well if not many times better than its archaic predecessor.

When Oracle7 first appeared in late 1992, the cost-based approach was touted as a dream come true. Developers no longer had to expend much energy optimizing SQL statements. At run time, Oracle would decide an execution plan based on statistics in the data dictionary. Since the cost-based approach is able to optimize statements based on the current data volumes and distribution of indexed column values, execution plans are more dynamic. As the data changes, so will the selected optimal plan.

To help invest in the cost-based approach, Oracle has provided a technique called hints. Using hints, you can influence choices made by cost-based optimization and experiment with different access paths to your data. Oracle has done its homework. Users have been provided with a new optimization technique and can now influence Oracle choices by using these hints. We offer the following guidelines to help you choose between the rule-based and cost-based optimization approaches:

- Applications that have migrated from earlier versions of Oracle (version 6 and earlier offer only rule-based optimization) should be left running rule-based.

- Experiment with the cost-based approach and familiarize yourself with using optimizer hints coupled with new hints in Oracle8 that expand on the set of hints used with Oracle7.

■ New application development and tuning exercises should use the cost-based approach.

■ Tune SQL statements using the tools we introduce in the next section of this chapter: **explain plan** coupled with a few of the members of the Oracle Expert family of performance monitoring tools embedded in the Oracle Enterprise Manager.

SQL Statement Processing

All SQL statements are processed in three phases—parse, execute, and fetch—regardless of the tool (e.g., Oracle Forms, Oracle InterOffice) that passed it to Oracle for processing. Let's look briefly at these phases.

Parse

Parse is the most time-consuming of the three phases, and the most costly. In the section of this chapter covering the shared pool, we will discuss ways to avoid parsing SQL statements prior to execution. During this phase, the optimizer does its job of selecting the most efficient access path and execution plan. Using the following SQL statement as an example, let's look at the tasks involved in this phase.

NOTE
This section offers an oversimplified explanation of the parse phase of SQL statement execution. It gives you a flavor of the amount of work involved. It is NOT the way Oracle directly processes your SQL statements.

```
select a.class_group, descr, sum(mon_amt + tue_amt + wed_amt + thu_amt +
                                 fri_amt + sat_amt + sun_amt)
  from timesheets a, classes b
 where a.class_group like 'CS%'
   and a.class_group = b.class_group
 group by a.class_group, descr;
```

The next four sections illustrate some of the processing required to parse every SQL statement.

	Component	Decision Made	Action Taken
1	a.descr	Not a reserved word	Store until the prefix "a." can be resolved
2	a.class_group	Not a reserved word	Store until the prefix "a." can be resolved
3	by	Reserved word	
4	group	Reserved word	
5	b.class_group	Not a reserved word	Store until the prefix "b." can be resolved
6	a.class_group	Not a reserved word	Store until the prefix "a." can be resolved
7	and	Reserved word	
8	'CS%'	Text enclosed in quotes	Nothing more to do
9	like	Reserved word	
10	a.class_group	Not a reserved word	Store until the prefix "a." can be resolved
11	where	Reserved word	
12	classes b	Not a reserved word	Must be an object name and its alias
13	timesheets a	Not a reserved word	Must be an object name and its alias
14	from	Reserved word	

TABLE 13-3. *Parse Phase Decisions*

Word Meaning

Oracle examines the code from the bottom to the top. It finds different kinds of words in the statement: words it knows as part of its own lingo (e.g., select or where), words that refer to your tables and their columns (e.g., timesheets a or class_grp), and all other miscellaneous words and punctuation (e.g., commas and parentheses). Table 13-3 outlines the decisions Oracle has to make using the last four lines of the previous listing.

Once Oracle works through the statement, bottom to top, it can start to put the whole thing together. Based on what it found, it deduces the following:

■ The objects in the SQL statement are timesheets and classes, using the aliases "a" and "b" respectively. Therefore, column names using one of those prefixes must reside in the appropriate object.

■ The columns enclosed in parentheses all belong to the timesheets object. Since they are being summed in the statement, they all must be defined as numeric.

Resolve Object Names

After learning what it has, Oracle then tries to find out what objects and columns are in the statement. Table 13-4 shows the decisions that must be made. The numbers in the Item column are the component numbers from Table 13-3.

Syntax Checking

Oracle checks the following to ensure the statement is syntactically correct:

■ Parentheses: some portions require parentheses.

■ Commas: members of lists are usually separated from one another by commas.

■ Location of reserved words: Oracle checks the placement of these words and verifies they are in the proper order and do not appear more times than permitted.

SQL statement syntax is verified and the objects mentioned in the statement are resolved.

Determination of the Execution Plan and Data Access Path

The execution plan is determined after the optimizer evaluates the available access paths. The choices the optimizer makes are influenced by the tables accessed in the SQL statement and the way the statements are worded. We discussed cost-based and rule-based optimization approaches earlier in this chapter. The execution plan selected by Oracle during the parse phase is influenced by the optimization approach in use.

Item(s)	Assumptions	Error If Not True
13	The user must have access to an object called timesheets	Table or view does not exist
12	The user must have access to an object called classes	Table or view does not exist
5	The classes table must contain a class_group column	Invalid column name
10, 6, and 12	The timesheets table must contain a class_group column	Invalid column name
1	The timesheets table must contain a descr column	Invalid column name

TABLE 13-4. *Resolving Object Names*

VIP

Over 75 percent of application tuning can be realized by avoiding the parse phase altogether. By using ready-parsed statements already in the shared pool, you are more than three-quarters of the way there.

As we discussed in Chapter 1, the shared pool consumes a significant part of the memory allocated to running the Oracle database. To use ready-parsed statements in the shared pool, you may need to allocate more memory to the shared pool.

VIP

You may have to work closely with your database administrator (DBA) to ensure there is adequate space in the shared pool to accommodate an optimal number of ready-parsed SQL statements.

Let's spend a little time on the data access path. When the optimizer parses a SQL statement, it evaluates possible access paths in order to use the best access path. To some degree, users can help the optimizer choose an access path through deliberate wording of SQL statements.

Let's use the following scenario to illustrate the concepts of access path and optimizer. Suppose you need to get from Montreal to Boston. Your goals are to realize as little wear and tear on your vehicle as possible, spend as little money as possible, and avoid traffic in any large urban centers along the way. The assortment of possible routes is similar to the access path. Like your data, there is a fixed number of ways to get from one end to the other (e.g., if a road has not been built, you cannot include it in your plans). In the midst of selecting the best route, you decide where the fewest bottlenecks are, and you avoid routes that pass through states with higher gasoline prices. You weigh the costs and benefits of each potential route and decide which is best.

With Oracle, this decision-making process is the job of the Oracle optimizer. In more detailed technical discussions of application tuning, we would highlight ways to influence Oracle while it chooses the most efficient access path to your data. For discussions on some of these issues, consult other publications, such as *Tuning Oracle* (Corey, Abbey, and Dechichio, Osborne/McGraw-Hill/Oracle Press, 1995).

VIP

Oracle chooses the access path that will yield the fastest results and consume the least amount of computer resources.

Execute

The reads and writes required to process the statement are performed during the execute phase. Oracle now knows how it will get at the data (based on the execution plan determined during the parse phase). It knows the optimal access path (as determined during the parse phase), and it is armed with all the information necessary to fetch the data that qualifies based on the selection criteria in the SQL statement. Locks are obtained, as required, if the SQL contains any update or delete operations.

Fetch

All rows that have qualified are retrieved during the fetch phase. If the query requires sorting, this is done now. The results are formatted and displayed according to the query's instructions.

VIP
The golden rule about processing SQL statements is: PARSE ONCE, EXECUTE MANY TIMES. By reusing parsed statements in the shared pool, you have made the biggest step toward application tuning.

Naming Variables

You need to adopt a standard convention when naming variables in your programs. Using the same name across SQL statements coupled with the coding conventions discussed in Chapter 10 helps ensure SQL statements you pass to Oracle will match ones already in the shared pool. When using a tool such as Oracle Forms, the names of variables, especially block names, must be standardized. We discuss coding conventions in Chapter 10. The same theory holds when choosing names for variables in your SQL and PL/SQL programs.

When programming using Oracle Forms, a block groups a number of fields on the screen together, permitting creation, modification, and deletions to database data. Fields within blocks and the block name together form what is referred to as *bind variables*. Referencing a block name and a field name prefixed by a colon allows direct manipulation of values in fields on a form. By standardizing block names, SQL statements using these bind variables may match statements already in the shared pool. For example, the first pair of statements in the following listing match, whereas the second pair differ. The same bind variable is used in the first two statements; the latter two may be referring to the same data, but they use different bind variable names.

```
select count(*) into :people.class_count from classif where class_1 =
:people.classif;
select count(*) into :people.class_count from classif where class_1 =
:people.classif;
```

```
select last_name||' '||first_name into :person.full_name from person;
select last_name||' '||first_name into :person.fnam from person;
```

VIP
*Even if two bind variables with different names
(e.g., ":nam" and ":name)" hold the same data
(e.g., the name Wilson), they are still treated
as different variables.*

TIP
*We recommend using block names that match
the table name they refer to. When the same
table is referenced in more than one block in a
program, call the blocks table_name_1 and
table_name_2.*

What Should Be Indexed?

Where to use indexes is a difficult decision. Using indexes properly
contributes to the application tuning process. Towards the end of this
chapter in "Tools of the Tuning Trade," we show you how to assess what
indexes are used as your applications operate. Indexes are optional
structures maintained by Oracle that provide rapid access to your data.
When you create an index, you specify the table name and one or more
columns to keep track of. Once an index is created, Oracle maintains it
automatically as data is created, changed, and deleted from your tables.
The following rules help you decide when to create indexes:

- You should index columns that are mentioned in the **where** or
  and sections (also referred to as the predicate) of a SQL statement.
  Suppose the first_name column in a personnel table is displayed
  as query results, but never as part of the predicate. The column,
  regardless of what values it contains, should not be indexed.

- You should index columns that have a range of distinct values.
  Here's the rule of thumb: if a given value in a table's column is
  present in 20 percent or less of the rows in the table, then the
  column is a candidate for an index. Suppose there are 36,000 rows

in a table with an even distribution (about 12,000 each) of values through one column in the table. The column is not a good candidate for an index. However, if there are between 2,000 and 3,000 rows per column value in another column in that same table (between 5 percent and 8 percent of the rows), then that column is a candidate for an index.

■ If multiple columns are continually referenced together in SQL statement predicates, you should consider putting these columns together in an index. Oracle will maintain single column indexes (those built on one column) or composite indexes (those built on more than one column). Composite indexes are also referred to as concatenated indexes.

Primary Key Constraints

Relational database theory dictates that one or more columns in a table that can uniquely identify each row in that table is the object's *primary key*. Creating primary keys for tables in the Oracle8 database assists the application tuning process since primary key definitions in the data dictionary ensure uniqueness between rows in a table. In addition, this alleviates the need for developers to implement their own individual method for uniqueness checking.

VIP
Data retrieval using entries stored in a primary key is faster than using an index that does not contain unique values.

Suppose that a person table uses its id column as a primary key, and the constraint has been set up using the code

```
alter table person add constraint person_pk primary key (id)
   using index storage (initial 1m next 1m pctincrease 0)
   tablespace prd_indexes;
```

While processing the following SQL statement:

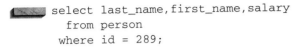
```
select last_name,first_name,salary
   from person
 where id = 289;
```

Oracle would proceed directly to the person_pk index when looking for a certain id column value. If it did not find the right index entry, Oracle would know the row does not exist. The primary key index offers the following two attractions:

- Since each entry in the index is unique, Oracle knows there can only be one entry with the desired value. If the desired entry is found, the search terminates at once.

- The sequential search of the index can be terminated as soon as an entry greater than the desired one is encountered; if a greater primary key index entry (in this case, anything over 289) is encountered, then the desired entry cannot exist.

Tools of the Tuning Trade

We have discussed SQL statement processing, execution plans, access paths, optimization, and indexes. We now show you how to peek at the contents of the shared pool. Once you know how to inspect the SQL statements in the pool, you can start coding SQL to match the statements already there. Then with a brief introduction to tools supplied with Oracle, you will be armed with enough knowledge to start, or continue, tuning applications. In this section, you will learn details on the following:

- How to issue an SQL statement to display the shared pool contents

- Using **explain plan** and **autotrace** to analyze the access path Oracle chooses to access your data

- How to present output from **explain plan** in a readable, tree-like fashion

- How to use SQL trace and the tkprof utility to report on SQL statement processing and CPU utilization

Seeing What Is in the Shared Pool

So far we have talked (or is it nattered at you on and on!) about the shared pool. We will now take the time to show you how to look around the pool and view its contents. Seeing the current contents of the shared pool may help you to make decisions about standardizing as outlined in this chapter as well as Chapter 11. A data dictionary view called v$sqlarea will serve our purpose. You are interested in a column called sql_text. The following code shows you what is in the shared pool:

```
rem *  The sql_text column is 1,000 characters wide so
rem *  set it to 80 for this display
col sql_text format a80
select sql_text from v$sqlarea where lower(sql_text)
        like lower('&text'||'%');
```

TIP

When comparing text against the values of the sql_text column in v$sqlarea, force your lookup string and the sql_text column to the same case (using one of the SQL functions lower and upper).

When this is run, you will see something similar to the following (the code you see will of course depend on what is happening in your database when the query is issued).

```
SQL>  select sql_text from v$sqlarea where lower(sql_text) like
  2>         lower('&text'||'%');
Enter value for text: last_name

old 2: select sql_text from v$sqlarea where lower(sql_text) like
lower('&text'||'%')
new 2: select sql_text from v$sqlarea where lower(sql_text) like
lower('last_name'||'%')
SQL_TEXT
----------------------------------------------------------------
-
select surname||' '||first_name into :person.fname from person
select surname||' '||first_name into :person.fnam from person
SQL>
```

NOTE
The v$sqlarea view is owned by Oracle user SYS, and you must be granted access to the v$ views manually.

explain plan

This utility inspects the indexes being used during the execution of **select**, **insert**, **update**, and **delete** statements. The output is presented as a list of operations describing the access mode for each table in the statement and the indexes Oracle used during processing. All too often, indexes are created on tables and never get used. **explain plan** is the way to detect which indexes are being used and the indexes you could just as well do without.

VIP
*Before you can run **explain plan**, you must own or have access to a table called plan_table. A script called utlxplan.sql in the %RDBMS80%/admin directory creates this table for you.*

This is how to run **explain plan** on the following SQL statement:

```
select last_name, first_name, descr
   from person a, classn b
 where pin = 123897
    and a.clssn = b.clssn;
```

1. Save the SQL statement to a file by entering the command **save sql_test replace** (we use the file name **sql_test**, but use whatever you want).

2. Edit the file called sql_test.sql and insert the text **explain plan set statement_id = 'statement_id'** for in front of your SQL statement. The **statement_id** is a one-character to 30-character name used to uniquely identify the code. The file **sql_test.sql** now contains (using a sample statement_id of **ST_ID**):

```
explain plan set statement_id = 'ST_ID' for
 select last_name, first_name, descr
   from person a, classn b
  where pin = 123897
    and a.clssn = b.clssn;
```

3. Run the following SQL script (we call it **expl.sql**) by entering the command **@expl statement_id**, using the statement_id name from when you loaded your SQL into the plan_table:

```
rem *  File name: expl.sql
spool expl
select decode(id,0,'',
        lpad(' ',2*(level-1))||level||'.'||position)||' '||
        operation||' '||options||' '||object_name||' '||
        object_type||' '||
        decode(id,0,'Cost = '||position) Query_plan
  from plan_table
connect by prior id = parent_id
   and statement_id = upper('&1')
  start with id = 0 and statement_id = upper('&1');
spool off
```

4. Interpret the output in the file expl.lst.

NOTE

The name of the file is based on the spool statement in the code shown in the previous listing. The filename extension .lst may be different on your platform.

The next listing shows the output of the statement loaded in this exercise. Table 13-5 explains the operations in the listing.

```
SELECT STATEMENT     Cost = 13
    2.0 NESTED LOOPS
      3.1 TABLE ACCESS FULL PERSON
      3.2 TABLE ACCESS BY ROWID CLASSN
        4.1 INDEX RANGE SCAN CLASSN_1 NON-UNIQUE
```

Operation	Meaning
Nested loops	Oracle loops through the column values returned by one set of rows, comparing them against those returned by a second set of rows. The rows that match the selection criteria are displayed; ones that do not qualify are discarded.
Table access full	Oracle reads the table from start to finish, one row at a time.
Table access by rowid	Oracle reads rows from a table by rowid after obtaining the rowid from that table's index.
Index range scan	Oracle retrieves one or more rowids from an index as the index is read in ascending order.

TABLE 13-5. *Explain Plan Output Operations*

VIP
As you become more experienced with **explain plan**, *you will notice that some operations almost always appear with each other. For example, prior to most index range scans, you will find a table access by rowid operation.*

Using set autotrace

Set autotrace provides a more automated way of using **explain plan** with your SQL statements. The process of explaining statements has been streamlined starting with release 7.3 of Oracle using the **autotrace** feature. The next listing shows the format of the set command to start autotracing your SQL.

```
SQL> set autotrace
Usage: SET AUTOT[RACE]  {OFF  |  ON  |  TRACE[ONLY]}  [EXP[LAIN]]
[STAT[ISTICS]]
```

Note how the command can be abbreviated to **set autot**. To set the SQL environment to automatically trace statements, issue the command **set autotrace on**. If you receive the following error message, you will have to ensure you have access to a plan_table to allow the set command to succeed.

```
SQL> set autotrace on
Unable to verify PLAN_TABLE format or existence
Error enabling EXPLAIN report
```

When the **set autotrace** command succeeds, you will get no feedback from Oracle. Now after each statement is issued, Oracle will produce trace output similar to that shown in the following session:

```
SQL*Plus: Release 4.0.3.0.0 - Production on Mon May 12 20:43:31 1998
Copyright (c) Oracle Corporation 1979, 1994, 1996.  All rights reserved.
Connected to:
Oracle8 Server Release 8.0.3.0.1 - Production
With the distributed, heterogeneous, replication, objects
and parallel query options
PL/SQL Release 3.0.3.0.1 - Production
SQL> select last_name,first_name,desce
  2  from person,dept
  3  where person.dept = dept.dept_no
  4  and pin = (select min(pin) from person);

LAST_NAME              FIRST_NAME           DESCE
--------------------   ------------------   --------------------
Abbey                  Michael              Eastern Region
Execution Plan
----------------------------------------------------------
    0        SELECT STATEMENT Optimizer=CHOOSE
    1     0    NESTED LOOPS
    2     1      TABLE ACCESS (BY ROWID) OF 'PERSON'
    3     2        INDEX (UNIQUE SCAN) OF 'PERSON_PK' (UNIQUE)
    4     3          SORT (AGGREGATE)
    5     4            INDEX (FULL SCAN) OF 'PERSON_PK' (UNIQUE)
    6     1      TABLE ACCESS (BY ROWID) OF 'DEPT'
    7     6        INDEX (UNIQUE SCAN) OF 'DEPT_PK' (UNIQUE)
Statistics
----------------------------------------------------------
        0  recursive calls
        0  db block gets
```

```
  5   consistent gets
  0   physical reads
  0   redo size
197   bytes sent via SQL*Net to client
286   bytes received via SQL*Net from client
  3   SQL*Net roundtrips to/from client
  0   sorts (memory)
  0   sorts (disk)
  1   rows processed
```

SQL>

NOTE

Using the expl.sql program from the "explain plan" section displays a Cost= figure which autotracing will not do. We like the expl.sql approach for this reason, though autotrace may be quicker.

SQL Trace and tkprof

These facilities provide performance information on SQL statements. It reports on times spent on the parse, execute, and fetch phases of statement execution. One Oracle technique that allows applications to perform well is the ability to keep significant amounts of data and data dictionary information in memory. As they operate, your applications will find a large part of the information they need in memory. If application-specific information can be found in memory, the I/O involved to retrieve that information can be bypassed. SQL trace also informs you of the percentage of logical reads (those satisfied by memory reads) and physical reads (those satisfied by reads from disk). To use SQL trace and tkprof:

1. Ensure the timed_statistics entry in your initialization parameter file is set to TRUE.

NOTE

If this parameter is not properly set, set it to TRUE, then you will have to restart the database to activate the changed value.

2. Enter the text **alter session set sql_trace = true;** at the top of your SQL program.

3. Run the SQL program to produce a trace file to be fed to tkprof. For this exercise, the name of the trace file is ora_11277.trc.

NOTE
The location of the trace file is defined by the initialization parameter file entry user_dump_dest. For help finding the name of the trace file, see the next section, "Finding Which Trace File Is Yours."

4. Run the command **tkprof80 ora00076.trc output=ora00076.out explain=person/password** to produce formatted SQL trace output.

5. Examine the output produced by tkprof. You then begin to see how much time Oracle is spending retrieving your data. When tkprof output is coupled with explain plan, you are presented with formatted output similar to the following.

```
******************************************************************
select ename,loc,hiredate
from emp a, dept b where a.deptno = b.deptno

call       count       cpu    elapsed     disk    query  current0      rows
-------   -------  --------  ---------  -------  -------  -------  --------
Parse          1     0.00       0.06        0        0        0       200
Execute        1     0.00       0.00        0        0        0       200
Fetch          1     0.00       0.06        0       57        2      2014
Rows      Execution Plan
-------   -------------------------------------------------------
     0    SELECT STATEMENT
    14      NESTED LOOPS
    14        TABLE ACCESS (FULL) OF 'EMP'
    14        TABLE ACCESS (BY ROWID) OF 'DEPT'
    28          INDEX (RANGE SCAN) OF 'DEPT_1' (NON-UNIQUE)
******************************************************************
```

The technical ins and outs of this output are too much to handle in this book. Suffice it to say, by looking at the Parse, Execute, and Fetch lines that appear in bold type, you can get a grasp of how your SQL statements are performing. Run tkprof, examine the results, and try to get the times for the three processing phases to an absolute minimum.

Finding Which Trace File Is Yours

Picture yourself figuring out which trace file to use for tkprof. You go to the directory where the trace files are deposited and find hundreds of files all starting with ora_ and ending with .trc. You issue the directory command for your operating system, and sit back and watch the show—screens and screens of filenames. Use the following technique to help you find which trace file is yours.

Oracle8 on Windows NT

The simple "dir" command is used on NT followed by inspection of the output for tthe appropriate time and date of the desired trace file. Most of the time, you will end up sending the output to a file with the ">{file_name}" convention.

```
D:\ORANT\RDBMS80\TRACE>dir
 Volume in drive D is DRIVE DEE
 Volume Serial Number is 2627-1D06
 Directory of D:\ORANT\RDBMS80\TRACE
04/20/97  09:21a         <DIR>          .
04/20/97  09:21a         <DIR>          ..
04/25/97  11:47a                 26,092 ORA00076.TRC
04/20/97  11:35p                  1,559 ORA00206.TRC
05/12/97  08:25p                 76,319 orclALRT.LOG
05/12/97  08:25p                  5,746 orclCKPT.TRC
05/12/97  08:25p                  5,746 orclDBWR.TRC
05/12/97  08:25p                  5,746 orclLGWR.TRC
05/11/97  02:47p                  3,211 orclPMON.TRC
05/12/97  08:25p                  5,746 orclRECO.TRC
05/12/97  08:25p                  5,746 orclSMON.TRC
05/12/97  08:25p                  5,239 orclSNP0.TRC
              12 File(s)         141,150 bytes
                          1,523,089,408 bytes free

D:\ORANT\RDBMS80\TRACE>
```

UNIX

At the top of your SQL script, after the line where you entered **alter session set sql_trace = true;**, place the UNIX host character "!". The segment of code with the alter session and the host character is

```
alter session set sql_trace = true;
!
```

This will position you at your operating system prompt. Using UNIX, issue the command **ps -fu yourname** to see the activity against your UNIX userid:

```
jrstocks  9824      1  0 15:44:14 tty0p5   0:00 -ksh
jrstocks 11276   2805  0 17:16:21 ttyp7    0:00 sqlplus
jrstocks 11277  11276  0 17:16:21 ?        0:00 oracledev (DESCRIPTION=(LOC)
```

The process identifier in the second column (in this output, it would be process 11277) can be used to build the trace filename for tkprof. The desired trace filename becomes ora_11277.trc.

VMS

In VMS, the SQL script uses the VMS host character $:

```
alter session set sql_trace = true;
$
```

and the VMS command **sh us oracle/full** yields output similar to

```
VAX/VMS User Processes at 39-FEB-2001 13:40:33.73
Total number of users = 1,  number of processes = 2
Username  Node   Process Name      PID      ÿ20Terminal
ORACLE7   NCR3   Database Admin.   2020103A  LTA840:  (LAT_AA000400442C)
ORACLE7   NCR3   ORACLE7_1         20201040  (subprocess of 2020103A)
```

The desired trace filename becomes ora_20201040.trc.

VIP
*If you turn on sql_trace during testing and program development, make sure the **alter session** statement and the host character **are removed** from the programs before they are used by end users. Forgetting to remove them can be disastrous!*

Oracle Trace

Oracle Trace offers a point of collection for performance-related information that can assist the application tuning process. Data collected can be used to report on system usage, details of transactions performed against the Oracle8 database, and can be used to diagnose problems before they occur or become catastrophes. The Oracle Trace Manager allows you to manage, report on, and purge trace information no longer required, and produce graphical output to assist the tuning process.

Oracle Trace is an event-based collector of performance and transaction information. Advanced application tuning needs timely raw data to assist the DBA and the application developer as they try to iron out bottlenecks that force systems to their knees. Some of its predecessors such as **explain plan** and **tkprof80** do their own thing in their own way, but Oracle Trace takes it that extra distance. Oracle Trace events are divided into two categories:

■ Duration events such as a transaction; by collecting start and end times, you can measure the length of a transaction and add impetus, where required, to the statement "That activity seems never-ending."

■ Point events that occur but have no duration, such as the raising of a space management request.

The key feature of Oracle Trace is the ability to predefine a stream of events, then measure the resources used as those events unfold. Oracle Trace can help, when necessary, to provide evidence to support a feeling that the user community has about activities in their online systems.

Suppose there was an ongoing discussion that a set of transactions in a financial application is never-ending. Users complain that it takes 30 to 40 seconds to return control to the screen after the Save button is pressed. Using Oracle Trace, you define an event that covers the time between the button press and the termination of the transaction. After data has been collected, you pass the information off to Oracle Trace to investigate where the bottleneck lies. We have experience in situations where a spot in an application is suspect, and after proper investigation we can determine that the problem is something else.

Table 13-6 shows some of the events that can be defined for the Oracle8 Server (used with permission of Oracle Corporation).

Oracle Trace adds the missing link to the advanced application tuning arena. So many requests for resources that lead to contention issues can be rectified once you have a tool at your disposal. Many third-party software vendors address backend performance bottlenecks: they allow the DBA to look at how the instance is behaving. They permit drill-down to levels of detail that provide the DBA with the information necessary to tune memory structures and read/write operations. Oracle Trace steps up to the plate. In mid-1995, one of us wrote a white paper for one of these vendors entitled "Application Tuning—the Missing Link." That link can now be closed with the likes of Oracle Trace.

What's Next

There is a wealth of information in technical publications, newsletters, magazines, and books on Oracle to help you get the most out of your applications. One of life's golden rules is so applicable when working with Oracle: do it right the first time. In an earlier book, *Tuning Oracle*, the following sentiments were quoted:

- You know, one of the things I like so much about Oracle is that it is so tunable.

- You know, one of the things I hate so much about Oracle is that it is so tunable.

Event	Description	Duration	Point
Connection	Records each connection to a database.		X
Disconnect	Records each disconnection from a database.		X
Error Stack	Code stack for core dump.		X
Migration	Session migration between shared server processes.		X
SQLSegment	Text of SQL statement.		X
Wait	Records a generic WAIT event. Context is provided in the event strings.		X
Parse Start	Start of event that contains SQL query information (actual text of query).	X	
Parse End	End of event that contains SQL query information.	X	
Execute Start	Start of event containing information for execution of SQL query plan.	X	
Execute End	End of event containing information for execution of SQL Query plan.	X	
Fetch Start	Start of event containing actual row retrieval information.	X	
PhysicalTX Start	Start of event marking a definite change in database status.	X	
PhysicalTX End	End of event marking a definite change in database status.	X	

TABLE 13-6.   *Oracle8 Server Events Defined for Oracle Trace*

When it comes to tuning your applications, you will find this to be all too true.

By reading the last three chapters of this book, we trust that you have become better equipped to write efficient Oracle applications (Chapters 10 and 12) and use some more sophisticated SQL syntax (Chapter 11). You should read on: in the next part of the book, "So You're the New DBA," you will read details on important database administrator (DBA) duties and round out your understanding of Oracle. We touch on database tuning which, alongside application tuning discussed here and in Chapter 11, provides for optimal system performance and efficient use of your computer's resources.

CHAPTER
14

DBA 101

n this chapter, we will discuss what you need to know to become a database administrator (DBA). The work of the DBA contributes to the effective operation of all systems that run with the Oracle database. The DBA offers technical support to everyone and is expected to become fluent in all technical issues that arise with the Oracle software. The DBA is responsible for the following:

- Day-to-day operations of the Oracle database

- Installation and upgrades of Oracle software

- Performance tuning

- Backup and recovery strategies

- Consultation with data administration personnel

- Consultation with developers

We will show you the tools of the trade: Server Manager and Enterprise Manager. With these tools, we will show you how to do the following:

- Start the database

- Shut down the database

- Give database access to new users

- Revoke database access from existing users

- Create tablespaces

- Add more space to a tablespace

We will lead you through some important concepts and guide you through the DBA's job using code samples. We will introduce some new terminology, and then use those technical terms as part of the DBA lingo in the rest of the chapter. This is designed to be an introduction, so we will not get into much technical detail. If you have problems, or if procedures do not work as expected, something may be wrong with your configuration or the way the Oracle software has been installed. Personal Oracle for Windows 95 specifics are covered at the end of the chapter. Chapter 18 covers these and some additional topics in more detail.

Becoming a Database Administrator

You may have already worked with Oracle as a developer, also called a programmer or programmer analyst. Or you may be starting from scratch with Oracle. As you become a DBA, you will find yourself becoming the focal point for all your installation's Oracle issues. The major components of your new role include the following responsibilities:

- Installation and upgrades of the Oracle Server and all its associated products

- Allocation of resources to support Oracle, including memory, disk space, and user account management, to name a few items

- Backup and recovery

- Tuning the Oracle database for optimal performance

- Liaising with Oracle Worldwide Customer Support to deal with technical issues requiring Oracle's intervention

- Staying current with Oracle's emerging product line and with new additions that may complement your existing applications

At the end of this chapter, you will have the knowledge to start working as a DBA. We strongly recommend that you read this book cover to cover, paying special attention to the following chapters which are of special interest to the DBA:

- Chapter 3
- Chapter 5
- Chapter 16
- Chapter 17
- Chapter 18

We also recommend reading *Tuning Oracle* by Corey, Abbey, and Dechichio (Osborne McGraw-Hill/Oracle Press, 1995) and the *Oracle DBA*

Handbook—7.3 Edition by Kevin Loney (Osborne McGraw-Hill/Oracle Press, 1994). These two works will enhance your understanding of the DBA role and will help you become an effective DBA. Both cover important issues such as the architecture of the Oracle database, database design, application tuning, and DBA roles and responsibilities.

Terminology

The following definitions will arm you with the technical jargon you need to make it through this chapter.

- When a program operates in *line mode*, it presents output one line at a time; the output scrolls up the screen every time you press the ENTER key. In this mode, information scrolls off the screen when room is required for further input.

- When a program operates in *full-screen mode*, it presents information on the screen, and you move around using the TAB key or a mouse and initiate activities based on where you are on the screen.

- *GUI* (graphical user interface) programs allow users to interact with them by clicking the mouse on an assortment of icons, menus, check boxes, radio buttons, etc. Products such as MS Word 6, WordPerfect for Windows, and Personal Oracle7 are GUI.

- An *instance* is a set of support processes and memory allocated for accessing an Oracle database. Throughout your experience as a DBA, you will hear the terms Oracle instance and Oracle database. Use these two terms synonymously.

- *Startup* is the action of placing an Oracle instance in a state that allows users to access the database to carry on their business. Startup initiates processes required for users to access the database, and it reserves a portion of your computer's memory within which Oracle operates.

- The command *connect internal* logs you onto the database as Oracle user SYS. One accesses the database in this fashion to perform activities such as startup and shutdown.

■ *Shutdown* is the action of taking an Oracle instance from a state that allows users to access the database to a dormant state; when the database is shut down, we say that it is closed. Shutdown terminates the processes required for users to access the database, and it releases the portion of your computer's memory within which Oracle was operating.

■ A *user name* is assigned to people when they require access to the Oracle database. It is also referred to as one's logon ID.

■ A *password* accompanies every user name and must be supplied to Oracle to connect to the database.

■ A *user* is associated with a person that is allowed access to an Oracle database. Many people are familiar with logging into a local area network at work by entering accounting information with a user name and password.

■ A *role* is a logical grouping of one or more Oracle users who end up performing similar tasks while they work with Oracle data. Suppose a handful of users in personnel required the same set of privileges to work with sensitive data that no other user had access to. You would group these users together in a role and make these people members of that role.

■ A *profile* is a set of resource consumption limits assigned to users of the Oracle database. Unless they are restricted by the DBA, users automatically have no limits on the resources they can consume so that they are not prevented from completing their day-to-day work.

■ A *job* is a set of one or more computer programs that perform a task. If you use Microsoft Word, you could say that saving your word processing document is a job.

■ *O/S* is a short form for operating system. An operating system is a collection of programs that permit a computer to manage the flow of information between its processor, peripherals (e.g., keyboard, screen, hard disk), and memory.

■ *Batch* is a facility available on most mini and mainframe computers that runs jobs for you unattended; the jobs are submitted to batch using an O/S-specific command. As batch jobs execute, they do not tie up your screen and terminal.

Enterprise Manager

This product, affectionately referred to as *OEM*, first appeared with Oracle 7.3 and has developed into a solid database administration tool—and then some. Since this is the first time we have really had a look at it, let's take a few minutes to examine the OEM console and some of its additional management tools.

NOTE
The first time you run OEM, you may be asked the question shown in Figure 14-1 about setting up the OEM and Software Manager repositories. Click OK to invoke setup, which takes a few minutes.

OEM Management Tools

Once OEM loads, you will view the main console with a screen similar to that shown in Figure 14-2. As the version of OEM changes, the look of the console, the position and look of the buttons, and the features of OEM may be different: the flavor of the product can be gleaned from this release.

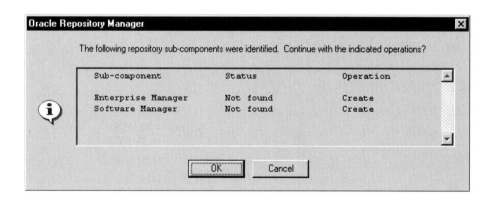

FIGURE 14-1. *Setting up the repository dialog box as OEM starts*

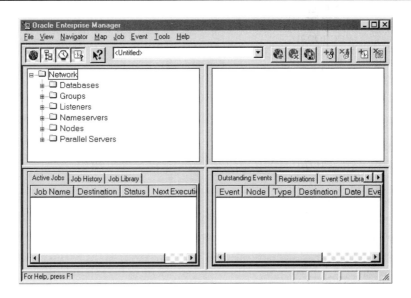

FIGURE 14-2. *OEM console*

Let's have a look at the options on the drop-down menu when "Tools" is selected on the menu bar at the top of the console.

VIP
*The OEM console must be open after successfully connecting to a repository **before** you can use any of the managers discussed in the next few sections.*

Instance Manager

As the name of the tool suggests, this manager is used to work with one or more Oracle instances to which you have access through OEM. You can start or stop an instance, inspect/change initialization parameter file entries, and monitor which users are connected to which database. We will be looking at a few tasks that can be accomplished with this manager a bit later in this chapter.

Schema Manager

This is the heart of OEM's object management toolset, where the DBA or other privileged users can work with the assortment of database objects we discussed in Chapter 4. The operator is able to create, edit, and inspect objects belonging to just about anyone in any available instance.

Security Manager

Managing users, roles, and profiles is done from this manager. These objects can be created, modified, and dropped.

Storage Manager

All tasks associated with managing storage items in an Oracle database are controlled from this tool. Instance support files that hold the data are created here; these files can be renamed if and when necessary using the assortment of dialog boxes presented as you work with this manager.

Backup Manager

This is where you can guide the instance through a series of backups. There is a backup wizard that takes you by the hand and leads you through an interactive dialog to perform just about any level of full database or database file backup.

Data Manager

This is where the operator can invoke export, import, or Oracle Loader. We looked at the load capabilities a bit more in Chapter 10 where we discussed moving data into the Oracle database using SQL*Loader, commonly referred to as Oracle Loader.

Recovery Manager

This tool is used to recover or restore a database. This is where you administer the redo log groups, and manage backups that can be written with the database open and accessible to the user community.

SQL Worksheet

For those of us who like to roll up our sleeves and get our hands dirty, this worksheet is where you can enter SQL commands, OEM DBA commands, and even run PL/SQL. There is a command history feature that allows you to scroll back and work again with commands passed to Oracle for processing.

Enterprise Manager: Invoking

OEM is started from the Windows NT start menu, or by clicking the appropriate icon in the Oracle Enterprise Manager folder. You must connect to the OEM repository before working with the main console shown in Figure 14-2.

VIP
*Each user that invokes OEM needs access to the two repositories displayed in Figure 14-1. If you invoke OEM as a user and do **not** want to set up a new set of repositories, enter the user name and password of an existing repository owner.*

Throughout this book, when we use OEM we are connecting to a local database on a Windows NT 4.0 workstation. If you use OEM to access a suite of instances all over a corporate network, the "Service" portion of the repository logon dialog box will have to be filled in.

Enterprise Manager: Connecting to the Repository

The dialog box shown in Figure 14-3 is how you connect to the OEM console. Notice that there are four entry areas in the box.

■ User name is where you enter the name of the user whose account you use to connect to the OEM repository.

■ Password is the text that was assigned when the user was created.

■ Service refers to a connect string to be used to hook up to a remote database.

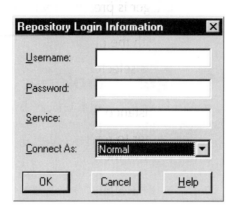

FIGURE 14-3. *Repository logon information*

- Connect As refers to the mode with which you wish to log into the repository. Most of the time, you select the "Normal" option, though the SYSOPER and SYSDBA options in the drop-down menu are used to perform startup and shutdown, for example.

Enterprise Manager: Startup

After entering logon information as OEM is invoked, do the following to start an Oracle8 database.

1. Proceed to the Tools option on the menu bar at the top of the OEM console.

2. Click on Applications, and then the Instance Manager option on the drop-down menu.

3. If informed that a database needs to be selected for this application, click on OK to enter that information.

4. Enter appropriate logon details, ensuring you select the SYSDBA option in the Connect As area of the login dialog box. We created a privileged user named **abbey** identified by **abbey** to perform these operations.

5. When the Instance Manager is presented, proceed to the Startup tab, as shown in Figure 14-4. Notice the indicator showing the instance is not running with the circle/line indicator.

6. Ensure Mount and Open is selected, and then click on Startup to start the operation.

7. Click OK to dismiss the Instance Started information box.

8. Leave the Instance Manager to return to OEM by clicking the close box in the top-right corner of the screen.

The database is now open and available for user connections.

Enterprise Manager: Shutdown

This task is similar to the previous one, save for the activity at hand. Perform the same steps 1 through 4, but then do the following.

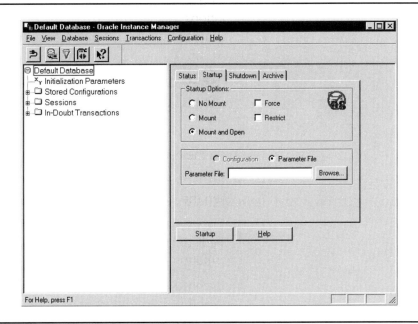

FIGURE 14-4. *Startup dialog box in the Instance Manager*

1. When the Instance Manager is presented, proceed to the Shutdown tab, as shown in Figure 14-5. Notice the indicator showing the instance is running.

2. Ensure Immediate is selected in the Shutdown Options area of the folder, then click OK to proceed.

3. Click OK to dismiss the shutdown information box.

4. Leave the Instance Manager to return to OEM by clicking the close box in the top-right corner of the screen.

The database is now closed, and inaccessible to the regular user community.

NOTE
For more ways to shut down a database using OEM, refer to a discussion in the Line-mode Server Manager: Shutdown section called "Problems Shutting the Database" in this chapter.

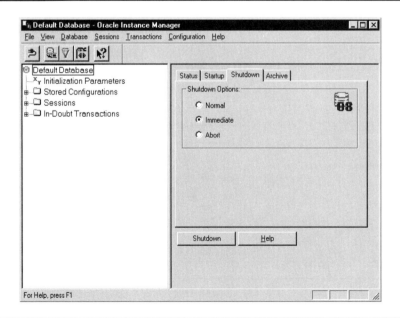

FIGURE 14-5. *Shutdown dialog box in the Instance Manager*

Enterprise Manager: Granting Access to a User

Enabling access is accomplished from the Security Manager under Applications in the Tools drop-down menu. After supplying appropriate logon information, perform the following to accomplish this task.

1. Right mouse click on the Users folder to bring up the dialog box shown in Figure 14-6.

2. Fill in the user name **polly** beside the Name prompt.

3. Ensure the Password option is selected in the Authentication box, and enter the text **gone** in the Enter Password area, then the same text in the Confirm Password area.

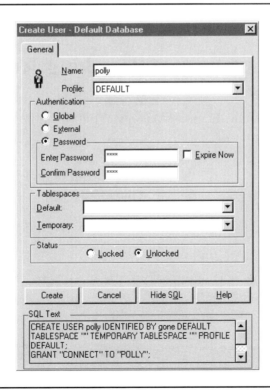

FIGURE 14-6. *Create user dialog box*

NOTE
We have selected the Show SQL option in this sheet; thus the bottom of the sheet shows the SQL statement passed to Oracle.

4. Pick a tablespace name from the Default Tablespace drop-down menu and one from the Temporary Tablespace list as well.

5. Click Create to finish.

User polly can now connect to the database.

VIP
The user will only be able to connect to the database within which he or she was created. If you manage more than one database in OEM, the user must be created manually in each instance.

Enterprise Manager: Revoking Access from a User

Again, this is done in the Security Manager. Follow these steps to accomplish this task.

1. Right mouse click on the user polly to be removed.

2. Select the Remove option from the drop-down menu displayed.

3. Click OK on the dialog box to confirm completion of the activity.

NOTE
If the user to be removed owns objects in the database, you will be reminded and must confirm that you want the user's objects removed as well.

4. Click on the Exit-X to leave the Security Manager.

User polly's access to the database is now removed.

Enterprise Manager: Creating a Tablespace

This is accomplished using the Oracle Storage Manager. After connecting to the desired database, perform the following to create a new tablespace.

1. Right mouse click on Tablespaces to display the dialog box shown in Figure 14-7.

2. Name the tablespace, then click Add in the Datafiles area.

3. Fill in the required information shown in Figure 14-8 to specify one or more datafiles that will make up the new tablespace.

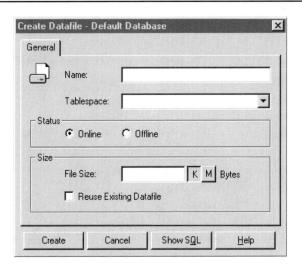

FIGURE 14-7. *Create the tablespace dialog box*

4. Click Create to send the tablespace creation command off for processing.

5. When you return to the Security Manager startup screen, the tablespace you just created will appear in the list of available tablespaces.

6. Click on the Exit-X to leave the manager.

The next time the instance is started, it will automatically acquire this dbtinc tablespace in the future.

Enterprise Manager: Adding Space to an Existing Tablespace

Again, this is done from the Storage Manager by performing the following.

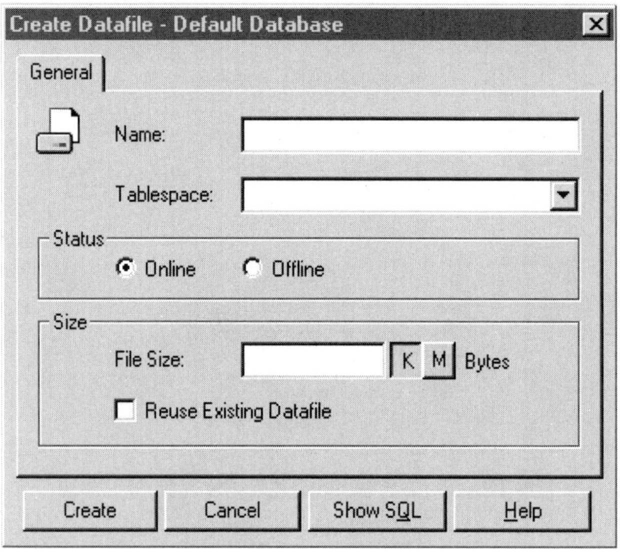

FIGURE 14-8. *Datafile specifications*

1. Right mouse click on the tablespace to which the file is to be added.

2. Pick the Add Datafile option on the drop-down menu to bring up the dialog box shown in Figure 14-9.

3. Click Create to add the new file to the existing tablespace.

4. Click the Exit-X on the Security Manager to return to OEM.

Now, wasn't that fun? Let's move on to look at another way to accomplish the work we did in this section.

Line-Mode Server Manager

This tool runs on any terminal regardless of its ability to support graphics. You can run jobs unattended using line-mode Server Manager, which first appeared with release 7.1.3.

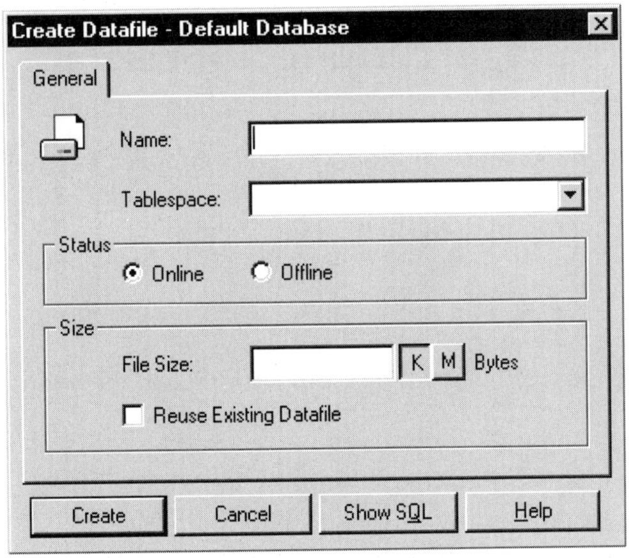

FIGURE 14-9. *Create the datafile dialog box*

Server Manager: Invoking

The command **svrmgr30** starts line-mode Server Manager and displays the following output:

```
Oracle Server Manager: Release 3.0.3.0.1 - Production
Copyright (c) Oracle Corporation 1994, 1995. All rights reserved.
Oracle Server Release 8.0.3.0.1 - Production
With the distributed, heterogenous, replication, objects
and parallel query options
PL/SQL Release 3.0.3.0.1 - Production
SVRMGR>
```

VIP

The name of the program that runs Server Manager on NT and some other platforms differs from "svrmgr30" as used in this section. For example, Windows 95 uses the name "svrmgr73" whereas NT uses the name "svrmgr30" with Oracle8.

Server Manager: connect internal Command

After starting line-mode Server Manager, enter **connect internal** and Oracle responds with one of two responses. If the instance is down when the command is issued, Server Manager responds with

```
Connected to an idle instance.
SVRMGR>
```

If the instance is started when the command is issued, Server Manager responds with

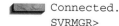
```
Connected.
SVRMGR>
```

You must connect to the Oracle database to perform all operations in Server Manager.

Server Manager: Startup

After starting line-mode Server Manager, follow these steps:

1. Enter **connect internal**.

2. Enter **startup**. Oracle responds with the following:

```
ORACLE instance started.
Database mounted.
Database opened.
Total System Global Area        4393640 bytes
              Fixed Size          46112 bytes
           Variable Size        3929736 bytes
        Database Buffers         409600 bytes
            Redo Buffers           8192 bytes
SRVRMGR>
```

The database is now started. We also refer to the database as being open or the database being up after this activity completes successfully. Using Server Manager to start your database is actually a three-step process—the startup command performs three distinct steps, as listed here:

```
startup nomount
alter database mount;
alter database open;
```

When starting your database with Server Manager (line-mode or full-screen), if any step in the startup process abends (i.e., does not complete successfully), the database is left in the condition it was in when the last step successfully completed. Following is an example of how this difference can affect your clients and what to do about it. Let's say your production database is shut down every morning at 2:00 AM for system backups. After the backups complete, you start the database with the command svrmgrl @startup_prd.sql. The startup_prd.sql file has the code

```
connect internal
startup
exit
```

In the morning, the users start logging onto the database and receive the following error message:

 ERROR: ORA-01033: ORACLE initialization or shutdown in progress

You attempt to connect to the database, but you get the same message. For some reason, one of the three operations Server Manager has performed during startup has aborted, leaving the database in its previous state. Perhaps the alter database mount operation has failed, and the database has been left unmounted.

NOTE

*If you use line-mode Server Manager to start your database, rather than using the command startup, you may wish to enter the three commands **startup nomount**, then **alter database mount;**, then **alter database open;** separately.*

Server Manager: Shutdown

After starting line-mode Server Manager, follow these steps:

1. Enter **connect internal**.

2. Enter **shutdown**. Oracle responds with the following:

```
Database closed.
Database dismounted.
ORACLE instance shut down.
SVRMGR>
```

The database is now closed.

Problems Shutting the Database

Early into your tenure as a DBA, you may run across a situation we have seen many times: You enter Server Manager, connect to the database, then issue the **shutdown** command. For the next few minutes (actually it feels like a few hours when it happens to you), you are looking at the following:

```
SVRMGR> shutdown
```
_

The cursor sits on the next line, flashing for an eternity. When you get tired of waiting, you press the terminal break key (usually mapped to CTRL-C) and get the following message from Oracle:

```
ORA-01013: user requested cancel of current operation
```

Since the shutdown did not complete, the database is left running.

There are two options you may use with the **shutdown** command when this happens to you: **immediate** and **abort**. Why would anyone need to shut down a database while users are connected? Look at the following scenario for one of many reasons:

- An accounts receivable manager inadvertently selects the wrong menu option from her system menu, and invokes a job that initiates year-end processing for a number of accounts. Noticing her error, she phones her IT (Information Technology) contact, who calls you in a panic. If other users are permitted to carry on with their regular business after this has happened, the integrity of the system is in question. You decide the database has to be shut down immediately before more harm is done. You log into Server Manager, connect internal, then issue the shutdown command, and guess what—blinking cursor! You return to your O/S and ask for a program status for the machine, and you find out that 17 users are logged onto the database doing various things.

- An introductory discussion to shutdown would be deficient without telling you about two of the shutdown options, immediate and abort; they are used in case the "blinking cursor" happens to you.

CAUTION
When any users are logged onto the database, you cannot close that database using the **shutdown** _command without using either the_ **immediate** _or_ **abort** _option._

IMMEDIATE OPTION   This is done by entering **shutdown immediate** while connected to your database. The database will not close at once—after Oracle performs some cleanup, the database will shut down. The sessions that were accessing the database are terminated gracefully, and any resources in use by those sessions are methodically freed up. When Oracle completes this work, the database will be shut down. Think of shutdown immediate as a small child's caregiver carrying the youngster up to bed, reading to the child, preparing the blanket and pillow, and then putting the child to bed and leaving the room.

NOTE
*Shutdown immediate is the most common way you will shut down your database when a normal shutdown does not work. The length of time for a **shutdown immediate** to complete depends on the number of users on the database when the command is issued. Be patient.*

ABORT OPTION   This is done by entering **shutdown abort** while connected to your database. The database will close at once. The sessions that were accessing the database are terminated abruptly. Think of that child in the previous scenario. **Shutdown abort** is like walking up to that same child, pointing your index finger up at the stairs, and saying "GO TO BED, NOW."

CAUTION
Shutdown abort should be used as a very last resort. You may wish to get some advice from colleagues before using this command.

With this advice in mind, there are definitely situations where you will have to use **shutdown abort**; you will have to use it from time to time when the need arises.

NOTE
*After doing **shutdown abort**, you may wait less than a minute, a few minutes, or as much as a few hours for the database to restart. If your database has not started in what you feel is "an expected amount of time," speak with a skilled colleague or Oracle before taking corrective action.*

The amount of time it takes the database to restart after a shutdown abort is an extension of what was going on (i.e., the number of users connected and how much activity they were in the midst of doing) when the **shutdown abort** command was issued.

VIP
*On a number of occasions, we have seen a database take six to eight hours to start after a **shutdown abort** was issued when there was a great deal of activity.*

Server Manager: Exiting

To exit, enter **exit** at the SVRMGR> prompt. Oracle responds with

 Server Manager complete.

Server Manager: Granting Access to a User

To set up a new user, start line-mode Server Manager, then follow these steps:

1. Enter **connect internal**.

2. Enter the command **grant connect to polly identified by gone;** and receive the response from Oracle:

```
Statement processed.
SVRMGR>
```

3. Enter **exit** to leave line-mode Server Manager.

In this example, *polly* is the user name and *gone* is the password. Thus, user polly may connect to the database after supplying the password *gone*.

Server Manager: Revoking Access from a User

After starting line-mode Server Manager, follow these steps:

1. Enter **connect internal**.

2. Enter the command **revoke connect from polly;** and receive Oracle's response.

```
Statement processed.
SVRMGR>
```

3. Enter **exit** to leave line-mode Server Manager.

When this completes, polly will no longer be able to access the database.

NOTE
*There are other ways to revoke access to the database from users; familiarize yourself when necessary with the **drop user** SQL statement.*

Server Manager: Creating a Tablespace

We will use the requirements shown in Table 14-1.
After starting line-mode Server Manager, follow these steps:

1. Enter **connect internal**.

2. Enter the command **create tablespace hold_my_data datafile '/usr/oradata/disk1/hmd.dbf' size 10m;** and receive the following response from Oracle

   ```
   Statement processed.
   SVRMGR>
   ```

3. Enter **exit** to leave line-mode Server Manager.

Every time you start the database, it will now acquire the hold_my_data tablespace.

Server Manager: Adding Space to an Existing Tablespace

We will now add another 10 megabytes (10,485,760 bytes) of space to the hold_my_data tablespace. When this completes, we will have a total of 20MB allocated. After starting line-mode Server Manager, follow these steps:

1. Enter **connect internal**.

2. Enter the command **alter tablespace hold_my_data add datafile '/usr/oradata/disk2/hmd2.dbf' size 10m;** and receive feedback from Oracle.

   ```
   Statement processed.
   SVRMGR>
   ```

3. Enter **exit** to leave line-mode Server Manager.

Tablespace Component	Detail
Name	hold_my_data
Datafile	hmd.dbf
Location	/usr/oradata/disk1
Size	10MB

TABLE 14-1. *Requirements for Tablespace Creation Exercise*

The hold_my_data tablespace now has an additional 10MB.

You will use line-mode Server Manager from day one. It works everywhere and provides a quick method of accomplishing many DBA-related tasks.

Full-Screen Server Manager

We now move on to another product in the DBA tools of the trade: full-screen Server Manager. In the client/server world, many administrators use Server Manager from Windows or Windows 95. Some DBAs use X-Terminal hardware and run a copy of full-screen Server Manager on the host. It is possible that your terminal configuration may not support Server Manager in this mode on the host. If you receive the following error message when invoking full-screen Server Manager, check with the system administrator at your installation.

```
TK2-04097: Oracle Toolkit II's connection to the window system
was refused
```

Full-screen Server Manager is the graphical companion to line-mode Server Manager. It is a comprehensive DBA tool with an interface that uses familiar check boxes and radio buttons; the look and feel is similar to Windows 3.1 and Windows 95.

Server Manager: Invoking

Enter the command **svrmgrm** to invoke full-screen Server Manager. You will then see the screen shown in Figure 14-10.

Server Manager: connect internal Command

After starting full-screen Server Manager, follow these steps:

1. In the Connect dialog box, click on the Normal drop-down button. A small dialog box appears with the choices Normal, SYSOPER, and SYSDBA.

2. Click on the SYSDBA option.

3. Click on Connect to complete the internal login. When logged in, you will be presented with the screen shown in Figure 14-11.

Notice the message near the bottom of the screen, telling you that you are connected as an internal user.

Server Manager: Startup

After starting full-screen Server Manager, follow these steps:

1. Connect to the database as SYSDBA, as described in the previous section.

2. Click on the Instance icon, then click on the Database folder to bring up the screen shown in Figure 14-12.

3. Click on Database at the top of the screen, then select Startup from the Database menu. The Startup Database dialog box appears, as shown in Figure 14-13.

4. Click on Startup Open.

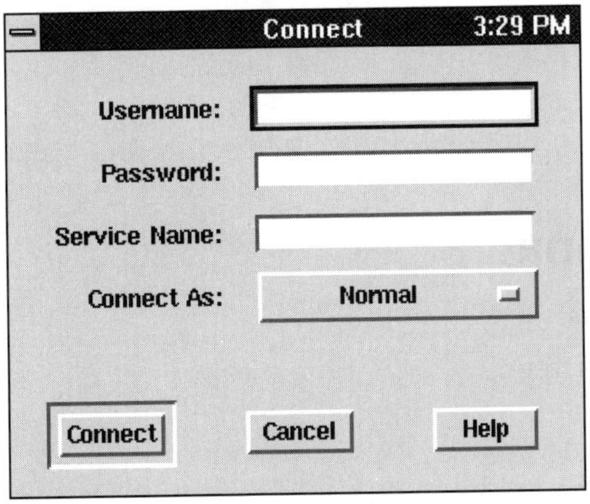

FIGURE 14-10. *Starting full-screen Server Manager*

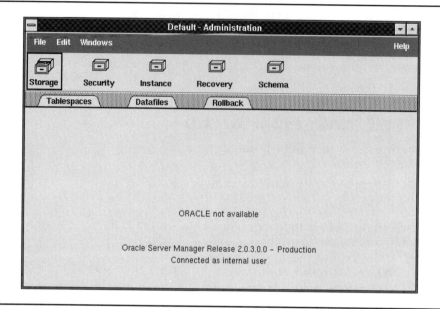

FIGURE 14-11. *Main screen after connecting to the database*

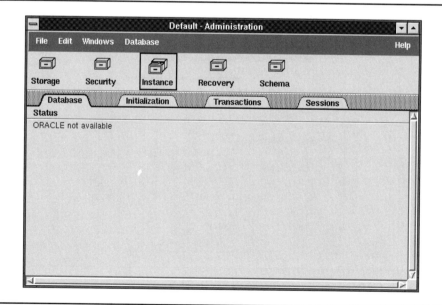

FIGURE 14-12. *Database folder in full-screen Server Manager*

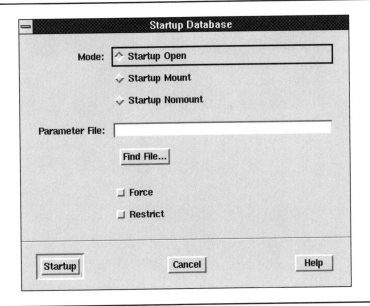

FIGURE 14-13. *Startup Database dialog box*

After the database has been successfully started, the screen shown in Figure 14-14 appears, displaying the components in the instance's SGA. We discussed the SGA (system global area) in Chapter 3.

Server Manager: Shutdown

After starting full-screen Server Manager, follow these steps:

1. Connect to the database as SYSDBA.

2. Click on the Instance icon, then click on the Database folder.

3. Click on Database at the top of the screen, then select Shutdown from the Database menu. The Shutdown Database dialog box appears, as shown in Figure 14-15.

4. Click on Normal.

5. After the database has been successfully shut down, the screen shown in Figure 14-12 appears.

6. Press CTRL-Q to leave Server Manager.

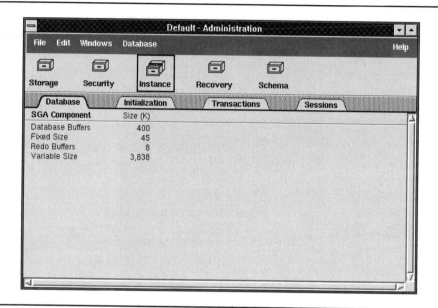

FIGURE 14-14. *Instance started with SGA display*

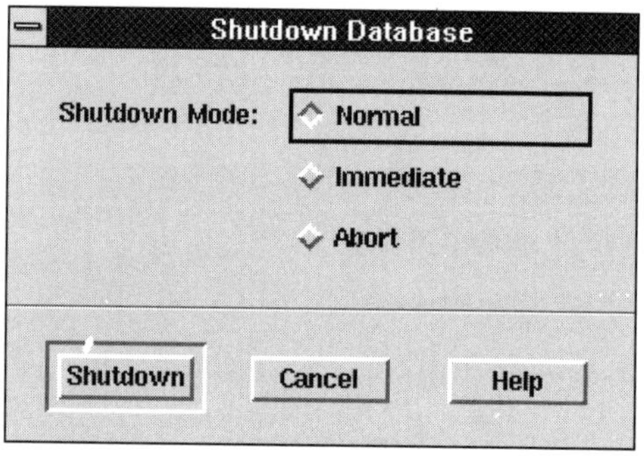

FIGURE 14-15. *Shutdown Database dialog box*

VIP
*Please refer to the section earlier in this chapter on line-mode Server Manager, in which we discuss the **shutdown** command, which includes some very important and useful information.*

Server Manager: Exiting

There are two ways to exit full-screen Server Manager. The shortcut key combination is CTRL-Q, which will drop you out of Server Manager regardless of what screen you are working with. Alternatively, you can select Quit from the File menu at the top of the screen shown in Figure 14-16.

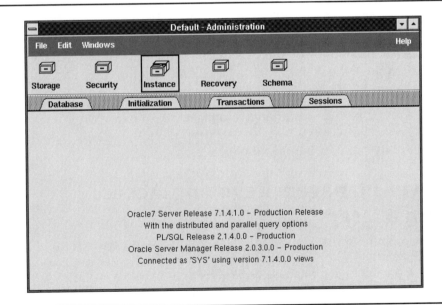

FIGURE 14-16. *Leaving full-screen Server Manager using the menu*

Server Manager: Granting Access to a User

After starting full-screen Server Manager, follow these steps:

1. Connect to the database as SYSDBA.

2. Click on the Security icon, then click on the Users folder.

3. Click on User at the top of the screen, then select Create from the User menu. The Create User dialog box appears.

4. Fill in the Create User dialog box, as shown in Figure 14-17.

5. Click on Create. The Users folder now looks like Figure 14-18. Note that polly is now a valid user.

6. Select Add Privilege to User from the User menu. The Add Privilege to User dialog box appears, as shown in Figure 14-19.

7. Click on CONNECT in the Defined Roles field.

8. Click on Add to complete this activity (the Add button is at the bottom of the dialog box but has scrolled off the screen shown in Figure 14-19).

9. Press CTRL-Q to leave Server Manager.

User polly can now log onto the database.

Server Manager: Revoking Access from a User

After starting full-screen Server Manager, follow these steps:

1. Connect to the database as SYSDBA.

2. Click on the Security icon, then click on the Users folder.

3. Scroll through the list of users, then click on the user you wish to remove.

4. Click on User at the top of the screen, then select Remove Privilege from User under the User menu. The Remove Privilege from User dialog box appears, as shown in Figure 14-20.

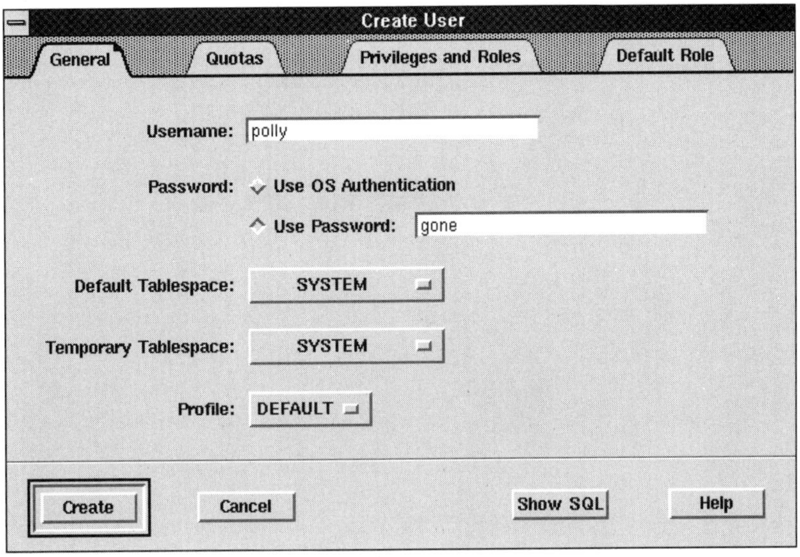

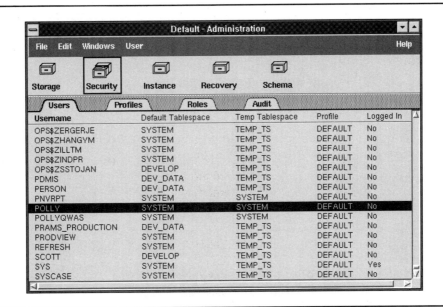

FIGURE 14-17.   *Create User dialog box*

FIGURE 14-18.   *Valid user list showing user polly just created*

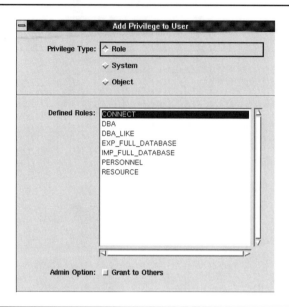

FIGURE 14-19. *Selecting privilege to give to a user*

FIGURE 14-20. *Remove Privilege from User dialog box*

5. Click on CONNECT in the Privileges and Roles field.

6. Click on Remove to complete this activity.

7. Press CTRL-Q to leave Server Manager.

User polly can no longer connect to the database.

Server Manager: Creating a Tablespace

After starting full-screen Server Manager, follow these steps:

1. Connect to the database as SYSDBA.

2. Click on the Storage icon, then click on the Tablespaces folder.

3. Click on Tablespace at the top of the screen, then select Create from the Tablespace menu. The Create Tablespace dialog box appears, as shown in Figure 14-21.

4. Type **hold_my_data** in the Name box as shown in Figure 14-22.

5. Click on Online in the Status field.

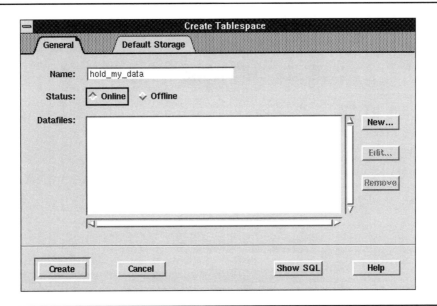

FIGURE 14-21. *Create Tablespace dialog box*

6. Click on New to bring up the New Datafile dialog box, as shown in Figure 14-22.

7. Enter **?/dbs/hmd.dbf** in the Filename box.

8. In the New File Size field, click on the drop-down list, select Mbytes, then enter **10** in the box.

9. Click OK. The Create Tablespace dialog box now looks like Figure 14-23.

10. Click on Create to finish this activity. Notice that when you return to the Tablespaces folder, the new tablespace is displayed, as shown in Figure 14-24.

11. Press CTRL-Q to leave Server Manager.

Notice the Show SQL button in Figure 14-23. To see the SQL that is passed from Server Manager to Oracle, click that button anytime. When the SQL is displayed as shown in Figure 14-25, a Hide SQL button appears, which closes the SQL statement display.

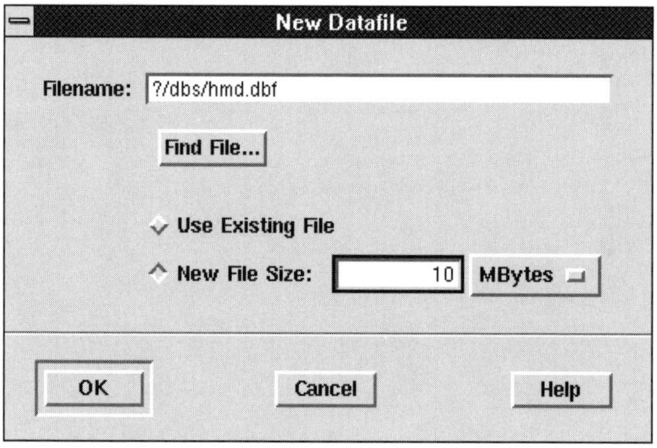

FIGURE 14-22. *New Datafile dialog box*

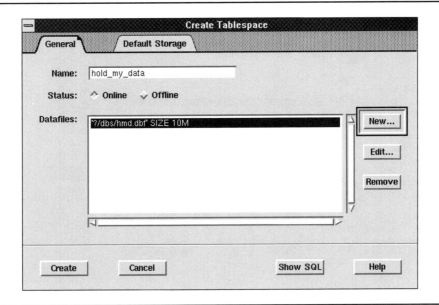

FIGURE 14-23.   *Create Tablespace dialog box filled in*

Tablespace	Status	Size (K)	Used (K)	Remain (K)	% Used
ATTEST	ONLINE	40,960	24,376	16,584	60
CASE5	ONLINE	51,200	29,464	21,736	58
CHARET	ONLINE	81,920	69,928	11,992	85
DEVELOP	ONLINE	163,840	67,344	96,496	41
DEV_DATA	ONLINE	409,600	197,432	212,168	48
HOLD_MY_DATA	ONLINE	10,240	8	10,232	0
INSIGHT	ONLINE	25,600	22,792	2,808	89
KUMARAN	ONLINE	20,480	8,680	11,800	42
MISC	ONLINE	20,480	248	20,232	1
ROLLBACK_SEGS	ONLINE	102,400	39,528	62,872	39
SQLOPDEV	ONLINE	15,360	3,240	12,120	21
SYSTEM	ONLINE	112,640	95,424	17,216	85
TEMP_TS	ONLINE	102,400	8	102,392	0
TRS	ONLINE	112,640	100,272	12,368	89

FIGURE 14-24.   *Created tablespaces in the Tablespaces folder*

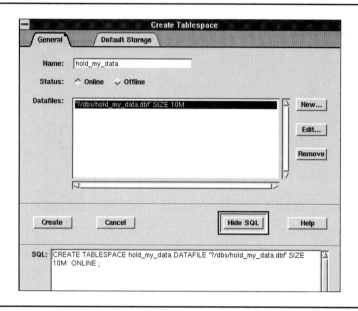

FIGURE 14-25. *Show SQL display*

TIP
Use the display SQL facility. It helps you become familiar with the SQL statements that accomplish the DBA's job.

Server Manager: Adding Space to an Existing Tablespace

After starting full-screen Server Manager, follow these steps:

1. Connect to the database as SYSDBA.

2. Click on the Storage icon, then click on the Tablespaces folder.

3. Click on Tablespace at the top of the screen, then select Add Datafile from the Tablespace menu. The Add Datafile dialog box appears, as shown in Figure 14-26.

4. Enter the filename **?/dbs/hmd2.dbf** in the Filename box.

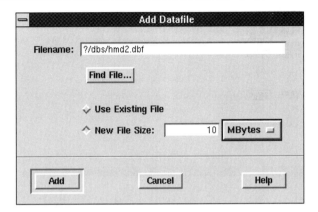

FIGURE 14-26.   *Add Datafile dialog box*

5. In the New File Size field, click on the drop-down list, select Mbytes, then enter **10** in the box.

6. Click the Add button. The Tablespaces folder shows the tablespace with additional space, as shown in Figure 14-27 (the size shows 20 megabytes—the original 10 megabytes plus the extra 10 we just added).

7. Press CTRL-Q to leave Server Manager.

Personal Oracle for Windows 95

We will now discuss how to perform the tasks outlined in this chapter with the Windows 95-based Personal Oracle. The activities discussed throughout this chapter for Server Manager are done in one of two ways on your personal computer:

1. Using the Server Manager, which can be run in a DOS window, using the techniques discussed in the "Line-Mode Server Manager" section of this chapter. There are two files in the \ORAWIN95\BIN directory, called *svrmgr.exe* and *svrmgr73.exe*. To hone your DBA skills, it would be a good idea to work with a local database using Server Manager on your PC.

Default - Administration					
File Edit Windows Tablespace					Help

Storage   Security   Instance   Recovery   Schema

Tablespaces	Datafiles		Rollback		
Tablespace	Status	Size (K)	Used (K)	Remain (K)	% Used
ATTEST	ONLINE	40,960	24,376	16,584	60
CASE5	ONLINE	51,200	29,464	21,736	58
CHARET	ONLINE	81,920	69,928	11,992	85
DEVELOP	ONLINE	163,840	67,344	96,496	41
DEV_DATA	ONLINE	409,600	197,432	212,168	48
HOLD_MY_DATA	ONLINE	20,480	16	20,464	0
INSIGHT	ONLINE	25,600	22,792	2,808	89
KUMARAN	ONLINE	20,480	8,680	11,800	42
MISC	ONLINE	20,480	248	20,232	1
ROLLBACK_SEGS	ONLINE	102,400	39,528	62,872	39
SQLOPDEV	ONLINE	15,360	3,240	12,120	21
SYSTEM	ONLINE	112,640	95,424	17,216	85
TEMP_TS	ONLINE	102,400	8	102,392	0
TRS	ONLINE	112,640	100,272	12,368	89

FIGURE 14-27.   *Storage folder showing additional space*

NOTE
We mention ORAWIN95\BIN in the above section; in fact, the text "ORAWIN95" refers to Oracle home that can be something other than ORAWIN95 if you entered the name of some other folder when installing Personal Oracle for Windows 95.

2. Using the assortment of shortcuts in the Oracle for Windows 95 folder in conjunction with the Oracle navigator shown in Figure 14-28.

Figure 14-29 shows the folder where the shortcuts referenced in the next few sections reside.

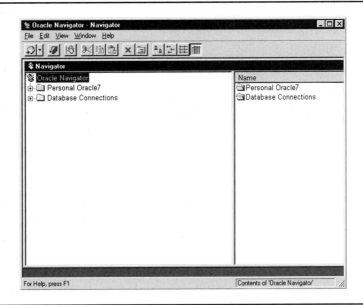

FIGURE 14-28.   *Oracle Navigator startup display*

FIGURE 14-29.   *Personal Oracle for Windows 95 shortcuts*

NOTE
If you have rearranged your shortcuts and packaged them in different folders, their organization may look different than what is shown here. The routines invoked when double-clicking these shortcuts will be exactly the same as those we describe in the next few sections.

Starting and Stopping the Database

With Personal Oracle for Windows 95, you start the database by doing the following.

1. Click on the "Start Database" shortcut.

2. Acknowledge any information boxes displayed by Oracle.

3. Click OK when presented with the Oracle7 Startup confirmation box.

You can stop the database by doing the following:

1. Click on the "Stop Database" shortcut.

2. Acknowledge any information boxes displayed by Oracle.

3. Click OK when presented with the Oracle7 Shutdown confirmation box.

Creating a User

To create a user (and thereby permit the user to access the Personal Oracle database), the database must be started using the "Start Database" shortcut. After the database is started, you create a new user by doing the following.

1. Click on the "+" sign beside the Personal Oracle7 selection shown in the Navigator displayed in Figure 14-26.

2. Click on the "Local Database" selection to bring up the options, as shown in Figure 14-30.

3. Right mouse click on the "User" selection to bring up the New User Properties sheet where the General tab is highlighted.

4. Fill in the user name, and then enter and confirm a password.

5. Highlight the "Role/Privilege" tab to bring up the sheet shown in Figure 14-31. Notice how the CONNECT role appears in the Granted part of the sheet. This means that polly is now permitted to connect to the Personal Oracle database.

6. Click OK to dismiss this property sheet and return to the Navigator.

Removing a User

You remove a user starting at the Navigator shown in Figure 14-30.

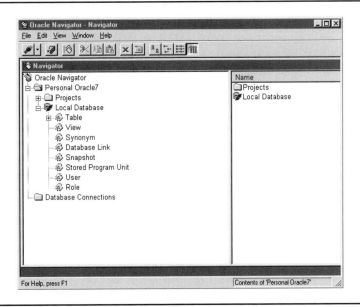

FIGURE 14-30. *Local Database selection expanded*

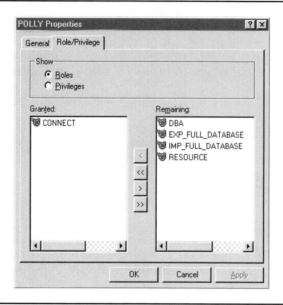

FIGURE 14-31. *Role/Privilege dialog box*

1. Click on the "User" folder, causing the Name section at the right of the screen to be populated with the list of users.

2. Right mouse click on the polly selection that pops up a menu from where the user can be modified, deleted, or copied.

3. Click on the Delete option on that menu.

4. Click OK to return to the Navigator with user polly erased. User polly can no longer log onto the Personal Oracle7 database.

Adding Space to an Existing Tablespace

The copy of Personal Oracle for Windows 95 that we downloaded from the Internet is actually a product bundle referred to as Personal Oracle Lite.

NOTE
Personal Oracle Lite has no GUI facility to accomplish the task at hand in this section.

To illustrate the portability of the DBA skill set, we are going to lead you through using the Server Manager program in a DOS window to add space to the USER_DATA tablespace.

1. Open up a DOS window.

2. Enter the command **svrmgr** and receive the following output from Oracle.

```
Oracle Server Manager Release 2.3.2.0.0 - Production
Copyright (c) Oracle Corporation 1994, 1995. All rights
reserved.
Personal Oracle7 Release 7.3.2.1.1 - Production Release
With the distributed and replication options
PL/SQL Release 2.3.2.0.0 - Production
SVRMGR>
```

3. Enter the command **connect internal** which logs you onto the database as user SYS.

4. Enter the SQL statement **alter tablespace user_data add datafile 'c:\orawin95\database\user2.dbf' size 10m;** and receive feedback from Oracle.

```
Statement processed.
SVRMGR>
```

5. Enter **exit** to return to the DOS prompt.

6. Enter **exit** to close the DOS window.

The 10 megabytes just added to the USER_DATA tablespace become immediately available for storage of user objects.

What's Next

Armed with the routines we examined in this chapter, you now know how to work with Enterprise Manager, Server Manager, and Personal Oracle for Windows 95 to perform the following tasks:

- Connect to the database
- Start up the database

- Shut down the database
- Grant access to a user
- Revoke access from a user
- Create a tablespace
- Add space to an existing tablespace

This is enough to get started, and this is also what you will have to do beginning with day one. To find out more about the DBA working with the Oracle database, read Chapter 18. Happy DBAing!

CHAPTER
15

Export and Import

xport and import are the most widely used utilities supplied with the Oracle software. All DBAs, whether seasoned or just getting started, need to be fluent with these two utilities. In Chapter 16, we discuss the role they play in making copies of your Oracle data. Knowing how to use them and why to use them (see the "What Export and Import Can Do for You" section in this chapter) will help further your understanding of Oracle as a whole. In this chapter, we will discuss the following:

- Uses for export and import

- Similarities and differences between export and import

- Methods of operation

- Modes of operation

- Error handling and problem-resolution techniques

Terminology

The following definitions will arm you with the technical jargon you need to make it through this chapter.

- A program runs *interactively* when it enters into a series of questions requiring the operator's response.

- Programs are said to be *parameter-driven* when you code a number of keywords and supply values for each parameter when the program is invoked.

- An *instance* is a separate set of processes and memory structures required to support an open Oracle database.

- An *extent* is a chunk of space in a tablespace that Oracle allocates to tables when they require additional space for new or changed data.

- *Defragmenting* a table is a process whereby you take all the data from all the extents allocated to the table and pack it into one larger extent. Figure 15-1 shows what defragmentation involves.

- *Roles* are used by Oracle to group user accounts together and thereby empower a collection of users to manipulate data or perform restricted activities with the database.

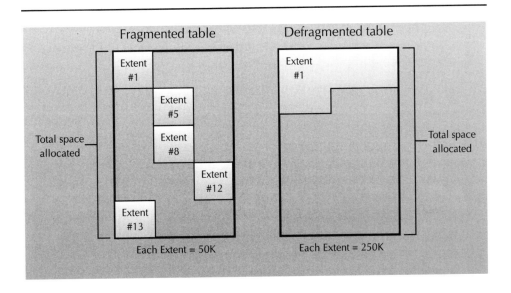

FIGURE 15-1. *Defragmenting extents allocated to a table*

What Export and Import Can Do for You

Export and import empower the DBA and application developers to make dependable and quick copies of Oracle data. Export (invoked using the command **exp80**) makes a copy of data and data structures in an operating system file. Import (invoked using the command **imp80**) reads files created by export and places data and data structures in Oracle database files. These two handy utilities are used primarily for the following reasons:

- As part of backup and recovery procedures (refer to Chapter 16 for details).

- For moving data between different instances of Oracle. You may export data from your production database and use import to move all or part of the data in that export file into your development database.

■ To move all or part of a user's data from one tablespace to another. Suppose userA has data residing in two tablespaces, tablespaceA and tablespaceB. You could move all of the data out of tablespaceB and place it in tablespaceA using export and import.

NOTE
There must be enough space in tablespaceA to accommodate the data being moved from tablespaceB. Import itself will not always add additional disk space to tablespaceA if it is not already there.

■ When the need arises to rebuild an existing database, export and import are the only way to preserve the current database data before it is recreated.

NOTE
After performing a full database export, a number of SQL statements and some additional SQL scripts have to be run before the new database is ready for import to reinstate the database's data.

Similarities Between Export and Import

Export and import behave in the same way, and learning one of the two will put you more than 80 percent of the way to mastering both products. These two tools are similar in the following ways:

■ Both can be run interactively or can read run-time parameters from a file.

■ Both accept keyword (parameters started with keyword_value=) or positional parameters (those that mean something based on their order on the command line).

■ Both work with Oracle read-only copies of data and data structures.

■ Both are used to move data among different Oracle accounts and hardware platforms.

Differences Between Export and Import

Even though export and import are similar, there are some differences. Some parameters are used only with export, others only with import. For example, the fromuser and touser parameters are only used with import. Likewise, the compress parameter is only coded when using export. These parameters are discussed in the "Parameter-Driven Export" and "Parameter-Driven Import" sections in this chapter.

■ Import may report on a wide assortment of Oracle errors, since it is creating and loading data into Oracle database files.

■ Export is sensitive to the amount of free space on a disk drive to which the export file is being written.

Even though these differences exist, export and import methods and modes of operation are the same. These two areas are the subject of the next two main sections in this chapter.

Methods of Operation

The methods we are about to discuss apply to export and import. Learning and experimenting with different methods is part of your job as a DBA. In this section, we will discuss:

■ Invoking interactive export with no parameters

■ Invoking interactive import with no parameters

■ How answers to prompts affect questions Oracle asks later on and the success/failure of import and export

■ Running parameter-driven export and import

■ Using the parfile keyword parameter

■ Mixing interactive and parameter-driven methods

When running export and import interactively, Oracle presents you with a list of questions. With export, the answers you give to those questions affect what is written to the export file. With import, these answers affect what data is retrieved from the export file. When export and import are parameter-driven, you instruct Oracle what you want written to or read from the export file based on values supplied with these parameters. Think of the parameter-driven method as a form you fill out when requesting reimbursement for expenses from a health insurance company; the questions you answer can affect the amount of coverage you are permitted. Later in this chapter, we discuss parameters that can be fed to export and import.

Interactive Export: Invoking with No Parameters

The next listing shows an example of the dialog between export and the user when export is invoked without any parameters.

```
D:\ORANT\BIN> exp80
Export: Release 8.0.3.0.1 - Production on Tue Nov 19 11:32:25 1998
Copyright (c) Oracle Corporation 1979, 1994.  All rights reserved.
Username: fin_man/drowssap
Connected to: Oracle8 Server Release 8.0.3.0.1 - Production Release
With the distributed, heterogeneous, replication, objects
and parallel query options
PL/SQL Release 3.0.3.1 - Production
Enter array fetch buffer size: 4096 > 102400
Export file: EXPDAT.DMP >
(2)U(sers), or (3)T(ables): (2)U > 3
Export table data (yes/no): yes >
Compress extents (yes/no): yes >
Export done in WE8ISO8859P1 character set and WE8ISO8859P1
       NCHAR character set
About to export specified tables via Conventional Path ...
Table(T) or Partition(T:P) to be exported: (RETURN to quit) > e_master
. . exporting table                E_MASTER                122 rows exported
Table to be exported: (RETURN to quit) >
Export terminated successfully without warnings.
```

You are asked to supply the information in the Meaning and Response column of Table 15-1 before Oracle commences the export.

Prompt Received from Oracle	Meaning and Response
Username	The user name and password of the person running export.
Enter array fetch buffer size	The size of the chunk of memory to use as a work area while export writes data to the export file. Normally, one enters values between 10240 (also called 10k) and 10485760 (also called 10m).
Export file	The name of the export file. Defaults to expdat.dmp but can be changed.
(2)U(sers), or (3)T(ables)	Oracle wants to know which method you wish to run. You will be asked for names of one or more users if you choose 2 or the names of one or more of your own tables if you answer 3.
Export table data (yes/no)	Instructions on what to write to the export file. Oracle always writes SQL statements necessary to create exported objects to the export file. Answering yes to this prompt tells Oracle to export the data in the objects as well.
Compress extents (yes/no)	Oracle wants to know if the create table statements written to the export file should include an initial space request capable of holding all the existing table data.
Table(T) or Partition(T:P) to be exported	The name of the table or partition name of a partitioned table to be exported.

TABLE 15-1. *Dialog When exp Is Invoked with No Parameters*

VIP
When defragmenting a table, answer yes to the compress extents prompt. Figure 15-1 shows what defragmentation involves.

Interactive Import: Invoking with No Parameters

To give you a flavor of Oracle7 and Oracle8 import, the next listing illustrates an Oracle7 dialog, and Figure 15-2 shows invoking import with Oracle8 without any parameters.

```
imp
Import: Release 7.1.4.0.0 - Production on Tue Nov  9 14:30:48 1995
Copyright (c) Oracle Corporation 1979, 1994.  All rights reserved.
Username: fin_man/drowssap
Connected to: Oracle7 Server Release 7.1.4.0.0 - Production Release
PL/SQL Release 2.1.4.1 - Production
Import file: expdat.dmp >
Enter insert buffer size (minimum is 4096) 30720>
Export file created by EXPORT:V07.01.04
List contents of import file only (yes/no): no >
Ignore create error due to object existence (yes/no): yes >
Import grants (yes/no): yes >
Import table data (yes/no): yes >
Import entire export file (yes/no): yes >
. importing FIN_MAN's objects into FIN_MAN
. . importing table "E_MASTER"                  122 rows imported
Import terminated successfully without warnings.
```

You are asked to supply the information in the Meaning and Response column in Table 15-2 before Oracle8 commences the import.

```
D:\ORANT\BIN> imp80
Import: Release 8.0.3.0.1 - Production on Fri Apr 15 11:53:59 1999
Copyright (c) Oracle Corporation 1979, 1994, 1996.  All rights reserved.
Username: fin_man/drowssap
Connected to: Oracle8 Server Release 8.0.3.0.1 - Production
With the distributed, heterogeneous, replication, objects
and parallel query options
PL/SQL Release 3.0.3.0.1 - Production
Import file: EXPDAT.DMP >
Enter insert buffer size (minimum is 4096) 30720>
Export file created by EXPORT:V08.00.03 via conventional path
List contents of import file only (yes/no): no >
Ignore create error due to object existence (yes/no): no > yes
Import grants (yes/no): yes > yes
Import table data (yes/no): yes > yes
Import entire export file (yes/no): no > yes
. importing FIN_MAN's objects into FIN_MAN
. . importing table            "E_MASTER"          122 rows imported
Import terminated successfully without warnings.
```

FIGURE 15-2. *Importing the entire export file*

VIP
If you answer no to the ignore create errors due to object existence prompt, then Oracle will not bring the table data in for tables that exist. Nearly all the time, you will answer yes to this prompt.

Prompt Received from Oracle	Meaning and Response
Username	The user name and password of the person running import.
Import file	The name of the file you want import to read. Defaults to expdat.dmp but can be changed.
Enter insert buffer size (minimum is 4096)	The size of the chunk of memory to use as a work area while import writes data to the database. Normally, one enters values between 10240 (also called 10k) and 10485760 (also called 10m).
List contents of import file only (yes/no)	Oracle will list the SQL statements written to the import file if you answer yes. If you answer no, import will bring the data and data definitions into the database.
Ignore create error due to object existence (yes/no)	Oracle wants to know what it should do when it encounters an object in the import file that already exists. If you answer yes, Oracle ignores the fact that an object exists and brings in its data anyway. Answering no causes Oracle to report an error and then move on to the next object when it encounters an object that already exists.
Import grants (yes/no)	Oracle wants to know whether to run the grant statements written to the import file after an object is imported.
Import table data (yes/no)	Oracle wants to know if it should bring in the table data (yes) or just run the SQL statements to create objects (no).
Import entire export file (yes/no)	Oracle wants to know if the complete file or only specified portions should be imported. If you answer yes, the import starts at once. If you answer no, Oracle will ask questions about what you wish to import.

TABLE 15-2. *Dialog When imp Is Invoked with No Parameters*

How Answers to Prompts Affect Further Dialog

After using export and import interactively, you will notice that the chain of questions that follow your responses depends on your answers. For example, when Oracle asks

```
Import entire export file (yes/no): yes >
```

and you answer **no**, Oracle then proceeds to ask you exactly what you want to import, as shown in Figure 15-3.

In Figure 15-2, we did not accept the default answer **no**, and changed it to **yes**, thereby asking Oracle8 to import the entire export file. The interaction with Oracle8 is different in the last eight lines of Figure 15-3, since we answer **no** to the same question. By answering **no**, we are telling Oracle8 not to import the complete export file. We then have to supply one or more table or table:partition names, as shown in the boldfaced lines in Figure 15-3. Again, inspect the next listing before Figure 15-3 showing an Oracle7 dialog.

```
imp /
Import: Release 7.1.4.0.0 - Production on Tue Nov  9 21:47:05 1995
Copyright (c) Oracle Corporation 1979, 1994.  All rights reserved.
Connected to: Oracle7 Server Release 7.1.4.0.0 - Production Release
PL/SQL Release 2.1.4.1 - Production
Import file: expdat.dmp >
Enter insert buffer size (minimum is 4096) 30720>
Export file created by EXPORT:V07.01.04
Warning: the objects were exported by PER_MAN, not by you
List contents of import file only (yes/no): no >
Ignore create error due to object existence (yes/no): yes >
Import grants (yes/no): yes >
Import table data (yes/no): yes >
Import entire export file (yes/no): yes > no
Username: /finman/drowssap
Enter table names. Null list means all tables for user
Enter table name or . if done: per_mast
Enter table name or . if done: .
. importing PER_MAN's objects into FINMAN
. . importing table "PER_MAST"              2134 rows imported
Import terminated successfully without warnings.
```

```
D:\ORANT\BIN> imp80
Import: Release 8.0.3.0.1 - Production on Fri Apr 15 11:53:59 1999
Copyright (c) Oracle Corporation 1979, 1994, 1996.  All rights reserved.
Username: other_user/opass
Connected to: Oracle8 Server Release 8.0.3.0.1 - Production
With the distributed, heterogeneous, replication, objects
and parallel query options
PL/SQL Release 3.0.3.0.1 - Production
Import file: EXPDAT.DMP >
Enter insert buffer size (minimum is 4096) 30720>
Export file created by EXPORT:V08.00.03 via conventional path
List contents of import file only (yes/no): no >
Ignore create error due to object existence (yes/no): no > yes
Import grants (yes/no): yes > yes
Import table data (yes/no): yes > yes
Import entire export file (yes/no): no > no
Username: finman/drowssap
Enter table(T) or partition(T:P) names. Null list means all tables for
user
Enter table(T) or partition(T:P) name or . if done: PER_MAST
Enter table(T) or partition(T:P) name or . if done: .
. importing PER_MAST's objects into FINMAN
. . importing table               "PER_MAST"         2134 rows imported
Import terminated successfully without warnings.
```

FIGURE 15-3. *Importing part of the export file*

VIP
The default response to "Ignore create errors due to object existence" has changed from Oracle7 to Oracle8. The Oracle7 default was **yes***, whereas the Oracle8 default is* **no***. Also, the default response to the question "Import entire export file" has changed. With Oracle7, the default was* **yes***, and with Oracle8 it has changed to* **no***.*

How Answers to Prompts Effect Success or Failure

In addition, export and import behave in different ways based on the responses given to the dialog. In the question

`Ignore create error due to object existence (yes/no): yes >`

if you had changed yes to no, the listing shown in Figure 15-4 would have occurred.

In Figure 15-3, accepting **yes** to the ignore create error due to object existence prompt means that as Oracle encounters the **create table** statement for per_mast, it carries on. In Figure 15-4, when the same **create table** statement is executed, an error condition is raised. As you work more with export and import, you will find there are things you can do with the utilities using the parameter-driven method, discussed in the next section, that cannot be done interactively.

```
imp /
Import: Release 7.1.4.0.0 - Production on Tue Nov  8 22:02:33 1994
Copyright (c) Oracle Corporation 1979, 1994.  All rights reserved.
Connected to: Oracle7 Server Release 7.1.4.0.0 - Production Release
PL/SQL Release 2.1.4.1 - Production
Import file: expdat.dmp >
Enter insert buffer size (minimum is 4096) 30720>
Export file created by EXPORT:V07.01.04
Warning: the objects were exported by PER_MAN, not by you
List contents of import file only (yes/no): no >
Ignore create error due to object existence (yes/no): yes > no
Import grants (yes/no): yes > no
Import table data (yes/no): yes > no
Import entire export file (yes/no): yes >
. importing PER_MAN's objects into FIN_MAN
IMP-00015: following statement failed because the object already exists:
"CREATE TABLE "FIN_MAST" ("FIN_ID" VARCHAR2(5) NOT NULL, "START_DATE" DATE,
"END_DATE" DATE, "FY_MAX" NUMBER(4, 0) PCTFREE 10 PCTUSED 90 INITRANS 1
MAXTRANS 255 STORAGE(INITIAL 16384 NEXT 8192 MINEXTENTS 1 PCTINCREASE 20
FREELISTS 1 FREELIST GROUPS 1) TABLESPACE "USERS""
Import terminated successfully with warnings.
```

NOTE

When run interactively, export and import suggest a response to most questions. Accept the suggested response by pressing ENTER.

```
D:\ORANT\BIN> imp80
Username: fin_mast/drowssap
Connected to: Oracle8 Server Release 8.0.3.0.1 - Production
With the distributed, heterogeneous, replication, objects
and parallel query options
PL/SQL Release 3.0.3.0.1 - Production
Import file: EXPDAT.DMP >
Enter insert buffer size (minimum is 4096) 30720>
Export file created by EXPORT:V08.00.03 via conventional path
List contents of import file only (yes/no): no >
Ignore create error due to object existence (yes/no): no >
Import grants (yes/no): yes >
Import table data (yes/no): yes >
Import entire export file (yes/no): no > yes
. importing PER_MAST's objects into FIN_MAST
IMP-00015: following statement failed because the object already exists:
"CREATE TABLE "PER_MAST" ("PER_ID" VARCHAR2(5) NOT NULL,
"START_DATE" DATE, "END_DATE" DATE, "FY_MAX" NUMBER(4,0))
PCTFREE 10 PCTUSED 40 INITRANS 1 MAXTRANS 255
LOGGING STORAGE(INITIAL 16384 NEXT 8192 MINEXTENTS 1
MAXEXTENTS 249 PCTINCREASE 20 FREELISTS 1 FREELIST GROUPS 1)
TABLESPACE "USERS"
Import terminated successfully with warnings.
```

FIGURE 15-4. *Interactive dialog with import, with a table create error*

You will find the more you use these utilities that the default answers Oracle suggests are usually the ones you will end up using.

TIP
Use the interactive method when getting started with export and import and experiment with different answers to Oracle's questions. This is the quickest way to familiarize yourself with using these utilities.

Parameter-Driven Export

In the parameter-driven export method, the exp command is issued with one or more parameters passed on the command line. This method is the most flexible. We recommend becoming fluent with this method early in your career as a DBA, as you will use it from day one. The format of the command is

```
exp80 keyword1=value1 keyword2=value2 keyword3=value3
```

By using keyword parameters, you instruct Oracle what to write to the export file. A quick list of keywords, their meanings, and their default values can be obtained by issuing the command **exp help=y** from your operating system prompt. The following shows the output from this command.

```
D:\ORANT\BIN> exp80 help=y
Export: Release 8.0.3.0.1 - Production on Fri Apr 5 12:58:52 1999
Copyright (c) Oracle Corporation 1979, 1994, 1996. All rights reserved.
You can let Export prompt you for parameters by entering the EXP
command followed by your username/password:
    Example: EXP SCOTT/TIGER
Or, you can control how Export runs by entering the EXP command followed
by various arguments. To specify parameters, you use keywords:
    Format:  EXP KEYWORD=value or KEYWORD=(value1,value2,...,valueN)
    Example: EXP SCOTT/TIGER GRANTS=Y TABLES=(EMP,DEPT,MGR)
             or TABLES=(T1:P1,T1:P2), if T1 is partitioned table
Keyword  Description (Default)      Keyword      Description (Default)
--------------------------------------------------------------------
USERID    username/password        FULL          export entire file (N)
BUFFER    size of data buffer      OWNER         list of owner usernames
FILE      output file (EXPDAT.DMP) TABLES        list of table names
COMPRESS  import into one extent (Y) RECORDLENGTH length of IO record
GRANTS    export grants (Y)        INCTYPE       incremental export type
INDEXES   export indexes (Y)       RECORD        track incr. export (Y)
ROWS      export data rows (Y)     PARFILE       parameter filename
CONSTRAINTS export constraints (Y) CONSISTENT    cross-table consistency
LOG       log file of screen output STATISTICS   analyze objects
                                                 (ESTIMATE)
DIRECT    direct path (N)
```

Table 15-3 discusses each of the export parameters.

VIP

*Use the **log** parameter on ALL parameter-driven exports. If something goes wrong, you need to study the log file to clean up the mess that may be left over by an unsuccessful export.*

Parameter	Meaning/Notes	Default
userid	The Oracle user name and password of the account running the utility. If you supply just the user name, Oracle will prompt you for the password.	None
buffer	The data buffer size in bytes. If you request too big a size, Oracle will carry on with whatever it can obtain.	10240
file	The name of the file being written to. If you do not specify a filename extension, Oracle assumes the .dmp extension.	Expdat.dmp
compress	Write storage parameters to the export file that would place all table data in one extent when the data is imported.	Y
grants	Write SQL grant statements to the export file.	Y
indexes	Write SQL create index statements to the export file.	Y
rows	Export the data in the tables' rows as well as the definition of the underlying objects.	Y
constraints	Write SQL statements to the export file needed to recreate declarative integrity when the objects are imported (for example, primary key and references statements).	Y
log	Instructs Oracle to write the screen I/O from the export to a disk file.	None
full	Controls whether Oracle writes SQL statements to the export file to recreate all the system associated datafiles, tablespaces, rollback segments, etc.	N
owner	Provides a list of Oracle accounts whose objects are to be written to the export file.	None
tables	Provides a list of tables whose definitions or data are to be written to the export file.	None
recordlength	Length in bytes of the record written to the export file.	Operating system-specific
inctype	Type of incremental export being performed.	None

TABLE 15-3. *Export Parameters and Their Defaults*

Parameter	Meaning/Notes	Default
record	Instructs Oracle to track the type of incremental export being written in some data dictionary views. This information is used when performing an import from an incremental export file.	Y
parfile	The name of a file containing parameters to be fed to export.	None
consistent	Instructs Oracle to maintain cross-table consistency. This ensures that export will make copies of table data as of the time the export started even if tables being exported are being used while the export runs.	N
statistics	Write SQL analyze statements to the export file.	Estimate
direct	Causes export to extract data by reading the data directly, bypassing the SQL command processing layer. This method can be much faster than a conventional path export.	N
feedback	Specifies that export should display a progress meter in the form of a dot for each x number of rows exported.	0

TABLE 15-3.   *Export Parameters and Their Defaults (continued)*

Parameter-Driven Import

The imp command is issued with one or more parameters passed on the command line. Parameter-driven import provides the most flexible and robust method for using import as part of your new skill set. The format of the command is

```
imp80 keyword1=value1 keyword2=value2 keyword3=value3
```

By using keyword parameters, you instruct Oracle what to bring in from the export file. A quick list of keywords, their meanings, and their default values can be obtained by issuing the command **imp80 help=y** from your operating system prompt. The following shows the output from this command. Table 15-4 discusses each of the import parameters.

Parameter	Meaning/Notes	Default
userid	The Oracle user name and password of the account running the utility. If you supply just the user name, Oracle will prompt you for the password.	None
buffer	The data buffer size in bytes. If you request too big a size, Oracle will carry on with whatever it can obtain.	30720
file	The name of the file being read from. If you do not specify a filename extension, Oracle assumes the .dmp extension.	expdat.dmp
show	Tells Oracle whether to perform the import or simply show the contents of the export file.	N
ignore	Instructs Oracle on how to deal with SQL create statements in the export file. If set to N, Oracle reports an error when trying to create a table that already exists. If set to Y, Oracle ignores the error condition raised when attempting to run a create table for one that already exists.	N
grants	Execute the SQL grant statements in the export file.	Y
indexes	Execute the SQL create index statements in the export file.	Y
rows	Import the data in the tables' rows as well as the definition of the underlying objects.	Y
log	Instructs Oracle to write the screen I/O from the import to a disk file.	None
destroy	Instructs Oracle to not overwrite a datafile during a full database import if a datafile contains a tablespace belonging to any database.	N
indexfile	Instructs Oracle to write all create table, create index, and create cluster statements to a user-supplied operating system filename. The table and cluster statements are commented out.	None

TABLE 15-4. *Import Parameters and Their Defaults*

Parameter	Meaning/Notes	Default
charset	The character set of the data in the export file.	NLS_LANG value in initialization parameter file
full	Controls whether Oracle executes the SQL statements in the export file to recreate all the system associated datafiles, tablespaces, rollback segments, etc.	N
fromuser	The owner(s) of the data that was written to the export file.	None
touser	The user(s) into which the data should be imported.	None
tables	A list of table names to be imported.	None
recordlength	Specifies the length of each record in the export file. May be necessary when moving data between platforms with different default record lengths.	Operating system-specific
inctype	The type of incremental export being read. Values are either RESTORE or SYSTEM.	None
commit	Instructs Oracle whether or not to commit after each array insert. This is very useful when importing large amounts of data that may cause rollback segment errors.	N
feedback	Specifies that import should display a progress meter in the form of a dot for each x number of rows imported.	0
parfile	The name of a file containing parameters to be fed to import.	None

TABLE 15-4. *Import Parameters and Their Defaults* (continued)

VIP

*Use the **log** parameter on ALL parameter-driven imports. If something goes wrong, you need to study the log file to clean up the mess that may be left over by an unsuccessful import.*

The parfile Keyword Parameter

This parameter deserves special attention. You may feed keyword parameter values to export and import by using this parameter with a filename afterwards. The format of the parfile parameter is either of the following:

```
imp80 parfile=my.parfile
```

or

```
exp80 parfile=my.parfile
```

You place a list of parameters in the file (in this case, "my.parfile") following the parfile keyword. This could be the contents of "my.parfile" being fed into export:

```
userid=fin_man/drowssap tables=(fin_mast,assignment)
buffer=102400 compress=y grants=y
```

This could be the contents of "my.parfile" being fed into import:

```
userid=fin_man/drowssap fromuser=fin_man touser=per_man
buffer=102400 grants=y
```

Both parameter files are a free-form format. The export parameter file shows two parameters on the first line, then three parameters on the second. You could as easily have done either of the following.

```
userid=fin_man/drowssap tables=(fin_mast,assignment)
buffer=102400 grants=y
compress=y
```

or

```
compress=y
userid=fin_man/drowssap
tables=(fin_mast,assignment)
buffer=102400
grants=y
```

Mixing Interactive and Parameter-Driven Methods

You may invoke export and import with a mixture of the two methods by doing the following:

```
exp80 fin_man/drowssap buffer=102400 compress=n
```

As soon as Oracle encounters at least one keyword parameter on the command line, it starts the import or export immediately and does not enter into the interactive dialog. For example, invoking import with the command **imp fin_man/drowssap file=finance** would start import without stopping to prompt for further parameter values. You must be careful when calling export or import this way. Let's say you want to perform a full database export. You call export with the command

```
exp80 fin_man/drowssap buffer=102400 rows=n
```

Oracle would not prompt you for any other parameters and would carry on with a user export.

TIP
Experiment with export and import so you are not caught off-guard by their behavior when you least expect it.

Export and Import Modes

You can run export and import in one of three modes, depending on what you want to accomplish. For example, if you want to create a copy of a table belonging to userA in userB's area, you would use one mode. On the other hand, if you want to preserve a complete copy of userA's data, you would use a different mode. By the end of this section, you will know details on the following:

- Table-mode export and import
- User-mode export and import
- Full database export and import

Table-Mode Export

When using table-mode export, you tell Oracle the names of one or more tables to export. Oracle writes the table data to the export file. The command

```
exp80 userid=fin_man/drowssap tables=(permast,finmast,stockmast)
file=fm.dmp
```

exports the three tables whose names are enclosed in parentheses belonging to Oracle user fin_man. The export file is called fm.dmp.

NOTE
When listing more than one table after the table keyword, the names are separated by commas and the whole list is enclosed in parentheses.

User-Mode Export

In user-mode export, Oracle exports all of a user's objects, including views, synonyms, triggers, procedures, database links, and tables. User-mode export is commonly used to defragment a tablespace. After all the user's objects are exported, the tablespace can be dropped and recreated. The command

```
exp80 userid=fin_man/drowssap owner=(fin_man,per_man,acc_man)
```

exports the three users whose names are enclosed in parentheses. The export file is called expdat.dmp.

NOTE
When listing more than one owner after the owner keyword, the owner names are separated by commas and the whole list is enclosed in parentheses.

Full Database Export

When using full database export, all users' data and database support file (datafiles, tablespaces, rollback segments, etc.) creation statements are written to the export file for every database user except SYS. This export file can be used for a full database import. The command

```
exp80 userid=system/manager full=y grants=y indexes=y
```

writes the full database export to a file called expdat.dmp.

NOTE
*Not every database user will be able to use the full keyword when trying to initiate a **full** database export. Most full database exports are run using the Oracle SYSTEM account.*

Table-Mode Import

When using table-mode import, you tell Oracle the names of one or more tables to import. Oracle writes the table data to the database. The command

```
imp80 userid=fin_man/drowssap tables=(permast,finmast,stockmast)
```

imports the three tables whose names are enclosed in parentheses belonging to Oracle user fin_man. The export file is called expdat.dmp.

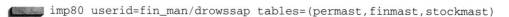
NOTE
*When listing more than one table after the **tables** keyword, the names are separated by commas and the whole list is enclosed in parentheses.*

User-Mode Import

In user-mode import, Oracle imports the specified users' objects, including views, synonyms, triggers, procedures, database links, and tables. User-mode import is commonly used after a tablespace has been recreated during a defragmentation exercise. The command

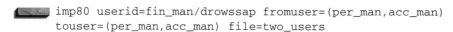
```
imp80 userid=fin_man/drowssap fromuser=(per_man,acc_man)
touser=(per_man,acc_man) file=two_users
```

imports the two users whose names are enclosed in parentheses. The export file is called two_users.dmp.

NOTE
When listing more than one user after the
fromuser *or **touser** keyword, the names are*
separated by commas and the whole list is
enclosed in parentheses.

Full Database Import

Full database import runs in two phases. During the first phase, all database
support file (datafiles, tablespaces, rollback segments, etc.) creation
statements in the export file are executed. When this phase is complete, the
complete structure of the database is in place. The second phase brings
users' objects into their appropriate tablespaces. The command

```
imp80 userid=system/manager full=y file=full_tst
```

performs a full database import from a file called expdat.dmp.

NOTE
Not every database user will be able to use the
full *keyword when trying to initiate a full*
database import. Most full database imports
are run using the Oracle SYSTEM account.

VIP
When running a full database import from the
system account, the password will be
***manager**, regardless of what it was when the*
full database export was run.

Switching among Modes

We have devised a hierarchy of export files to illustrate how an export file
written using one mode can be used by import in another mode. By
assigning a weighting factor to each mode of export (3=full, 2=user,
1=table), you may use a file produced by a higher-numbered mode to run
import in a lower- or equal-numbered mode. Table 15-5 summarizes which
export files can be used for the three modes of import.

Requirement	Can export file written by export mode be used?		
	Table	User	Full
Table mode import	Y	Y	Y
User mode import	N	Y	Y
Full database import	N	N	Y

TABLE 15-5.   *Export Modes Used in Different Import Modes*

Thus, a full database export file can be used to do a table-mode, user-mode, or full database import. A user-mode export file can be used to do a user-mode or table-mode import. A table-mode export file can only be used to do a table-mode import.

When to Use Each Mode

Table 15-6 illustrates what export and import can do for you, including a few scenarios and the suggested mode to use with export and import. Although the tasks can easily (and sometimes better) be accomplished using SQL*Plus, we use export and import here.

Using Export and Import with Partitioned Tables

The objects of most export or import sessions are tables, and with the partitioning capabilities of Oracle8, you can specify partitioned objects as source data. Exports of selected partitions are accomplished using partition-level export, and a command similar to the following:

```
exp80 system/manager file=export.dmp
tables=(scott.b:px, scott.b:py, mary.c, d:qb)
```

where the table names include partitions **px** and **py** belonging to table **b** owned by user **scott**, table **c** belonging to user **mary**, and partition **qb** belonging to the user running the export.

Requirement	Export Mode	Import Mode	Reason
Defragment user's tablespace	User	User	We need to get all the user's objects; table mode would ignore view, synonyms, procedures, etc.
Move a copy of the personnel table from development to test	Table	Table	We want one table. This can also be accomplished using the user mode, but table mode is faster.
Move a copy of the salary table from a full database export of production into development	Full	Table	The table we are looking for is in the full database export file. By importing in table mode, we extract only the desired table and data.
Recover the objects belonging to user from last night's full database export after inadvertently dropping a user	Full	User	We need all of the user's objects. Since he or she no longer exists in the data dictionary, we are unable to collect a list of them and run in table mode. User mode will extract all the user's objects from the full database export file.
Move the personnel system views from one user to another user	User	User	A table export does not extract SQL view creation statements. You must do this in user mode.

TABLE 15-6.   *Export and Import Scenarios*

NOTE
Each partition name must be specified with its corresponding table name.

Oracle8 partition-level import imports one or more exported partitions of a table or the export of a non-partitioned table into a partitioned or non-partitioned target table. Import reads from the dump file only the data rows from the specified source partition(s). These specifications are delivered on the command line as import is invoked, or read from a parameter file.

VIP

Partition level import will not bring rows into a specified target partition if the rows in the export file fall outside the allowable range within which the target partition was defined.

Source and target partitions must have the same table name. In other words, data from one partition of a table can be imported into only another partition of the same table.

Requirements for Running Export and Import

As the DBA, you must ensure the two programs exp and imp are accessible to you and your developers. The requirements for a few common environments are outlined in the following table.

Operating System	Requirements
Windows	The executables must be in a directory in the current path and the appropriate values must be set in the oracle.ini initialization file.
VMS	World must have read and execute permissions (W=RE).
UNIX	The executables' file permissions must be set to 744 (execute for all users).

Error Conditions and Their Solutions

Yes, you are going to have problems with export and import. We all do! Most of them are a result of coding errors. This section of the chapter will show you how to deal with errors caused by the following situations:

- Trying to run export or import when the database is not open

- Trying to read an export file written by a DBA user

■   Trying to run a full database export or import with insufficient privileges

Oracle Not Running

The Oracle instance you are using export or import against must be running to use these programs. The following is encountered if the instance is not running:

```
D:\ORANT\BIN> imp80 userid=/ full=y
Import: Release 8.0.3.0.1 - Production on Mon Nov 23 11:39:01 1998
Copyright (c) Oracle Corporation 1979, 1994,1996.  All rights reserved.
IMP-00003: ORACLE error 1034 encountered
ORA-01034: ORACLE not available
ORA-07318: smsget: open error when opening sgadef.dbf file.
HP-UX Error: 2: No such file or directory
IMP-00021: operating system error - error code (dec 13, hex 0xD)
IMP-00000: Import terminated unsuccessfully
```

Reading Your DBA-Created Export File

When you, as the DBA, create an export file, only other DBA-privileged users may read that file for import regardless of the mode (table, user, or full) used to create the export. The following will occur if a user (no DBA role) tries to read an export file you created as the DBA.

```
D:\ORANT\BIN> imp80 userid=userx/drowssap full=y
Import: Release 8.0.3.0.1 - Production on Mon Nov 23 11:39:01 1998
Copyright (c) Oracle Corporation 1979, 1994,1996.  All rights reserved.
Connected to: Oracle8 Server Release 8.0.3.0.1 - Production
With the distributed, heterogeneous, replication, objects
and parallel query options
PL/SQL Release 3.0.3.0.1 - Production
Export file created by EXPORT:V08.00.03
IMP-00013: only a DBA can import a file exported by another DBA
IMP-00021: operating system error - error code (dec 2, hex 0x2)
IMP-00000: Import terminated unsuccessfully
```

Unable to Initiate a Full Database Export

You must start a full database export from your account with the DBA role or an account that you have given the role **exp_full_database**.

```
D:\ORANT\BIN> imp80 userid=/ full=y rows=n
exp userid=/ full=y rows=n
Import: Release 8.0.3.0.1 - Production on Mon Nov 23 11:39:01 1998
Copyright (c) Oracle Corporation 1979, 1994,1996.  All rights reserved.
Connected to: Oracle8 Server Release 8.0.3.0.1 - Production
With the distributed, heterogeneous, replication, objects
and parallel query options
PL/SQL Release 3.0.3.0.1 - Production
EXP-00023: must be a DBA to do Full Database export
EXP-00222:
System error message
(2)U(sers), or (3)T(ables): (2)U >
EXP-00030: Unexpected End-Of-File encountered while reading input
EXP-00222:
System error message
EXP-00000: Export terminated unsuccessfully
```

Relationship Between Parameters

You will soon learn that there are certain parameter values with export and import that cannot be coded together. The most common occurrence is with export running in table mode. Suppose you wanted to export one table from userA and two tables from userB in the same export session. The first cut at calling export may be done using the following command:

```
exp80 userid=fin_man/drowssap owner=(userA,userB)
tables=(table1A,table1B,table2B)
```

After pressing ENTER, Oracle responds with

```
EXP-00026: only one parameter (TABLES, OWNER, or FULL) can be specified
EXP-00222:
System error message 2
EXP-00000: Export terminated unsuccessfully
```

and the export aborts.

In the next listing, we are asking Oracle not to export the table data (**rows=n**) and to compress the extents (**compress=y**). Since the compress keyword is not on the command line, Oracle defaults it to **Y**, as shown in Table 15-3.

```
D:\ORANT\BIN> exp80 userid=/ rows=n file=partial
Import: Release 8.0.3.0.1 - Production on Mon Nov 23 11:39:01 1998
```

```
Copyright (c) Oracle Corporation 1979, 1994,1996.  All rights reserved.
Connected to: Oracle8 Server Release 8.0.3.0.1 - Production
With the distributed, heterogeneous, replication, objects
and parallel query options
PL/SQL Release 3.0.3.0.1 - Production
EXP-00035: Cannot specify Rows=N and Compress=Y
EXP-00222: System error message
EXP-00000: Export terminated unsuccessfully
```

In the next listing, you see that Oracle insists you enter the **fromuser** and **touser** parameters in the call to import, issue the keyword **full=y**, or provide some table names using the **tables=** keyword parameter.

```
D:\ORANT\BIN> exp80 userid=/ file=prod
Import: Release 8.0.3.0.1 - Production on Mon Nov 23 11:39:01 1998
Copyright (c) Oracle Corporation 1979, 1994,1996.  All rights reserved.
Connected to: Oracle8 Server Release 8.0.3.0.1 - Production
With the distributed, heterogeneous, replication, objects
and parallel query options
PL/SQL Release 3.0.3.0.1 - Production
Export file created by EXPORT:V08.00.03
IMP-00031: Must specify FULL=Y or provide FROMUSER/TOUSER or TABLE
           arguments
IMP-00021: operating system error - error code (dec 2, hex 0x2)
IMP-00000: Import terminated unsuccessfully
```

UNIX Specifics

We have run across the following UNIX caveats with import and export. Enclosing a list of table names in parentheses when using table mode raises an error, since the operating system interprets rather than reads the leading parenthesis. The solution is to put the keyword and its qualifiers in single quotes or use the UNIX escape character \ (backslash). This forces UNIX to read the parentheses.

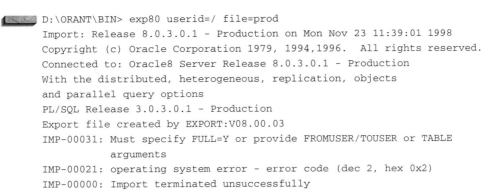

NOTE
*This section uses release 7.3.3 on UNIX as an example; hence the name **exp** and **imp** rather than **exp80** and **imp80** for the executables running export and import.*

```
exp userid=/ tables=(table_q,table_r)
ksh: syntax error: '(' unexpected
```

Either of the following will work.

```
exp userid=/ tables='(table_q,table_r)'
```

or

```
exp userid=/ tables=\(table_q,table_r\)
```

If you code an **ops$** account prefix on the command line call to export or import, you get the following error even though, using this example, the account **ops$francesl** with the **drowssap** password is valid.

```
exp userid=ops$francesl/drowssap
Export: Release 7.3.3.2.0 - Production on Mon Nov 20 12:07:28 1999
Copyright (c) Oracle Corporation 1979, 1994.  All rights reserved.
Connected to: Oracle7 Server Release 7.3.3.2.0 - Production Release
PL/SQL Release 2.3.2.0 - Production
EXP-00004: invalid username or password
EXP-00222:
System error message
Username:
```

As above, you must either enclose the user name and password in single quotes or use the UNIX escape character \ (backslash). Either of the following will solve the problem.

```
exp userid=ops\$francesl/drowssap
```

or

```
exp userid='ops$francesl/drowssap'
```

Examples

We now introduce some real-life export and import situations, and we will present a listing of the parameter file to use with each. As you become more fluent in using these utilities, you will specify the **parfile=** keyword more and more and place the appropriate parameters in a file.

Sample Scenario #1

Export my person, acc_rec, fin_mast, and letters tables into a file called recs. The contents of the parameter file would be

```
userid=/ file=recs tables=(person,acc_rec,fin_mast) buffer=10240
```

Import userA's objects into userB's schema using export file frank. Some of the objects already exist in userB's schema, but we want to bring the data in for existing objects as well.

```
userid=/ ignore=y file=frank buffer=102400 fromuser=userA touser=userB
```

Sample Scenario #2

Export three of userA's tables and two of userB's tables.

```
userid=/
tables=
(userA.table_1,userA.table_2,userA.table_3,userB.table_1,userB.table_2)
```

Sample Scenario #3

Make a copy of the tables exported in the previous example in userC's schema.

```
userid=userc/drowssap fromuser=(userA,userB) touser=(userC,userC)
```

What's Next

We have stressed throughout this chapter the importance of export and import and how they are integrated into your DBA skill set. In Chapter 16, we will highlight how to use these utilities as part of your backup and recovery procedures. Export and import have been around for years—they are dependable and integral to the set of utilities you receive with the Oracle Server product. Very early in your career as a DBA, you will wonder how you could ever live without them.

CHAPTER
16

Backup and Recovery

h yes! Backup and recovery—two of the biggest issues with any system, regardless of the software. Oracle has implemented sophisticated backup and recovery mechanisms that allow you to protect your precious data in case all or part of your database is inoperable. By the time you finish this chapter, you will be able to implement a standard backup and recovery plan for your installation. We include details on the following topics:

- Overview of Oracle Enterprise Backup Manager

- Making image backups of your database

- Leaving the database open and accessible while making backups

- Running the database in ARCHIVELOG mode

- Performing complete and incomplete database recovery

- Integrating backup with export and import

All too often, DBAs look at backup and recovery procedures only when it's too late. One of our clients lost a production database before they "got around" to taking the time to implement routines that would have allowed the necessary protection. Keep in mind that there are two steps to initiating backup and recovery procedures. The first (the backup step) makes copies of the Oracle data; the second (the recovery step) copies the data created from the backup step and restores the database to its operable status.

Terminology

The following definitions will arm you with the technical jargon you need to make it through this chapter.

- A *checkpoint* causes information to be written from memory to the database files to which they belong. During this activity, the state of the datafiles, redo logs, and control files is synched, and the instance is in a consistent state.

■ Oracle keeps an internal transaction log referred to as the *SCN* or system change number. Using an internal set of rules, Oracle assigns an SCN to transactions and, when performing a log switch, records the highest SCN in each redo log as it is archived.

■ The Oracle database is in a *consistent state* when the information in the control files (e.g., the last time the datafiles were updated) is the same as the information contained in the datafiles themselves.

■ A tablespace is *online* when it is accessible to the users of the Oracle instance. In contrast, when a tablespace is *offline*, it is available for maintenance and cannot be accessed by the user community until it is brought back online.

Protection Provided by Backup

We need to spend some time explaining some concepts and theory before we discuss how and what to back up. Essentially, Oracle offers two types of backup protection. After we discuss both and present a complete backup plan, you will know how to secure your installation with bulletproof protection against just about anything.

Protection against Loss of an Object

Backing up data with export and import (which will be discussed in the "Export and Import Backup" section coming up) provides protection against loss of objects. How could that happen, you ask? Picture yourself as a developer for a large bank in Germany. You use Oracle's network product, Net8, which allows you to work with databases on a remote machine. You have just finished some cleanup before final installation of a new system in production, and you connect to the production database using Net8. You are called out of the office for a few minutes, and when you come back, you realize that you have forgotten to remove a table from the development database, so you enter the command **drop table account_master;**. Less than five minutes later, your phone rings, and guess what? The account_master table is missing in production. Now, how did that happen?

VIP
Export and import provide protection against loss of tables that get dropped inadvertently from the database. In other words, they provide protection against loss of all or part of one or more tables.

When a table needs to be recovered from an export file, bring it back using the table mode of import (this is discussed in Chapter 15 in the "Switching among Modes" section). If the export was made at 2:00 a.m. and a table is inadvertently dropped at 3:00 p.m. the next day, any new or changed rows in the table after 2:00 a.m. are not restored as the table is recreated. Sound impossible? Believe us, it happens.

VIP
While import allows protection against losing a table, the import will only restore the table to the condition it was in when the export file was written.

Protection against Loss of the Database

Protection against loss of the database also means protection against loss of a datafile or tablespace. This protection is related directly to the redo or transaction logs we discuss in many places throughout this book, especially the "Redo Logs—The Transaction Log" section of Chapter 3. Picture the following situation that happened to us a few years ago. It's morning, and everyone is happily working with the database. There is a phone call to the help desk from a user saying that Oracle is asking her for her user name and password. Interesting! When she usually logs onto the machine, the first screen she sees is the main menu for her system. We investigate, and find out that Oracle is not running! We look around and do some exploring, and we receive the following message from Oracle:

```
ERROR: ORA-01034: ORACLE not available
ORA-09243: smsget: error attaching to SGA
```

Panic! Something has gone wrong with one of the disks, and Oracle has shut itself down. This illustrates the second type of backup protection. In this situation, there is a problem with the hardware (disk pack, in this case) and we may have lost the datafiles on the bad disk. Unlike losing one or more objects, here the physical structure of the database is damaged.

Protection for this type of problem is provided by running the database in ARCHIVELOG mode, which will provide you with roll-forward capabilities. The redo or transaction logs record every transaction against the database. By saving copies of the redo logs before they are overwritten, they can be reapplied to the database as if the transactions had been entered by the users. We discuss what can be done when an instance runs in ARCHIVELOG mode in more detail in the "Recovery" section in this chapter.

VIP

ARCHIVELOG provides protection against an assortment of hardware problems that happen periodically. You can restore a backup of the database and recover all the transactions, since the backup was written using your archived redo logs.

Oracle Enterprise Manager Backup

We have already spoken throughout a number of chapters of the Oracle Enterprise Manager (*OEM*) set of tools for the database administrator. Let's get started looking at the Backup Manager. From the Enterprise Manager main console, select Tools from the menu bar, then Applications. Select the Oracle Backup Manager from the drop-down list to be presented with the screen shown in Figure 16-1.

Notice that there are two folders on this screen. The first is used to display a list of tablespaces in the Oracle database, the second the set of online redo log groups and members. Double-click on Tablespaces, then do the same on Redo Logs Groups to bring up the screen shown in Figure 16-2.

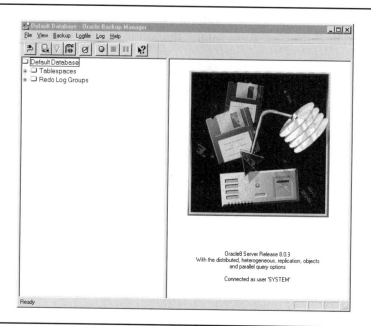

FIGURE 16-1. *Oracle Backup Manager main screen*

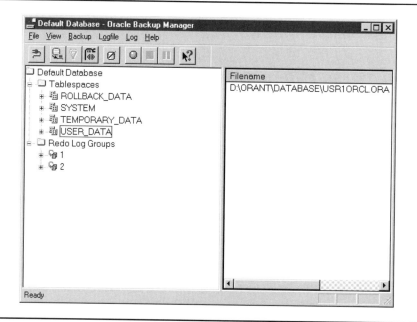

FIGURE 16-2. *Backup Manager showing Tablespaces and Redo Log Groups*

We are going to take this opportunity to look at one of many wizards in the manager tools accessible through OEM. The backup Wizard can be invoked in one of two ways:

1. Clicking the Backup Wizard button (fourth from the left in Figure 16-1).

2. Selecting Backup, then Backup Tablespace Wizard from the menu bar at the top of the main console.

Backup Wizard

There are four screens to this wizard; let's look at each one in turn to get an idea of how they are put together.

1-Tablespace Status Dialog

The wizard wants to know the status of the tablespace(s) being backed up. This screen is shown in Figure 16-3.

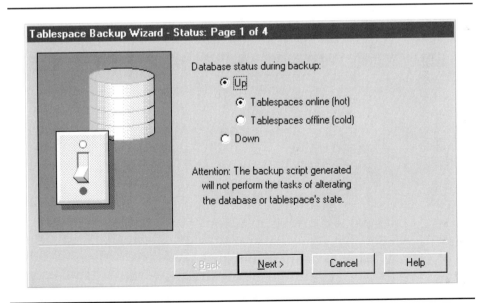

FIGURE 16-3.   *Tablespace(s) status dialog*

You are asked to specify whether the database is up and running while the backup is to be written, or if it is closed and inaccessible to the user community. Oracle refers to the task of backing up an online tablespace as a *hot backup* and an offline tablespace as a *cold backup*. The dialog box informs you that the script that will be generated as a result of this dialog will not alter the status of any tablespaces being backed up. It is your responsibility to do this yourself. Click Next to move to the next screen.

VIP
*Placing tablespaces online and offline is accomplished using the command **alter tablespace ...I offline;** followed later by an **alter tablespace ...I online;**.*

2-Tablespaces Dialog

Using the familiar point-and-click interface, this is where you specify what tablespace(s) to include in the backup. This is shown in Figure 16-4.

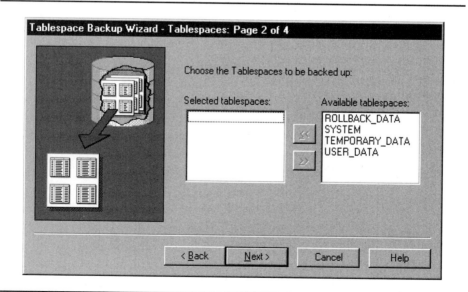

FIGURE 16-4. *Specify Tablespace(s) to include in backup*

Double-click a tablespace name in the Available Tablespaces section of this screen to transfer a name to the Selected Tablespaces section. Alternately, highlight a name, then click the double arrow to move a tablespace name from one box to the other.

3-Method Dialog

The next screen asks you to specify whether you wish to write the backup to disk, to tape, or the nature of your operating system archiving utility to be used for the backup activity. This screen is shown in Figure 16-5.

When writing to disk, you enter the location to which the backup should be written after selecting the Write to Disk option. If you wish to go directly to tape, after selecting the Write to Tape option, specify the ID of the tape device attached to the machine from which the backup is being written. In Figure 16-5 we have specified the Windows NT pkzip command for the archiving utility using the text **pkzip ora8nt %s.**

4-Save Backup Script Dialog

This screen is where you specify the name of the script within which the backup commands you have just built will be stored. OEM suggests a name

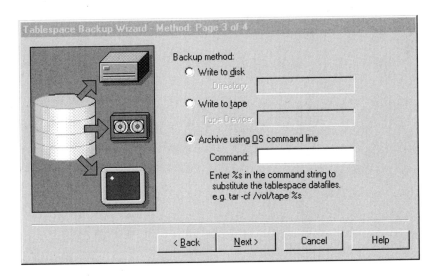

FIGURE 16-5. *Specifying a method for the Backup Manager*

as shown in Figure 16-6, but you can enter a name over the one displayed, or click on the Save As box beside the area where you specify the filename. Click on Finish as shown in Figure 16-6 to complete this activity.

The wizard then writes the appropriate commands to the file specified in the third dialog box. The backup job is then run from the job subsystem available through the OEM console. The next listing is a sample of the job commands written by the dialog we carried on in this section.

```
EM Wizard Backup Tcl Script Ver. 1.1
$SMP_USER/$SMP_PASSWORD@$SMP_SERVICE
"UP"
{\"ONLINE\"}
{{ {ROLLBACK_DATA} {USER_DATA} {TEMPORARY_DATA} }}
{{ {1} {1} {1} }}
{{ {D:\ORANT\DATABASE\RBS1ORCL.ORA} {D:\ORANT\DATABASE\USR1ORCL.ORA}
{D:\ORANT\DATABASE\TMP1ORCL.ORA} }}
{{{pkzip ora8nt %s}}}
CopyFilesUsingCommand
```

FIGURE 16-6. *Naming backup script*

Preparing for Backups with Database Open

One of the biggest mistakes DBAs make when managing backups for the Oracle databases is writing what they think are useful backups that turn out to be useless. This is most commonly caused when a DBA neglects to enliven the appropriate log mode, and carries out backups with the database running. The secret to backing up an open database is ensuring that the files that are part of the backup are consistent as they are copied to disk or tape. Under normal circumstances this is impossible since Oracle writes information to the various database tablespace files as users work with objects in those containers. Look at the following logic to see how Oracle maintains interfile consistency as it backs up one or more tablespaces in an open database.

```
if database is in archivelog mode then
    if backup is turned on for selected tablespace
        loop until tablespace is taken out of backup mode
            write information destined for that tablespace to
                the online redo logs
        end loop
        take tablespace out of backup mode
        dump appropriate information from redo logs to tablespace
            now out of backup mode
    else
        write information directly to appropriate tablespace data
            files as systems operate
    end if
else
    allow online tablespace backup with no intervention (thereby
        the DBA ends up writing an unusable backup)
end if
```

The secret here involves a two-step process:

1. Initiating a process that will archive online redo logs as they fill.

2. Place the Oracle database in ARCHIVELOG mode.

Let's do the first using Oracle Backup Manager, and the second using Server Manager.

Starting the Archiving Process

From the main console of the Backup Manager as shown in Figure 16-1, select the Logfile option from the menu, then click on Enable Automatic Archiving; OEM responds with the information shown in Figure 16-7.

Placing the Database in Archivelog Mode

After opening up a DOS window, start Server Manager with the command **svrmgr30** and do the following.

1. Connect to the instance using the command **connect internal**, then enter the secure password you selected during installation of Oracle8 for Windows NT.

2. Close the database using the command **shutdown**.

3. Issue the command **startup mount** to ready the database for the pending log mode switch.

4. Enter the command **alter database archivelog;**.

5. Enter the command **alter database open;** to make the instance available to the users.

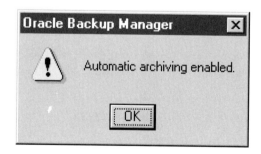

FIGURE 16-7. *Archiving enabled information*

The next listing shows the dialog and the responses from Oracle.

```
Oracle Server Manager Release 3.0.3.0.1 - Production
Copyright (c) Oracle Corporation 1994, 1995. All rights reserved.
Oracle8 Server Release 8.0.3.0.1 - Production
With the distributed, heterogeneous, replication, objects
and parallel query options
PL/SQL Release 3.0.3.0.1 - Production
SVRMGR> connect internal
Password:
Connected.
SVRMGR> shutdown
Database closed.
Database dismounted.
ORACLE instance shut down.
SVRMGR> startup mount
ORACLE instance started.
Total System Global Area          8030448 bytes
Fixed Size                          44584 bytes
Variable Size                     7510728 bytes
Database Buffers                   409600 bytes
Redo Buffers                        65536 bytes
Database mounted.
SVRMGR> alter database archivelog;
Statement processed.
SVRMGR> alter database open;
Statement processed.
```

The status of archive logging can be checked anytime using the command **archive log list;**, the output from this command is shown in the next listing.

```
SVRMGR> archive log list
Database log mode            Archive Mode
Automatic archival           Enabled
Archive destination          D:\ORANT\RDBMS80\
Oldest online log sequence   36
Next log sequence to archive 37
Current log sequence         37
SVRMGR>
```

After this brief overview of tweaking the environment to permit the writing of consistent backups when the Oracle database is open, let's look at the role played by export and import in a total backup strategy.

Export and Import Backup

We discuss export and import in Chapter 15 (we thought these two utilities were so important that they warranted their own chapter). If you refer to the "Export and Import Modes" section in Chapter 15, you will see how export and import play a role in most standard backup procedures.

Classically, most backups are done in the quiet hours. When deciding how to use export as part of your backup, examine what we call your "window of opportunity." This window is the amount of time during which everything is quiet on your computer (i.e., there are no reporting jobs or system backups running to interfere with the resources required to do an export), and no users are accessing the database. Most of our clients have a window of between six and seven hours. In some situations, however, that window is as small as 30 minutes or as large as nine hours. We suggest you use export according to the guidelines in the next two sections as part of your backup routines.

VIP

If you can do a full database export within this window of opportunity, the full database export must be part of your Oracle backups.

When the Window Is Long Enough

If the window is long enough to accommodate a nightly full database export, run the command **exp parfile=full_nightly.parfile;** the parameter file contents are the following:

```
userid=system/manager full=y file=full_sys
buffer=102400 log=full_sys grants=y indexes=y
```

Run this export every night, and you will have all the protection you could ever want against losing an object.

When the Window Is Not Long Enough

One important question needs to be answered when deciding what to export and when: "Which tables experience the highest activity?" With the answer to that question, you can decide to export those tables on a regular basis and other not-so-active ones less frequently. Examine Table 16-1 to see how this could be mapped to the largest and most strategic data in a communication company's database.

Armed with this information, you then produce the code that will run the export routines. You always add two more parts to the backup procedures, as shown in Table 16-2. Part 5 exports all the data not done in parts 1 through 4, and part 6 makes a copy of the makeup of the database but does not export any data.

VIP
Based on your configuration, you may have more or fewer parts after you analyze your requirements.

Use the following guidelines when implementing the procedures (the part numbers referred to are from Tables 16-1 and 16-2):

- Each part (numbered 1 to 4) must complete successfully before the next component runs. Thus, if part 2 does not complete on a Tuesday night, part 2 is run again Wednesday night, and part 3 waits one more night for its turn.

- These procedures must run unattended; thus, export must be run using the parfile= parameter (discussed in Chapter 15). Using part 3 from Table 16-1 as an example, the export command would be **exp parfile=sys_part3.parfile** and the parameter file would contain the following:

```
userid=b_inventory/secure file=sys_part3 buffer=102400
grants=y indexes=y log=part3_systables=loc_master
```

Table Name	Owner	Approximate Size	Part
customers	b_cust	8,000,000	1
phones	b_numbers	12,000,000	2
loc_master	b_inventory	615,000	3
interurban	b_ld	7,500,000	4

TABLE 16-1. *Large Objects Part of Export Cycle*

Component	Part
Other data not part of 1 to 4	5
Full system no rows	6

TABLE 16-2. *Other Parts of Database To Export*

- Part 5 exports all the data not done in parts 1 through 4.

- Part 6 runs every night and writes an export file containing all the SQL statements required to recreate your database. No data is written to the export file during this operation. Assuming the job runs from the Oracle SYSTEM account using the command exp parfile=full_no_rows, the contents of the parameter file are

```
userid=system/manager full=y rows=n compress=n file=full_sys
buffer=102400 log=full_sys grants=y indexes=y
```

Keep a log of your export backups. A sample is shown in Table 16-3. Notice how part 3 was scheduled to run June 13, but did not complete. As a result, part 3 was rescheduled to run June 14. Had part 3 run to completion on the 13th, part 4 would have run on the 14th. Even though parts 5 and 6 run nightly, you still should track their successful completion.

Recovery from an Export File

Once the export files are written as described in the previous sections, restoring one or more objects from the export is done when required. Let's look at a few situations that may come up and how to use import to rebuild one or more missing objects.

NOTE
We recommend doing object restoration from the Oracle SYSTEM account.

Restoring a Single Object

Using the appropriate export file as input, follow these steps to restore the complete contents of the loc_master:

Date	Part Scheduled	Completed	Written to Tape
June 11	1	Y	Y
June 11	5	Y	Y
June 11	6	**N**	**N**
June 12	2	Y	Y
June 12	5	Y	Y
June 12	6	Y	Y
June 13	3	**N**	**N**
June 13	5	Y	Y
June 13	6	Y	Y
June 14	3	Y	Y
June 14	5	Y	Y
June 14	6	Y	Y
June 15	4	Y	Y
June 15	5	Y	Y
June 15	5	Y	Y

TABLE 16-3. *Export Log*

1. Log into SQL*Plus using the SYSTEM account, and enter the command **truncate table b_inventory.loc_master;** to clean out the table. If the table has been dropped, the truncate command will return Oracle error "942:table or view does not exist."

2. Leave SQL*Plus, and enter the command **imp userid=system fromuser=b_inventory touser=b_inventory commit=y file=sys_part3 buffer=102400 tables=loc_master ignore=y log=sys_rest**. You will be prompted for the password missing from the command line.

NOTE
*Use the parameter **commit=y** to ensure that the import runs to completion. When you are restoring a large table, this ensures Oracle has enough rollback segment space to handle a large import.*

3. Log into SQL*Plus as the b_inventory user and verify the grants on the table by issuing the command **select grantee, privilege from user_tab_privs_made where table_name = 'LOC_MASTER';**. If there seem to be some privileges missing, ascertain what they are and give them out again.

Restoring Multiple Objects

This exercise is similar to the previous section, except that you have to delete rows from more than one table before bringing the table back from the export file. In addition, the command used to invoke import is **imp userid=system fromuser=(b_inventory,b_cust) touser=(b_inventory,b_cust) commit=y file=sys_part2 buffer=102400 tables=(loc_master,customers) ignore=y log=sys_rest**. You will be prompted for the password missing from the command line. In this command, the Oracle user names owning the tables are listed with **fromuser** and **touser** in parentheses separated by commas. The tables being brought back are listed in parentheses separated by commas as well.

Image Backups

Let's move from export and import to image backups. Image backups play an important role in your backup and recovery procedures. They make copies of some or all of your datafiles, redo logs, and control files. In this section, we will discuss making consistent (cold) backups and online (hot) backups.

Consistent (Cold) Backups

Cold backups are made with the database closed. Any file, be it datafile, redo log, or control, is part of this backup. Usually, disk space permitting, the files are copied somewhere on a disk, then backed up to tape during the quiet hours in the middle of the night. We recommend running the following program in SQL*Plus, as it will create output that can be used to make a cold backup. The bolded text in the following listing may change to suit your database.

```
SQL*Plus: Release 4.0.3.0.0 - Production on Sun May 11 12:20:12 1999
Copyright (c) Oracle Corporation 1979, 1994, 1996.  All rights reserved.
Connected to:
```

```
Oracle Server Release 8.0.3.0.1 - Production
With the distributed, heterogeneous, replication, objects
and parallel query options
PL/SQL Release 3.0.3.0.1 - Production
SQL> -- You must have select privileges on the v$parameter
SQL> -- v$logfile v$dbfile and v$controlfile data
SQL> -- dictionary views belonging to SYS to run
SQL> -- this program
SQL> set pages 0 feed off echo off
SQL> col a new_value b
SQL> col c new_value d
SQL> select value a,sysdate c
  2      from v$parameter
  3    where name = 'db_name';
SQL> prompt g:
SQL> prompt cd \oradb\backups
SQL> spool cold.backup
SQL> prompt
SQL> prompt Cold backup for "&b" database on &d ...
SQL> prompt
SQL> prompt rem Redo logs
SQL> prompt
SQL> select 'copy '||member
  2      from v$logfile;
SQL> prompt
SQL> prompt rem Datafiles
SQL> prompt
SQL> select 'copy '||name
  2      from v$dbfile;
SQL> prompt
SQL> prompt rem Control files
SQL> prompt
SQL> select 'copy '||name
  2      from v$controlfile;
SQL> spool off
SQL> exit
```

In the listing, the name of the output file is cold.backup; if this does not conform to the filenaming rules on your computer, the spool command filename will have to be changed. The output from the listing is shown next.

```
Cold backup for "prd" database on 12-JUN-99 ...
Rem Redo logs
copy d:\orant\database\log1orcl.dbf
copy d:\orant\database\log2orcl.dbf
```

```
Rem Datafiles
copy d:\orant\database\dbs1orcl.dbf
copy d:\orant\database\temporcl.dbf
copy d:\orant\database\usersorcl.dbf
copy d:\orant\database\toolsorcl.dbf
Rem Control files
copy d:\orant\database\ctl1orcl.dbf
copy d:\orant\database\ctl2orcl.dbf
```

Online (Hot) Backups

Hot backups are made with the database running in ARCHIVELOG mode. To find out how to switch your database into this mode, consult the "Tuning Online Backups" section in *Tuning Oracle* by Corey, Abbey, and Dechichio (Osborne/McGraw-Hill/Oracle Press, 1995).

Hot backups do not copy the online redo logs, since they are being archived and backed up as part of your nightly backups anyway. The database is open, and an online backup can be performed while the users are working with the database. Hot backups are done by placing a tablespace in backup mode, copying it somewhere else on disk or to tape, and then taking the tablespace out of backup mode. After the tablespaces are backed up in this manner, you can back up your control file.

VIP

You can provide users with 24-hour database availability by running in ARCHIVELOG mode and making hot backups. Even though the database is open and may be in use, the backup is consistent and may be used for recovery, as discussed later in this chapter.

Sample Hot Backup

Table 16-4 shows a database against which we will be doing a hot backup.

Tablespace	Datafile(s)
system	d:\orant\database\d1\dbs1.dbf
users	d:\orant\database\d1\users1.dbf
	d:\orant\database\d1\users2.dbf
temp	d:\orant\database\d1\temp.dbf
rollback_segs	d:\orant\database\d1\rbs1.dbf
	d:\orant\database\d1\rbs2.dbf
tools	d:\orant\database\d1\tools.dbf

TABLE 16-4. *Database for Backing Up*

The following SQL*Plus script can be used (make modifications where necessary if your operating system is not Windows NT):

```
SQL*Plus: Release 4.0.3.0.0 - Production on Sun May 11 12:20:12 1999
Copyright (c) Oracle Corporation 1979, 1994, 1996.  All rights reserved.
Connected to:
Oracle Server Release 8.0.3.0.1 - Production
With the distributed, heterogeneous, replication, objects
and parallel query options
PL/SQL Release 3.0.3.0.1 - Production
SQL> -- We inform Oracle that we are backing up a tablespace
SQL> -- before doing the copy. This is done one tablespace
SQL> -- at a time. After the tablespace is put in backup
SQL> -- mode, make a copy of its datafile(s). By forcing
SQL> -- a checkpoint after each tablespace is backed up,
SQL> -- we synch the registering of the backup internally
SQL> -- to Oracle.
SQL>
SQL> alter tablespace tools begin backup;
Tablespace altered.
```

```
SQL> $ copy d:\orant\database\d1\tools.dbf d:\backups\d1\tools1.dbf
SQL> alter tablespace tools end backup;
tablespace altered.
SQL> alter system checkpoint;
System altered.
SQL> alter tablespace temp begin backup;
Tablespace altered.
SQL> $ copy d:\orant\database\d1\temp.dbf d:\backups\d1\temp.dbf
SQL> alter tablespace temp end backup;
Tablespace altered.
SQL> alter system checkpoint;
System altered.
SQL> alter tablespace rollback_segs begin backup;
Tablespace altered.
SQL> $ copy d:\orant\database\d1\rbs1.dbf d:\backups\d1\rbs1.dbf
SQL> $ copy d:\orant\database\d1\rbs2.dbf d:\backups\d1\rbs2.dbf
SQL> alter tablespace rollback_segs end backup;
Tablespace altered.
SQL> alter system checkpoint;
System altered.
SQL> alter tablespace users begin backup;
Tablespace altered.
SQL> $ copy d:\orant\database\d1\users1.dbf d:\backups\d1\users1.dbf
SQL> $ copy d:\orant\database\d1\users2.dbf d:\backups\d1\users2.dbf
SQL> alter tablespace users end backup;
Tablespace altered.
SQL> alter system checkpoint;
System altered.
SQL> alter tablespace system begin backup;
Tablespace altered.
SQL> $ d:\orant\database\dbs1.dbf d:\backups\d1\dbs1.dbf
SQL> alter tablespace system end backup;
Tablespace altered.
SQL> alter system checkpoint;
System altered.
SQL> alter database backup controlfile to
  2    'd:\backups\d1\control.bkp' reuse;
Database altered.
```

Recovery

So far in this chapter, we have discussed export and import, the role they play in your backup procedures, and how to restore an object from an export file. We have also discussed image backups. Now comes the meat of this chapter: recovery. Strap yourself in; this is the heart of Oracle's backup and recovery strategy, and it can prove quite stimulating!

In this section, we will lead you through some exercises and show you how to perform recovery. You will need a "practice" database to do these exercises. Following is a sample create database script you can use as a skeleton SQL script to build your own database. It is included to get you started; the text that is bolded needs modifications to suit your configuration:

```
Oracle Server Manager Release 3.0.3.0.1 - Production
Copyright (c) Oracle Corporation 1994, 1995. All rights reserved.
Oracle Server Release 8.0.3.0.1 - Production
With the distributed, heterogeneous, replication, objects
and parallel query options
PL/SQL Release 3.0.3.0.1 - Production
SVRMGR> connect internal
SVRMGR> spool scratch.log
SVRMGR> set echo on
SVRMGR> startup nomount pfile=d:\orant\database\initprac.ora
SVRMGR> create database prac
     2    datafile 'd:\orant\database\dbs1prac.dbf      size 10m
     3    logfile  'd:\orant\database\log1prac.dbf',
     4             'd:\orant\database\log2prac.dbf'     size 300k
     5            maxlogfiles     20
     6            maxlogmembers    4
     7            maxdatafiles    30
     8            maxinstances     1
     9            maxloghistory 100;
Statement processed.
SVRMGR> create rollback segment temp
     2       tablespace system
     3    storage (initial 50k minextents 10 maxextents 10);
Statement processed.
SVRMGR> shutdown
SVRMGR> startup pfile=d:\orant\database\initprac.ora
 SVRMGR> alter tablespace system default storage (pctincrease 0);
SVRMGR> set echo off
SVRMGR> set termout off
SVRMGR> @d:\orant\rdbms80\admin\catalog.sql
SVRMGR> @d:\orant\rdbms80\admin\catexp.sql
SVRMGR> @d:\orant\rdbms80\admin\catldr.sql
SVRMGR> @d:\orant\rdbms80\admin\catproc.sql
SVRMGR> connect system/manager
SVRMGR> @d:\orant\rdbms80\admin\catdbsyn.sql
SVRMGR> connect internal
SVRMGR> shutdown
```

What Is Recovery?

Recovery is a process whereby an image backup of the database (done, let's say, at 7:00 a.m.) is rolled forward to a later point in time (let's say 2:00 p.m.) using the archived redo logs. Roll forward applies changes recorded in the redo logs; then, using the rollback segments, undoes any transactions that were recorded in the redo log but were not committed. We discussed the redo logs in Chapter 3, pointing out how they record all activities against the database. Say a system had been used by twelve people between 7:00 a.m. and 2:00 p.m. Everything these people did to the database was written to the redo logs; thus, the redo logs are a mirror image of the activities of those twelve people during those seven hours.

Redo Log Types

There are two types of redo logs: online redo logs and archived redo logs. Online redo logs are the pool of two or more redo logs written to as the database operates. We discussed in Chapter 3 how Oracle cycles between the online redo logs. When running the database in ARCHIVELOG mode, before reusing a redo log, Oracle copies it elsewhere and adds it to the pool of archived redo logs. Every redo log is allocated a sequence number when Oracle does a log switch. In Table 16-5, we show how the status of redo logs cycles between active, being archived, and inactive.

In Table 16-5, after the second log switch, a redo log belonging to group 1 is archived, and that copy is referred to as an archived redo log. Notice that when the fourth log switch occurs, redo log group 1 becomes active once again, and any information in the log is overwritten. This is not a problem, since the previous contents of the redo log have become an archived redo log.

Types of Recovery

Every time you start the database, Oracle looks through its online redo logs to see if there is any recovery it should perform based on the information in those logs. If it finds any information, it applies it to the database before it is opened. This feature is called automatic database instance recovery. When you take a mixture of archived and online redo logs and recover all or part of the database, this is called either complete media recovery or incomplete media recovery.

Event	Log Sequence	Redo Log Group	Status
log switch #1	18	1	active
		2	inactive
		3	being archived
log switch #2	19	1	being archived
		2	active
		3	inactive
log switch #3	20	1	inactive
		2	being archived
		3	active
log switch #4	21	1	active
		2	inactive
		3	being archived

TABLE 16-5.   *Cycling of Redo Logs Through Four Log Switches*

Complete media recovery can be performed on the database, a tablespace, or one or more datafiles. Recovery stops with the application of the most recent redo log. Incomplete media recovery can only be performed on the whole database. The term incomplete is used because, with this type of recovery, not all of the redo logs are applied. You specify when the recovery process is to stop; when Oracle applies enough redo logs to reach that point, the recovery stops. Table 16-6 summarizes what can be recovered using complete and incomplete recovery.

Recovery Type	Database	Datafile	Tablespace
Complete	X	X	X
Incomplete	X		X

TABLE 16-6.   *What Can Be Recovered Using Complete and Incomplete Recovery*

VIP
Incomplete tablespace recovery is only supported in Oracle8; it cannot be accomplished using the Oracle Enterprise Manager. It must be done with line-mode Server Manager.

Performing Complete Recovery

We will now lead you through a complete recovery session. The database we are recovering has the following makeup:

Tablespace	Datafile(s)
system	f:\ora8db\dbs1book.dbf
rollback	f:\ora8db\rbook.dbf
users	f:\ora8db\users.dbf
tools	f:\ora8db\tools.dbf
temp	f:\ora8db\temp.dbf

In this scenario, the database is backed up at 4:40 a.m. nightly. The archived redo logs are copied to the directory d:\orant\arc. Image backups are written to the directory d:\sys\backups and written to tape from there at 6:00 a.m. At noon, there is a problem with one of the disk packs, and the database shuts itself down.

Before doing the recovery, you must restore the image backup from wherever it resides to the correct location on your disks. Using our sample database, the following five commands copy the image backup to its proper location:

```
copy d:\sys\backups\rbook.dbf f:\ora8db\rbook.dbf
copy d:\sys\backups\users.dbf f:\ora8db\users.dbf
copy d:\sys\backups\tools.dbf f:\ora8db\tools.dbf
copy d:\sys\backups\temp.dbf f:\ora8db\temp.dbf
copy d:\sys\backups\dbs1book.dbf f:\ora8db\dbs1book.dbf
```

To perform the complete recovery, follow these steps:

I. Invoke line-mode Server Manager with the command **svrmgrl**.

2. Enter the command **connect internal**, followed by **startup mount**.

3. Check the status of the database by entering the command **alter database open;** and receive the following feedback from Oracle:

```
alter database open
*
ORA-01113: file 1 needs media recovery
ORA-01110: data file 1: 'f:\ora8db\dbs1book.dbf'
SVRMGR>
```

4. Enter the command **recover database;** and receive the following feedback from Oracle:

```
ORA-00279: Change 9964 generated at 12/21/99 14:37:06 needed...
ORA-00289: Suggestion : d:\orant\arc\arch_383.arc
ORA-00280: Change 9964 for thread 1 is in sequence #383
Specify log: {<RET>=suggested | filename | AUTO | CANCEL}
```

5. Press ENTER to accept the log filename presented (d:\orant\arc\arch_383.arc, in this case).

As Oracle suggests each archived redo log filename, keep pressing ENTER to accept the suggestions made. When the recovery is complete, Oracle presents you with this message:

```
Log applied.
Media recovery complete.
SVRMGR>
```

You then issue the command **alter database open;** and the database recovery is complete! Bravo—nice job.

When presented with the name of the first redo log to apply, you could have entered the word auto (notice it is one of the suggestions in the specify log prompt), and Oracle would have run the recovery without need for further intervention. The last log file prompt is shown below, and the recovery complete message follows.

```
ORA-00279: Change 10029 generated at 12/21/99 14:43:13 needed...
ORA-00289: Suggestion : d:\orant\arc\arch_399.arc
ORA-00280: Change 10029 for thread 1 is in sequence #399
ORA-00278: Logfile 'd:\orant\arc\arch_399.arc' no longer...
Log applied.
Media recovery complete.
SVRMGR>
```

Performing Incomplete Recovery

Incomplete recovery is one of the most interesting features of Oracle's recovery mechanisms. Review the exercise we went through in the previous section, in which Oracle asked for names and locations of archived redo logs, then look at the following listing:

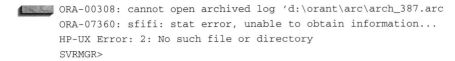

```
ORA-00308: cannot open archived log 'd:\orant\arc\arch_387.arc
ORA-07360: sfifi: stat error, unable to obtain information...
HP-UX Error: 2: No such file or directory
SVRMGR>
```

Uh oh! Oracle wants archived redo log file with sequence number 387—panic (why did you want to be a DBA anyway?). Confident that Oracle just messed up, you try the job again and, lo and behold, it happens again. No problem. Just drop back to the operating system, find the missing log file, and all will be well. You issue the command **dir/w** and receive the following output:

```
arch_382.arc   arch_386.arc   arch_391.arc   arch_395.arc   arch_399.arc
arch_383.arc   arch_388.arc   arch_392.arc   arch_396.arc   arch_400.arc
arch_384.arc   arch_389.arc   arch_393.arc   arch_397.arc   arch_401.arc
arch_385.arc   arch_390.arc   arch_394.arc   arch_398.arc
```

Notice that the file arch_387.arc is not there. This is why incomplete recovery exists.

VIP

Incomplete recovery recovers the database to a point in time in the past. In our example, the database can only be recovered to the transaction at the end of archived log sequence number 386.

There are three ways to perform incomplete recovery: change-based recovery, cancel-based recovery, and time-based recovery. We will run through each one in the next sections. Hold on.

Change-Based Recovery

To do change-based recovery, you need to know the highest system change number (SCN) written to the archived redo log just before the missing log. You can then issue the recovery statement recover database until change scn_number; where the scn_number is that SCN written to archived redo log file sequence number 386 (i.e., one less than the missing log sequence number 387). You can get that SCN information from a view called v$log_history owned by Oracle user SYS, which looks like the following:

```
RECID                                    NUMBER
STAMP                                    NUMBER
THREAD#                                   NUMBER
SEQUENCE#                                 NUMBER
FIRST_CHANGE#                             NUMBER
FIRST_TIME                               DATE
NEXT_CHANGE#                              NUMBER
```

NOTE
Since v$log_history stores the first SCN for each archived redo log, you need to decrease the first_change# from the next highest sequence# log file by 1. Since we are looking for the last SCN for sequence number 386, we use sequence# 387 as the desired log file number.

Using the query **select first_change#-1 from v$log_history where sequence# = 387;**, you can find out the desired SCN. The output from this query is the following:

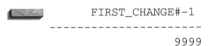

```
    FIRST_CHANGE#-1
---------------------
              9999
```

Now that you know the SCN, let's perform the recovery, using these steps:

1. Invoke line-mode Server Manager with the command **svrmgrl**.

2. Enter the command **connect internal**, followed by **startup mount**.

3. Enter the command **recover database until change 9999;** and receive feedback from Oracle similar to when you started complete recovery.

4. Enter the word **auto** in response to Oracle's suggestion for the first archived redo log. Oracle stops recovery before it looks for arch_387.arc and informs you of the following:

```
ORA-00289: Suggestion : d:\orant\arc\arch_387.arc
ORA-00280: Change 9999 for thread 1 is in sequence #387
ORA-00278: Logfile 'd:\orant\arc\arch_386.arc' no...
Log applied.
Media recovery complete.
SVRMGR>
```

The final step in this recovery exercise is to open the database. After we have covered all three incomplete recovery types, we will show you how to open the database in the section called "Opening the Database after Incomplete Media Recovery."

Cancel-Based Recovery

Cancel-based recovery proceeds until you enter the word **cancel** to a prompt Oracle gives you suggesting the name of an archived redo log. So far in our discussions, you have seen the following prompt from Oracle:

```
Specify log: {<RET>=suggested | filename | AUTO | CANCEL}
```

Using the cancel option as the prompt suggests, let's do our recovery again. You are logged into Server Manager and have issued **connect internal** and then **startup mount**. When you enter the command **recover database until cancel;**, Oracle suggests the name of the first archived redo log it requires. Press the ENTER key to accept the name, and keep going until Oracle asks for log with the sequence number 387. Enter the word **cancel**, and recovery stops, as Oracle tells you the following:

```
ORA-00289: Suggestion : d:\orant\arc\arch_387.arc
ORA-00278: Logfile 'd:\orant\arc\arch_386.arc' no...
Specify log: {<RET>=suggested | filename | AUTO | CANCEL}
cancel
Media recovery cancelled.
```

Again, the final step in this recovery exercise is to open the database, which we will cover in the "Opening the Database after Incomplete Media Recovery" section following our discussion of all three incomplete recovery types.

Time-Based Recovery

To use time-based recovery, you need to know the time recorded in v$log_history for archived redo log sequence 387 (the missing redo log). By issuing the query **select time from v$log_history where sequence# = 387;**, you get the following time:

```
TIME
------------------
12/21/98 14:42:04
```

Let's do the recovery now. You are logged into Server Manager and have issued **connect internal** and then **startup mount**. When you enter the command **recover database until time '1998/12/21:14:42:04';**, Oracle suggests the name of the first archived redo log it requires. Enter the reply **auto** and Oracle applies archived redo logs until the sequence number 387. You are then told the following:

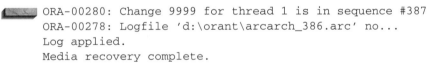
```
ORA-00280: Change 9999 for thread 1 is in sequence #387
ORA-00278: Logfile 'd:\orant\arcarch_386.arc' no...
Log applied.
Media recovery complete.
```

VIP

When using time-based recovery, the format for the time is YYYY/MM/DD:HH24:MI:SS and it is enclosed in single quotes.

Opening the Database after Incomplete Media Recovery

Before we tell you how to do this, we need to go over some pseudo-legal stuff. The command we are about to show you must **never be run against any database (other than your practice database) without speaking with Oracle worldwide customer support**. Issuing this command against a database after incomplete media recovery will allow you to open the database but **the backup you recovered from will not be usable**. If you attempt a recovery again using the same image backup, you will receive the following error:

```
ORA-00283: Recovery session canceled due to errors
ORA-01190: control file or data file 1 is...RESETLOGS
ORA-01110: data file 1: 'd:\orant\arc\dbs1book.dbf'
SVRMGR>
```

The problem is that Oracle knows when the database was last opened with the resetlogs option, and any backups written before that time are unusable. We cannot stress this enough. The command alter database open resetlogs; is used to get a database open, but it can be very dangerous.

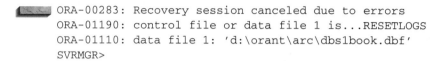

VIP

Do not use the command alter database open resetlogs; without speaking with Oracle worldwide customer support FIRST!

You have been warned.

A Complete Backup Plan

We now present a sample backup plan, using a combination of export and image backup. The database is running in ARCHIVELOG mode and the window of opportunity is about two hours.

Even though the makeup of the database is fairly static, we use the following SQL and PL/SQL script to write the program to do the hot backup (the bolded text may have to be changed if your operating system is other than Windows NT):

```
set serveroutput on size 100000
set echo off feed off pages 0
spool hot.backup
select 'File created '||to_char(sysdate,'dd-Mon-yy hh24:mm:ss')
  from dual;
prompt
begin
  declare
    target_dir varchar2(100) := 'g:\oracle\backups';
```

```
    source_file varchar2(100);
    ts_name varchar2(100);
    prev_ts_name varchar2(100);
    cursor mycur is
      select file_name,lower(tablespace_name)
        from sys.dba_data_files
       where instr(file_name,'temp') = 0
       order by 2;
  begin
    prev_ts_name := 'X';
    open mycur;
    fetch mycur into source_file,ts_name;
    while mycur%found loop
      if ts_name <> prev_ts_name then
         dbms_output.put_line ('#######################');
         dbms_output.put_line ('# Tablespace '||ts_name||'. . .');
         dbms_output.put_line ('#######################');
         dbms_output.put_line ('sqlplus '||
         '@d:\orant\sysman\start.sql '||
                                ts_name);
      end if;
      dbms_output.put_line ('copy '||source_file||' '||target_dir);
      prev_ts_name := ts_name;
      fetch mycur into source_file,ts_name;
      if ts_name <> prev_ts_name then
         dbms_output.put_line ('sqlplus '||
         '@d:\orant\sysman\end.sql '||
                                prev_ts_name);
      end if;
    end loop;
    dbms_output.put_line ('sqlplus @d:\orant\sysman\end.sql '||
                              prev_ts_name);
  end;
end;
/
```

The output from this PL/SQL code resembles the following:

```
File created 19-May-99 11:05:20
#######################
# Tablespace rollback_data. . .
#######################
sqlplus @d:\orant\sysman\start.sql rollback_data
copy D:\ORANT\DATABASE\RBS1ORCL.ORA g:\oracle\backups
```

```
sqlplus @d:\orant\sysman\end.sql rollback_data
#######################
# Tablespace system. . .
#######################
sqlplus @d:\orant\sysman\start.sql system
copy D:\ORANT\DATABASE\SYS1ORCL.ORA g:\oracle\backups
sqlplus @d:\orant\sysman\end.sql system
#######################
# Tablespace temporary_data. . .
#######################
sqlplus @d:\orant\sysman\start.sql temporary_data
copy D:\ORANT\DATABASE\TMP1ORCL.ORA g:\oracle\backups
sqlplus @d:\orant\sysman\end.sql temporary_data
#######################
# Tablespace user_data. . .
#######################
sqlplus @d:\orant\sysman\start.sql user_data
copy D:\ORANT\DATABASE\USR1ORCL.ORA g:\oracle\backups
sqlplus @d:\orant\sysman\end.sql user_data
```

The program **start.sql** referenced in this listing puts a tablespace in backup mode. It contains the code:

```
alter tablespace &1 begin backup;
exit
```

The program **end.sql** takes a tablespace out of backup mode. It contains the code:

```
alter tablespace &1 end backup;
exit
```

NOTE
*The &1 text in start.sql and end.sql allow passing of a parameter to each program. Since you place a tablespace name after **alter tablespace**, the &1 would translate to a tablespace name.*

In the "Substitution Variables in SQL*Plus" section of Chapter 12, we showed how the & character is used. By placing the &1 substitution variable in a SQL*Plus program, you can pass a value to a program. Thus, the command sqlplus @start system is expanded into the following:

```
SQL> alter tablespace &1 begin backup;
old    1: alter tablespace &1 begin backup;
new    1: alter tablespace system begin backup;
SQL>
```

Notice how the text system from the command sqlplus @start system is accepted into the program, and replaces the substitution variable &1.

The complete backup plan we have presented here is to be used as a starting point. As you can see by examining Table 16-7, export, import, and hot backups play a role when developing a full backup strategy. Backup and recovery are two of the most popular topics at Oracle technical

	Component	Time	Notes
1	Export	2:00 a.m.	Full database export from the SYSTEM account.
2	Hot backup	3:30 a.m.	Same as the 12:05 p.m. and 8:00 p.m. backups, except all archived redo logs are moved to another directory.
3	Tape copy	5:00 a.m.	Image backup is written to tape as well as the directory to which the archived redo logs were moved at 3:30 a.m.
4	Control file	6:30 a.m.,	Control file contents are written to a trace file using the command **alter system backup controlfile to trace;**.
5	Export	7:30 a.m.	Full database export with **rows=n compress=n** whose output can be used to create the structure of the database (i.e., the tablespaces, rollback segments, users, etc.).
6	Hot backup	12:05 p.m.	All tablespaces in the database except temp and ones containing objects protected by the nightly export.
7	Hot backup	8:00 p.m.	Same as 12:05 p.m. hot backup.

TABLE 16-7. *Full Backup Procedures*

conferences. Users and Oracle Corporation personnel present papers and lead workshops on these ever-so-important topics.

What's Next

Perhaps you have noticed the amount of ground we have covered in this chapter. We believe that with guidance you can start doing some remarkably intense work with Oracle from day one as a DBA. In the next chapter, we will discuss tuning the Oracle database to help you get maximum performance from this robust software.

CHAPTER
17

Database Tuning

his chapter deals with tuning your database, not your applications. We will discuss the major items that will allow you, as a database administrator, to get an extra 20 to 30 percent throughput from your Oracle-based systems. We do touch briefly on the cost-based approach to SQL statement processing as it can have a profound effect on how your database performs.

But first, let's discuss what database tuning cannot do. It is not a substitute for good application design—remember that old saying, "Garbage in leads to garbage out." A system that is designed badly will perform badly. The bottom line: good performance out of your database starts with good application design. With this in mind, we will take a look at the key steps you can take to get that extra boost of performance from your system.

In this chapter we will cover the following subjects:

- The initialization parameter file init.ora

- Which key initialization file settings to change

- How to determine current initialization parameter file settings

- How to change the current initialization file settings

- The key input/output stream

- Key tablespaces and their contents

- How indexes work

Terminology

The following definitions will arm you with the technical jargon to make it through this chapter:

- A *database administrator*, or DBA, is responsible for the technical management of a database, including installation, performance tuning, and computer resource management. The DBA classically serves as an advisor on application design to maximize system throughput.

- The *initialization parameter file* (commonly called init.ora) is read by Oracle when starting the database; its values help determine resource utilization. The best analogy to this is your win.ini file in Windows or your autoexec.bat file when you boot your PC.

- A *database instance* is an amount of main memory and a set of support processes required to access an Oracle database.

- *sqldba* is a tool used by database administrators to go about their day-to-day work with an Oracle database. Starting with version 7.3, sqldba has been replaced by line-mode Server Manager. For readers using Oracle 7.2 or earlier, sqldba is featured in Appendix A of this work.

- A *cache* is a segment of computer memory allocated to holding specific pieces of information. For example, while Oracle operates, it maintains a data cache that contains most recently read data.

- A *table* is defined in Oracle's data dictionary, and it groups rows of information together in the database. A list of your fellow workers' names, numbers, and hire dates is an example of a table.

- An *index* is a structure Oracle uses to permit rapid access to your tables.

Initialization Parameter (init.ora) File

There are many tools available to you for tuning the database; the initialization parameter file is a good place to start. At startup, every database reads its initialization parameter to configure itself. Think of this file as the key to a lock. Before you can enter the room, you must first use the key. Before a database instance can start up, it must read the initialization parameter file. There are over 100 different changeable entries, all affecting how your database and processes that run against your database work. By making changes to this file, you will change the way your database uses and allocates resources.

VIP
All changes you make to the initialization parameter file only take effect the next time the database is started.

Let's investigate working with entries in the initialization parameter file; first we look at the types of entries in the initialization parameter file, then working with those entries using Oracle Enterprise Manager/Instance Manager with Oracle8 on Windows NT. Next, we look at doing the same work with Server Manager and a simple text editor.

VIP
Regardless of which way you decide to do it, it is wise to note previous values before making changes in case the new parameter values have a negative rather than a positive effect on performance tuning.

Types of Entries in the Initialization Parameter File

The initialization parameter file is like any other text file on your computer—pick your favorite editor and make the changes. The order of the entries within the initialization parameter file does not matter.

VIP
If you do not have an entry listed in your initialization parameter file, Oracle configures the missing value to a default setting.

There are three types of initialization parameter file entries:

■ **Strings:** A number of parameters are enclosed in single quotes, some in double quotes, and some need not be in any quotes. Most of the string parameter values you enter will need no quotes. If one requires quotes of either type and you leave them out, Oracle will inform you when you start the database.

■ **Integer:** Some parameters are looking for an integer. There are no quotes.

■ **Boolean:** Some parameters are looking for the value TRUE or FALSE with no quotes.

Oracle8 Instance Manager—Viewing Settings

Viewing of settings can be done from the Oracle8 Instance Manager. Invoke the Instance Manager by double-clicking on the NT Instance Manager shortcut in your Oracle8 for Windows NT folder. When presented with the Instance Manager main console, click on the Initialization Parameters folder to display the screen shown in Figure 17-1.

Notice how there are two property sheets underneath this folder.

1. Basic Tuning parameters are normally standard between different instances of the Oracle8 database. The Running Value shows the current setting.

2. Instance Specific parameters are specific to the instance being viewed. The control_files entry displaying the text "D:\ORANT\DATABASE\ctlorcl..." and the db_name parameter displaying the value "oracle" are examples of this type of entry. For different instances, these values would most likely be different, though not necessarily always.

Server Manager—Viewing Settings

Before you begin making changes to the initialization parameter file, it is important you know how the parameters are currently set. The simplest way to see how the entries are set is to use Server Manager. Using Oracle8 for Windows NT and Server Manager, enter the command **svrmgr30** to begin. Once in Server Manager, issue the command **connect internal** followed by the secure database password you selected when installing Oracle8. Oracle responds with the following feedback:

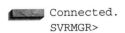
```
Connected.
SVRMGR>
```

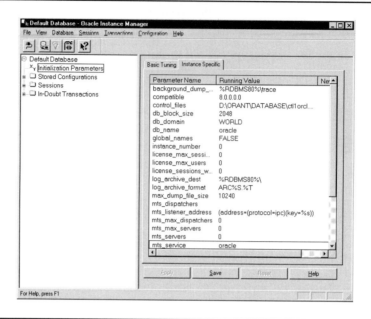

FIGURE 17-1. *Initialization parameter display*

Viewing All Parameter Values

To view all the parameters, enter the command **show parameters**. This displays all the possible entries and values in the initialization parameter file. The parameters are listed in alphabetical order, and the top of the output resembles the following:

```
NAME                          TYPE              VALUE
--------------------------    ---------------   ------------------
audit_trail                   string            NONE
background_dump_dest          string            %RDBMS80%\trace
checkpoint_process            boolean           FALSE
cleanup_rollback_entries      integer           20
commit_point_strength         integer           1
```

Viewing Some of the Parameter Values

Often, you are only interested in a particular type of parameter. For example, you might be interested in all the parameters that contain the word "buffer." Once connected to the instance in Server Manager, enter **show parameters**, followed by another word. Oracle will do a character match on the word. For example, to see all the parameters that contain the word "buffer", you type the command **show parameters buffer** and receive output similar to the following:

```
NAME                          TYPE              VALUE
----------------------------  ----------------  ------------------
db_block_buffers              integer           400
log_archive_buffer_size       integer           127
log_archive_buffers           integer           4
log_buffer                    integer           65596
```

Initialization Parameter File—What to Change

In this section, we list the key parameters you should consider tweaking. In our experience, these are the parameters that need changing 99 percent of the time.

db_block_buffers

This is your data cache. Before any process can look at, inspect, correct, or delete a piece of data, it must first reside in this data cache. The higher the value of the cache, the more data blocks Oracle is able to hold in memory. The lower the value, the fewer data blocks it can hold. If the data is not in memory, Oracle issues the needed I/O requests to obtain the data. I/O is one of the slowest operations a computer can do.

To summarize, the larger the number you choose for db_block_buffers, the larger your data cache. A large data cache is a very desirable situation. In fact, in a perfect world, you might want to make your db_block_buffers large enough to hold your entire database. In this situation, the need to go to the actual disk might be eliminated.

VIP
Set the db_block_buffers as high as possible for your operating environment in order to hold as much data in memory as possible.

This parameter is a memory hog. It very quickly increases the size of the SGA. Do not allow the SGA to go beyond 50 percent of the available memory of the computer.

shared_pool_size

This is your program cache and data dictionary cache. The data dictionary is information that Oracle needs to manage itself. For example, when a user logs onto the database, a number of data dictionary tables are referenced to determine the validity of the user's request to log on. Before that user can look at a row of information, a number of data dictionary tables are referenced to determine that database user's privileges. The program cache is where Oracle stores programs that work with the database. For example, every SQL statement you run in SQL*Plus must be placed into the program cache before it can be executed.

The larger the cache, the more likely your statement will be found in memory. The smaller the cache, the more often Oracle has to place the program into memory. A program cannot make requests from the database until it has been placed into this cache.

VIP

Set the shared_pool_size as high as possible. It is very desirable for performance reasons to have a program cache that is very large.

Again, this parameter is a memory hog. It very quickly increases the size of the SGA. Do not allow the SGA to go beyond 50 percent of the available memory of the computer.

sort_area_size

This is the parameter that controls the allocation of chunks of memory for sorting activities. SQL statements that include the **order by** and **group by** clauses generate sort activity. In addition, activities like **create index** also generate sort activity.

When the Oracle database cannot acquire enough memory to complete the sort, it completes the process on disk. An inadequate value for this parameter causes excessive sorts on disk (disk access is very slow compared to memory access). It has been our experience that the default setting is too low. We typically start off by doubling it.

VIP

*Try doubling your sort_area_size parameter
value. The default value is much too small.*

The value coded for sort_area_size is allocated on a per-user basis. It does not take effect until you restart the database.

checkpoint_process

A checkpoint is an event that happens periodically when the Oracle database writes information from its buffers in memory to the appropriate database files. Refer to the discussion on checkpoints in the "Database Support Processes" section of Chapter 3 for more information. When this event happens, an area in the datafiles is updated to record the event. The writing of this information is done by the log writer (lgwr) or a dedicated checkpoint (ckpt) process.

If the initialization parameter file parameter checkpoint_process is set to FALSE, the checkpoint event is done by the log writer. On systems with a heavy transaction load, having the log writer have the additional job of checkpointing the database may slow down or halt processing momentarily. Setting the checkpoint_process to TRUE instructs Oracle to activate an additional process whose sole responsibility is to handle checkpoints. It's like being given an additional set of hands. In our experience, there is no down side to activating the checkpoint_process.

VIP

*Activate the checkpoint_process by setting its
initialization parameter file value to TRUE.*

processes

This parameter defines the maximum number of processes that can simultaneously connect to an Oracle database. The default value of 50 is only acceptable for a very small system. Keep in mind that the Oracle background processes are included in this number. In addition, if an application spawns processes recursively, all the spawned processes count toward this number.

The only reason you keep this value low is to limit the number of users for a business reason or because of hardware/software capacity issues. Otherwise, it is highly recommended that you overestimate this value.

NOTE

We recommend setting this parameter to 200 when Oracle8 is installed. Our experience shows this value is more than necessary for most implementations.

open_cursors

This parameter is the maximum number of cursors a user can have open at a time. Think of a cursor as a chunk of memory that Oracle allocates to the user process for SQL statements. The default value for this is much too small. When you run out of cursors, your application stops. We recommend setting this value to 250 to start with.

VIP

Set this value very high to start. If it is set too low, your application will come to a stop.

db_writers

This parameter controls the number of processes that write information to the database concurrently. On many UNIX platforms, you have the option of having multiple database writers. This greatly improves your ability to write information to the database. If you are on an operating system that supports additional database writers, the first thing you should do is increase the number of database writers that are activated. Many DBAs are under the misconception that this is limited by the number of CPUs; this is not true. In fact, we recommend you set db_writers to two per datafile.

VIP
If you are on an operating system that supports additional database writers, the first thing you should do is increase the number of database writers.

timed_statistics

This parameter tells the database to record additional information about itself as it is running. This is quite useful information in a test environment; in a production environment, we recommend you turn it off. Since this is additional overhead, it has a performance impact on your system.

optimizer_mode

This parameter has a major impact on how your database chooses to execute SQL statements. You have four possible choices for this parameter:

- **FULL_ROWS or ALL_ROWS:** These two modes instruct Oracle to use the cost-based optimizer (*CBO*) approach (discussed as well in the "Cost-Based Approach" section of Chapter 13). With this setting, Oracle takes into account table sizes when you issue SQL statements. For example, your database knows that your customer table has 10,000 rows of information and your phone_type table has three rows. It takes this into account when executing SQL statements.

- **RULE:** This is the way Oracle databases have traditionally determined how SQL statements would execute. There is a weighting system that Oracle uses to determine how a SQL statement will execute. For example, a table that contains an index will be favored over a table that has no indexes.

- **CHOOSE:** This is the default setting. This tells the database to use the cost-based optimization approach when you have the necessary information. Without that information, use the rule-based method.

WHAT APPROACH TO USE FOR EXISTING SYSTEMS   If not already using the cost-based optimizer approach with your Oracle systems, we recommend looking at its performance after implementing a statistic collection system similar to one we discussed in the "Methodology for Statistic Collection" section of Chapter 13. Many systems that have been around since Oracle version 5 and 6 perform well with the rule-based optimization. It can prove disastrous to suddenly switch the optimization approach without adequate preparation.

VIP
For systems that were designed and tuned using the rule-based approach, set **optimizer_mode=rule** *in your initialization parameter file. Gather statistics for the database objects and benchmark the performance of CBO before switching.*

WHAT APPROACH TO USE FOR NEW SYSTEMS   We unequivocally recommend using the cost-based approach with new system development. CBO is sensitive to the row counts in application tables, and the distribution of column values in those tables; inspect the information in Table 17-1 to see the access path used by Oracle and CBO to process a query against the last_name (an indexed column) in a 2,450,000-row table.

When tuning the performance of the applications as well as the instance, using CBO can improve throughput of online and reporting systems based on its flexible nature of processing SQL statements. The first word (cost) in the name of this optimization approach is key to

Selection Criterion	Qualifying Rows	% Qualifying	Access Path
last_name like 'J%'	187,501	7.65	full table scan
last_name like 'JO%'	87,232	3.56	index range scan
last_name like 'JOR%'	19,231	0.78	index range scan
last_name = 'JORDAN'	4,891	0.19	index range scan

TABLE 17-1.   *Comparison of Percentage of Qualifying Rows and Access Path*

understanding why Oracle sometimes performs a full table scan and other times decides to do an index lookup, then go fetch the qualifying rows' information.

VIP
After weighing the cost of alternative access paths, the cost-based optimizer will choose a path that costs the least, where cost is a measurement of resource consumption.

Changing Parameter Values in Oracle8 Instance Manager

To change a parameter value, double-click on the appropriate property sheet to bring up the dialog box shown in Figure 17-2.

The value in effect for shared_pool_size is now 6500000, and we are going to change it to 8000000. When the change has been made, the dialog box is dismissed, and the Instance Manager displays the updated information in the New Value section of the Basic Tuning property sheet.

NOTE
There may be operating system specific maximums that can be set for certain parameters. Consult documents related to your specific operating system for details.

Edit Initialization Parameter	✕

Name:	shared_pool_size
Current Value:	6500000
New Value:	

| OK | Cancel | Help |

FIGURE 17-2. *Changing a parameter value in the Instance Manager*

Changing Entries Using a Text Editor

With this in mind, we now give you an example of each type of entry. We include db_block_buffers (integer type), db_name (string type), and checkpoint_process (boolean type):

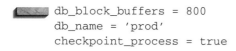

```
db_block_buffers = 800
db_name = 'prod'
checkpoint_process = true
```

It all sounds so simple. Take your favorite editor, change the entry, and you are on your way. Well, almost. Here are the pitfalls:

- **Fat fingers (also called typos):** If you make one, the entire initialization parameter file is rejected. In other words, your database won't start until the typo is corrected.

- **Domino effect:** In some situations, a change to one parameter affects other parameters.

VIP

Changing parameter values in the initialization parameter file is no trivial exercise. Look at the effect changes may have on other parameters, and make changes with caution.

With all this in mind, one word describes how you should proceed: s l o w l y. Tuning a database takes time. At first, it is best if you make one change at a time. Edit the file, then try to start the database. This way, if you have made a typo, you at least know which entry is causing the database not to start. As you will see, Oracle is not always very gracious in telling you where the problem is. Use Server Manager and issue the **show parameters** command to see what changes have occurred. Try to develop your own checklist to help you determine if your changes are improving performance. We refer you to *Tuning Oracle* by Corey, Abbey, and Dechichio (Osborne McGraw-Hill/Oracle Press, 1995) for details on how to tune your database.

Viewing the Current Size of the SGA

As you make changes to the initialization parameter file, the changes affect how the database uses resources. One of the things you realize early on in the tuning process is that tuning is all about trade-offs. The more memory Oracle uses, the less memory is available for other processes. Many of the changes to the initialization parameter file affect the size of the SGA and how much memory the current database needs to operate. The command **show sga** tells you the current allocation of memory for the database:

```
Total System Global Area      4817701 bytes
Fixed Size                      28376 bytes
Variable Size                 3904532 bytes
Database Buffers               819200 bytes
Redo Buffers                    65596 bytes
```

VIP

The Oracle database is one of many processes that must live, share, and breathe all available resources. With this in mind, the SGA should never take over 50 percent of the available memory of the computer.

Spooling Results

Many times you will find it helpful to spool the results of your Server Manager session. We find it especially helpful to capture the output of the **show parameters** command; you can then use this output for your first attempt at customizing an initialization parameter file. By using the captured output as a starting point, you eliminate "fat fingers" (typos).

VIP

A misspelled entry in the initialization parameter file will prevent the database from starting up.

To start recording your actions while in Server Manager, do the following:

1. Enter the command **spool file_name** where the filename conforms to the rules of your computer. Oracle redisplays the SVRMGR> prompt after the spool file is opened.

2. Go about your job in Server Manager, then close the file by entering the **spool off** command and Oracle closes the output file and redisplays the Server Manager prompt.

This the output from the **show sga** command spooled to "example.log":

```
SVRMGR> show sga
Total System Global Area          4767460 bytes
               Fixed Size           36432 bytes
            Variable Size         3846292 bytes
         Database Buffers          819200 bytes
             Redo Buffers           65536 bytes
SVRMGR> spool off
```

I/O Stream

What is a database? A database is a place where information is organized, received, and dispensed. A disk drive is the physical location where a database holds information. To take this one step further, the major task of a database is to read and write data to the disks. The problem you face is that I/O (input/output) from a disk drive is slow. In fact, it is one of the slowest operations a computer can do. Even though CPUs keep getting faster and faster by comparison, I/O has not kept up the pace. Let's now take a look at some things you can do to minimize your I/O.

Tables and Indexes

All the data you place in an Oracle database is stored in an object called a table. Whenever a request is made to the database to read or write information, a record is read from a table or inserted into a table. There is another database object called an index (we also discuss indexes in the "Data and Index Tablespaces" section of Chapter 3). As we explained earlier, an index is used to speed up access to particular columns of information in a table. Think of an index as a minitable. For example, let's say you create an index on the customer table on the column last_name. There are two major reasons why an index access is faster:

- When you read a record from a table, you must read in every column of information associated with that table. If you had a very large customer table with 300 fields associated with it, even though you just want the last_name column, you are forced into the additional overhead of reading every column of the table. For example, a concatenated index on last_name, first_name only contains two columns. It is faster to read two columns than 300 columns.

- Indexes are in presorted order. While data in an Oracle table is stored in the order it was loaded, data in an Oracle index is stored in a sorted order. This is part of the requirement of an index.

There are two major things you can do to improve your database's ability to access data. The first is to properly index your tables. In the long run, this will have the greatest impact on performance. The second is to make sure your tables and indexes are stored on separate physical devices. We recommend you create a separate tablespace to hold tables. In addition, you should create another tablespace to hold indexes.

VIP

Put tables on a separate disk from their indexes.

This point is important even if you have a limited number of disks at your disposal (i.e., one to three). Separating tables from their indexes allows for quicker access, since reading and writing to the index and the table may happen simultaneously.

VIP

Large tables in your database should have at least one index on them.

When we say "large," we mean tables with anything over 1,000 rows; our experience dictates that over 90 percent of the tables in an Oracle database are indexed.

VIP
*Create separate tablespaces to hold data
and indexes.*

System Tables

Before an Oracle application can even look at a table or its contents, it must first talk to the Oracle data dictionary. The data dictionary contains information as to what is stored in the database, where it is stored, and who has the privilege to look at it. The tables and database objects that make up the Oracle data dictionary are owned by a database user called SYS. They are stored in a tablespace called system. This is a major I/O stream for the database. In a perfect world, you would place the system tablespace on its own disk drive.

VIP
*Do not allow other users to place database
objects in the system tablespace.*

Temporary Segments

Temporary segments are objects the database periodically creates to help it finish transactions. For example, when you issue a SQL statement with a **group by** clause, the database will likely create some temporary objects to help it in its work. It is very important that you keep temporary objects in their own tablespace. By doing so, you will eliminate the performance problems associated with having temporary segments mixed with other database objects.

VIP
*Create a separate tablespace to hold
temporary segments.*

Rollback Segments

A rollback segment is a database object that holds information when a user does an **insert**, **update**, or **delete**. This rollback information is recorded so that the database can undo or rollback the transaction in the case of failure. Since all transactions are not equal in size, these rollback segments have a tendency to grow and shrink.

VIP
Create a separate tablespace for your rollback segments.

Online Redo Logs

The online redo logs are your transaction logs. Every action that occurs in an Oracle database is recorded into these special files called online redo logs (discussed as well in the "Redo Logs—The Transaction Log" section of Chapter 3).

VIP
Since I/O can be one of the slowest operations, place online redo logs on a separate disk.

Summary

I/O is one of the slowest operations a computer can do. However, it is also one of the most important operations. In a perfect world, you would place every tablespace in a database on a separate disk drive. We don't live in a perfect world, but you should still create these separate tablespaces, even if they are on the same disk. Then, utilizing the tools available to you within Oracle and the operating system, balance the I/O load as best you can. If, over time, you are able to obtain additional disk drives, then you are ready for them.

What's Next

Tuning is a double-edged sword. Be careful how you handle it. Tuning is about choices. Each choice has its good points and its bad points. If you increase db_block_buffers to expand the data cache, then you are able to hold more data in memory. On the other hand, the system now has less free memory to do its own work. So, as you go down the tuning path, you will constantly have forks in the road to consider.

We have introduced you to the two major areas of database tuning: the initialization parameter file and tuning the I/O stream. We talked about the most common items to change in the initialization parameter file. In the "I/O Stream" section, we stressed the fact that I/O is slow. We encouraged you to look closely at indexes and a standard strategy for laying out your database. Now it's up to you. Tune slowly. The tortoise wins this race every time.

Our next chapter, "Advanced DBA," will prove helpful to your expanding knowledge of the Oracle database. We guide you through some advanced tasks you will be responsible for as a DBA and show you how to . . . better still, keep reading!

CHAPTER
18

Advanced DBA

erhaps, up until now, you have been quite content with not being a DBA. Well, it looks like somebody stole the DBA and, guess what, you're the new DBA! In Chapter 14, we pointed you in the right direction. We showed you how to do some DBA stuff you will be asked to do from day one (if not sooner). We discussed and walked you through how to start the database, shut down the database, create a tablespace to hold Oracle data, add more space to a tablespace, grant access to a user, and revoke access from a user.

Database administration is pretty much the same regardless of the hardware you are using—Windows NT on a Pentium, an Amdahl mainframe, or a VAX. Oracle releases port-specific documentation that highlights the differences you can expect to run across on different hardware platforms. These manuals are referred to as the port-specific System Release Bulletin (SRB) and Installation and Configuration Guide (ICG). There is a wealth of information on everything discussed in this chapter in the Oracle8 Server Administrator's Guide. Database installation and tuning are two DBA responsibilities that are not discussed in this chapter; they are highlighted in Chapter 5 and Chapter 17. By the end of this chapter, you will know more terminology as well as some advanced details on how to do the following:

- Start up the database

- Perform additional user management

- Perform additional tablespace management

- Manage redo log file groups

- Add control files

- Drop control files

- Find your way around the data dictionary

- Classify error messages

- Work with Oracle Corporation's Worldwide Customer Support

In Chapter 14, we showed you how to use Server Manager and Enterprise Manager to perform the basic DBA activities; this chapter uses line-mode Server Manager for the startup section, then Enterprise Manager for all the hands-on work.

NOTE
Line-mode Server Manager is on the Oracle8 distribution medium, as it has been since release 7.1.

Terminology

The following definitions will arm you with the technical jargon you need to make it through this chapter:

■ The *archiving status* of the database controls what Oracle does with redo log files before it reuses them. When this status is ARCHIVELOG, Oracle automatically copies a redo log file to a destination you specify before it is reused. When the status is NOARCHIVELOG, Oracle does not save a copy of each redo log file before it is reused. This is discussed in more detail in Chapter 16.

■ A tablespace is *online* when it is accessible to all users and therefore available for storage of new objects, and for querying and modifying data.

■ The *system tablespace* holds all the data dictionary information required to access the database. It must be online and accessible when the database is open.

■ A tablespace is *offline* when its data is unavailable for any access. An offline tablespace must be brought back online before users may access it again.

■ *Backup* is a procedure that makes a secondary copy of Oracle data (usually on tape) and helps provide protection against hardware, software, or user errors; backup minimizes data loss if and when problems arise.

■ *Recovery* is a procedure whereby data is read from a backup in an effort to restore the database to a past or current point in time.

■ *Redo logs* are written by Oracle and contain a record of all transactions against a database. They are written automatically as Oracle operates.

- The *active redo log group* is the group to which Oracle is currently writing information. All members of the active group are written to simultaneously.

- *Rollback* is the event that Oracle performs when, for an assortment of reasons, a transaction is not completed. The rollback restores the data to the state it was in before the transaction started.

- A *rollback segment* is a portion of a tablespace that contains undo information for each transaction in the database; this undo information is kept until a transaction is committed or rolled back.

- An *extent* is a chunk of space in a datafile of an Oracle database; it is measured in bytes, kilobytes (1,024 bytes), or megabytes (1,048,576 bytes). Extents are allocated based on keywords used when objects (e.g., tables, rollback segments) are created.

- A database is *up* when it has been opened and is accessible to users. A database is *down* when it has been closed and is inaccessible to users.

Startup Options

Most of the time, when you start up your database, you simply start Server Manager, connect to the database, and type **startup** to get things going. In this section, we will discuss additional startup options, using these options in sqldba, and when you may need or want to use one of these options.

Startup Normal

This is the default startup mode (you almost always omit the word "normal"). We showed you how to start up the database in Chapter 14. Use the output in the next listing as a reference point for the following discussion on startup options.

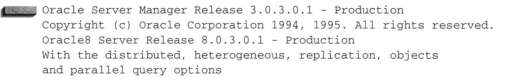

```
Oracle Server Manager Release 3.0.3.0.1 - Production
Copyright (c) Oracle Corporation 1994, 1995. All rights reserved.
Oracle8 Server Release 8.0.3.0.1 - Production
With the distributed, heterogeneous, replication, objects
and parallel query options
```

```
PL/SQL Release 3.0.3.0.1 - Production
SVRMGR> connect internal
Password:
Connected.
SVRMGR> startup
ORACLE instance started.
Total System Global Area        8030448 bytes
Fixed Size                        44584 bytes
Variable Size                   7510728 bytes
Database Buffers                 409600 bytes
Redo Buffers                      65536 bytes
Database mounted.
Database opened.
SVRMGR>
```

Startup Mount

This mode is used to change the archiving status of the database or perform recovery. The database is not open, and therefore access by users is not permitted. After starting Server Manager, do the following:

1. Enter **connect internal**.

2. Enter the secure database password **oracle**.

3. Enter **startup mount**, and receive feedback from Oracle, as shown in the next listing. Notice that there is no message about opening the database after it is mounted.

```
ORACLE instance started.
Total System Global Area        8030448 bytes
Fixed Size                        44584 bytes
Variable Size                   7510728 bytes
Database Buffers                 409600 bytes
Redo Buffers                      65536 bytes
Database mounted.
SVRMGR>
```

4. Enter **exit** to leave Server Manager.

The database is left in a mounted condition; users are not able to log on in this state.

Startup Nomount

This mode is used to recreate a control file (discussed in the "Control File Responsibilities" section of this chapter) or recreate the database from scratch. The database is not open, and therefore access by users is not permitted. After starting Server Manager, do the following:

1. Enter **connect internal**.

2. Enter the secure database password **oracle**.

3. Enter **startup nomount**, and receive feedback from Oracle, as shown in the next listing.

```
ORACLE instance started.
Total System Global Area        8030448 bytes
Fixed Size                        44584 bytes
Variable Size                   7510728 bytes
Database Buffers                 409600 bytes
Redo Buffers                      65536 bytes
SVRMGR>
```

4. Enter **exit** to leave Server Manager.

The response from Oracle is similar to when the database is started and mounted, except the database mounted and database opened messages are suppressed.

Startup Restrict

This mode is used to start up the database, but access is restricted to a privileged set of users that you have defined. The output from this command is the same as when the database is started up in non-restricted mode. The database is open, but if nonprivileged users attempt to log on, they will obtain the following error message:

```
SQL*Plus: Release 4.0.3.1.1 - Production on Tue Dec 18 22:14:09 1999
Copyright (c) Oracle Corporation 1979, 1996.  All rights reserved.
Enter password:
ERROR: ORA-01035: ORACLE only available to users with RESTRICTED SESSION privileges
Enter user-name:
```

Let's discuss changing the database access mode from restricted to unrestricted. The first is done with the database open, the other by restarting the database.

Change Status with Database Open

After starting Server Manager, do the following:

1. Enter **connect internal**.

2. Enter the secure database password **oracle**.

3. Enter **alter system disable restricted session;** and receive feedback from Oracle, as shown in the next listing.

```
SVRMGR> alter system disable restricted session;
Statement processed.
SVRMGR>
```

4. Enter **exit** to leave Server Manager.

When this is done, the database is running in unrestricted access mode and users will be able to log on once more.

Change Status by Restarting the Database

After starting Server Manager, do the following:

1. Enter **connect internal**.

2. Enter the secure database password **oracle**.

3. Enter **startup**.

4. Enter **exit** to leave Server Manager.

Regardless of the method you choose, the database will be open and ready for access by all once the steps are completed.

Startup Force

This option is used in the rare situation when you are unable to shut down a database. It shuts the database, then starts it with no options; the startup operation is the same as having issued the **startup** command alone. This is accomplished by starting Server Manager and doing the following:

1. Enter **connect internal**.

2. Enter the secure database password **oracle**.

3. Enter **startup force** and receive feedback from Oracle, as shown in the next listing.

```
SVRMGR> startup force
ORACLE instance started.
Total System Global Area      8030448 bytes
Fixed Size                      44584 bytes
Variable Size                 7510728 bytes
Database Buffers               409600 bytes
Redo Buffers                    65536 bytes
Database mounted.
Database opened.
```

4. Enter **exit** to leave Server Manager.

When this operation is complete, your database will be open and accessible to the user community.

Startup pfile

This option with the startup command does not affect the mode of the database operation; it defines the name and location of the initialization parameter file (pfile). As we have discussed elsewhere, the initialization parameter file is read by Oracle as it opens a database. Oracle expects the default initialization parameter file to be in a location and called a name that is dependent on the hardware on which the database operates. In Oracle8 for NT, for example, Oracle builds the default initialization parameter filename using the environment variable "%RDBMS80% and appends the text "initorcl.ora". If you wish to start your database using an initialization parameter file other than the default, follow these steps after starting Server Manager:

1. Enter **connect internal**.

2. Enter the secure database password **oracle**.

3. Enter **startup pfile=*parameter_file_name*** and receive feedback from Oracle as shown in the next listing.

```
SVRMGR> startup pfile=c:\orant\database\initorcl.ora
ORACLE instance started.
Total System Global Area        8030448 bytes
Fixed Size                        44584 bytes
Variable Size                   7510728 bytes
Database Buffers                 409600 bytes
Redo Buffers                      65536 bytes
Database mounted.
Database opened.
SVRMGR>
```

NOTE
Fill in the appropriate parameter file name with the pfile option, replacing the bold and italicized text after the "=" sign.

4. Enter **exit** to leave Server Manager.

From time to time, you may use the pfile option to start your database with some initialization parameter file values different than usual. For example, when running a large data load, you may wish to instruct Oracle to allocate much more memory for sorting than you normally request.

NOTE
If you have started your database using the pfile option, remind yourself to shut it down and use the regular initialization parameter file when the job completes.

Nothing will go wrong if you leave your database running with an initialization parameter file other than the file you normally use.

VIP
More than 99 percent of the time, you will start up a database with no options.

Operation Modes

Table 18-1 summarizes the operating modes and indicates what can be accomplished with the database in each mode—open, mount, nomount, and closed. If you attempt to issue a SQL command and the database mode of operation does not support the command, Oracle will inform you.

Shutdown Options

When an Oracle database is not running, we refer to it as down. You shut down the database for a number of reasons. Some installations bring the database down for backups. Certain Oracle software requires that Oracle be shut down while you are running the upgrade or installation session. In Chapter 14, we talked about shutdown normal, immediate, and abort (a discussion of shutdown is not complete without mentioning these two extra options). There is nothing more frustrating than being told to shut down your database with the **shutdown** command only to find it does not work!

Mode	Activities That Can Be Accomplished
closed	Add, drop, or move a control file (with modifications made in the initialization parameter file to reflect the changes)
	Backup the database—all datafiles, online redo logs, and control files
nomount	Create a database
	Create a control file
mount	Perform database, datafile, or tablespace recovery
	Rename any database file
	Change redo log archival mode (ARCHIVELOG or NOARCHIVELOG)
	Add, drop, or rename redo log groups or redo log file members
open	All users can access the database and go about their normal business
	Export full database, one or more users, or specific database objects
	Import full database, one or more users, or specific database objects

TABLE 18-1. *Tasks with the Database in Each Mode*

VIP
*Refer to the section on line-mode sqldba in Chapter 14, in which we discuss shutdown—there is some **very** important and useful information there.*

VIP
You will use shutdown immediate more than 90 percent of the time.

As a last resort, you may have to use the **shutdown abort** command. Sometimes, there are situations when nothing else works, and you have no choice.

CAUTION
If you shut down a database with the abort option, start it up immediately, then do a normal shutdown. Experience dictates this is the best way to care for a database shut down with this abort option.

Additional User Management Responsibilities

Coupled with the tasks discussed in Chapter 14, the exercises we highlight in this section will round out your user management skills. By the end of this section, you will know how to do the following:

- Give privileges to a user, allowing him or her to perform secure operations
- Create a profile and assign it to one or more users
- Create a role and sign up one or more users to that role

Let's get started with Enterprise Manager. The next three sections assume that you have started OEM and brought up the Security Manager.

Giving Privileges to Database Users

Privileges, when given out to users, allow them to perform activities in the Oracle8 database they would be unable to do without them. To give privileges to a user, do the following:

1. Right mouse click on top of one of the users; it does not matter which one you are over.

2. Select the Add Privileges to User option on the ensuing drop-down menu to display the dialog box shown in Figure 18-1.

3. Highlight a user in the Users list.

4. Highlight one or more privileges at the bottom, then click on Apply to complete the activity. Notice in Figure 18-1 that we have chosen to give user SCOTT the EXP_FULL_DATABASE and IMP_FULL_DATABASE privileges.

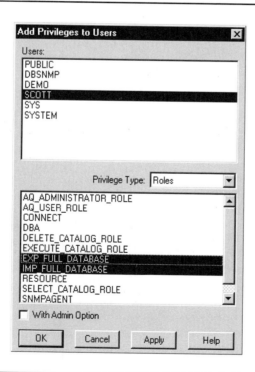

FIGURE 18-1. *Add privileges to user*

5. Click Cancel or the close box to dismiss this box and return to the Security Manager console.

Creating and Assigning a New Profile

For the sake of this exercise, we have decided that the users of the database spend long periods of time doing nothing, and we would like to disconnect them from the server after 15 minutes of inactivity. Let's do this one a little differently: start by clicking Profiles on the menu bar at the top of the Security Manager screen.

1. Select the Create option off the drop-down menu that appears.

2. Give the new profile a name when the Create Profile dialog box appears, as shown in Figure 18-2.

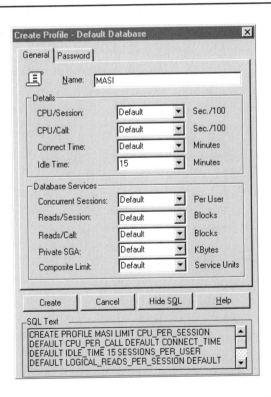

FIGURE 18-2. *Create profile*

3. Give the profile the name **masi** or any other name of your choice.

4. Proceed to the Idle Time position in the Details area, then select 15 from the pick list displayed.

NOTE
We have clicked the Show SQL button in this dialog box, which displays the SQL as shown at the bottom of the screen.

5. Click Create to finish the task at hand.

When you return to the Security Manager console, expand the list under the Profiles folder; you will notice that the new profile just created appears.

Creating and Assigning a New Role

We continually use roles as database administrators to make the activity of granting object privileges easier to manage. To start, right mouse click over the Roles folder in the Security Manager, then do the following:

1. Enter the name **dbtech** for the role, as shown in Figure 18-3.

2. Click Create to finish the activity.

3. Click Cancel to return to the Security Manager.

Now when you're granting privileges on application tables to users, rather than giving out the grants individually, you simply give them to the dbtech role as shown in the next listing.

```
grant dbtech to ops$masi;
grant dbtech to ops$puff;
-- Now when privileges are given to the dbtech role, ops$masi
-- and ops$puff assume the privileges based on their membership
-- in the dbtech role.
grant select, insert, update, delete on spoon to dbtech;
```

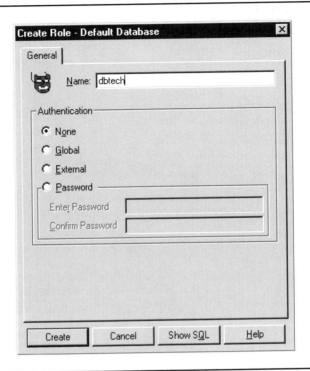

FIGURE 18-3. *Create role*

Additional Tablespace Maintenance Responsibilities

In Chapter 14, we discussed creating a tablespace and adding more space to one that already exists. By the end of this section, you will also know how to move the datafile that makes up a tablespace (i.e., rename a datafile) as well as drop a tablespace. For the following few sections, we assume you have loaded Enterprise Manager and are ready to position yourself at the Storage Manager console to start the work.

Adding More Space to a Tablespace

Either by plan, or when forced to do so in anticipation of something like a
large data load, you may need to add a datafile to an existing tablespace.
This table shows the requirements for the exercise:

Tablespace name	hold_my_data
Datafile to add	hmd2.dbf
New datafile size	1m
Location	c:\orant\database

From the Storage Manager main console, do the following:

1. Click on the Tablespace folder to bring up the list of tablespaces
   shown in Figure 18-4.

2. Right mouse click over the HOLD_MY_DATA tablespace in that
   list, then select the Add Datafile option from that drop-down menu.

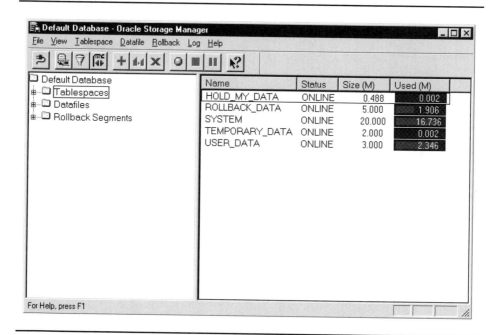

FIGURE 18-4. *Tablespaces in tablespace folder*

3. When the Create Datafile dialog box appears, fill in **c:\orant\database\hmd2.dbf** beside Name.

4. Bring up the drop-down list beside Tablespace, and select the HOLD_MY_DATA tablespace.

5. Leave the Status radio button as is with Online selected.

6. In the Size box, enter the number **1**, then ensure the "M" is selected beside Bytes. The completed dialog box is shown in Figure 18-5. Notice we have selected the Show SQL option that illustrates the command passed to Oracle via this dialog box.

7. Click Create to finish the activity.

When you have returned to the Storage Manager console, click the Datafiles folder, and you will notice the filename (c:\orant\database\

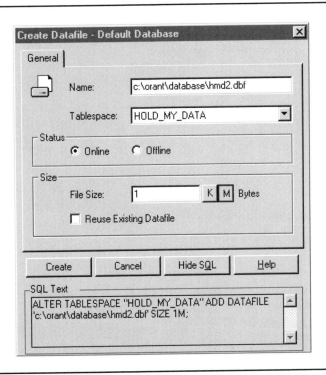

FIGURE 18-5. *Create datafile dialog box*

hmd2.dbf) appears in the list of files associated with the database. Let's now look at dropping a tablespace.

Dropping a Tablespace

Once a user's data is no longer required, you may want to get rid of the data and even the tablespace the data now resides in.

VIP

PLEASE BE CAREFUL: when dropping a tablespace and clicking OK on the information box shown in Figure 18-6 below, the DATA IN THE TABLESPACE BEING DROPPED ARE GONE; TOAST; ARE NO MORE; GIVEN UP THE GHOST; PASSED ON; HISTORY!!!

From the main console of the Storage Manager do the following:

1. Bring up the list of tablespaces, if it is not already showing, by clicking on the tablespace folder.

2. Proceed to the tablespace you wish to drop; in the example we use the HOLD_MY_DATA tablespace.

3. Right mouse click to bring up the drop-down menu underneath.

4. Select Remove, and answer the question shown in the information box in Figure 18-6.

5. Click OK to remove the tablespace.

6. Click the close box to leave the Storage Manager.

VIP

Dropping a tablespace does not erase the datafile it was using. The datafile must be removed using an operating system command. Erase the datafile from the dropped tablespace immediately. If you decide to do this some other time, more than likely you will forget!

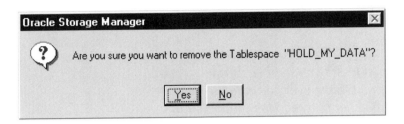

FIGURE 18-6. *Drop tablespace confirmation*

Managing Redo Log Groups

Oracle writes transaction information to redo log files. Picture a redo log as a passbook that records all changes to the database as if it were a checking account. With Oracle, we speak of redo log file groups. If you define more than one member for a redo log group, Oracle writes to each member simultaneously. This protects you against problems if a redo log file is damaged; Oracle continues to write to another member of the group that is still intact. In this section, we will discuss how to do the following:

- Mirror your redo logs
- Add a redo log group
- Drop a redo log group

We're going to use the Enterprise Manager to do this exercise, with a little twist we know you'll like—let's use the SQL Worksheet tool. For those of you familiar with line-mode sqldba, Server Manager, or SQL*Plus, Oracle has never delivered a command history feature with any tool the DBA has ever used. Along comes the SQL Worksheet—ta da! Here we go!

Mirrored Redo Logs

When instructed, Oracle will maintain mirrored copies of all online redo logs. A redo log group is made up of one or more equally sized redo log files. Each redo log group is assigned a number when created and Oracle writes to all members of each group at the same time. In the next section, we show you how to add a new redo log group to set up this mirroring.

When the database operates in ARCHIVELOG mode, Oracle archives only one member of a redo log group before the whole group is reused.

TIP
Have at least two members in each redo log group. If Oracle ever has difficulty writing to one member of a redo log group, it will carry on, satisfied to write to another member of the same group.

The status of your database redo log groups and members is viewed using the v$logfile data dictionary view and the following query in the worksheet, as shown in Figure 18-7.

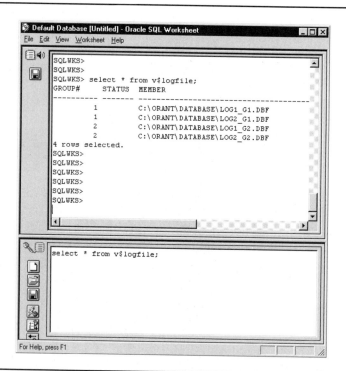

FIGURE 18-7. *Getting list of current redo log members*

Use the following conventions when setting up mirrored redo logs:

■ Ensure there are the same number of members in every redo log group.

■ Ensure each member of each redo log group is the same size.

■ Embed the member number and group number in the name of each redo log file. For example, the second member of redo log group 2 in the previous listing is called log2_g2.dbf.

■ Whenever possible, place members of each redo log group on separate disks. For example, the two members of redo log group 2 in Figure 18-7 could be on separate drives if more than one resides on your NT server.

NOTE
*You may have difficulty when you try to add a third member to your redo log groups. The parameter **maxlogmembers** controls the number of members in a redo log group.*

The value of **maxlogmembers** can be increased by recreating the database control file.

NOTE
*If you wish to increase the value for **maxlogmembers**, you can recreate your control file, as discussed in the "Building a New Control File" section of this chapter.*

Adding a New Redo Log Group

For this exercise, we need to add redo log group 3 with two redo log file members of 500K each. On the SQL Worksheet, do the following:

1. Enter the command shown in Figure 18-8.

2. Press the Execute button (the one with the letter **E** pointing to it) to execute the command entered.

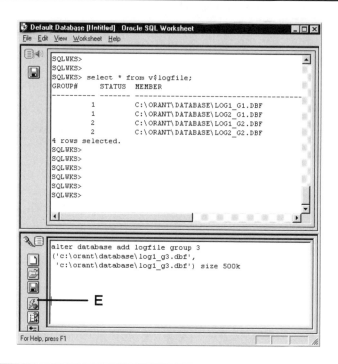

FIGURE 18-8. *Command to add redo log group 3*

When the command finishes successfully, you will see the worksheet, as shown in Figure 18-9.

Notice in Figure 18-9 how the names of the redo log file members are enclosed in single quotes. In addition, the two redo log file member names are separated by a comma and enclosed in parentheses. We now have three redo log groups associated with the database.

TIP

When building a redo log file member name, embed the group number and member number in the filename. That is why we named the files log1_gr3 and log2_gr3 in this exercise.

FIGURE 18-9. *Redo log group added successfully*

Dropping an Existing Redo Log Group

You have just upgraded your hardware, and you find yourself with one less disk for Oracle and its associated database files. You used to have three disks, and now you have two. On the SQL Worksheet, enter the command **alter database drop logfile group 3;**. Redo log group 3 is no longer part of the database. Note how the SQL statement in the previous sentence makes no mention of any redo log file member names as the group is dropped.

Problems Dropping Redo Log Groups

There are two problems that commonly occur when attempting to drop a redo log group. If one of these happens to you, follow our advice and then reissue the command to drop the group.

- You may be attempting to drop a redo log group (let's call it redo log group 2) that would leave Oracle with less than two groups. If this happens, you must add a third group before you can drop group 2. When you drop group 2, that leaves groups 1 and 3, which satisfies Oracle's requirements.

- You may be attempting to drop a redo log group that is active. You must wait until the group is no longer active before it can be dropped. This is shown in Figure 18-10.

Rollback Segments

You may remember that these segments are used to store undo information when you update or delete data in Oracle tables. Managing these segments

FIGURE 18-10. *Problems dropping redo log group 3*

is part of your DBA responsibility. In this section, we show you how to do the following:

■ Acquire a rollback segment using the initialization parameter file

■ Create a rollback segment

■ Change the status of a rollback segment

■ Drop a rollback segment

Acquiring a Rollback Segment

Oracle8 for Windows NT uses the term "configuration files" synonymously with what we have called "initialization parameter files." There are two ways to acquire a rollback segment.

■ At instance startup time, ensuring the rollback segment you wish to acquire is mentioned in the initialization parameter file in the "rollback_segments" entry

■ Bringing the rollback segment online from the Storage Manager

Let's look at the latter method, which will be used more frequently. Once positioned at the Storage Manager console, do the following:

1. Click the Rollback Segments on the main console.

2. Right mouse click the rollback segment you wish to acquire.

3. When the drop-down menu appears, there are two options that can be used to accomplish the task at hand:

■ Click Online to bring up a confirmation box, then click OK to bring the segment online.

■ Click Quick Edit to bring up the dialog box shown in Figure 18-11.

4. Using the Quick Edit option, ensure Online is selected, and click OK to finish and return to the console or Apply to bring the segment online, leaving the dialog box in place.

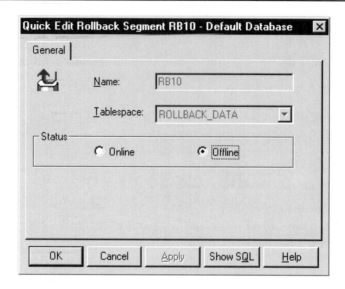

FIGURE 18-11. *Quick Edit*

When returned to the console, the segment brought online is so indicated.

Creating a Rollback Segment

We discussed rollback segments in greater detail in Chapter 4. As the DBA, you will quickly become more familiar with the nuances of working with them. From the Storage Manager main console, perform the following to create a rollback segment:

1. Right mouse click the Rollback Segment folder to display the drop-down menu.

2. When the dialog box appears, as shown in Figure 18-12, fill in the segment name and the tablespace name within which it is to reside.

3. Ensure the Online option is highlighted and click Create.

When returned to the console, the rollback segment you just created appears in the list.

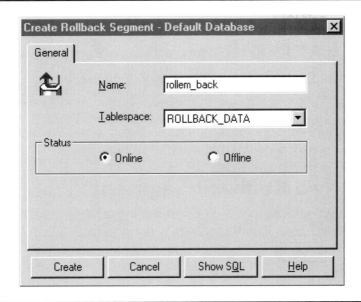

FIGURE 18-12. *Create Rollback Segment dialog box*

The name of the rollback segment must be unique and the tablespace you are placing it in must be accessible.

VIP
We recommend that you build one or more tablespaces to hold nothing other than rollback segments. This is the default behavior of Oracle8 on Windows NT.

Changing the Status of a Rollback Segment

As we have seen in a few previous exercises, rollback segments are either online or offline. To change the status of a rollback segment, do the following:

I. Right mouse click on the desired segment in the rollback segment list.

2. Select the Quick Edit option from the drop-down menu that appears.

3. Highlight the Online or Offline button to toggle the Status, then click OK to alter the segment.

Let's now look at dropping a rollback segment, which will pretty much round out our newly acquired rollback segment knowledge.

Dropping a Rollback Segment

Dropping a rollback segment can be a frustrating activity: there are a number of situations in which Oracle may not do exactly what you expect. If you try to drop a rollback segment with the online status, then you will receive the error message "ORA-01545: rollback segment 'RBS3' specified not available." Also, if you try to take a rollback segment offline to drop it, and someone is using it when you issue the command, then the rollback segment will not come offline until that user is done with it.

Initialization Parameter File

This file can be one of the most mystifying components of the Oracle database. Many articles in magazines and presentations at technical conferences deal with this file and what it does for the Oracle database. This section will discuss details on the following:

- What the initialization parameter file is used for

- Format of parameters in this file

- Displaying values of entries in this file

- Changing parameters in this file

- Parameters most commonly changed

This file is read by Oracle when an instance is started. It is also called init.ora or the pfile. There are entries in this file that are specific to the database you wish to access, and they control the environment Oracle will

set up during startup. The parameters in this file can be used to do
the following:

- Define the name and location of files used by the database.

- Control the size of portions of computer memory allocated to
  support the database configuration.

- Specify the number of concurrent sessions that may access
  the database.

When Oracle starts the database, much of its operating environment is
based on the values of entries in this file. When entries list the name and
location of files the instance needs to open at startup, these files are
checked. Oracle needs to ensure the files mentioned exist where they are
supposed to, and can be accessed without error. In addition, the settings of
some of the parameters in this pfile affect the performance of your database.

Format for Entries in
the Initialization Parameter File

There are two kinds of parameters in this parameter file (hereafter referred
to as pfile); explicit parameters have an entry in the pfile; implicit
parameters do not appear in the pfile and assume the default until (if ever)
you place a value for them in the pfile. In the next listing, all the values
except the first (dml_locks) have no entry in the pfile.

```
dml_locks                          integer 1200
gc_db_locks                        integer 75
gc_files_to_locks                  string
gc_rollback_locks                  integer 20
gc_save_rollback_locks             integer 20
row_locking                        string default
temporary_table_locks              integer 80
```

The format for parameters is

```
pfile_keyword = keyword_value
```

and, for some entries, you need to enclose parameter values in appropriate punctuation such as parentheses () or double quotes " ". If parameters span more than one line, they require a continuation character, as follows:

```
rollback_segments = (rollback_disk1,rollback_disk2, rollback_disk3, \
                     rollback_disk4)
```

Examining Contents of the Initialization Parameter File

This section returns to line mode Server Manager for a few minutes; Enterprise Manager can be used to do the following, but we suggest staying familiar with your options and continually popping back and forth between tools. A complete list of parameters (implicit and explicit) is available by doing the following in Server manager:

1. Enter **connect internal**.

2. To see a list of the values for all entries, enter the command **show parameters** and Oracle displays a list, the end of which is shown in the next listing.

```
tape_asynch_io                         boolean TRUE
temporary_table_locks                  integer 60
text_enable                            boolean FALSE
thread                                 integer 0
timed_os_statistics                    string off
timed_statistics                       boolean FALSE
transaction_auditing                   boolean TRUE
transactions                           integer 66
transactions_per_rollback_segment      integer 11
user_dump_dest                         string %RDBMS80%\trace
utl_file_dir                           string
```

You can look at a subset of parameters (implicit and explicit). For this exercise, we want all the parameters that contain the word "sort." After starting Server Manager, follow these steps:

1. Enter **connect internal**.

2. Enter the command **show parameters sort** and receive the feedback
from Oracle as shown in the next listing.

```
nls_sort                        string
sort_area_retained_size         integer 0
sort_area_size                  integer 65536
sort_direct_writes              string AUTO
sort_read_fac                   integer 20
sort_spacemap_size              integer 512
sort_write_buffer_size          integer 32768
sort_write_buffers              integer 2
```

Changing Parameter Values

When Oracle is first installed on all platforms, it builds an initialization
parameter file to start the database. As your knowledge of Oracle grows,
you may change some initialization parameter entry values. Some of them
can be changed; others must be left as is. Details about changing pfile
parameter values are covered in the Oracle8 Server Administrator's Guide
(commonly referred to as the OSAG). The manual gives advice and
recommendations about what can be changed and the acceptable range of
values. For example (used with permission of Oracle Corporation), the
following advice is given about the shared_pool_size entry.

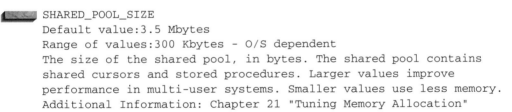

```
SHARED_POOL_SIZE
Default value:3.5 Mbytes
Range of values:300 Kbytes - O/S dependent
The size of the shared pool, in bytes. The shared pool contains
shared cursors and stored procedures. Larger values improve
performance in multi-user systems. Smaller values use less memory.
Additional Information: Chapter 21 "Tuning Memory Allocation"
```

Perhaps the most important advice given is whether you are
permitted to even change a parameter value: many should be left as is
and never changed.

NOTE
*Changes to any entries in the initialization
parameter file will not take effect until the next
time the database is started.*

Parameters Most Commonly Changed

Over 130 parameter values are recorded in the data dictionary view v$parameter. This view lists the values in effect as the database operates, and it serves as the source for the query output displayed by the **show parameters** command. Table 18-2 highlights the four entries in the initialization parameter file you will change most often.

NOTE

When you change an entry in the pfile, comment the old one with the "#" character. This will help you keep track of what changed, why, and when.

Parameter	Meaning	Most Common Changes
shared_pool_size	The number of bytes of memory allocated to the shared pool	As the size of your concurrent user community grows, you may increase this value periodically.
rollback_segments	The name of one or more rollback segments to acquire when the database is started	When transaction volume increases or decreases over a period of time, you may add or remove the name of a rollback segment from this list.
sessions	The maximum number of concurrent sessions that may access the database	Needs increasing as more and more users come onboard.
processes	The maximum number of concurrent processes that may access the database	Needs increasing as more and more users come onboard.

TABLE 18-2.   *Most Common Changes in the Initialization Parameter File*

Control File Responsibilities

Coupled with the initialization parameter file, control files are read by Oracle every time you start the database. Their file information is vital to opening the database. In this section, you will learn details on the following:

- How Oracle uses the control file

- Adding a new control file

- Dropping an existing control file

- Moving an existing control file

- Building a new control file

As the DBA, you will bear complete responsibility for managing control files. Think of control files as the transmission in your car. When both behave themselves, they require no attention, but when both misbehave, they can cause major headaches!

Use of the Control File

Every Oracle database has one or more control files. The control file holds information about the database creation time, the name of the database, and the location and names of all files used when the database is running. You instruct Oracle to maintain as many copies of a database control file (usually two or more) as you deem necessary. The control files are written to as Oracle operates, and they are key to database startup and shutdown. Every time you perform maintenance operations, such as adding a datafile or configuring redo log file groups, the control files are automatically modified to reflect the change. Some control file maintenance is performed with the database down; some maintenance is performed with the database in a nomount status. When you start the Oracle database, the control file is opened first. Oracle then verifies the existence and status of all the files needed to operate, and it ensures all redo log files are accessible. As the DBA, you are responsible for ensuring Oracle can open its control files when it needs them. As we discuss in the "Building a New Control File" section of this chapter, making a copy of the control file is included in your backup procedures.

Adding a Control File

You may decide to add a control file when a new disk is added to the disk farm. This can be accomplished in the Instance Manager by following these steps:

1. After entering appropriate login information, and connecting as SYSDBA, proceed to the Shutdown folder.

2. With the Immediate option selected, click Shutdown. As Oracle shuts down, the status indicator will change to red with a slash through the O8 text.

3. Click on the Initialization Parameters folder on the main console.

4. Click the Instance Specific tab to bring up the screen shown in Figure 18-13.

5. Highlight the control_files parameter, then double-click to bring up the Edit Initialization Parameter form.

6. Enter the name of the current control file already displayed, plus the new one **d:\orant\database\ctl2orcl.ora**, so the entry looks as it does in Figure 18-14.

7. Click OK to return to the Instance Specific sheet.

8. Click OK to save the updated configuration with the new control filename in place.

9. In the Save Configuration dialog box, enter a name (e.g., **control2**), some descriptive comments, and then click OK to return to the main console.

VIP

We recommend entering comments for this and all other activities; one never knows how long it will be until you revisit one of these screens and the comments can sometimes help explain why you ended up doing something a certain way.

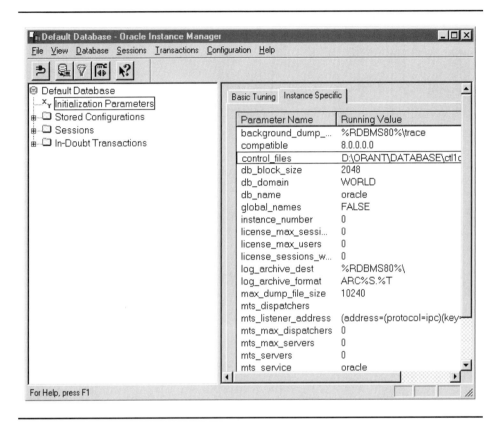

FIGURE 18-13. *Initialization Parameters file entries display*

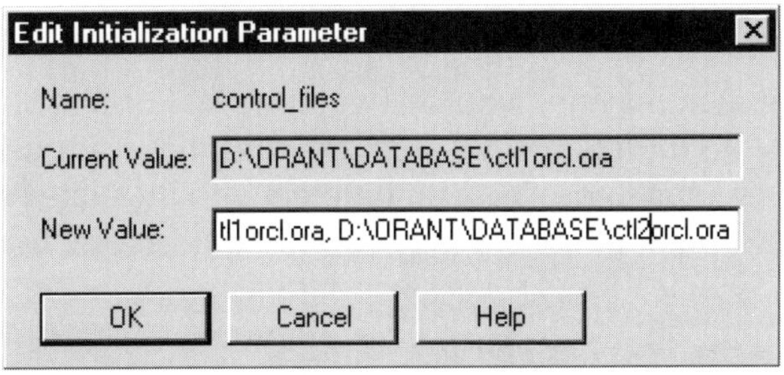

FIGURE 18-14. *Entry of additional control file*

When returned to the main console, click Stored Configurations in the Default Database folder, and you will see your newly entered configuration in place.

VIP
Before you start the instance with the additional control file, you must copy the present control file (usually but not always **ctl1orcl.ora***) to create the new control file named in the dialog box shown in Figure 18-14. When this has been done, you will have two identical control files, which is exactly what we hoped to accomplish.*

Let's quickly look at working with the new configuration during instance startup. To start using the control2 configuration, do the following from the Instance Manager.

1. Click Default Database, then the Startup tab.

2. Bring up the drop-down menu beside the Configuration prompt, then select control2 from the list displayed. The screen now looks like Figure 18-15.

3. Click Startup to finish starting the database.

Using this configuration feature, you may have different parameters and values depending on what you are trying to accomplish.

Dropping a Control File

Once in a while, you may find yourself with one less disk at your disposal. This requires you to drop one of your control files that was positioned on that disk. We are going to do this a bit differently to illustrate how there always seems to be more than one way to go about accomplishing something with Oracle8 for NT. Let's get started.

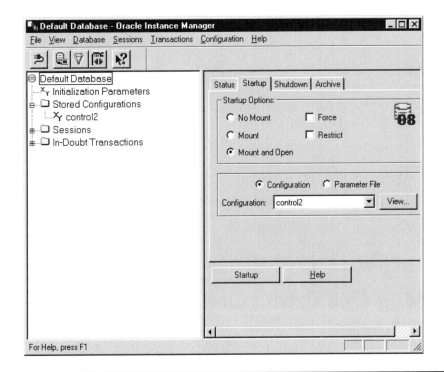

FIGURE 18-15. *Startup with control2 configuration selected*

1. Open up an MS-DOS window, then enter the command **svrmgr30** to start Server Manager.

2. Enter **connect internal**, then the password **oracle** when prompted.

NOTE
The secure password is **oracle** *by default, but may have been changed by you or a colleague.*

3. Enter **shutdown** to shut the database.

4. Enter **exit** to leave Server Manager.

5. Proceed to the directory where the database initialization parameter file is located.

6. Edit the file looking for the entry that specifies **control_files =**. The parameter value could resemble the following (suppose the bold and italicized name is the one to be removed).

```
control_files = (c:\orant\database\ctr1orcl.ora,
                 c:\orant\database\ctr2orcl.ora)
```

7. Remove the name of the control file to be dropped. The parameter value then becomes

```
control_files = (c:\orant\database\ctr1orcl.ora)
```

8. Follow steps 1 and 2, then enter **startup** to start the database.

9. Enter **exit** again to leave Server Manager.

10. Erase the unwanted control file.

Your database is now running with one less file in its pool of control files.

Moving an Existing Control File

If your system administrator needs to change the name of a disk where you have a control file, you too will have to inform Oracle of the name of the new location. Again, let's do this in Server Manager. This can be accomplished by following these steps:

1. Open up an MS-DOS window, then enter the command **svrmgr30** to start Server Manager.

2. Enter **connect internal**, then the password **oracle** when prompted.

3. Enter **shutdown** to shut the database.

4. Enter **exit** to leave Server Manager.

5. Proceed to the directory where the database initialization parameter file is located.

6. Edit the file, looking for the entry that specifies **control_files =**. The parameter value could resemble the following (suppose the bold and italicized name is being moved).

```
control_files = (c:\orant\database\ctr1orcl.ora,
                 c:\orant\database\ctr2orcl.ora)
```

7. Change the name of the second control file, at which point the
entry becomes:

```
control_files = (c:\orant\database\ctr1orcl.ora,
                 d:\orant\data\prd\ctr2orcl.ora)
```

8. Move the original control file into its new location using
the command:

```
move c:\orant\database\ctr2orcl.ora
d:\orant\data\prd\ctr2orcl.ora
```

9. Follow steps 1 and 2, then enter **startup** to start the database.

10. Enter **exit** again to leave Server Manager.

VIP
*The database **must** be closed when performing
this and the previous task.*

As the database starts, it reads the control_files value from the
initialization parameter file using the control file in the new location as
created by step 8.

Building a New Control File

If and when a control file is damaged, Oracle cannot open your database.
This is why in a number of places throughout this book, we recommend
you have more than one control file. If the need arises to build a
control file, you place the following routine somewhere in your nightly
backup procedures.

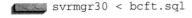
```
svrmgr30 < bcft.sql
```

where "bfct.sql" contains the following three lines

```
oracle
alter database backup controlfile to trace;
exit
```

VIP
*The first line in "bfct.sql" contains the secure password to enable login to the instance using the **connect internal** command. Please ensure when using a program similar to this that the privileges on the file are set such that all users of the server cannot read this file.*

This writes a trace file in the directory defined by the initialization parameter file entry user_dump_dest. The trace file will have the text "ora_" as the prefix and the text ".trc" as the file extension. Embedded in this trace file will be the SQL statements required to build a control file from scratch.

```
# The following commands will create a new control file and use it
# to open the database.
# Data used by the recovery manager will be lost. Additional logs may
# be required for media recovery of offline data files. Use this
# only if the current version of all online logs are available.
startup nomount
create controlfile reuse database "oracle" noresetlogs noarchivelog
    maxlogfiles 32
    maxlogmembers 2
    maxdatafiles 32
    maxinstances 16
    maxloghistory 1630
logfile
  group 1 'd:\orant\database\log2orcl.ora'  size 200k,
  group 2 'd:\orant\database\log1orcl.ora'  size 200k
datafile
  'd:\orant\database\sys1orcl.ora',
  'd:\orant\database\usr1orcl.ora',
  'd:\orant\database\rbs1orcl.ora',
  'd:\orant\database\tmp1orcl.ora'
;
# Recovery is required if any of the datafiles are restored backups,
# or if the last shutdown was not normal or immediate.
recover database
# Database can now be opened normally.
alter database open;
```

There are three distinct parts to this statement, which give you a better understanding of the use of the control file:

- The name of the database and its environment, e.g., the database name and the maximum number of members in a redo log group

- The location and size of all redo log groups and their members

- The location and size of all the datafiles associated with the instance

TIP
Make this routine part of your daily backup procedure immediately. It can prove a lifesaver many times during your career as a DBA.

We use this routine as part of all backup procedures we have placed at all our clients' installations. We use the SQL statements in the trace file created with this feature regularly.

NOTE
This command only works for Oracle7/8. It is not available with version 6.

Getting the Most from Your Error Messages

Unfortunately, something *will* go wrong when you're working with software. In this case, Oracle feeds an error message back to you with a message number followed by some descriptive text about the problem. Most of the time, you will also get a suggestion or two about how to fix the problem. In this section, we will discuss the following:

- Ranges of messages you will deal with as a DBA

- Obtaining error message text online

- Recognizing Oracle internal errors and what to do with them

As the DBA, you will become familiar with common error conditions, where to look for their resolution, and what to do about them. As time marches on, you will surprise even yourself with how quickly you react to common messages. You will begin to spout error text at coffee breaks: "I looked where the clerk told me, and then got 942'ed" or "If I get asked to take on any more responsibilities before vacation, I'm gonna 1547." The Oracle8 Server Error Messages and Codes Manual will start following you around.

Popular DBA Message Ranges

As the DBA, you will become familiar with a whole new series of error messages in the following ranges—they relate to your new areas of responsibility. These are the bounds of the assortment of error messages you will spend your time with:

```
00000-00100: Oracle Server
00101-00149: Multi-threaded Server
00150-00159: Oracle*XA Messages
00160-00199: Distributed Transaction Messages
00200-00249: Control File Messages
00250-00299: Archiving and Recovery Messages
00300-00369: Redo Log File Messages
00390-00399: Redo Log File Messages
00600-00639: Oracle Exceptions Messages
00640-00699: SQL*Connect Messages
00700-00709: Dictionary Cache Messages
00816-00816: Message Translation Messages
00900-00999: SQL Parsing Messages
01000-01099: User Program Interface Messages
01100-01250: Oracle Files Messages
01400-01489: SQL Execution Messages
01490-01499: Miscellaneous, ANALYZE, SQL Parsing, Execution Messages
01500-01699: Oracle Commands Messages
01700-01799: SQL Parsing Messages
01800-01899: The Date Function Messages
01900-02039: SQL Parsing Messages
02040-02099: Distributed Transactions Messages
02140-02299: SQL Parsing Messages
02351-02375: SQL*Loader in Direct Path Mode Messages
02376-02399: Oracle Resources Messages
02401-02419: EXPLAIN PLAN Command Messages
02420-02429: Schema Messages
02430-02449: Constraint Enabling & Disabling Messages
02476-02479: Parallel Direct Loader Messages
```

```
02480-02489: Trace Facility Messages
02490-02499: Resizeable Datafile Messages
02700-02874: UNIX Two-Task Messages
02875-02899: IBM RS/6000 Messages
03000-03099: Features Not Implemented Messages
03100-03199: Two-Task Interface Messages
03200-03289: Extent Allocation and Other Space Management Messages
03290-03295: TRUNCATE Command Messages
03296-03299: Resizeable Datafiles
04000-04019: Invalid Command Parameter Messages
04020-04029: Library Object Lock Messages
04030-04039: System Memory Messages
04040-04059: Stored Procedure Messages
04060-04069: Stored Procedure Execution Messages
04070-04099: Trigger Messages
06000-06429: SQL*Net Messages
06500-06580: PL/SQL Messages
06600-06699: SQL*Net Messages
07200-07499: UNIX Messages
07500-07999: VAX/VMS Messages
08000-08174: Data Accessing Messages
08401-08499: PL/SQL Utility Packages for Procedural Gateway Messages
08600-09099: SQL*Connect Messages
09100-09199: Oracle Gateways Messages
09200-09499: DOS, OS/2, and Novell Messages
09700-09999: UNIX Messages
10000-10999: Internal Messages
12000-12099: Table Snapshot Messages
12100-12299: SQL*Net Messages
12500-12699: SQL*Net Messages
12700-12799: National Language Support Messages
12800-12849: Parallel Query/Index Creation Messages
13000-13199: Spatial Data Option Messages
14000-14119: Partitioned Objects - Parsing Messages
14400-14499: Partitioned Objects - Execution Messages
14500-14999: Partitioned Objects - ANALYZE Messages
19500-19998: Server Managed Recovery Messages
19999-21099: Stored Procedure Messages
21100-21299: Internal Messages
22800-22849: Object SQL Messages
22850-22879: Object SQL DDL Messages
22880-22899: Object SQL REF/DEREF Support Messages
22900-22919: SQL Nested Tables and Collections Messages
23300-24299: DBMS PL/SQL Package Messages
25000-25099: Trigger Messages
```

```
25100-25199: Parse Messages
27000-27299: Unix Messages
27500-27650: IPC Messages
28000-28499: Security-Related Messages
28500-28549: Heterogeneous Option Messages
28750-29249: Security Service Messages
29250-29399: DBMS_SQL Messages
29400-29499: Oracle Data Cartridge Messages
```

Online Error Messages

You will become familiar with these ranges, and in a short time period you will know what you have on your hands immediately by where a message number falls in this list. In UNIX operating systems, you can access error text using a program called **oerr**. When you use **oerr**, enter the text **ora** followed by the message number of the error: for example, **oerr ora 1547**. You will receive output similar to the following:

```
01547, 00000, "failed to allocate extent of size %s in tablespace '%s'"
// *Cause: Tablespace indicated is out of space
// *Action: Use ALTER TABLESPACE ADD DATAFILE statement to add one or more
//    files to the tablespace indicated or create the object in other
//    tablespace if this happens during a CREATE statement
/oracle:prod>
```

ORA-00600 Internal Errors

Getting one of these errors is the "rite of initiation" to being a DBA, of sorts. The 0600 error is a "catch-all" message returned when Oracle encounters some internal difficulty. It is a generic message followed by up to six arguments enclosed in brackets []. The majority of the arguments in the square brackets are numbers, but sometimes you may find text. The arguments 12387 and 34503 shown in the example below should point Oracle support to the exact reason the error was raised.

```
ORA-00600: internal error code, arguments: [12387],
[34503],[],[],[],[]
```

VIP
*Almost all 0600 error messages are not fatal.
In our experience, the occurrence of an 0600
that impedes the operation of your database
is very rare.*

Report these errors to Oracle Worldwide Customer Support. They will explain the condition, tell you what to do about it, and reassure you that "yes, you do enjoy being a DBA!"

The Data Dictionary

The data dictionary resides in the system tablespace. Its information enables Oracle to manage its resources as well as track information such as who can log into the database and what files are required to run the database. You need to familiarize yourself with the data dictionary; it's remarkable how much of your DBA work uses the information it contains. In this section, we will do the following:

■ Discuss the four types of data dictionary views

■ See how objects appear in a different user's snapshot of the dictionary

■ Highlight the most important dba and v$ views

You will become more fluent with the makeup of the data dictionary in a surprisingly short time period. There is no magic in the Oracle database. Just about everything is stored somewhere in a table, or it can be displayed on the screen in some format. The Oracle data dictionary belongs to user SYS. The data dictionary is your friend—get to know it.

Types of Dictionary Views

You now need to concern yourself with types of dictionary views. Their names start with the prefix shown in Table 18-3, and the pieces of their names are connected with the underscore character "_".

The following list shows how the information in these views is interrelated.

```
SQL> select * from dict where table_name like '%OBJECTS';
TABLE_NAME                      COMMENTS
--------------------            ----------------------------------
ALL_OBJECTS                     Objects accessible to the user
DBA_OBJECTS                     All objects in the database
USER_OBJECTS                    Objects owned by the user

SQL>  select * from dict where table_name like '%_QUOTAS';
TABLE_NAME                      COMMENTS
--------------------            ----------------------------------
DBA_TS_QUOTAS                   Tablespace quotas for all users
USER_TS_QUOTAS                  Tablespace quotas for the user

SQL> select * from dict where table_name like '%_SYNONYMS';
TABLE_NAME                      COMMENTS
--------------------            ----------------------------------
ALL_SYNONYMS                    All synonyms accessible to the user
DBA_SYNONYMS                    All synonyms in the database
USER_SYNONYMS                   The user's private synonyms

SQL>
```

Dictionary View Prefix	Meaning
all	Returns information on all objects accessible to a user.
user	Returns information on all objects owned by a user.
dba	Returns a database-wide list (for all users) similar to the user category.
v$,	Dynamic performance views updated by Oracle as it runs. Performance information and the status of files and memory being used by Oracle is available by querying these views.

TABLE 18-3.   *Data Dictionary View Prefixes*

Most Useful dba and v$ Views

Unless you put access in place, users do not have privileges to view information in the v$ and dba views belonging to SYS. You need to grant select to everyone to allow them to see these views; the information they contain is invaluable to the novice as well as the seasoned DBA. These are the most useful dba_views, and the ones you need to become familiar with in order to get started.

```
TABLE_NAME                  COMMENTS
--------------------        ---------------------------------------
DBA_DATA_FILES              Information about database files
DBA_DB_LINKS                All database links in the database
DBA_EXTENTS                 Extents comprising all segments in the database
DBA_FREE_SPACE              Free extents in all tablespaces
DBA_INDEXES                 Description for all indexes in the database
DBA_IND_COLUMNS             COLUMNs comprising INDEXes on all TABLEs and
                            CLUSTERs
DBA_OBJECTS                 All objects in the database
DBA_ROLLBACK_SEGS           Description of rollback segments
DBA_SEGMENTS                Storage allocated for all database segments
DBA_SEQUENCES               Description of all SEQUENCEs in the database
DBA_SYNONYMS                All synonyms in the database
DBA_TABLES                  Description of all tables in the database
DBA_TABLESPACES             Description of all tablespaces
DBA_TAB_COLUMNS             Columns of all tables, views, and clusters database
DBA_TAB_GRANTS              All grants on objects in the database
DBA_TAB_PRIVS               All grants on objects in the database
DBA_TS_QUOTAS               Tablespace quotas for all users
DBA_USERS                   Information about all users of the database
DBA_VIEWS                   Text of all views in the database
```

Table 18-4 highlights the most useful v$ views, and the ones you need to become familiar with to get started.

View	Contains
v$datafile	Information on the datafiles used by the database; same as the information in the control file(s).
v$librarycache	Information on management of SQL statements in the shared pool.
v$lock	Information about locks placed on objects by sessions that access the database. Locks are used to prevent users from changing data in the database another user may have already started changing.
v$log	Information extracted from the control file about redo logs.
v$logfile	Information about the location and names of the instance redo log files.
v$parameter	The values of all entries in the initialization parameter file.
v$process	Information regarding current processes.
v$rollname	Rollback segment information.
v$rollstat	Statistics about online rollback segments.
v$rowcache	Information about data dictionary activity/performance in memory.
v$session	Information about active sessions.
v$sesstat	Statistics about active sessions reported in v$session.
v$sqlarea	Statistics about cursors currently held in the shared pool. Cursors are chunks of memory opened by Oracle for the processing of SQL statements.
v$statname	The meaning of each statistic reported in v$sesstat.
v$sysstat	System-wide statistics based on currently active sessions.
v$waitstat	Details on situations encountered where more than one session wants access to data in the database. There can be wait situations when more than one session wishes to manipulate the exact same information at the same time.

TABLE 18-4. *Information in the Most Useful v$ Dictionary Views*

Working with Oracle Worldwide Customer Support

As the DBA, you will end up being the central contact point for your organization and technical support requests. To expedite the logging of support calls, Oracle needs the following information when you call.

- Your appropriate customer number for the configuration and tool for which you require support.

- A complete list of version numbers; telling support you are using Oracle version 8 is helpful, but knowing it's 8.0.3 is better, and 8.0.3.2 is better still (if the version number even goes to this fourth qualification level). This is especially true with the Oracle tools: there are significant differences between using Oracle Forms versions 4.0.13 and 4.5.

- A list of any Oracle errors that caused your logging the support request. These can begin with an assortment of prefixes such as **ora**, **frm**, or **dba**.

- Descriptive information about "what was going on" when the error was detected.

Oracle will do one of four things when you call. We prefer the first solution (by far the most frequent).

1. Tell you what to do to remedy the situation, and send you on your way a satisfied, enthusiastic customer.

2. Keep you online while they search a number of support databases looking for a similar situation and, after finding a match, provide you with a number of workarounds.

3. Keep you online while they search a number of support databases looking for a similar situation, and, after finding no match, get back to you in an amount of time that varies directly with the severity of your call (i.e., if the problem inhibits smooth operation of your business, you will be dealt with in a shorter period of time).

4. Record pertinent information and call you back at some later time.

Feel free to call and check on the status of your call whenever you feel the need.

"But I Can't See the Forest for the Trees"

You are poised to embark on a journey into the unknown. This DBA job you are starting (or is it "have been saddled with") is not going to wreck your social life. No, contrary to what you have heard, you will not be up until all hours of the night wrestling with the database. Yes, people will come to you for answers. Why do you think it's called Oracle? Perhaps they were thinking of you: you are the oracle that sees, says, and solves all.

Become fluent with what we have discussed in this chapter. Read technical magazines. Attend user conferences (ever wanted to go to Japan? Europe? or perhaps Australia?). Frequent Oracle forums and information services on CompuServe, the Internet, and World Wide Web servers. If you don't understand something or you are boggled by a new routine, idea, or concept, just ask! Between the two of us, we have over 20 years of experience using Oracle. We still learn things from each other. Believe it: we know a developer (thanks Lise!) who showed us some tricks with SQL*Forms version 3 a while back that we had never been aware of. If you figure out how to do something that you are excited about, let everybody know. One of the interesting things about Oracle is that it is such a complex product, you may just have mastered doing something that four other DBAs all over the world have been tearing their hair out trying to figure out for the past two years. Enjoy!

CHAPTER
19

Data Warehouse
Features

n this chapter, we will briefly discuss the concept of data warehousing, and highlight some of the features of Oracle8 that blend so nicely with this approach to information management. Data warehousing and the management of large volumes of static data are distinct features of the Oracle8 database management solution. Release 7.3 (circa early 1996) delivered many of the bells and whistles that have matured with Oracle8.

NOTE
Headings will display the appropriate version numbers (7 or 8) to indicate what versions support features we discuss in this chapter.

Let's first look at some terminology.

Terminology

The following definitions will arm you with the technical jargon you need to make it through this chapter:

- A *data warehouse* is a data repository designed to support the decision-making process for an organization. Unlike its operational system counterpart, the information can be stored many times in many different locations. Its primary purpose is to provide management with the information it needs in order to make intelligent business decisions.

- A *CPU* is the central processing unit of a computer that is responsible, in conjunction with the operating system, for coordinating work and managing the resources available as software operates.

- An *operational system* (commonly referred to as OLTP) is a partner with a business' data warehouse. These systems allow employees to go about their daily business. For example, let's suppose a company maintains a large inventory of automobile supplies. The system that manages part supply, reorder, and stock depletion notification is an OLTP system. The system that allows executives to analyze customer purchasing habits and make long-term business decisions is in the decision support arena where the data warehouse resides.

■ An *enterprise-wide data warehouse* is a homogeneous collection of data designed to facilitate the decision-making process across a company's business units.

■ A *full table scan* involves reading an Oracle table from start to finish. Each row of information is read sequentially, from beginning to end.

■ An *index range scan* is an operation in which Oracle selects rows from a table by scanning the index, then fetching rows from the table whose column values match a query's selection criteria. The scan is two-phase: first the index, then the data. Under many circumstances, an index range scan can be many times faster than a full table scan.

■ A *datamart* is a subset of an organization's decision support information that focuses on a specific area of interest. The datamart caters to a smaller portion of an organization's user community, and has a time-to-market that is far shorter than that of the enterprise-wide data warehouse.

■ *Data normalization* involves ensuring data is stored in only one place and updated centrally. When data is normalized, it conforms to the relational model we discussed in Chapter 1.

■ *Denormalizing* is a process used throughout the data warehouse that involves undoing a data normalization exercise. When data warehouse architects look at the reporting and analysis requirements of their user community, they go through a systematic denormalization of OLTP data to satisfy the community's reporting needs.

■ *Data mining* is a knowledge discovery in database exercise. Data mining efforts analyze vast quantities of information, looking for patterns and trends in behavior that can be used by organizations when they are designing targeted marketing initiatives and new product releases.

■ *OLAP* stands for online analytical processing, and relates to a set of end user query tools that allow drill-down, aggregation, and collection of various levels of summarization. OLAP tools facilitate slicing and dicing of data warehouse information in ways unique to the decision support requirements of users of an information warehouse.

- *Parallelization* is a process whereby work to be performed by a computer is split amongst different processes. These processes work simultaneously on a task, and the results of the work are merged when complete to appear the same as if the work had been done by only one process.

Oracle has built a handful of warehouse-centric enhancements into its Oracle8 offering. These features are designed to speed the mechanisms involved in storing vast amounts of data as well as Oracle8's ability to retrieve that information. The details of all the features are too many and too technical to discuss at great length in this work, but we encourage you to look at *Oracle Data Warehousing* (Corey and Abbey, Osborne/McGraw-Hill/Oracle Press 1997) for a more detailed look at Oracle's offerings in this arena. Let's highlight a few features to give you a flavor of some Oracle internal mechanisms specially designed to enhance the performance of the Oracle7/8 software supporting the data warehouse.

Bitmap Indexing (7.3.2 and 8)

Many decision support queries are worded in the following way: "How many people who purchased an automobile bought a ____ within the same calendar year?" or "What is the likelihood that marketing efforts in the northeast quadrant of the continent will____?" These are translated by a query tool into SQL statements similar to **select count(*) from auto_sales where car_year = other_part_year;** and **select count(sales) from sales_summary where quadrant = 'NE';**.

Indexes are used by Oracle to provide rapid access to information. Think of an index on an Oracle table as the index to a book, because Oracle uses an index in the same way as you may use the index to an encyclopedia to locate a desired topic. Bitmap indexing is simply a stream of bits, where each bit corresponds to a row in a table. Picture a simplified example to satisfy the query shown above.

The building of a bitmap index is a two-step process:

1. Decide the number of unique values in the desired column (looking at Table 19-1, there are five values in Car_Year and three values in Other_Part_Year).

2. Build a compressed bit stream for each value in the bitmap indexed column.

Using the same data shown in Table 19-1, Oracle would build five bit streams on the former column, and three on the latter. Table 19-2 and 19-3 show these bit stream indexes.

Oracle8's bitmap indexing implementation allows rapid access to statistics about warehouse data since the search on a compressed bitmap index can execute in a fraction of the time required to search data based on a more traditional indexing approach.

Optimizer Histograms (7.3.2 and 8)

So many queries sent off to a data warehouse for processing are requests for rollups of large amounts of numeric data. Questions like "How many people in the sales organization in the southern hemisphere earned commissions of over $7,500 last year—break down by the four major geographical areas and display running totals for each quadrant" can best be answered after the data warehouse administrator builds histograms on parts of the warehouse data.

VIP
*Optimizer histograms are only beneficial on table columns with a nonuniform distribution of data that are frequently used in the **where** portion of an SQL statement.*

Row #	Car_year	Other_part_year	Row #	Car_year	Other_part_year
1	1995	1995	5	1993	1993
2	1995	1996	6	1995	1995
3	1996	1995	7	1994	1996
4	1994	1995	8	1992	1993

TABLE 19-1. *Years of Purchase*

Row #	1992 stream	1993 stream	1994 stream	1995 stream	1996 stream
1	0	0	0	1	0
2	0	0	0	1	0
3	0	0	0	0	1
4	0	0	1	0	0
5	0	1	0	0	0
6	0	0	0	1	0
7	0	0	1	0	0
8	1	0	0	0	0

TABLE 19-2. *Bitmap Indexes for Purchase Data*

Histograms are nothing new to mathematics, but their implementation in the Oracle7.3 and Oracle8 optimizer is. They record the distribution of data within an Oracle table, and can enhance SQL statement processing in situations where there is nonuniform distribution. Inspect the next listing, which shows a histogram with the same weight to each bucket.

```
   |   |   |   |   |   |   |   |   |   |   |
   +----+----+----+----+----+----+----+----+----+----+
   1   10   20   30   40   50   60   70   80   90  100
```

Row #	1993 stream	1995 stream	1996 stream
1	0	1	0
2	0	0	1
3	0	1	0
4	0	1	0
5	1	0	0
6	0	1	0
7	0	0	1
8	1	0	0

TABLE 19-3. *Bitmap Indexes for Other Parts Purchases*

The optimizer would easily deduce that the data is distributed evenly throughout the table, thus the number of records in the table whose column values lie between 41 and 50 is exactly the same as those between 91 and 100. Suppose the histogram looked like this.

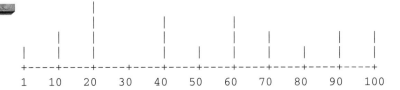

Using this histogram, without even reading the table or index data, one can see that twice as many rows fall into the 50-60 range as do the 70-80 range (using the upper bound of the bucket as the determining factor). Before moving on, let's briefly look at how optimizer histograms are built.

Building the Histogram

The SQL **analyze** command with the following syntax is used to build a histogram.

```
analyze table outlet
    compute statistics for columns province size 10;
```

Let's pick apart the statement:

1. The table name (shown in italics) is usually owned by the user collecting information for the histogram.

2. The column name upon which the histogram is being built (shown underlined) is specified prior to the number of buckets.

3. The number of buckets (shown in bold) is specified at the end of the statement. The bucket size is not required; if it is not included it defaults to 75.

Investigate optimizer histograms if they seem appropriate for your applications. They appeared in release 7.3 and are in Oracle8.

Parallelization

As far back as International Oracle User Week in Orlando (1993), Larry Ellison, President, CEO, and Chairman of the Board at Oracle Corporation, talked about *parallel everything*. Significant advances appeared in parallelization in release 7.1 in early 1994. As the size of Oracle databases increases, parallelization of operations is a significant component of the support for these very large databases that Oracle8 provides. The following operations highlight the type of processes that, when parallelized, contribute to improved performance and response times of information repositories using Oracle.

■ Read/write operations, commonly referred to as *I/O* (input/output), when performed in parallel, reduce the amount of time from when the I/O request is initiated, and the resulting set of information becomes available.

■ Sort operations are a matter of fact in warehouse query resolution. The end users of the warehouse continually require presentation of the qualifying data in various ways. Oracle7 and Oracle8 are capable of taking advantage of multi-CPU machines, leveraging their ability to perform tasks in parallel.

The familiar adage "more bang for the buck" comes to mind when looking at parallelization features, as does "two heads are better than one."

Query Processing

More and more hardware vendors are releasing these multi-CPU machines, and we have worked on a number with multiple processors. Oracle8 allows the database administrator to control how aggressively the optimizer will attempt to parallelize query processing. In a nutshell, this is a simplified version of how Oracle processes queries in parallel:

1. Inspects the degree of parallelization for the objects involved in the join operation. This degree is set as illustrated in the following two listings (with the keywords in bold).

```
-- Set degree of parallelization at creation time
create table account (acc_num      number,
                       owner_id     number,
                       address_id   number,
```

```
          ...
            ...
             ... )
     parallel (degree 8);

-- Set degree of parallelization later or change a degree
previously set
alter table account parallel (degree 16);
```

2. Look to see if the instance is running with multiple parallel query processes and, if it is, selects one of these processes to act as dispatcher for the parallel processing. On a UNIX machine, for example, the following command and output could answer this question. It looks for the parallel query server process with ID "p000" which is assigned to the first process spawned as the instance is started.

```
ps -ef | grep oracle | grep p000
```

3. The dispatcher partitions the workload amongst the number of parallel query processes up to the number specified in the table's degree of parallelization. Suppose there are 16 parallel query processes, and a table's degree of parallelization is 8. Oracle uses the following logic to determine how many query processes to use.

```
if degree of parallelization set for table then
   if number of query server processes >= that degree
      dispatch that number of query server processes to process query
   else
      dispatch as many query server processes as are available
   end if
else
   process query using one and only one server process
end if
```

4. Assembles qualifying data, receiving chunks from each participant query process. As the participating query server processes finish their work, each passes qualifying data back through the dispatcher process.

5. Merges the chunks of data into a consistent set of qualifying data under the supervision of the dispatcher.

6. Passes the data back to the user process that initiated the query.

Picture a situation when, for whatever reason, the work passed off to parallel query process P001 was not as intensive as that passed to process P002. As a result, say P001 finished its work early while P002 was only half done with its task. Oracle uses a dynamic load balancing system such that query processes that finish early will rob work from processes involved in retrieving data from the same query.

VIP
This dynamic load balancing is one of the most important characteristics of a successful approach to parallel query processing.

Load Operations

In a data warehouse, large volumes of data end up being moved into the warehouse during partial or complete refreshes. We dedicated Chapter 10 to Oracle Loader, directing you here to look at how to parallelize loader routines. Suppose you wanted to load 7,000,000 rows into a table in your warehouse, and the data resided in a fixed-length text file. The next listing shows a few lines from that file.

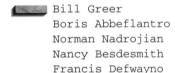

```
Bill Greer            CEO           Bunque Systems International
Boris Abbeflantro     President     BJA Holdings
Norman Nadrojian      Senior VP     Communications Directorate Ltd.
Nancy Besdesmith      Trainer       Silver Institute
Francis Defwayno      Conductor     Chapel Philharmonic
```

Notice the number of characters reserved for name, position, and company; hence the term fixed-length. To perform a parallel load (using three parallel processes in this example, though you can use more or less), do the following:

1. Extract the data from its source repository into three separate output files. Select a column from the source data such that, for example, records whose state code starts with A to H are in one file, I to M in another, and N to Z in the third.

2. Create three separate control files to feed to Oracle Loader. We discussed the control file in Chapter 10, and included some examples.

3. Initiate three Oracle Loader sessions to run concurrently, using something similar to the following program in UNIX. The "&" character tells UNIX that the job should run without tying up the terminal (also referred to as running in the *background*).

```
sqlldr userid=tom/scholz control=parr1 parallel=true &
sqlldr userid=tom/scholz control=parr2 parallel=true &
sqlldr userid=tom/scholz control=parr3 parallel=true &
```

From our experience, load sessions run in parallel complete in significantly less time even though they are loading data into the same table(s) concurrently.

Table and Index Creation

Data warehouse load and data transformation personnel continually create tables and indexes as the repository is refreshed. You can parallelize these two operations using parallel processing and the following syntax.

```
create table blah_blah (...) parallel 2;
create index blah_blah_1 on blah_blah (...) parallel 2;
```

Previously in the "Query Processing" section, we spoke of setting a degree of parallelization for a table. There, the parallel keyword was used in the **parallel (degree..)** construct, whereas here it is simply **parallel n**, where **n** is an integer representing the number of parallel processes to utilize.

Partitioning Objects (8)

As the size of the enterprise data warehouse grows, the bounds of very large objects are being stretched. Picture the metrics illustrated in Table 19-4, using the megabyte (1,048,576 bytes as the unit of measurement).

NOTE
Using this table, think of an exabyte as 1,152,921,504,607,000,000 bytes—perhaps some of us will have the opportunity to support a 16 exabyte data warehouse some day!

Measure		Units	Of
megabyte	=	1,024	kilobytes
gigabyte	=	1,024	megabytes
terabyte	=	1,024	gigabytes
petabyte	=	1,024	terabytes
exabyte	=	1,024	petabytes

TABLE 19-4. *Units of Measurement*

It does not take too long to realize the sheer size of many data warehouse implementations when you start talking about a repository in the neighborhood of a few hundred terabytes (the same as a few thousand gigabytes or a few ten thousand megabytes). Some day-to-day operational system repositories' data swells well into many gigabytes, if not terabytes. Oracle8 mechanisms address very large database requirements using a scheme of partitioning we will touch on in the next few sections. *Partitioning* is the deliberate separation of a very large object into smaller, more manageable chunks. Oracle8 permits partitioning of data and index segments using some of the syntax we are about to cover.

Why Partition Objects

Partitioning is a smart approach, because breaking up large objects provides so many benefits, including:

- Less chance of losing data when it is partitioned—the chance of experiencing total data destruction in a partitioned object is exponentially lower than in a nonpartitioned object.

- Ease of load balancing—the breakup and deliberate separation of partitions can assist in the process we all go through of ensuring there is a balance of read/write operations between all the disks upon which our Oracle8 database resides.

- Backup and recovery—when an Oracle8 database design maps pieces of partitioned objects across multiple data files, it becomes easier to plan an optimal.

■ Ease of archival—when objects are partitioned by column values, older data can be more easily moved offline as time marches on. Say an organization partitions by fiscal year and is committed to keeping current and two previous years accessible at all times. As the calendar flips from December 31, 1998 to January 1, 1999, the data in the 1996 fiscal year can be easily moved to the archives.

Partitioning is one of the biggest trends in the industry regarding management of very large databases. All the vendors are getting on the bandwagon, not just Oracle.

Working with Partitioned Objects

We looked at some of the syntax for creating partitioned objects in a few other places around this book. Let's look at the flexibility offered by a partitioned object approach and how it fits so nicely into the management of very large objects. The following is a sample of five common operations you can do with partitioned tables and other objects:

■ Table partitions can be moved from one device to another to assist the I/O balancing exercise. The **alter table account move partition p2…;** keywords are the heart of this operation.

■ Index partitions can be moved as well, except the movement of one or more pieces of a partitioned index requires rebuilding the index or each partition individually. The **alter index account_1 rebuild partition p2;** construct is how this is accomplished.

■ Partitions can be added to tables and indexes using the **alter table account add partition p2;**. When a partition is added to an existing partitioned table, the corresponding indexes, if any, are further partitioned to match.

■ Table partitions can be dropped after deleting their rows. This is accomplished using the **alter table account drop partition p3;** command. Index partitions cannot be manually dropped; they are dropped implicitly when the data they refer to is dropped from the partitioned table.

■ Rows can be truncated from a partition using the **alter table account truncate partition p3;** command. The corresponding index partitions are truncated at the same time as the table to which the index belongs.

Partition Views (7.3 and 8)

As data is moved from operational systems into the data warehouse, design personnel find themselves bombarded with vast amounts of data many times more voluminous than the original information. Data is denormalized when moved into the data warehouse: as the nature of how the data is stored changes, it inevitably takes up more space. The best way to illustrate the wonder of partition views is to look at a common implementation of a sales datamart.

VIP

Partition views are an entirely different concept than building partitioned tables, as covered in the previous section. When using a partition view, the data resides in separate tables and is brought together at run time. The secret to the view is using the **union all** *to splice the tables together.*

Suppose information in the datamart has a time component that resides in a denormalized SALES table. The next listing shows the makeup of a few key columns in SALES:

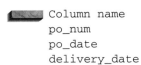
```
Column name
po_num
po_date
delivery_date
```

As data is moved into a warehouse, utilizing partition views involves the following steps:

■ Analyze the source data, determining how the information can be split to build a number of separate partitions or tables.

■ Move the data from the operational system into the warehouse using that column as a selection criterion.

Suppose we selected PO_DATE as the partitioning column, and discovered the earliest date in the operational sales system is January 21, 1994, and the data goes up to the present day. Inspect the following abstract of a few SQL statements used to build the SALES datamart partition.

```
create table SALES_94 as
select * from PURCHASE_ORDER where po_date between
       to_date('21-JAN-1994','DD-MON-YYYY')
       and to_date('31-DEC-1994','DD-MON-YYYY')
       and line_item <= 3;
create table SALES_95 as
select * from PURCHASE_ORDER where po_date between
       to_date('01-JAN-1995','DD-MON-YYYY')
       and to_date('31-DEC-1995','DD-MON-YYYY')
       and line_item <= 3;
create table SALES_96 as
select * from PURCHASE_ORDER where po_date between
       to_date('01-JAN-1996','DD-MON-YYYY')
       and to_date('31-DEC-1996','DD-MON-YYYY')
       and line_item <= 3;
create table SALES_97 as
select * from PURCHASE_ORDER where po_date between
       to_date('01-JAN-1997','DD-MON-YYYY')
       and to_date('31-DEC-1997','DD-MON-YYYY')
       and line_item <= 3;
create table SALES_98 as
select * from PURCHASE_ORDER where po_date between
       to_date('01-JAN-1998','DD-MON-YYYY')
       and to_date('31-DEC-1998','DD-MON-YYYY')
       and line_item <= 3;
create table SALES_99 as
select * from PURCHASE_ORDER where po_date between
       to_date('01-JAN-1999','DD-MON-YYYY')
       and to_date('31-DEC-1999','DD-MON-YYYY')
       and line_item <= 3;
create view SALES as
select * from sales_94
union all
select * from sales_95
union all
select * from sales_96
```

```
union all
select * from sales_97
union all
select * from sales_98;
union all
select * from sales_99;
```

And now, the magic begins. There are two main features that come into play when a query is passed to Oracle that accesses a view using this facility:

■ Suppose an analysis were being done that looked for data in the SALES partition view for calendar year 1997. The partitions built on all calendar years other than 1997 would be skipped by the process scanning the data. This is called *partition elimination,* and by nature can drastically reduce the amount of data being scanned. Let's say the total number of rows in the partition view was 12,000,000 rows, and the 1997 partition contained 1,500,000. The execution plan and retrieval of information from the view would scan less than 15% of the total number of rows in the view.

■ If more than one partition is scanned as a query is processed, the optimizer may end up using a different execution plan to fetch information from different partitions. It may choose a full table scan for one or more partitions, and do an index range scan on others.

Star Query Optimization (7.3 and 8)

In many data warehouses, designers build a star schema that can be characterized by a very large table (called the *fact* table) and two or more smaller tables (called *dimension* tables) that contain information about attributes in the large fact table. These dimension tables used to be called lookup tables. The optimizer recognizes queries built on a star schema when it encounters the following:

■ A join operation (merging data from two or more tables) where one table is very large compared to the other tables involved in the operation.

■ There is a network of foreign keys sitting in the very large table pointing at all of the smaller dimension tables.

■ The very large table has a composite index (i.e., index built on more than one column).

Once Oracle detects these three characteristics of a query, special star query processing routines come into play. The cost-based optimizer uses a transformation technique to process star queries; this transformation specifically rewords a query (without changing the intent) to take advantage of speed-enhancing objects such as bitmap indexes discussed previously in this chapter.

VIP

*When supporting an Oracle8 database, star query transformation and processing routines will come into play when the initialization parameter file entry STAR_TRANSFORMATION_ENABLED is set to **true** and the instance restarted.*

The star transformation is a good example of why Oracle's optimization approach is called *cost-based*. The optimizer decides the cost of using or not using the transformation by:

■ Generating the best plan it can produce without the transformation and placing it away for safekeeping.

■ Applying the transformation (if enabled), if applicable, and generating the best plan using the transformed query.

■ Comparing the cost estimates of the best plans for the two versions of the query.

■ Selecting the transformed or nontransformed plan, whichever is best (i.e. costs the least).

Most works that discuss data warehouse design, management, and deployment spend time talking about the star schema and why it makes so much sense in the decision support environment. *Building the Data Warehouse* (Inmon, John Wiley & Sons, 1996; ISBN 0-471-14161-5) is one of many.

What's Next

Data warehousing—a new phenomenon or simply a new way of saying an old thing? We lean toward the latter. We believe that what makes data warehousing seem so new is the sheer volume of data being managed in the present day. In the next chapter, we will look at network computing, specifically Oracle's solution. We think that network computing is the next-generation client/server technology looming on the horizon, rushing toward us at a blistering pace...duck!

CHAPTER
20

NC and Architecture

he shot heard 'round the world is a term you heard quite often if you grew up in New England. It represents the first shot fired during the American Revolution. Fact: a tiny colony was able to make a stand against the mighty empire of England, an empire so large that, somewhere within the empire, the sun was always shining. This analogy comes to mind when we think of what Larry Ellison, the founder of Oracle Corporation, was able to accomplish with his vision of the NC. Did anyone ever envision that great corporate giants like Microsoft, HP, and IBM would be so shaken by a concept that they would rethink and restructure their pricing, alliances and future strategies based on Ellison's vision of the NC? Yes, this vision is a shot heard around the world. Even if the NC had never become a reality, the impact it has had on technology companies would have been remembered for many, many years. Let's take a closer look at the Network Computer, but first review some terminology that will be very useful in order to help you understand this chapter better.

NOTE
We will use the acronym "NC" from here on to refer to the NC (odd how enamored we have all become with these abbreviations!).

Terminology

The following definitions will arm you with the technical jargon you need to make it through this chapter.

- An *end user* is the person using a canned application on the PC. A CPA using an Excel spreadsheet is an example of an end user. These are people who use computers to accomplish day-to-day tasks, but who have not been trained on the inner workings of a PC.

- A *fat client* is your traditional PC system. If purchased today it would have at least 16 megabytes of memory, 1.2 gigabytes of disk storage, a Pentium-based chip and an internal CD-ROM drive—in other words, your typical PC purchase. In the client/server world, a fat client would contain all the code/programs locally.

- An *intranet* site is where one or more applications reside that were built using Internet technologies. To access the application, you use a universal browser like Netscape Navigator or Microsoft Internet Explorer. Since it is an intranet site, the applications reside within the company firewall and are accessed using Internet technologies, like TCP/IP, HTML or Java. The primary purpose of intranet sites is to service internal customers.

■ An *Internet* site is where one or more applications reside that were built using Internet technologies. To access the application, you typically use a universal browser like Netscape Navigator or Microsoft Internet Explorer. Since it is an Internet site, the applications reside outside the firewall and are accessed using Internet technologies, like TCP/IP, HTML or Java. The primary purpose of Internet sites is to service external customers. A typical Internet URL is "http://www.dbtinc.com". An average Internet site typically contains marketing information.

■ A *firewall* is another term for a router. Its primary purpose is to inspect network traffic and prevent unauthorized traffic from passing through. In other words the router inspects requests coming from external sources and determines if they are appropriate to pass into internal systems. For example, an e-mail message sent to George Noll would only be allowed to enter into the system if you actually have an employee with that name. In addition, a firewall can also determine what types of services will be allowed through. For example, it might not allow a Telnet session to run.

■ A *Network Computer* or *"NC"* is a thin client by nature with as little as 4MB of Ram and no hard drive, but with any range of microprocessors from a Pentium to a 32-bit RISC chip that will retail for under $1000.00. Since the average user of a PC only uses it for functions like e-mail and word processing, why put an expensive "FAT Client/PC" on the desktop when only 10 percent of its functionality is ever really being used? Instead you can put a machine on the desktop that only has to deal with the presentation of information, which means that it only needs a very small operating system, small amount of memory, very fast processor and little or no disk storage. Unlike the dumb terminals of the past, the NC does have its own processor. The best analogy to this device is the telephone. It might have some limited functionality on its own, but it is useless unless it is hooked up to the phone network.

■ The *Network Computing Architecture* is Oracle's answer to surviving the information-enabled age. With the introduction and establishment of the Internet as a viable commercial platform for computing, Oracle took a hard look at the kind of architecture that would be needed to harness and manage software development and deployment in the age of network computing. They established a three-tier architecture, with a thin client for the presentation layer, an application server for business rules, and a database server for data storage and manipulation. The goal is to have a common set of technologies that will allow all PCs, NCs, and any other client devices to work with all database servers, application servers and Web servers over any network.

■ An *open system* is one that is built on open standards, as compared to a proprietary system. The classic example of this is UNIX. You can purchase the UNIX operating system from many sources, each of which is based on a core industry standard. It is interesting to note that each vendor, as a practice, always tries to put unique enhancements on its own version of the UNIX system, in order to lock you into their "open" offering.

■ A *proprietary system* is one that is built upon a company-unique standard or capability. Systems built on the Digital Computers VMS operating system or the IBM MVS operating system are examples of proprietary systems. If you want to use these operating systems, you must go to either the source or one of their licensees.

■ A *thin client* is a device with minimal internal memory and little or no hard disk storage, but typically has a microprocessor of some sort. In the future thin clients will range from Personal Data Assistants (PDAs) to NCs.

■ A *URL* is an Internet address. An example of a URL is "http://www.dbtinc.com". Think of this as your roadmap to any given Internet site. The acronym URL actually stands for *uniform resource location.*

■ A computer *virus* is a software program written to disrupt and annoy the computer systems that it "infects." Sometimes these viruses can be very harmful and initialize hard disks or even cause entire systems to crash.

- The *World Wide Web* is the graphical portion of the Internet. Since the creation of universal browsers like Netscape Navigator and Microsoft Inernet Explorer, the Internet can now easily deal with all types of data from sound to video to text. With this newfound graphical capability, anyone can easily navigate the Internet. Browsers have taken the Internet from the once-sacred realm of the highly technical person to John and Jane Q. Public. The advent of their massive embrace of Web surfing has created an extremely viable commercial platform on which to do business.

- *Zero administration for Windows* is an announcement by Microsoft to deliver software to substantially bring down the administrative costs associated with desktops. It's Microsoft's answer to combat the NC. With zero administration, Microsoft hopes that the day-to-day attention many PCs and the software they run requires will be reduced. With a reduction in the need for human intervention, the administrative nightmare could be reduced to zero.

The Network Computer "NC"

This dream is becoming a reality. Lets take a closer look at Larry Ellison's vision. Larry Ellison has been quoted as saying "all mature networks like TV and telephone have the same model—simple appliances with sophisticated and powerful networks…Users shouldn't have to worry about the underlying technology. Developers shouldn't be left out in the cold by a proprietary standards battle, and corporate customers shouldn't be left stranded with old technologies that don't work together."

In his vision of the future, he feels that it's about time the industry built an inexpensive device (a unit that sells for about $500) that hooks up to the network and is capable of meeting most users' needs. This device must be as simple to use as a telephone, and like the telephone, unless it's hooked up to the network, it is useless. When it is on the network, however, it becomes a very powerful tool. Another term the industry uses for this type of device is *thin client*. By design, this device would have 4 megabytes of RAM, no hard drive, and most likely some sort of Intel-based microprocessor. The reason this device can be so lean is due to the fact that the complexity of the technology is pushed onto the network.

Does Everyone Really Need a Fat Client?

Many of the users today who have fat clients on their desktops (or, in other words, a traditional PC system which if purchased today would have at least 16 megabytes of memory, 1.2 gigabytes of disk storage, a Pentium-based chip and an internal CD-ROM drive) neither need nor want to deal with all that complexity. A typical user who almost exclusively uses his or her computer for e-mail and word processing would be much happier with a NC: the simpler, the better. In today's world, these users have no choice but to purchase a fully equipped PC. How many times have we heard users talk about that big paperweight on their desk?

Ever had to deal with a broken PC? Think about what happens if your NC breaks down; if at your place of work, you are issued a new one. At a cost of about $500, it makes sense to have a spare waiting—after all, most of us have extra phones in our homes. Compared to the PC, the NC is really a very simple device. The things that typically break down on a PC are not part of an NC: there is no CD-ROM drive, no $3\frac{1}{2}$ inch drive, and no hard drive. When a PC breaks down, someone generally has to come in and fix it. When the NC breaks down, you put in a new one. Ever try to use a PC right out of the box? Good luck! You'll spend an entire day just getting the network card compatibility issues solved. With the NC, the complexity is pushed out to the network, and the end user does not have to deal with compatibility issues.

How many times have we heard that a critical piece of information resides only on a disk drive that just broke down? Far too many times. The reason is clear: most people who use computers are very good at their jobs, but not very good at backing up or even working with PCs beyond canned software like e-mail or Microsoft Word. Perhaps the machine never breaks down. What about the complexity of upgrading the software every nine months? Does a typical end user really need to deal with all these issues? Does it make sense every time a software vendor releases a new version to force our end users to upgrade their software? Do we trust that they have the necessary skill set to upgrade the software and troubleshoot the upgrade when things go wrong? Does it make sense for support people to go out to hundreds of PCs and individually upgrade them? Is this really the best use of their time and skill set? Never mind the fact that you might be doing all of these activities for someone who only uses e-mail. How many times has a network been infected with a computer virus by someone who only needs the PC to e-mail? Even if we have software that helps automate those problems, a typical fat client is a very complex device. Can you really expect to troubleshoot these problem remotely and keep it all running?

VIP

Larry Ellison, commenting on the PC versus the NC, said it best: "You might have running water in your home, but that doesn't mean you need a well."

Certainly, there is a class of users out there that need PCs, and by all means, they should have access to PCs. But if you asked most users to explain what all the icons mean on their PC, they couldn't tell and couldn't care less. So why force them to pay for all that unused and unnecessary capability? Clearly, they don't need to have all those unused applications residing on their desktops.

When was the last time you were given (or more than likely demanded) a more powerful desktop at your place of work? Did the upgrade take you from a mere 386 DX66 up to a Pentium or perhaps a Pentium Pro? What was the cost of that upgrade? When one extrapolates the cost (let's settle on about $4,000 for a powerful Pentium Pro with gobs of memory and local storage) across an enterprise of 400 users; all of a sudden the most recent personal computer hardware upgrade checks in at $160,000. We know this could easily happen again, thanks to the advances in computer technology that are happening as we speak.

VIP

Think about it—the NC makes even more sense in the workplace. Let the server provider in the three-tier architecture do the expensive upgrades, and let the NC keep doing what it does best—provide the user interface.

Economics at Work

Evaluating the economics of the situation is a very reliable way to determine industry and technology trends. Everyone loves a good deal. Ever go to an auction and watch people buy things just because the opening bid is so low? Ever go to a store sale and watch people buy things they really don't need just because they are on sale? These two examples validate the point that money is a very powerful motivating tool. What caused the immense popularity of the rightsizing/downsizing movement? The answer is simple: economics. It became cheaper for corporations to migrate their legacy systems onto to an open system, reengineer the applications, and have the return on investment (*ROI*) pay for itself in three to five years. This caused the corporate world to wake up and rightsize.

VIP

Economics is the source of many of our technology trends. Those technology trends with the highest ROI will typically be dominant trends.

The Internet explosion is another example of economics at work. Today it is possible for people to create an Internet store at a very low cost and have access to over 100,000,000 people. Now that corporations see the Internet as a commercially viable platform, there is a massive trend toward the creation of corporate Internet strategies. The fact that the Internet offers the perfect client, is free, and can be deployed and maintained cheaply is the reason for this trend toward Internet/intranet-aware applications.

When you take a look at the economics of the NC, you notice that it is a lot cheaper to purchase and maintain in comparison with the PC. Unlike a dumb terminal, the NC has the full presentational capabilities of a PC. This economic fact alone will force the corporate world to take notice. In Larry Ellison's words, "The administration costs of our NC are identical to the administration costs of your television and telephone. If that's not true, we screwed up."

This statement is the very reason every PC vendor has announced price cuts and a commitment to develop a PC for under $1000 or has committed to build NCs. This is the very reason we see corporate giants like Microsoft announce new strategies and alliances to defend themselves against the Network PC. The recent study by the Gartner Group has many vendors scared.

The Gartner Group recently did a survey to determine the yearly administration cost of a PC, which they found to be $12,000. Intel Corporation commissioned its own study and announced the yearly administration costs to be $8,000. Whether the costs are $8,000 or $12,000, you can see why they are all nervous. The economics of the PC versus the NC doesn't look good for the PC. The only winner in this game is the customer, and Intel, who will only sell more chips. Imagine yourself as the CIO of a corporation defending the purchase of expensive fat clients to the budget-minded CEO. With these economics at work, things are going to change quickly.

What is Zero Administration?

As we have already mentioned, Microsoft itself is reacting to the NC, fearing that their adoption will cause it to lose its stronghold over the marketplace. Microsoft is afraid the monopoly they have over the desktop might come to an end, just as IBM's stronghold on the marketplace ended many years ago. In this era, every two to three years you are forced to replace your PC, even though it works perfectly well. The Microsoft business model relies on this planned obsolescence. How do they do it? Easy: they put out a new version of the operating system, let's call it Windows 95. They start reducing support of previous versions, let's say Windows 3.1. Due to the way the software is written, certain computers are incapable of running Windows 95. Since Windows is the only game in town, guess what? You pay up. You are forced to upgrade to newer versions of the Microsoft family of software which, in turn, forces you to upgrade computers if you want your desktop software to keep running.

Frankly, the NC computer scares them, and what scares them most is its compelling financial model. As we have already discussed, economics makes the industry move quickly. They realize that when you evaluate the costs associated with acquiring and maintaining a PC as compared to a NC, they are in big trouble.

Using an old trick of IBM's, Microsoft has announced a new product offering before it actually exists. Microsoft knows that many people in the marketplace will wait to purchase an NC simply because of this promise to deliver. What's ironic is that Microsoft has known about the high administration costs associated with PCs for many years, but only now that a competing product exists are they concerned about these high costs.

The Microsoft solution to this problem is the "Zero Administration for Windows" initiative, which is Microsoft's promise to build a core set of tools to give information system professionals new control over the desktop by automating such tasks as updating operating systems and installing applications, profiling users, and locking down desktop systems. This solution, if it really works, only addresses a small part of what the NC is all about. You would still be "overpurchasing" a system for the majority of the end user community, and still have an inherently complex configuration of technology to keep working. You still have to deal with the obsolescence of the PC every two to three years, which is something that these vendors are counting on. The majority of the potential PC users in the world are not using technology. We feel this is because we don't yet have a mature network in place; a mature network would be easy to access at very high speeds, and be available virtually 24 hours a day, seven days a week.

Many people believe the model of deploying on the desktop has not changed in twenty years; perhaps it's time for a new model. The NC represents the next logical evolution of the desktop.

NC—The Paradigm Must Change

As the next potential desktop evolution, the success of the NC is so likely that the corporate giants are reacting very quickly to its possibilities. The world is changing due to technology, and technology is changing due to the world. The world has an insatiable hunger for information, and the desktop is the key to getting at that information. The desktop paradigm must and will change to meet this need. Larry Ellison said it best when he said that until a mature network is established, we will never see a worldwide adoption of technology that is possible. Larry Ellison is right—the model is going to change. For example, look at the explosion of the Internet. As soon as a universal browser was in existence, which made it easy to navigate the Internet, the world embraced the Internet. The browser, in many ways, hides and simplifies the complexity of the Internet for the average end user. The browser represents an open standard which makes it easy for all vendors to build and deploy software. Many of the reasons the universal browser has been so successful will be put into practice when Oracle publishes the Network Computing Architecture: they understand the power of an open standard that vendors can embrace.

Clearly, the complexity needs to be pushed back to the network, where the end user is insulated from it. With a mature network, this will be possible; only through centralization of this network will we ever be able to support the needed infrastructure. There simply are not enough specialists to deploy at every desktop: we need to be able to concentrate specialists in central locations, instead of trying to spread them around to every fat client. With the complexity of fat clients pushed back to the mature network, we can concentrate on building devices that everyone will be able to use.

Imagine trying to keep a telephone system working if every user had access to the internals of the phone network. With the mature network model in place, the end user would not be dealing with issues like computer viruses, backups, or upgrades. Under the mature network model, these items would be handled in central locations by trained professionals. Given the potential marketplace value, we are surprised that the mature network model has not been embraced sooner.

Recognizing that the paradigm is changing, Oracle realizes we need a new architecture that is ready to deal with Network Computing. Oracle knows that the corporate world is looking for this roadmap, which will enable them to survive in the Web-enabled world. That thirst for information will never be quenched until we have an architecture than can support it. Next, we will discuss Oracle's Network Computing Architecture, which will enable us to build and maintain the information age.

The Network Computing Architecture

The Network Computing Architecture or *NCA* is just what the name implies—an architecture for building and integrating applications within a networked computing environment. Remember, the World Wide Web is a Network Computing environment. By publishing this architecture, Oracle wants to make it as easy as possible for companies to adopt and develop solutions based upon this standard. The success of the universal browsers alone is proof as to why an open standard that people can build to makes sense. Oracle's early development of this well-needed architecture has placed Oracle Corporation and its technologies in the center of the Network Computing movement and positioned Oracle as the Internet solutions company.

VIP
*The Network Computing Architecture, "NCA,"
is exactly what its name implies: Oracle's
stated architecture for building and integrating
applications within a networked computing
environment. Remember, the World Wide
Web is a Network Computing environment.*

What Oracle was very quick to realize was that the combination of
Web computing and the NC requires a new architecture and that the
corporate world is crying out for the "how to do it." The Network
Computing Architecture provides corporations with the framework for the
information age: one that is portable, scaleable, extensible (able to deal
with the widest range of data types from text to video), and provides
corporations with a clear migration path from client/server to
Network-enabled computing.

Unlike the client/server model, which is based on a two-tier
architecture, Oracle has developed NCA architecture, which is based
on three separate tiers. The client/server architecture consists of :

- A client tier responsible for the presentation (including user
  interface issues) and the application itself.

- A server tier in which the data resides (e.g., the Oracle Universal
  Server).

The NCA architecture has three tiers consisting of:

- A thin client tier responsible for the presentation of information. In
  the Network Computing Architecture it assumes these are thin clients.

- An application server tier which is the layer responsible for all the
  business rules. In the Network Computing Architecture, it is assumed
  that this is a fat client.

- A database server tier which is responsible for the manipulation and
  storage of data. Data ranges from text to number, to video on demand.

The Network Computing Architecture is also designed to take advantage of all operating systems and all hardware platforms, which allows users to choose the operating system and hardware that gives them the best price performance.

By separating the presentation tier from the application layer, the PC functionality can now reside on a thin client. Remember our definition of a thin client—as little as 4MB of RAM and no hard drive but with any range of microprocessors, from a Pentium to a 32-bit RISC chip, that will retail for under $1,000.

The application tier now resides on a separate server from the database server tier. These would be put on machines with a very heavy footprint: minimally, they would be on a fat client. Remember our definition of a fat client: it would have at least 16 megabytes of memory, 1.2 gigabytes of disk storage, a Pentium-based chip and an internal CD-ROM drive. The point is that the application server and the database server can be moved to a machine with a lot more resources, perhaps a very big UNIX machine. These machines would be placed in a central location and managed by trained specialists. The end user is shielded from all the complexity.

VIP

The Network Computing Architecture is made up of the layers—the thin client layer, the application server layer and the database server layer. You can use different operating systems and hardware platforms with Network Computing Architecture.

So far we have discussed the Network Computing Architecture in its most simple form. The NCA envisions a world in which the database server and application server all are networked together as well as to thin clients. As you can see, there is a lot more to the architecture than that. At the heart of this architecture are data cartridges. The Network Computing Architecture also includes the necessary protocols that define how and what communications take place and when they should take place. As you can see in Figure 20-1, the builders of the NC Architecture envisioned a lot of data cartridges.

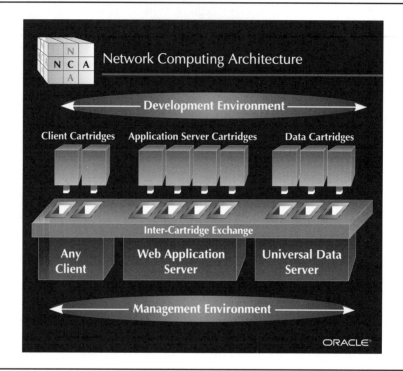

FIGURE 20-1. *Oracle's Network Computing Architecture*

What Is a Data Cartridge?

As we stated before, the Network Computing Architecture envisions a world in which the database server and application server all are networked together as well as to thin clients. It also envisions a world where vendors create software cartridges which can be plugged into the client tier, the application server tier, or even the database server tier. So today as published, the architecture envisions three types of cartridges:

- Client cartridges
- Application server cartridges
- Data cartridges

The cartridges are component-based software. Simply put, a cartridge is a program component. To use a cartridge, it must be installed and registered. This means an application cartridge is installed on the application server and registered. A database cartridge is installed on the database server and registered and so forth. As we stated, cartridges are component-based software, which means that cartridges would be built with PL/SQL, SQL, C++, JAVA, or even Visual Basic. A cartridge is software.

VIP

A cartridge is software. Cartridges can be built using SQL, JAVA, etc. To be used, they must be installed on the appropriate server and registered.

All cartridges will be able to take advantage of any other cartridge's services. The only difference is that an application cartridge will be installed on the application server, a database cartridge will be installed on the database server and so forth.

These cartridges allow applications to become very extensible. Developers can add more features by writing additional cartridges or by taking advantage of the services of other cartridges. Since the developer has the choice of where the cartridges reside, you are given more control over the various tiers.

The Inter-Cartridge Exchange

The backbone to this whole architecture is the inter-cartridge exchange. This is the bus that gives cartridges the ability to talk to other cartridges. With this backbone in place, cartridges anywhere in the network can take advantage of the services of any other cartridge.

Summary

Oracle has given us an architecture that can meet the challenge of the information age. We are facing a new paradigm: a world with thin clients where we have true Web-enabled computing. The Network Computing age is upon us. If we hope to truly realize the potential of technology, then we need to be doing a few things differently. We have no right to call this the information age when most of the world has no access to that information. The goal of this book is to give you enough information so that you can make a balanced decision on what is right for your business. After a thorough evaluation, we see the thin client playing a much stronger role in information technology.

Where Should You Go from Here?

This wraps up the final chapter in the *Oracle8: The Beginner's Guide* saga. We have covered a lot of material in this and the previous 19 chapters. Oracle8 is upon us. Many installations are still using previous releases of Oracle7 and some even V6. Whichever level of use you find yourself concerning the solutions Oracle provides, you know they have been and will continue to be a major force in enabling the information age. A theme that keeps recurring in many works about this age is the organization and presentation of data as it becomes information. Keep coming back to this book for reminders about Oracle (the company), Oracle (the solutions provider), and Oracle (the software manufacturer). Let's leave with a rhetorical question, and our comeback:

Q. Is Oracle doing anything especially unique and different than the host of other information technology vendors?

A. Yes and no. No—they have similar solutions, even though they are crafted in their unique way. Yes—they are a leader and are adding much greater impetus to the word *total* when they speak of their commitment to providing *total solutions.*

APPENDIX
A

SQL*DBA

ppendix A is dedicated to the former best friend of the database administrator—SQL*DBA. SQL*DBA was introduced with Oracle6 when it first hit the streets, and combined the ability to perform secure database administration activities coupled with monitoring capabilities formerly done through the Oracle Display System, affectionately called *ODS* in release 5. Beginning with release 7.1, Oracle delivered both SQL*DBA and Server Manager; we have featured and discussed the latter throughout the chapters of this book. With 7.3, Oracle stopped supplying SQL*DBA, forcing the technical community to start using Server Manager. For the sake of the readers using Oracle7 release 7.2 and lower, this appendix rolls all SQL*DBA-based discussions into one place. You may have noticed that it was missing from the two DBA chapters you have already come to love!

SQL*DBA operates in line or full-screen mode. The full-screen version imitates a Windows interface, with a menu bar at the top of the screen and a handful of drop-down menus underneath.

NOTE
*Starting now, we will use the name **sqldba** instead of SQL*DBA. We have architected this chapter to resemble the flow of the two DBA chapters, and we have left in the preamble to each section to allow DBAs supporting release 7.2 and earlier to use this appendix as a stand-alone guide to DBA activities.*

Line-Mode sqldba

Line-mode sqldba is a tool that is invaluable to any DBA: it is the program most commonly used to start up and shut down the database. It runs on any terminal, regardless of its ability to support graphics. For this reason, we introduce it first and suggest you use it as a starting point on your journey into DBA-land. You can run unattended jobs using line-mode sqldba.

Invoking

The command **sqldba lmode=y** starts line-mode sqldba and displays the following output:

```
SQL*DBA: Release 7.2.3.2.2 - Production on Tue Dec 11 12:34:20 1999
Copyright (c) Oracle Corporation 1979, 1994, 1995.  All rights reserved.
Oracle7 Server Release 7.2.3.2.2 - Production Release
PL/SQL Release 2.2.3.2.0 - Production
SQLDBA>
```

You are now positioned at the SQLDBA> line-mode prompt, and prepared to work with the database. The basic commands and their output are discussed in the next few sections.

NOTE

*You can also enter line-mode sqldba using the command **sqldba mode=line**.*

connect internal Command

After starting line-mode sqldba, enter **connect internal** and Oracle responds with

```
Connected.
SQLDBA >
```

You must connect to the Oracle database to perform all operations in sqldba. Every session in line-mode sqldba will start with this command.

Startup

After starting line-mode sqldba, follow these steps:

1. Enter **connect internal**.

2. Enter **startup**. Oracle responds with the following:

```
ORACLE instance started.
Database mounted.
Database opened.
Total System Global Area       4393640 bytes
              Fixed Size         46112 bytes
           Variable Size       3929736 bytes
        Database Buffers        409600 bytes
             Redo Buffers          8192 bytes
Export and Import SQLDBA>
```

The database is now started. We also refer to the database as being open or the database being up after this activity completes successfully.

Shutdown

After starting line-mode sqldba, follow these steps:

1. Enter **connect internal**.

2. Enter **shutdown**. Oracle responds with the following:

   ```
   Database closed.
   Database dismounted.
   ORACLE instance shut down.
   ```

VIP
Toward the start of the "Line-mode Server Manager" section of Chapter 14, there is a discussion about shutting down an Oracle database. Please refer to the section "Problems Shutting the Database" for important details.

Exiting

To exit, type **exit** at the SQLDBA> prompt. Oracle responds as shown here:

 ```
SQL*DBA complete
```
```

Granting Access to a User

You will need to perform this task as soon as you accept DBA responsibilities. To set up a new user, start line-mode sqldba, then follow these steps:

1. Enter **connect internal**.

2. Enter the command **grant connect to polly identified by gone;** and Oracle will respond with

   ```
   Statement processed.
   SQLDBA>
   ```

3. Enter **exit** to leave line-mode sqldba.

In this example, polly is the user name and gone is the password. Thus, user **polly** may connect to the database after supplying the password **gone**.

NOTE
The grant connect command only allows users to log onto the database; they can work with systems and other users' data, but they have no other privileges. Giving users the capability to have their own data is discussed in Chapter 18.

Revoking Access from a User

After starting line-mode sqldba, follow these steps:

1. Enter **connect internal**.

2. Enter the command **revoke connect from polly;** and receive Oracle's response.

   ```
   Statement processed.
   SQLDBA>
   ```

3. Enter **exit** to leave line-mode sqldba.

When this completes, user polly will no longer be able to access the database.

Creating a Tablespace

Creating a tablespace is a common activity for the new DBA, because almost as soon as you ascend to this throne, someone somewhere will need more space. The specifics for the following exercise are shown in Table A-1.

The location specified is a UNIX type; if you are using another O/S, the directory and filename may be different. After starting line-mode sqldba, follow these steps:

1. Enter **connect internal**.

2. Enter the command **create tablespace hold_my_data datafile'/usr/oradata/disk1/hmd.dbf' size 10m;** and receive Oracle's response.

   ```
   Statement processed.
   SQLDBA>
   ```

3. Enter **exit** to leave line-mode sqldba.

NOTE
The name of the datafile and its location are entered together, enclosed in single quotes. The space requested is mentioned after the filename, using the letter "m" to indicate megabytes (a megabyte is 1,048,576 bytes). The statement is free-form; it appears on two lines here as an example.

Tablespace Component	Detail
Name	hold_my_data
Datafile	hmd.dbf
Location	/usr/oradata/disk1
Size	10MB

TABLE A-1. *Requirements for Tablespace Creation Exercise*

Every time you start the database, it will now acquire the hold_my_data tablespace.

Adding Space to an Existing Tablespace

We will now add another 10 megabytes (10,485,760 bytes, or 10MB) of space to the hold_my_data tablespace. When this is done, we will have a total of 20MB allocated. After starting line-mode sqldba, follow these steps:

1. Enter **connect internal**.

2. Enter the command **alter tablespace hold_my_data add datafile'/usr/oradata/disk2/hmd2.dbf' size 10m;** and receive feedback from Oracle.

```
Statement processed.
SQLDBA>
```

3. Enter **exit** to leave line-mode sqldba.

You will find that line-mode sqldba is an important tool as you go about your DBA business. Some computer programs are referred to as "quick and dirty," and line-mode sqldba definitely falls into this category: it's dependable, easy to learn, and always comes packaged with Oracle up to and including release 7.2.

Full-Screen sqldba

Now we will move on to discussing full-screen sqldba, which provides an interface with check boxes and dialog boxes and allows you to accomplish the same tasks introduced in the previous section. After filling in blanks and pressing ENTER or the OK button, the SQL commands you have built are passed to Oracle for processing. Thus, the end result of using full-screen sqldba is the same as using the line-mode version.

Full-screen sqldba is a tool that provides a GUI-like environment with which you can perform all the same tasks as in the previous line-mode sqldba section. When using full-screen sqldba, you'll find a menu at the top of the screen which you can only access by pressing a key that Oracle calls "Menu." You will not, however, find a key on your keyboard called "Menu" because this is a name Oracle uses. When Oracle asks you to use the "Menu" key, you will most likely press the 0 key on your numeric keypad.

Invoking

Enter the command **sqldba** to start full-screen sqldba. You are presented with the screen shown in Figure A-1.

connect internal Command

After starting full-screen sqldba, enter **connect internal**. Oracle responds as shown in Figure A-2.

You are now connected to the database.

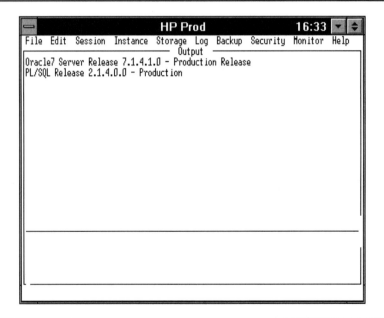

FIGURE A-1. *Starting full-screen sqldba*

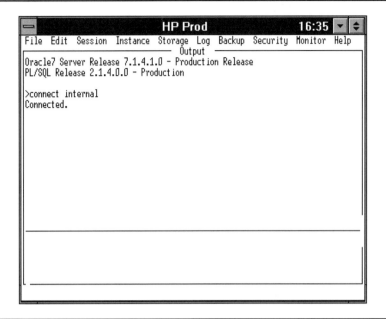

FIGURE A-2. *Connecting to the database using full-screen sqldba*

Startup

After starting full-screen sqldba, follow these steps:

I. Enter **connect internal**.

2. Enter **startup**. Oracle responds as shown in Figure A-3.

NOTE
Full-screen sqldba awaits your input when the box at the bottom of the screen is empty and the cursor is available for your input. Usually this happens just after Oracle has processed your command and given you feedback on its operation.

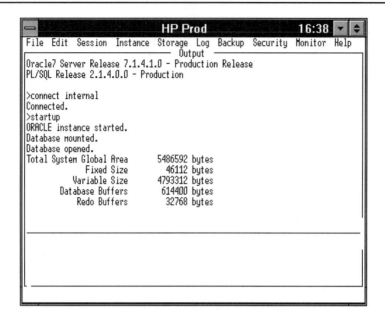

FIGURE A-3. *The startup command in full-screen sqldba*

The database is now started.

Shutdown

After starting full-screen sqldba, follow these steps:

1. Enter **connect internal**.

2. Enter **shutdown**. Oracle responds as shown in Figure A-4.

The database is now closed.

VIP
Toward the start of the "Line-mode Server Manager" section of Chapter 14, there is a discussion about shutting down an Oracle database. Please refer to the section "Problems Shutting the Database" for important details.

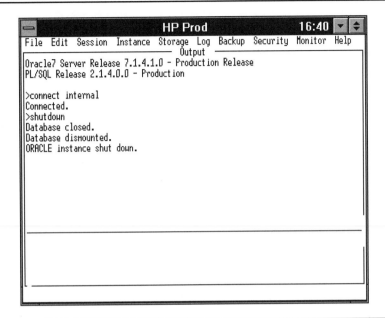

FIGURE A-4. *The shutdown command in full-screen sqldba*

Exiting

There are three ways to exit full-screen sqldba. The first, and quickest, way is to type the command **exit** and press ENTER. Alternatively, you can do one of the following:

1. Press ESC-Q. The Exit dialog box appears as shown in Figure A-5, with the OK selection highlighted. Press ENTER.

2. Press the Oracle Menu key, then select Quit from the File menu, as shown in Figure A-6. The same dialog box from Figure A-5 appears. Press ENTER.

Granting Access to a User

To set up a new user, start full-screen sqldba, then follow these steps:

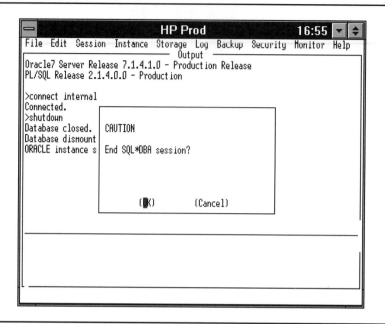

FIGURE A-5. *Exiting full-screen sqldba*

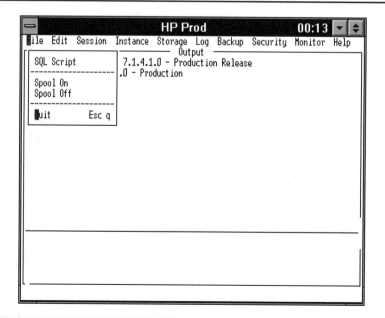

FIGURE A-6. *Exiting full-screen sqldba from the menu bar*

1. Enter **connect internal**.

2. Press the Oracle Menu key.

3. Select Create User from the Security menu. The Create User dialog box appears, as shown in Figure A-7.

4. Type **polly** beside the Name prompt, and **gone** beside the Use Password Authentication prompt as shown in Figure A-7. Move between fields using the TAB key.

5. Tab to OK and press ENTER to complete the command. Oracle closes the dialog box and shows you the command it has just executed.

6. Press the Oracle Menu key once again.

7. Select Grant System Privileges/Roles from the Security menu. The Grant System Privileges/Roles dialog box appears, as shown in Figure A-8.

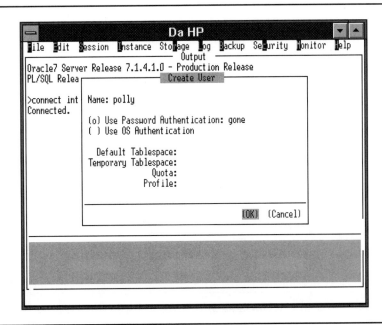

FIGURE A-7. *Create User dialog box*

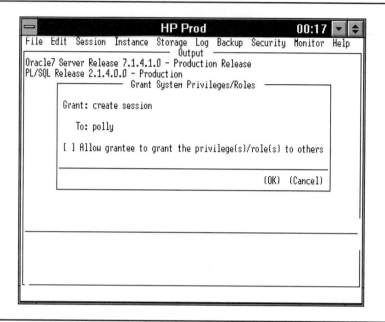

FIGURE A-8. *Grant Privileges and Roles dialog box*

8. Fill in **create session** beside Grant and **polly** beside To, as shown in Figure A-8.

9. Tab to the OK box and press ENTER to complete the command. Oracle closes the dialog box and shows you the command it has just executed.

10. Enter **exit** to leave sqldba.

User polly can now log onto the database. In Chapter 18 we discuss a number of other user management responsibilities.

Revoking Access from a User

After starting full-screen sqldba, you can revoke access by following these steps:

1. Enter **connect internal**.

2. Press the Oracle Menu key.

3. Select Revoke System Privileges/Roles from the Security menu. The Revoke System Privileges/Roles dialog box appears.

4. Fill in **connect** beside Revoke and **polly** beside From, as shown in Figure A-9.

5. Tab to the OK box and press ENTER to complete the command. Oracle closes the dialog box and shows you the command it has just executed.

6. Enter **exit** to leave sqldba.

Creating a Tablespace

We will use the requirements listed earlier in Table A-1. After starting full-screen sqldba, follow these steps:

1. Enter **connect internal**.

2. Press the Oracle Menu key.

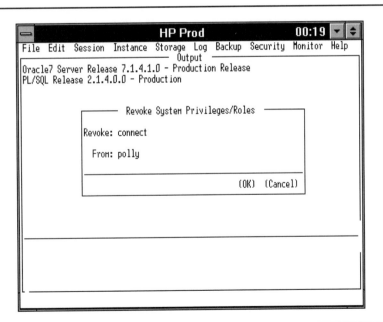

FIGURE A-9. *Revoke System Privileges/Roles dialog box*

3. Select Tablespace from the Storage menu. The Tablespace submenu appears, as shown in Figure A-10.

4. Select Create from the Tablespace submenu. The Create Tablespace dialog box appears, as shown in Figure A-11.

5. Fill in **hold_my_data** beside Name and **'/usr/oradata/disk1/ hmd.dbf' size 10m;** beside Data Files, as shown in Figure A-11.

6. Tab to the OK box and press ENTER to complete the command. Oracle closes the dialog box and shows you the command it has just executed.

7. Enter **exit** to leave sqldba.

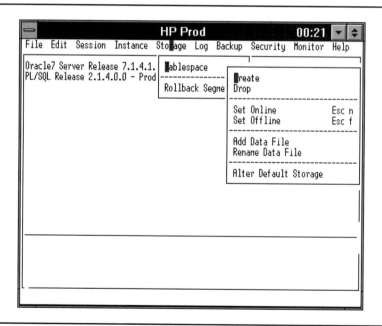

FIGURE A-10. *Tablespace submenu*

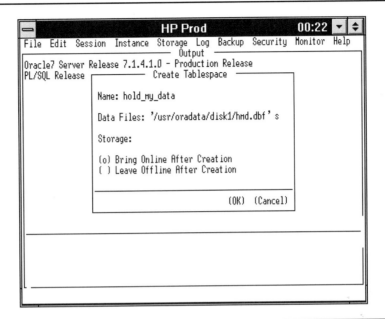

FIGURE A-11. *Create Tablespace dialog box*

NOTE
The name of the datafile and its location are entered together, enclosed in single quotes. The space requested is entered on the same line as the filename, using the letter **m** *to indicate megabytes (the size is specified at the end of the Data Files line that has scrolled off the screen in the figure).*

Every time you start the database, it will now acquire the hold_my_data tablespace.

Adding Space to an Existing Tablespace

After starting full-screen sqldba, follow these steps:

1. Enter **connect internal**.

2. Press the Oracle Menu key.

3. Select Tablespace from the Storage menu to open the Tablespace submenu.

4. Select Add Data File to Tablespace from the Tablespace submenu. The Add Data File to Tablespace dialog box appears, as shown in Figure A-12.

5. Move through the list of tablespaces using the DOWN ARROW key.

6. Press SPACEBAR to select HOLD_MY_DATA.

7. Enter the text **'/usr/oradata/disk2/hmd2.dbf' size 10m** in the dialog box as shown in Figure A-12.

8. Enter **exit** to leave sqldba.

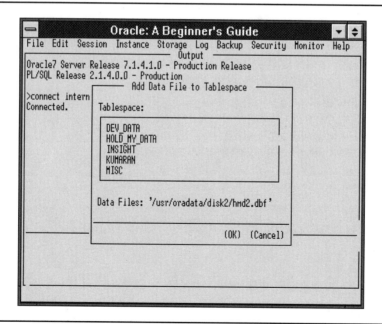

FIGURE A-12. *Add Data File to Tablespace dialog box*

The hold_my_data tablespace now has an additional 10MB of space within which tables can be stored.

Full-screen sqldba is useful as a learning tool; using the menu system and the dialog box method of data entry, you may find yourself getting more accomplished than when you used line-mode sqldba alone. Always study the commands passed to Oracle when you are finished with a full-screen sqldba dialog box.

Advanced Work with Full-screen sqldba

In this section, we will concentrate on full-screen sqldba (we will just use the term sqldba rather than full-screen sqldba). There are two interfaces in full-screen dba:

1. The dual-window facility: the bottom third of the screen is where you enter SQL commands and the top two-thirds is where Oracle displays and then responds to commands.

2. The menu dialog box facility: you use the top menu bar with drop-down menus to present boxes that you fill in with SQL statement details.

We will use the dual-window approach—we feel you can learn more by rolling your sleeves up and typing SQL commands manually.

 NOTE
You may find that using the dual-window method is many times faster than the menu/dialog box approach.

Startup Options

Most of the time you start your database, you simply start sqldba, connect to the database, and type **startup** to get things going. In this section, we will discuss additional startup options, using these options in sqldba, and when you may need or want to use one of these options.

Startup Normal

This is the default startup mode (you almost always omit the word "normal"). We showed you how to start up the database using Server Manager and the Enterprise Manager in Chapter 14. Use the output in Figure A-13 as a reference point for the following discussion on startup options.

Startup Mount

This mode is used to change the archiving status of the database or perform recovery. The database is not open, and therefore access by users is not permitted. After starting sqldba, follow these steps:

1. Enter **connect internal**.

2. Enter **startup mount**. Oracle responds with the output as shown in Figure A-14.

3. Enter **exit** to leave sqldba.

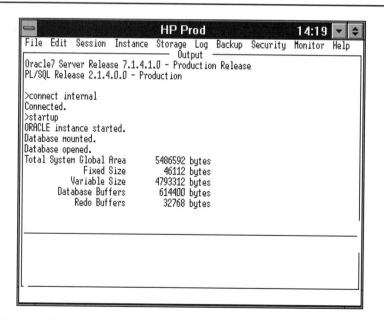

FIGURE A-13. *Startup normal in sqldba*

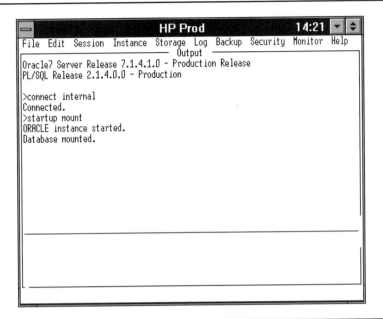

FIGURE A-14.   *Startup with the mount option*

The database is left in a mounted condition; users are not able to log on in this state. Notice in Figure A-14 that there is no message about opening the database or the size of the system global area.

Startup Nomount

This mode is used to recreate a control file or recreate the database from scratch. The database is not open, and therefore access by users is not permitted. After starting sqldba:

1. Enter **connect internal**.

2. Enter **startup nomount**. Oracle responds with the output as shown in Figure A-15.

3. Enter **exit** to leave sqldba.

The response from Oracle is similar to Figure A-14, except the Database mounted message is suppressed.

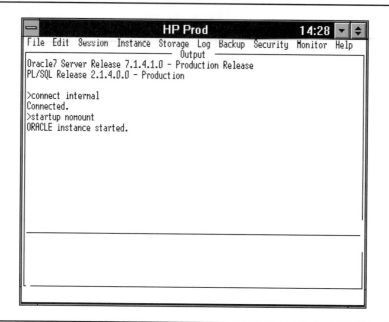

FIGURE A-15. *Startup with the nomount option*

Startup Restrict

This mode is used to start up the database, but access is restricted to
a privileged set of users that you have defined. The output from this
command is the same as shown in Figure A-13. The database is open,
but if non-privileged users attempt to log on, they will obtain the following
error message.

```
SQL*Plus: Release 3.2.3.5.1 - Production on Tue Dec 28 22:14:09 1999
Copyright (c) Oracle Corporation 1979, 1994.  All rights reserved.
Enter password:
ERROR: ORA-01035: ORACLE only available to users with RESTRICTED SESSION
privileges
Enter user-name:
```

Let's discuss changing the database access mode from restricted to
unrestricted. The first is done with the database open, the other by
restarting the database.

CHANGE STATUS WITH DATABASE OPEN   After entering sqldba:

1. Enter **connect internal**.

2. Enter **alter system disable restricted session;** and receive Oracle's response as shown in Figure A-16.

3. Enter **exit** to leave sqldba.

When this is done, the database is running in unrestricted access mode and users will be able to log on once more.

CHANGE STATUS BY RESTARTING THE DATABASE   After entering sqldba:

1. Enter **connect internal**.

2. Enter **shutdown**.

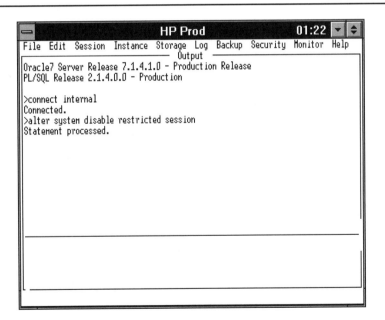

FIGURE A-16.   *Disabling restricted access*

3. Enter **startup**.

4. Enter **exit** to leave sqldba.

Regardless of the method you choose, the database will be open and ready for access by all once the steps are completed.

Startup Force

This option is used in the rare situation when you are unable to shut down a database. It shuts the database, then starts it with no options; the startup operation is the same as having issued the startup command alone. After starting sqldba, follow these steps:

1. Enter **connect internal**.

2. Enter **startup force**. You receive the feedback from Oracle as shown in Figure A-17.

3. Enter **exit** to leave sqldba.

When this operation is complete, your database will be open and accessible to the user community.

Startup pfile

This option with the startup command does not affect the mode of the database operation; it defines the name and location of the initialization parameter file (pfile). As we have discussed elsewhere, the initialization parameter file is read by Oracle as it opens a database. Oracle expects the default initialization parameter file to be in a location and called a name that is dependent on the hardware on which the database operates. In SCO-UNIX, for example, Oracle builds the default initialization parameter filename using the environment variable "$ORACLE_HOME", and appends the text "init", then the Oracle system identifier, and terminates the name with the file extension ".ora". Thus, a database with the system identifier "nau" uses a default initialization parameter file name of "initnau.ora". To

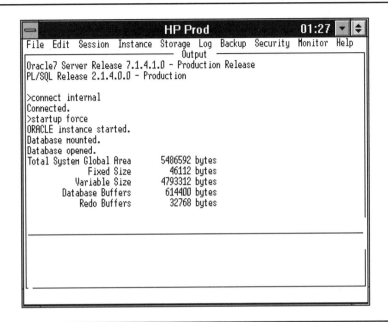

FIGURE A-17.   *Startup force*

start a database using an initialization parameter file other than the default, follow these steps after starting sqldba:

1. Enter **connect internal**.

2. Enter the command **startup pfile=?/dbs/tstother.ora** and receive feedback from Oracle as shown in Figure A-18. The text that follows **pfile=** is a directory name and filename of the initialization parameter file to be used for startup.

3. Enter **exit** to leave sqldba.

From time to time, you may use the pfile option to start your database with some initialization parameter file values different than usual. For

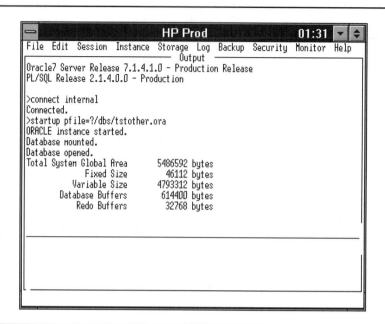

FIGURE A-18. *Startup with pfile*

example, when running a large data load, you may wish to instruct Oracle to allocate much more memory for sorting than you normally request.

NOTE
If you have started your database using the pfile option, remind yourself to shut it down and use the regular initialization parameter file when the job completes.

Nothing will go wrong if you leave your database running with an initialization parameter file other than the file you normally use.

VIP
More than 99 percent of the time, you will start up a database with no options.

Additional User Management Responsibilities

In this section we will round out your user management skills using sqldba. By the end of this section, you will know how to do the following:

- Assign a default tablespace for a user's objects
- Give users permission to acquire space in a tablespace
- Point users at a central tablespace for sorting

In the following sections, we'll have a user named *polly* with the password *gone*. The examples refer to the tablespace named *hold_my_data*.

Assign a Default Tablespace

Recall from Chapter 14 (in the three "Granting Access to a User" sections) that when you allowed a user access to the database, polly was permitted to log onto the database—but allowed to do nothing else. When the time comes to allow polly to occupy space in a tablespace in the database, she will do so by issuing SQL **create table** commands. By assigning polly a default tablespace, all her tables will end up in the hold_my_data tablespace by default. After starting sqldba, assign polly a default tablespace by following these steps:

1. Enter **connect internal**.

2. Enter the command **alter user polly default tablespace hold_my_data;** and receive the feedback from Oracle shown in Figure A-19.

3. Enter **exit** to leave sqldba.

Oracle assumes that the user (polly, in this case) exists, and the tablespace (hold_my_data) also exists. If either of these is not true, the command will return an error message.

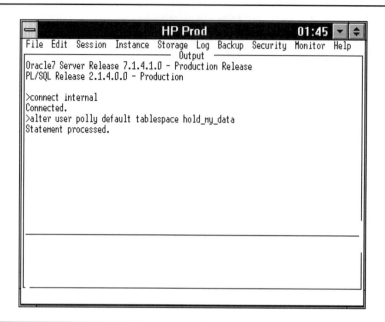

FIGURE A-19. *Pointing a user at a default tablespace*

TIP

It is easier to manage user tables when they are permitted to place all of their tables in a single tablespace. You will default tablespace assignment frequently.

Assign Space Quota to a User

This process allows the specified user to occupy space in a tablespace. It differs from the previous process, which points her tables at hold_my_data. That previous command alone does not allow her to occupy space in hold_my_data until this command is executed. After starting full-screen sqldba, follow these steps:

1. Enter **connect internal**.

2. Enter the command **alter user polly quota 10m on hold_my_data;** and Oracle responds as shown in Figure A-20.

3. Enter **exit** to leave sqldba.

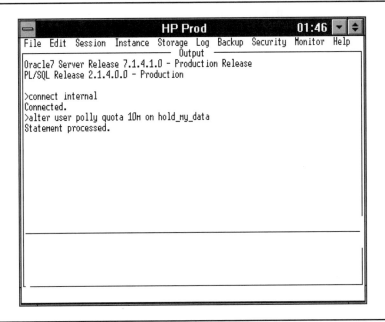

FIGURE A-20.   *Assigning a quota to a user*

Both the user to whom you are giving the space and the tablespace being assigned must exist when issuing this statement. If either the user or tablespace does not exist, the command will return an error message. The space in this statement is allocated in either megabytes (1,048,576 bytes), kilobytes (1,024 bytes), or the actual number of bytes (e.g., 10240) with no commas.

VIP
Oracle does not verify that the tablespace within which the quota is assigned has that amount of space available. You could (if you wish) assign a user quota of 100m in a tablespace that is only 500k.

Assign a Tablespace for Sorting

As Oracle runs and users make requests for data, sometimes information needs to be sorted. Most of the time, when there is sufficient memory available, Oracle does this work in memory. When Oracle needs more space than memory can satisfy, it uses work space in a tablespace. This tablespace is referred to as the *temporary segment,* since any objects Oracle creates for the work it does for the user are deleted after the sort completes. After starting sqldba, follow these steps:

1. Enter **connect internal**.

2. Enter the command **alter user polly temporary tablespace temp_ts;** and receive feedback from Oracle as shown in Figure A-21.

3. Enter **exit** to leave sqldba.

TIP
*Create a separate tablespace for sorting and assign it using the above command to **all** users of the database.*

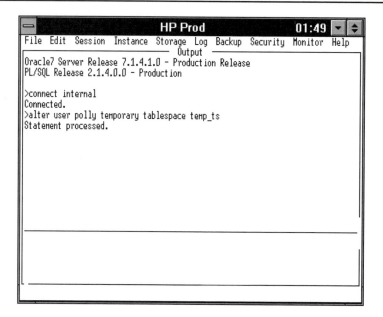

FIGURE A-21. *Pointing user at a tablespace for sorting*

Oracle assumes that the user (polly, in this case) exists and the tablespace (temp_ts) also exists. If either of these is not true, the command will return an error message.

Stacking the Three Previous Commands

The commands in the previous three sections (i.e., setting a default tablespace, assigning a quota, and a tablespace for sorting) can be stacked together in one statement. After starting sqldba, you can enter the command and then receive the feedback from Oracle as shown in Figure A-22. There are no rules governing the order of these commands.

Additional Tablespace Maintenance Responsibilities

In Chapter 14, we discussed creating a tablespace and adding more space to one that already exists. By the end of this section, you will also know

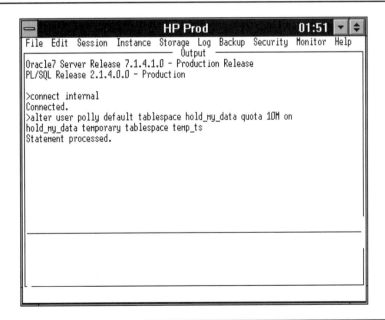

FIGURE A-22. *Three alter user commands together*

how to move the datafile that makes up a tablespace (i.e., rename a datafile) as well as drop a tablespace.

Moving a Datafile

Either by plan, or when forced to do so, you may need to move the datafile a tablespace occupies. You may find yourself with one less disk at your disposal and may need to move a tablespace to another disk. In the following code, these are the specifications:

Tablespace name	hold_my_data
Datafile	hmd.dbf
Current directory	?/dbs
New directory	?/oracle_dev

After starting sqldba, follow these steps:

1. Enter **connect internal**.

2. Enter the command **alter tablespace hold_my_data offline;** and receive feedback from Oracle as shown in Figure A-23.

VIP
The tablespace will not go offline if any users are currently using its data.

3. Using your operating system command, copy the datafile to its new location.

4. Enter the command **alter tablespace hold_my_data rename datafile '?/dbs/hmd.dbf' to '?/oracle_dev/hmd.dbf';** and receive feedback from Oracle as shown in Figure A-24.

5. Bring the tablespace online with the command **alter tablespace hold_my_data online;** as shown in Figure A-25.

6. Enter **exit** to leave sqldba.

After you leave sqldba, use an operating system command to delete the old file you are no longer using.

Oracle: A Beginner's Guide 14:13
File Edit Session Instance Storage Log Backup Security Monitor Help
Output
Oracle7 Server Release 7.1.4.1.0 - Production Release
PL/SQL Release 2.1.4.0.0 - Production
>connect internal
Connected.
>alter tablespace hold_my_data offline
Statement processed.

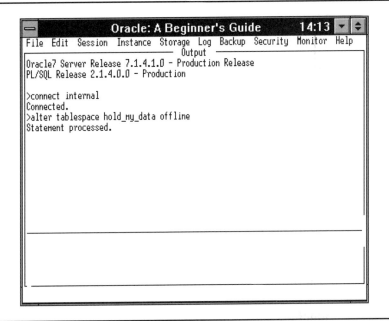

FIGURE A-23. *Taking tablespace offline*

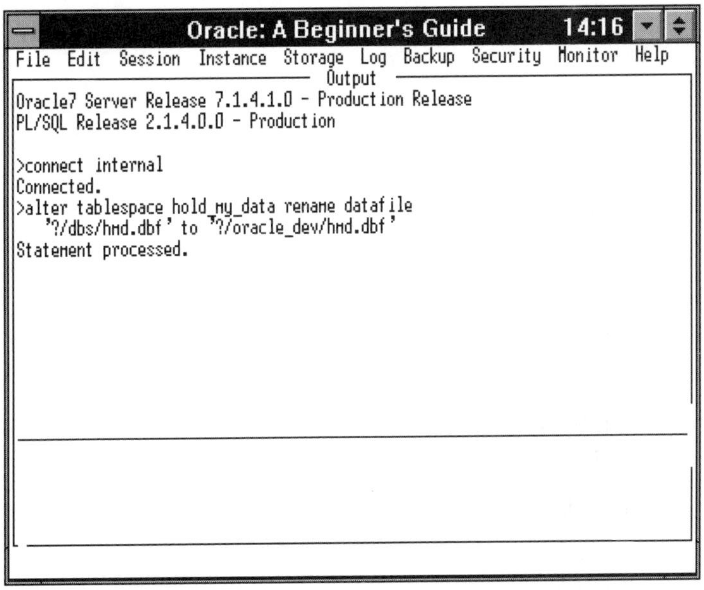

Oracle: A Beginner's Guide 14:16
File Edit Session Instance Storage Log Backup Security Monitor Help
Output
Oracle7 Server Release 7.1.4.1.0 - Production Release
PL/SQL Release 2.1.4.0.0 - Production
>connect internal
Connected.
>alter tablespace hold_my_data rename datafile
'?/dbs/hmd.dbf' to '?/oracle_dev/hmd.dbf'
Statement processed.

FIGURE A-24. *Renaming a datafile*

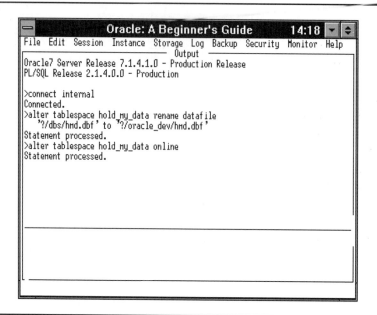

FIGURE A-25. *Bringing tablespace online*

Dropping a Tablespace

Once a user's data is no longer required, you may want to get rid of the data and even the tablespace the data now resides in. After starting full-screen sqldba, follow these steps:

1. Enter **connect internal**.

2. Enter the command **drop tablespace hold_my_data;** as shown in Figure A-26 and receive feedback from Oracle.

3. Enter **exit** to leave sqldba.

VIP
You are not allowed to drop a tablespace containing any objects. The SQL statement will fail if the tablespace still contains any tables. You must either drop those objects first or use the including contents option with the SQL statement as shown in Figure A-26.

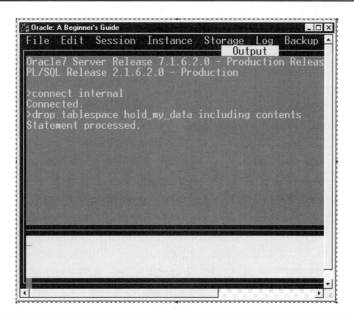

FIGURE A-26.   *Dropping a tablespace*

You will find that dropping a tablespace's objects and then dropping the tablespace is much faster than using the **drop tablespace including contents;** statement.

VIP
Dropping a tablespace does not erase the datafile it was using. The datafile must be removed using an operating system command. Erase the datafile from the dropped tablespace immediately. If you decide to do this some other time, more than likely you will forget!

Managing Redo Log Groups

Oracle writes transaction information to redo logs files. Picture a redo log as a passbook that records all changes to the database as if it were a checking account. With Oracle, we speak of redo log file groups. If you define more than one member for a redo log group, Oracle writes to each member simultaneously. This protects you against problems because if a redo log file is damaged, Oracle continues to write to another member of the group that is still intact. In this section, we will discuss how to do the following:

- Mirror your redo logs
- Add a redo log group
- Drop a redo log group

Mirrored Redo Logs

When instructed, Oracle7 will maintain mirrored copies of all online redo logs. A redo log group is made up of one or more equally sized redo log files. Each redo log group is assigned a number when created and Oracle writes to all members of each group at the same time. In the next section, we show you how to add a new redo log group to set up this mirroring. When the database operates in ARCHIVELOG mode, Oracle archives only one member of a redo log group before the whole group is reused.

TIP

Keep at least two members in each redo log group. If Oracle ever has difficulty writing to one member of a redo log group, it will carry on, satisfied to write to another member of the same group.

The status of your database redo log groups and members is viewed using the v$logfile data dictionary view and the following query.

```
SQL> select * from v$logfile;
    GROUP# STATUS  MEMBER
---------- ------- ------------------------------------------
         1         /lor/prd_log/log1prd_g1.dbf
         1         /data/log_shadow/log2prd_g1.dbf
         1         /picard/log_shadow/log3prd_g1.dbf
         2         /oracle/dbs/log1prd_g2.dbf
         2         /data/log_shadow/log2prd_g2.dbf
         2         /picard/log_shadow/log3prd_g2.dbf
         3         /lor/prd_log/log1prd_g3.dbf
```

```
3          /data/log_shadow/log2prd_g3.dbf
3          /picard/log_shadow/log3prd_g3.dbf
4          /oracle/dbs/log1prd_g4.dbf
4          /data/log_shadow/log2prd_g4.dbf
4          /picard/log_shadow/log3prd_g4.dbf
5          /data/log_shadow/log2prd_g5.dbf
5          /lor/prd_log/log1prd_g5.dbf
5          /picard/log_shadow/log3prd_g5.dbf
6          /oracle/dbs/log1prd_g6.dbf
6          /data/log_shadow/log2prd_g6.dbf
6          /picard/log_shadow/log3prd_g6.dbf
```

Use the following convention when setting up mirrored redo logs:

1. Ensure there are the same number of members in every redo log group.

2. Ensure each member of each redo log group is the same size.

3. Embed the member number and group number in the name of each redo log file. For example, the third member of redo log group 6 in the previous listing is called log3prd_g6.dbf.

4. Place members of each redo log group on separate disks. For example, the three members of redo log group 6 in the previous listing are on three separate drives: oracle, data, and picard.

 NOTE
You may have difficulty when you try to add a third member to your redo log groups. The parameter maxlogmembers controls the number of members in a redo log group.

The value of maxlogmembers can be increased by recreating the database control file.

Adding a New Redo Log Group

For this exercise, we need to add redo log group 3 with two redo log file members of 1MB (1,048,576 bytes) each. After starting sqldba, follow these steps:

1. Enter **connect internal**.

2. Enter the command **alter database add logfile group 3 ('log1_gr3','log2_gr3') size 1m;** and receive feedback from Oracle as shown in Figure A-27.

3. Enter **exit** to leave sqldba.

Notice in Figure A-27 how the names of the redo log file members are enclosed in single quotes. In addition, the two redo log file member names are separated by a comma and enclosed in parentheses. We now have three redo log groups associated with the database.

```
                  Oracle: A Beginner's Guide      15:53
 File  Edit  Session  Instance  Storage  Log  Backup  Security  Monitor  Help
─────────────────────────── Output ───────────────────────────
Oracle7 Server Release 7.1.4.1.0 - Production Release
PL/SQL Release 2.1.4.0.0 - Production

>connect internal
Connected.
>alter database add logfile group 3 ('log1_gr3','log2_gr3') size 1m
Statement processed.
```

FIGURE A-27.   *Adding redo log group*

TIP
When building a redo log file member name, embed the group number and member number in the filename. That is why we named the files log1_gr3 and log2_gr3 in this exercise.

Dropping an Existing Redo Log Group

You have just upgraded your hardware, and you find yourself with one less disk for Oracle and its associated database files. You used to have three disks, and now you have two. After starting full-screen sqldba, follow these steps:

1. Enter **connect internal**.

2. Enter the command **alter database drop logfile group 3;** and receive feedback from Oracle as shown in Figure A-28.

3. Enter **exit** to leave sqldba.

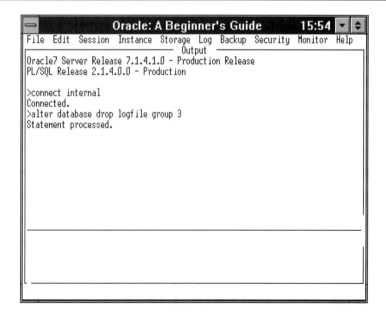

FIGURE A-28. Dropping redo log group 3

Redo log group 3 is no longer part of the database. Note how the SQL statement in Figure A-28 makes no mention of any redo log file member names as the group is dropped.

> **NOTE**
> *Dropping redo log file group 3 does not erase the disk files that made up that group. You must use the appropriate operating system command to delete these files.*

Problems Dropping Redo Log Groups

There are two problems that commonly occur when attempting to drop a redo log group. If one of these happens to you, follow our advice and then reissue the command to drop the group.

■ You may be attempting to drop a redo log group (let's call it redo log group 2) that would leave Oracle with less than two groups. If this happens, you must add a third group before you can drop group 2. When you drop group 2, that leaves groups 1 and 3, which satisfies Oracle's requirements.

■ You may be attempting to drop a redo log group that is active. You must wait until the group is no longer active before it can be dropped.

Rollback Segments

You may remember that these segments are used to store undo information when you update or delete data in Oracle tables. Managing these segments is part of your DBA responsibility. In this section, we will show you how to do the following:

■ Acquire a rollback segment using the initialization parameter file

■ Create a rollback segment

■ Change the status of a rollback segment

■ Drop a rollback segment

Acquiring a Rollback Segment

When you start up your database, it can be forced to acquire rollback segments by an entry in your initialization parameter file. This is done using a text editor (we use the UNIX "vi" editor as an example) and the following steps.

1. Invoke the editor, passing it the name of the initialization parameter file, as in **vi initprd.ora**. A few lines are shown in the next listing; the "…" indicate skipped parameters.

```
# initprd.ora    Created by MASI Inc.  September 1998
#                Ottawa Canada
db_block_size = 8192
db_name = prd
...
...
rollback_segments = (rbs01, rbs02)
```

2. Change the rollback_segments entry to include a new rollback segment, such that the entry now looks like the following, with the additional rollback segment bolded.

```
rollback_segments = (rbs01, rbs03, rbs02)
```

3. Save the updated initialization parameter file by exiting vi with your favorite exit sequence (be it SHIFT-Z-Z or ":X").

To complete this section, note the following points:

■ The names of the rollback segments are enclosed in parentheses.

■ The names of the rollback segments are separated by commas.

■ The rollback segments will not be acquired based on this entry until the database is shut down and started up.

■ The existence of the rollback segments mentioned in the entry is not checked by Oracle when you save the initialization parameter file.

If the rollback segments you placed in the initialization parameter file do not exist the next time you start up your database, you will receive an error.

Creating a Rollback Segment

We discussed rollback segments in greater detail in Chapter 3. As the DBA, you will quickly become more familiar with the nuances of working with them. After starting sqldba, follow these steps:

1. Enter **connect internal**.

2. Enter the command **create rollback segment rbs05 tablespace misc storage (initial 100k next 100k minextents 10 maxextents 10);** and receive the feedback from Oracle as shown in Figure A-29.

3. Enter **exit** to leave sqldba.

The SQL statement is made up of the following parts:

- The name of the rollback segment

- The tablespace in which the rollback segment is placed

- The storage parameters the rollback segment will assume

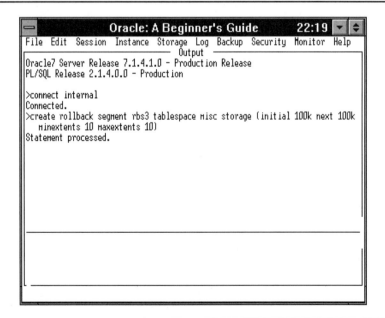

FIGURE A-29. *Creating a rollback segment*

The name of the rollback segment must be unique and the tablespace you are placing it in must be accessible.

VIP
We recommend you build one or more tablespaces to hold nothing other than rollback segments.

Changing the Status of a Rollback Segment

Rollback segments are either online or offline. Suppose the rollback segment rbs1 exists; the status of a rollback segment is changed by doing the following.

 1. Enter **connect internal**.

 2. Enter the command **alter rollback segment rbs3 online;** and receive the feedback from Oracle as shown in Figure A-30.

The status of your rollback segments can be obtained from the query shown in Figure A-31. A rollback segment must be online to be used by Oracle.

Dropping a Rollback Segment

When the need arises, after starting sqldba, do the following.

 1. Enter **connect internal**.

 2. Enter the command **alter rollback segment rbs3 offline;** followed by **drop rollback segment rbs3;** and receive the feedback from Oracle as shown in Figure A-32.

Notice how you need to take a rollback segment offline before it can be dropped. Dropping a rollback segment can be a frustrating activity because there are a number of situations where Oracle may not do exactly what you expect. If you try to drop a rollback segment with the online status, you will receive the error message "ORA-01545: rollback segment 'RBS3' specified

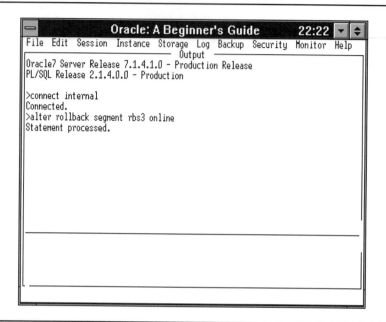

FIGURE A-30. *Bringing a rollback segment online*

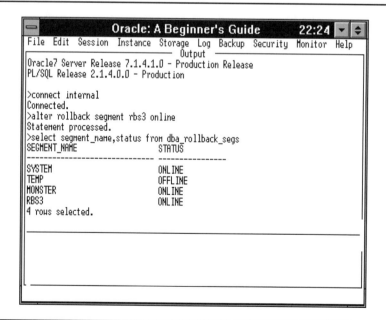

FIGURE A-31. *Listing status of rollback segments*

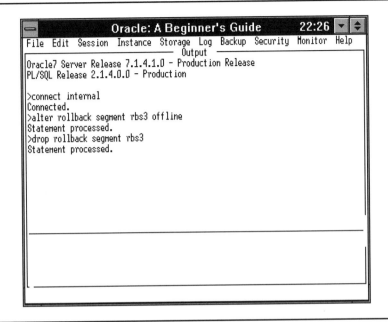

FIGURE A-32.   *Dropping a rollback segment*

not available." Also, if you try to take a rollback segment offline to drop it, and someone is using it when you issue the command, then the rollback segment will not come offline until that user is done with it.

Wrapup

So many have cut their teeth on Oracle7 database administration using some mode of sqldba. When you upgrade to release 7.3 and subsequently Oracle8, your instance management will more than likely be done from some form of Oracle Enterprise Manager.

INDEX

751

KMS.

Get Your **FREE** Subscription to Oracle Magazine

Stay informed and increase your productivity with every issue of *Oracle Magazine*. Inside each FREE, bimonthly issue, you'll get:

- Up-to-date information on the Oracle RDBMS and software tools
- Third-party software and hardware products
- Technical articles on Oracle platforms and operating environments
- Software tuning tips
- Oracle client application stories

Three easy ways to subscribe:

1 MAIL: Cut out this page, complete the questionnaire on the back, and mail to: *Oracle Magazine,* 500 Oracle Parkway, Box 659952, Redwood Shores, CA 94065.

2 FAX: Cut out this page, complete the questionnaire on the back, and and fax the questionnaire to **+ 415.633.2424.**

3 WEB: Visit our Web site at **www.oramag.com.** You'll find a subscription form there, plus much more!

If there are other Oracle users at your location who would like to receive their own copy of *Oracle Magazine,* please photocopy the form on the back, and pass it along.

☐ YES! Please send me a FREE subscription to Oracle Magazine. ☐ NO, I am not interested at this time.

If you wish to receive your free bimonthly subscription to *Oracle Magazine,* you must fill out the entire form, sign it, and date it (incomplete forms cannot be processed or acknowledged). You can also subscribe at our Web Site at ⌕ **http://www.oramag.com/html/subform.html** or fax your application to *Oracle Magazine* at **+415.633.2424.**

SIGNATURE (REQUIRED) ✓ | **DATE** |

NAME _____ TITLE _____

COMPANY _____

STREET/P.O. BOX _____

CITY/STATE/ZIP _____

COUNTRY _____ TELEPHONE _____

You must answer all eight of the questions below.

1 What is the primary business activity of your firm at this location?
(circle only one)
01. Agriculture, Mining, Natural Resources
02. Communications Services, Utilities
03. Computer Consulting, Training
04. Computer, Data Processing Service
05. Computer Hardware, Software, Systems
06. Education—Primary, Secondary, College, University
07. Engineering, Architecture, Construction
08. Financial, Banking, Real Estate, Insurance
09. Government—Federal/Military
10. Government—Federal/Nonmilitary
11. Government—Local, State, Other
12. Health Services, Health Institutions
13. Manufacturing—Aerospace, Defense
14. Manufacturing—Noncomputer Products, Goods
15. Public Utilities (Electric, Gas, Sanitation)
16. Pure and Applied Research & Development
17. Retailing, Wholesaling, Distribution
18. Systems Integrator, VAR, VAD, OEM
19. Transportation
20. Other Business and Services ____

2 Which of the following best describes your job function? *(circle only one)*
CORPORATE MANAGEMENT/STAFF
01. Executive Management (President, Chair, CEO, CFO, Owner, Partner, Principal, Managing Director)
02. Finance/Administrative Management (VP/Director/Manager/Controller of Finance, Purchasing, Administration)
03. Other Finance/Administration Staff
04. Sales/Marketing Management (VP/Director/Manager of Sales/Marketing)
05. Other Sales/Marketing Staff ____
TECHNICAL MANAGEMENT/STAFF
06. Computer/Communications Systems Development/Programming Management

07. Computer/Communications Systems Development/Programming Staff
08. Computer Systems/Operations Management (CIO/VP/Director/Manager MIS, Operations, etc.)
09. Consulting
10. DBA/Systems Administrator
11. Education/Training
12. Engineering/R&D/Science Management
13. Engineering/R&D/Science Staff
14. Technical Support Director/Manager
15. Other Technical Management/Staff
_____

3 What is your current primary operating system environment?
(circle all that apply)
01. AIX
02. HP-UX
03. Macintosh OS
04. MPE-ix
05. MS-DOS
06. MVS
07. NetWare
08. OpenVMS
09. OS/2
10. OS/400
11. SCO
12. Solaris/Sun OS
13. SVR4
14. Ultrix
15. UnixWare
16. Other UNIX
17. VAX VMS
18. VM
19. Windows
20. Windows NT
21. Other ____

4 What is your current primary hardware environment? *(circle all that apply)*
01. Macintosh
02. Mainframe
03. Massively Parallel Processing
04. Minicomputer
05. PC (IBM-Compatible)
06. Supercomputer
07. Symmetric Multiprocessing
08. Workstation
09. Other ____

5 In your job, do you use or plan to purchase any of the following products or services
(check all that apply)
SOFTWARE

	Use	Plan to buy
01. Accounting/Finance	☐	☐
02. Business Graphics	☐	☐
03. CAD/CAE/CAM	☐	☐
04. CASE	☐	☐
05. CIM	☐	☐
06. Communications/Networking	☐	☐
07. Database Management	☐	☐
08. Education	☐	☐
09. File Management	☐	☐
10. GIS	☐	☐
11. Image Processing	☐	☐
12. Laboratory Control	☐	☐
13. Materials Resource Planning (MRP, MRP II)		☐
14. Multimedia Authoring Tools	☐	☐
15. Office Automation	☐	☐
16. Order Entry/Inventory Control	☐	☐
17. Programming/Systems Development	☐	☐
18. Project Management	☐	☐
19. Scientific and Engineering	☐	☐
20. Spreadsheets/Financial Planning	☐	☐
21. Systems Management Products	☐	☐
22. Workflow	☐	☐
HARDWARE		
23. Macintosh	☐	☐
24. Mainframe	☐	☐
25. Massively Parallel Processing	☐	☐
26. Minicomputer	☐	☐
27. PC (IBM-Compatible)	☐	☐
28. Supercomputer	☐	☐
29. Symmetric Multiprocessing	☐	☐
30. Workstation	☐	☐
PERIPHERALS		
31. Bridges/Routers/Hubs/Gateways	☐	☐
32. CD-ROM Drives	☐	☐
33. Disk Drives/Subsystems	☐	☐
34. Tape Drives/Subsystems	☐	☐
35. Video Boards/Other Multimedia Peripherals	☐	☐
NETWORK/COMMUNICATIONS		
36. Communications Controllers	☐	☐
37. Local Area Networks	☐	☐
38. Modems	☐	☐
39. Wide Area Networks	☐	☐
SERVICES		
40. Computer-Based Training	☐	☐
41. Education/Training	☐	☐
42. Maintenance	☐	☐
43. Online DatabaseServices	☐	☐
44. Support	☐	☐
45. **None of the above**	☐	☐

6 What Oracle products are in use at your site? *(circle all that apply)*
SERVERS
01. Oracle7
02. Oracle Media Server
03. Oracle7 Workgroup Server
04. Personal Oracle7
05. Oracle Rdb
TOOLS
06. Designer/2000 (CASE)
07. Developer/2000 (CDE, Forms, Reports, Graphics)
08. Oracle Media Objects
09. Oracle Power Objects
APPLICATIONS
10. Oracle Financials
11. Oracle Human Resources
12. Oracle Manufacturing
13. Other ____
14. **None of the above**

7 What other database products are in use at your site? *(circle all that apply)*
01. CA-Ingres
02. DB2
03. DB2/2
04. DB2/6000
05. dbase
06. Gupta
07. IMS
08. Informix
09. Microsoft Access
10. Microsoft SQL Server
11. Progress
12. Sybase System 10
13. Sybase System 11
14. Sybase SQL Server
15. VSAM
16. Other ____
17. SAP
18. Peoplesoft
19. BAAN
20. **None of the above**

8 During the next 12 months, how much do you anticipate your organization will spend on computer hardware, software, peripherals, and services for your location? *(circle only one)*
01. Less than $10,000
02. $10,000 to $49,999
03. $50,000 to $99,999
04. $100,000 to $499,999
05. $500,000 to $999,999
06. $1,000,000 and over

OMG